Heroines of Sport

Heroines of Sport looks closely at different groups of women whose stories have been excluded from previous accounts of women's sports and female heroism. It focuses on five specific groups of women from different places in the world – South African women; Muslim women from the Middle East; Aboriginal women from Australia and Canada; and lesbian and disabled women from different countries worldwide. It also asks searching questions about colonialism and neo-colonialism in the women's international sport movement.

The particular groups of women featured in the book reflect the need to look at specific categories of difference – relating to class, culture, disability, ethnicity, 'race', religion and sexual orientation. In her account, Jennifer Hargreaves reveals how the participation of women in sport across the world is tied to their sense of difference and identity. Based on original research, each chapter includes material that relates to significant political and cultural developments.

Heroines of Sport will be invaluable reading for undergraduate and postgraduate students of sport sociology, and will also be relevant for students working in women's studies and other specialized fields, such as development studies or the politics of Aboriginality, disability, Islam, race, and sexuality.

Jennifer Hargreaves is Professor of Sport Sociology at Brunel University. She was one of the early pioneers of sport sociology and has edited the watershed text *Sport, Culture and Ideology*, and written the award-winning book *Sporting Females: Critical Issues in the History and Sociology of Women's Sports*; both are published by Routledge.

Heroines of Sport

The politics of difference and identity

Jennifer Hargreaves

London and New York

First published 2000
by Routledge
11 New Fetter Lane, London EC4P 4EE

Simultaneously published in the USA and Canada
by Routledge
29 West 35th Street, New York, NY 10001

Routledge is an imprint of the Taylor & Francis Group

Typeset in Goudy by Taylor & Francis Books Ltd
Printed and bound in Great Britain by Clays Ltd, St Ives plc

British Library Cataloguing in Publication Data
A catalogue record for this book is available from the British Library

Library of Congress Cataloging in Publication Data
Hargreaves, Jennifer, 1937–
Heroines of sport : the politics of difference and identity / Jennifer
Hargreaves.
p. cm.
Includes bibliographical references and index.
1. Sports for women–Social aspects. 2. Sports for women–Cross-cultural
studies. 3. Feminist theory. I. Title.

GV709 .H35 2001
796'.082–dc21

00-044633

ISBN 0–415–22848–4 (hbk)
ISBN 0–415–22849–2 (pbk)

To all the heroines of sport in this book

Contents

Abbreviations and acronyms

ADD	Action on Disability and Development
AFAHPER	African Association of Health, Physical Education and Recreation
AIATSIS	Australian Institute of Aboriginal and Torres Strait Islander Studies
ANC	African National Congress
ANZAF	Australia, New Zealand and Friends
ATSIC	Aboriginal and Torres Strait Islander Commission
BASA	British Amputee Sports Association
BBBC	British Boxing Board of Control
BCODP	British Council of Organisations of Disabled People
BD	Brighton Declaration
BDSC	British Deaf Sports Council
BGLSF	British Gay and Lesbian Sports Federation
BOA	British Olympic Association
BPA	British Paralympic Association
BWSF	British Wheelchair Sports Federation
CAAWS	Canadian Association for the Advancement of Women and Sport and Physical Activity
CAHPER	Canadian Association of Health, Physical Education and Recreation
CEDAW	Convention to Eliminate Discrimination Against Women
CIAD	Commission for Inclusion of Athletes with a Disability
CISS	Le Comité International Sportif pour les Sourds (International Committee of Sports for the Deaf)
CP-ISRA	Cerebral Palsy-International Sport and Recreation Association
CPS	Cerebral Palsy Sport
DAI	Danish Workers Sports Association
DAW	Division on Advancement of Women
DPI	Disabled Peoples' International
DSE	Disability Sport England
EFDS	English Federation of Disability Sport

EGLSF	European Gay and Lesbian Sport Federation
ENGSO	European Non-Government Sport Organizations
EPC	European Paralympic Committee
FWSAC	Finnish Workers' Sports Association of Canada
GAGM	Global Anti-Golf Movement
GISAH	Gay Integration through Sports and Arts Holland
HIVOS	Humanists' Institute for Development Cooperation Foundation
IAAF	International Amateur Athletic Federation
IAPESGW	International Association of Physical Education and Sport for Girls and Women
IBSA	International Blind Sports Association
ICHPER	International Council for Health, Physical Education and Recreation
ICI	International Committee on Integration of Athletes with a Disability
ICSSE	Islamic Countries Sports Solidarity Congress
ICSSPE	International Council of Sport Science and Physical Education
ICWSSC	Islamic Countries Women's Sports Solidarity Council
ICWSSG	Islamic Countries' Women's Sports Solidarity Games
IFSD	International Fund Sports Disabled
IOC	International Olympic Committee
IPC	International Paralympic Committee
IRNA	Islamic Republic News Agency
ISHPES	International Society for the History of Physical Education and Sport
ISMGF	International Stoke Mandeville Games Federation
ISMWSF	International Stoke Mandeville Wheelchair Sports Federation
ISOD	International Sports Organization for the Disabled
IWG	International Working Group
LPGA	Ladies' Professional Golf Association
LSA	Leisure Studies Association
MBE	Member of the British Empire
MCC	Marylebone Cricket Club
MWL	Muslim Women's League
NAIG	North American Indigenous Games
NASF	National Aboriginal Sports Foundation
NBA	National Basketball Association
NOC(SA)	National Olympic Committee (of South Africa)
NSC	National Sports Council
NWBA	National Wheelchair Basketball Association (US)
NWT	Northwest Territories
OBE	Order of the British Empire

OTCATSI	Olympic Training Centre for Aborigines and Torres Strait Islanders
RAWA	Revolutionary Association of the Women of Afghanistan
RDP	Reconstruction and Development Programme
RESPO DS-DI	Recreational Sports Development and Stimulation Disabled International
SACOS	South African Council on Sport
SAN-ROC	South African Non-Racial Olympic Committee
SWSI	Socialist Workers' Sports International
UKSMPMH	United Kingdom Association for People with Mental Handicap
UN	United Nations
UNESCO	United Nations Educational, Scientific and Cultural Organization
UPIAS	Union of the Physically Impaired Against Segregation
USOC	United States Olympic Committee
WHO	World Health Organization
WIN	World Indigenous Nations
WISC	Women's International Sports Coalition
WSF	Women's Sports Foundation
WSI	WomenSport International

Acknowledgements

I have a huge number of people to thank for helping me either directly or indirectly with the production of this book. Most important are those women, and some men, who have talked to me – either person-to-person, or on the telephone, or through email conversations – and helped me to understand the real-life situations that affect the participation in sport of women from marginalized groups. Other people have also helped – by putting me in touch with subjects; by collecting data for me; sharing their ideas; transcribing interviews; reading the first draft of chapters and commenting on my arguments and analysis; proofreading, and so on. Ann Hall laboriously read the whole manuscript and I am very grateful to her for her insightful comments and constant encouragement. Because so many people have been involved, I have just listed names below. I am sure there are other people whom I should acknowledge and have left out by mistake, and for reasons of space I simply cannot list everyone.

Sausan Youssef Abdou; Nafaa Abeer; Nabilah Ahmed Abdelrahman; Frances Abele; Thelma Achilles; Haleh Afshar; J. (Jugs) Akoojee; Fatma Yass Al-Hashimy; Julie Anderson; Barry Andrews; Mona El-Ansary; Jane Asher; Jim Atkinson; Isabel Azavedo-Burton; Linda Balboul; Audrey Bambra; Josfina Vibar Bauzon; Leon Beech; Tansin Benn; Rebeccah Bornemann; Patricia Bowen-West; Celia Brackenridge; Avtar Brah; Richard Broome; Alison Burchill; Libby Burrell; Bert Burnap; Campbell Burnap; Cora Burnett; Richard Cashman; Jayne Caudwell; Miia Chambers; Karen Christiansen; Gill Clarke; Luda Coff; Dara Culhane; Cara Currie; Shahizah Daiman; John Daly; Elizabeth Darlison; Simeon Davies; Barbara Drinkwater; Pauline Dunn; Noel Dyck; Jessica Edwards; Henning Eichberg; Mona El-Ansary; Nour El-Houda Karfoul; Zyad Darwish El-Kordy; Nicole Emzin-Boyd; Susan Emerson; Dina Engelbrecht; Penny Enslil; Janice Forsyth; Carole Gildenhuys; Eva Gloudon; Darren Godwell; Annelise Goslin; Kathleen Graham; Liam Graham; Juliet Gray; Susan Greendorfer; Tanni Grey; Simone Gristwood; Iris de Haas; Ann Hall; Jorn Hansen; Joan Hardy; Janie Hargreaves; Chris Holmes; David Howe; Pendukeni Iivula-Ithana, Lorraine Jacobs; Nour El-Huda Karfoul; Poppy Khala; Cheryl Kickett-Tucker; Nellie Kleinsmidt; Fadila Ibrahimbegovic-Gafic; Carol Isherwood; Lorraine

Jacobs; Carla Jones; Denise Jones; Ellen Katzenellenbogen; Allette Kraus; Leena Laine; Vicky Lambert; Andrew Lawrence; Patrick Lineham; Ian McDonald; Gail McDaniel; Jim McKay; Hala Joussef Mandour; Jillian Marsh; Busie Mbuyisa; Winnie Meiring; Rachel Melitz; Tembela Mgijima; Emily Mojafi; Jorn Moller; Michael Moloto; Frank Montemurro; Greg Moon; Sally Moon; Carol Motjuwadi; Kerel Motsjwedi; Sally Munt; Kathy Myburgh; Isabel Nell; Claire Nicholson; Nawal El-Moutawakel Bennis; Abeer Nafaa; Magda Nagy; Anne Nare; Zodwa Nglobo; Claire Nicholson; Carole Oglesby; Donny Ohlson; Pearly Ohlson; Mmuli Padi; Fraser Pakes; Diana Palmason; Catherine Palmer; Victoria Paraschak; Manorama Persad; Hazel Petersen; Imelda Petersen; Jerry Petersen; Gertrud Pfister; Zachariah Pooe; Farshad Pourhaddadi; Brenda Prince; Sam Ramsamy; Roland Renson; Dusty Rhodes; Roland Renson; Cheryl de la Rey; Cheryl Roberts; Angus Robertson; Sheila Robertson; Corne Rossouw; Johann Roux; Jean Runciman; Daniel Salee; Tessa Sanderson; Nazek Simbel; Diar Soma; Jasmat Soma; Loggie Soma; Andrew Sparkes; Elizabeth Stone; Tina Stout; Jane Swan; Margaret Talbot; Colin Tatz; Sadik Farag Thiab; Kedi Tshoma; Candan Tureyen; Sharda Ugra; Helen Van Graan; Gilbert Vander; Gerd Von der Lippe; Margaret Waite; Kristin Walset; Caz Walton; Kevin Wamsley; Helen Watson; Ida Webb; Barbara Wegg; Linda Weil-Curiel; Gabrielle van der Westhuizen; Anita White; Tricia White; Sylvia Wilkinson; Rod Windover; Cheryl Winn; Linda Yhukutwana; Alaia Zouhdy; Phindile Zwane.

1 Introducing heroines of sport

Making sense of difference and identity

Introduction

Who are the 'heroines of sport'? This book does not provide a simple answer. It is not a straightforward celebration of the feats of individual women, as the question might suggest. The concept of the heroic is examined through analysis of the struggles and achievements of specific groups of women whose stories have been excluded from previous accounts of women's sports and female heroism. It focuses on five specific groups of women from different places in the world – South African women; Muslim women from the Middle East; Aboriginal women from Australia and Canada; and lesbian and disabled women from different countries worldwide. The women selected for investigation are from historically marginalized groups who have had to struggle against particularly harsh forms of discrimination to take part in sport and have constructed their own sporting identities in changing and difficult conditions. Their struggles in sport are social as well as personal, linked to specific cultural, economic, political and religious contexts and to global processes. *Heroines of Sport* interrogates topical and polemical situations and has a strong international dimension. It is, fundamentally, about human agency.

The question of the heroine

A culture is remembered for its heroes and heroines, and sport constructs them and influences our perceptions of them continuously. In popular consciousness, heroes and heroines are men and women who are 'larger than life', 'inspirational icons', special people with extraordinary qualities that are constructed and represented in particular ways to encourage us to admire and idealize them. In other words, heroes and heroines are socially constructed through discourses and meanings and values that change over time. But heroes are more easily defined than heroines and there is greater social importance attributed to the production and celebration of male heroism. Bob Connell (1987: 249) argues that hegemonic masculinity is naturalized in the form of the hero who is conventionally strong, aggressive and brave. Muscular tension is associated with human endeavour and struggle – climbing mountains and fighting dragons – and heroism is symbolized in the muscular male body. Sportsmen, then, easily transform into heroes. Athletes in ancient Greece were seen as heroes, their exploits functioning symbolically as heroic feats. Kenneth Dutton (1995: 26) explains that 'The athlete modelled himself on the *hero* of myth, and in doing so took on much of the symbolism of heroic stature.' Sportsmen today are readily heroised when they break physical barriers, endure adverse conditions, overcome seemingly impossible obstacles, drive their bodies to the limit, risk death, and go further, higher and faster than any other living men. Pat Griffin (1998: 25) suggests that 'For many people the male team-sports hero is the epitome of masculinity: strong, tough, handsome, competitive, dating or married to the most desirable woman.'

Heroines are usually defined differently. It has been argued (with reference to literary heroines) that 'there is a basic contradiction in the idea of the heroine. She [is] required to be both heroic – superior or exemplary in some way – and female – inferior by definition' (Thompson 1993: 397). Selfless and courageous acts of humanity, associated with caring, kindness, motherliness and morality – essentially 'feminine' attributes – are ascribed to the traditional heroine. According to these characteristics, there is inconsistency in becoming a sporting heroine. 'Yet', Tuttle (1988: 10) argues, 'women are often, undeniably, and visibly, heroic, even according to male definitions of heroism.' Certainly, throughout the history of modern sport, there has always been a small number of adventurous women who have transgressed gender roles, taken up 'manly' sports, such as boxing, baseball, car racing, flying, mountaineering and soccer, and shown consummate skill and broken records equivalent to those of male sporting heroes. But the public response has been ambivalent. Since the 1920s, characterized as the 'Golden Age of Sport', the media has transformed top female performers into folk heroines and figures of international stature, and some of them became household names throughout the Western world. But according to Creedon (1994: 114), writing about the USA, they were portrayed as 'feminine and fashionable, health conscious in their leisure pursuits, as goddesses rather than as athletic heroines'. The small numbers of women who took part in aggressive, muscular, traditional male sports had their sexuality denied, were labelled 'mannish' or 'freakish', presented as androgynous or, more usually, as 'super-feminine'. There was always a feminizing code – as Tuttle (1988: 10) puts it – 'to neutralize the effect of the transgressive act'. Sally Munt (1998: 3) refuses the term 'heroine' because of its inferior gendered status, evaluated always 'in relation to', and a female version of, the prototype masculine hero. I continue to use it in order to suggest that the women I am writing about can reclaim it as a specifically female term relating to their own struggles and achievements.

The small but growing volume of women's sporting histories (e.g. Cahn 1994; Festle 1996; Jones 2000; Stell 1991)[1] illustrates clearly that women have been much more a part of the sporting lives of different nations in the world than has previously been believed, taking part in a wide range of activites. Today, throughout the West, and to a lesser extent in other parts of the world, women are bending mainstream definitions of gender and taking part in all types of sports, including masculinized sports in dramatically increased numbers. They are boxers, soccer and rugby players, bodybuilders and weightlifters, and they take part in the macho and risky worlds of free climbing, iron-man events and eXtreme sports ... and so on. Sportswomen in the new millennium are breaking the physical boundaries of the past (Hargreaves 1994; Vertinsky 1990) and producing new cultural and sporting identities. They do so as part of their everyday lives. However, those who are successful become 'ambiguous' heroines, treated differently from men and still struggling for equal support and recognition. Take, for example, mountain climbing and the quest to reach the summit of K2 – the second highest mountain in the world after Everest. K2 is known as the 'Killer Mountain' – for approximately every three to four climbers who reach its summit, one will die. In August 1995, Alison Hargreaves' name was added to the list of victims of K2 when she was swept away in violent winds on her descent from the summit. Three months earlier she had become the first ever woman (and the second person) to make a solo ascent of Everest without oxygen and she had wanted (and became) the first person to climb the world's two highest peaks in the same calendar year. On both occasions, the fact that Alison Hargreaves was a mother of two young children was highlighted in the British media. However, whereas following the successful Everest climb her identity as a mother did not prevent the media from constructing her at the same time as a national (British) heroine, the first woman to achieve such a spectacular feat, her death on K2, described by a reader as 'an irresponsible act', began a furious debate about 'motherhood, ambition and risk' (Rose and Douglas, *Observer* 8/8/99). Because climbing has the potential for accidents and deaths, there has been fierce opposition to female participation, and because Alison Hargreaves was a mother of two young children the debate focused on whether she should have been on K2 at all. She had behaved like a man, arguably putting her sport and the excitement, danger and fame it entailed before her children and her role as a mother. Her heroism was conditional upon her safe return to her children. No such condition is placed upon men – their deaths are the purest symbols of heroism. No comparable comments about fatherhood were made in the British press about the four men who died on the mountain the same day.

Controversy surrounds the differential treatment of men and women in sport: the glorification of male achievements and the downgrading of women's achievements. Gendered heroism is being constantly challenged by women who are appropriating the narratives of maleness and transforming themselves from victims into superstars. According to many feminists, to claim an identity that used to be exclusively male in a macho, sexist culture is symbolically heroic. However, what is often forgotten is that the fierce concern for equality props up the violence, corruption, commercialization and exploitation that plague men's sports. Jeff Benedict (1997: 217) argues that, 'At a time when society is searching for legitimate heroes, the traditional credentials of heroism – courage, honesty, bravery, self-sacrifice – are being replaced by visibility, wealth, and fame.' Furthermore, there is a trend for hypermasculine sportsmen who are the perpetrators of extreme violence and serious abuse to be allowed to continue their careers as public heroes (1997: 217). There is no evidence that female sports stars are equivalently violent, but they are constructed via the same imperatives of the sports industry and the same ideologies of aggressive and exploitative competition that construct the male sport hero. The modern-day popularized heroines of sport are trained and marketed for entertainment and spectacle; they are the products of a system which consistently induces them to abuse their bodies, tempts them to use unsporting and damaging performance-enhancing agents, and produces them as sexualized commodities for a global audience. In many respects, modern-day heroines of sport are manufactured clones of each other.

The liberal sport feminist position which argues for equality of participation and resourcing on a par with men through the removal of the social impediments that prevent female participation, has failed systematically to challenge the established and destructive principles of mainstream sport (M.A. Hall 1996: 90–1; Hargreaves 1994: 26–9). Liberal feminism, then, implicitly supports the creation of commodified and glamorized heroines of sport, a position which is opposed by radical sport feminists who question sport's global relations of power and exploitation and the values upon which the production of modern-day sport heroes and heroines is based. For example, Helen Lenskyj – a Canadian academic – takes an openly radical feminist stance. She opposes the destructive values inherent in the dominant model of competitive, aggressive sport, in particular the ideology of violence inherent in elite male sport (1992, 1994). She is one of a growing body of women – including academics, campaigners, journalists – whose relationship to sport is based on ethical and welfare criteria. Working outside the mainstream facilitates the creation of new models of sport authentically connected to power, knowledge and emotional life. For example, sport has been integrated into the women's health movement. 'Race for the Cure' (USA); 'Against the Tide' (USA) and 'Race for Life' (UK) are fun runs and fun swims that encourage a positive, healthy and holistic approach to exercise, raise consciousness about cancers that affect women, and raise money for research. These are shared political activities that bring into the open women's experiences of their bodies and that treat the body as subject, in contrast to the objectified body of the heroine of elite sport. They make the knowledge and experience of bodies important and central to identity, but in ways that feature sensuous pleasure and control rather than commodification, denial or estrangement. In this perspective, competitive individualism is replaced by a shared culture of caring and ethical lifestyle.

Women have also been active in the fields of humanism and biopolitics. For example, the movement known as 'Mothers and Others for a Livable Planet' has supported a campaign to stop sports goods manufacturers using cheap child labour in developing countries (*Green Guide* 21/3/97). They have also opposed the environmental hazards associated with golf courses that despoil the land and habitat and spread contamination to surrounding areas. There is a struggle in sport between environmentalists and those who wield economic and political power. Women are active in this struggle and have played a crucial role in questioning the modernist conception of progress and the domination of nature by rich developers. In many and varied locations, sport is a despoiler of nature. The Himalayas – including Mount Everest and K2 – are examples of sport locations that are being systematically despoiled by the increasing numbers of 'package climbers' – including women – who are part of a growing sport leisure industry. But remarkably few of our 'media heroines' of sport connect their roles as stars with politics and ethics. Most of them have been 'selfish heroines' who seek individual glory and financial gain; most of them have failed to speak out openly to oppose the damaging features of modern-day sport – even the ones that may affect their own specific sport or event. The main thrust of women in sport has been to follow the men and to ignore the 'dark side of sport'. Because popular heroic narratives are so concerned with the creation and representation of the individual, collective struggles and achievements are underplayed and often ignored. Women who take a stand – often against fierce opposition – and argue for new uses of sport that are humane and intrinsically enriching, and who speak out and take action on such issues as health and the environment, are generally little-known actors. They are the 'unsung heroines'. There is a strong argument for returning to the 1970s' anti-individualistic feminist principle that commodified heroines/stars should be replaced by 'real' women (Munt 1998: 2).

As well as masking the harmful features of modern sport, popularizing the individual heroine tends also to legitimate inequalities. The production of the heroine implies that the system allows success and makes everything possible. Her visibility exhorts us to believe that she is representative, not just of something special, but of 'our' nation, 'our' community. But women are not homogeneous. The creation of heroines of sport withdraws attention from the general position of the majority of women in sport; it masks the differences between different groups of women both within nations and between nations. Constructing heroines removes guilt. This book looks closely at different groups of women about whom very little is known and very little has been written. By telling their stories, the significance of diversity and difference among women in sport becomes apparent and, specifically, the categories of difference relating to class, culture, disability, ethnicity, 'race', religion and sexual orientation. *Heroines of Sport* recognizes the complexities and multiplicities of late capitalist/postmodern/postcolonial societies and engages with recent debates around 'identity politics' and the 'politics of difference', with the particular as opposed to the general.

Exclusion, difference and identity

Most histories and sociologies of sports, as well as popular books on sports, are written by men about male sports. But even when women *are* the focus of attention, another process of exclusion is taking place. On the one hand, deriving from the project of 'modernity', is the unified conception of women – as distinctly different from, and subordinate to, men – reflecting a struggle against patriarchy as the major mechanism of power and oppression. Much of the early sport feminism adopted this oppositional form of discourse, framed by the gender equity debate. It is what Ellen Staurowsky (1998b: 7) describes as 'adversarial, in both tone and nature, as seen in linguistic devices such as the "battle of the sexes", a "dispute", a "fight", and a "tug-of-war" '. Intrinsic to this approach was the concept of 'women in sport', implying that sportswomen are a homogeneous group with a common, shared culture. Since the dominant female sports culture is assumed to be White, Western, middle-class, heterosexual and able-bodied, women who come from minority groups and from countries outside the West have been marginalized, and their experiences, problems, struggles and achievements have been excluded from mainstream history and practice. The concept of homogeneity systematically excludes particular groups and discourses by treating them as 'Others'. The method is to treat White, Western, middle-class, heterosexual, able-bodied women's experiences as the norm and other women's experiences as 'different'. Cassidy *et al.* (1995: 32–3) explain that universalizing whiteness in feminism:

> includes thinking, imagining, and speaking as if whiteness described the world. Racism, for example, engenders white solipsism by allowing White women the power to make it seem as if their own experience is wholly representative of all women's experience. Black women, Native women, disabled women, in fact, most other women, are left out without anyone noticing they are absent.

Avtar Brah (1991: 171) asks the question, 'How may "difference" be conceptualized?' In answer to her own question, she goes on:

> At the most general level 'difference' may be construed as a social relation constructed within systems of power underlying structures of class, racism, gender and sexuality. At this level of abstraction we are concerned with the ways in which our social position is circumscribed by the broad parameters set by the social structures of a given society. ... Difference may also be conceptualized as experiential diversity. Here the focus is on the many and different manifestations of ideological and institutional practices in our everyday life.

Brah is pointing here to the way in which difference is constructed at different levels – at the level of the subject and at the level of institutions and politics. *Heroines of Sport* recognizes both and explores the relationship between the two. It recognizes that a sense of difference and patterns of exclusion arise from diverse mechanisms of power and oppression which are complexly articulated one with another. The construction of some groups of women as outsiders which stems originally from structures of domination and subordination can result in very personal and poignant experiences. The sense of *exclusion* can be strongly felt even within radical programmes specifically aimed at *in*clusion, explained here by an Aboriginal sportswoman who was a member of an ethnically mixed team on a sports scholarship: 'I just *feel* different ... it's to do with belonging ... Mainstream women make us feel different. They don't have to say anything ... it's just the way they talk about the world and the way they talk *to* us – you know – not *with* us.'

In the 1960s, the powerful sense of difference and exclusion experienced by Black Afro-Americans, as a result of personal and structural oppressions, initiated the growth of civil rights and Black power struggles. They in turn fostered the development of other 'new' social movements, including the women's liberation movement and the gay and lesbian liberation movement (see Chapter 5). Previously clear-cut distinctions between the private and the public were broken down and the lives of people from oppressed or marginalized groups became inescapably politicized. The new social movements were connected to people's lived experiences, and through difference *and* sameness a radical form of identity politics developed. Zaretsky (1995: 244) explains as follows:

> Sparked by the African-American and other freedom struggles, and by the women's liberation movement, a new type of politics emerged in the United States, Canada and Europe in the 1960s. 'Multiculturalism', 'class, race and gender', 'identity politics' and the 'politics of difference' are among the concepts and slogans it has generated. Its defining idea is that no superordinate group appellation, such as 'man', 'humanity', 'the working class' or 'the American people', should be used without recognizing the *differences* that exist within the aggregate – such differences as male and female, abled and disabled, native born and immigrant, and so forth. The term 'identity' is associated with emphasis on the particular as opposed to the general. 'Difference' connotes the refusal to homogenize or aggregate.

Identity embodies sameness *and* difference – consolidated from the late 1960s through being a member of an oppressed or marginalized group. Through the construction of difference, identities were recognized that had previously been 'hidden from history'. The politics of difference and identity have led to a questioning of the essentialist notion of a single and fixed identity and a recognition that identities are diverse and fluid, affected by changing political, social and cultural conditions. Stuart Hall (1996a: 4) asserts that:

> Identities are never unified and, in late modern times, increasingly fragmented and fractured; never singular but multiply constructed across different, often intersecting and antagonistic, discourses, practices and positions. They are subject to a radical historicization, and are constantly in the process of change and transformation.

During the twentieth century there was been a tendency to define identity in terms of culture. Zaretsky (1995: 248) claimed that 'Mass consumption and mass culture emerged as basic spheres for the formation of personal identity.' Through the globalization of culture and the spread of self-consciousness about the body, sport has become increasingly important in defining female identity in recent years. *Heroines of Sport* explores the link between identity and the particularities of women's sporting histories and cultures, in particular as they relate to such differences as disability, ethnicity and 'race', and sexual orientation. It is about how identities are produced and how they are performed (Butler 1990).

Stories of sport are almost exclusively stories of those in power. My intention in writing *Heroines of Sport* is to bring attention to groups of women who have been excluded from, or on the margins of, mainstream sport theory and practice. I wanted to break with the history of cultural imperialism, Eurocentric discourses, and the universalized accounts of 'women in sport'; and I wanted to examine the ways in which women's participation in sport is tied to their sense of difference and identity. I had speculated that, because we know so little about certain groups of women in sport, their struggles have been greater and, by virtue of their exclusion, their achievements have been heroic. In other words, my starting point for the book was that these women might be recognized as the ordinary, everyday, hidden heroines of sport. There are so many groups of women in sport about whom we know so little and about whom I would have liked to write – they are members of minority groups in the multicultural societies of the West and women from the whole of the rest of the world (M.A. Hall 1996: 42–3). But I had to be highly selective for reasons of space, time and logistics. Two of the first feminist scholars of sport who were critical of exclusionary 'White' research were Susan Birrell (1989) and Yevonne Smith (1992) from the USA (see M.A. Hall 1996: 42–4). They represent a slowly emerging field of feminist scholarship about women from non-hegemonic groups (see, for example, Laine 1993). But the body of work remains *very small* and feminist sport historians and sociologists and research students should once more be urged to look at various marginalized women in sport so that we can build up a picture of the particular histories, experiences, traditions and cultures of women in sport from all countries and social groups and in all their complexities.

The experiences of the particular groups of women that I have selected for this book – Black women in South Africa; Muslim women in the Middle East; Aboriginal women in Australia and Canada; lesbians; and disabled women – challenge the modernist notion that identities are fixed and determined for us by history. *Heroines of Sport* gives accounts of the struggles of women who are 'on the margins' of mainstream sport; it investigates how they understand themselves and construct personal and group identities through sport; how their identities are constructed relationally through contact with other people and communities of people; why they make certain allegiances and not others; and how their identities are socially and historically constructed within culture and through cultural discourses. The book is fundamentally to do with relations of power, dominance and subordination related to different social divisions, including disability, ethnicity, 'race' and sexuality. The approach is resistant to a 'victim' paradigm. The characterization of the victim is someone with no point of view, someone who is a passive recipient of culture and prejudice. In contrast, the women who are the subjects of this book have been *active agents* negotiating specific social barriers and discriminatory discourses. I explore the ways they do so in detail, and assess the extent to which the women are autonomous and how far they are assimilated into structures of power outside their control.

Methodology

Heroines of Sport is based on original material collected from a number of research methodologies. Doumentary evidence includes archival material, official reports and programmes, newspaper and magazine reports, correspondence, personal memorabilia, films, videos and material from the Internet. In some contexts, participant observation was possible, but the main method of investigation was interviewing – part of the interactionist tradition placing the meaningfulness of social action at the centre of any kind of explanation. It took a few years to complete interviews with around 150 women drawn from each of the groups under investigation. I carried out individual and group interviews, face-to-face or on the telephone. I was lucky to be able to speak in person to women from all ethnic backgrounds when I travelled to different parts of South Africa, including the townships; to Muslim women mostly from the Middle East, when I was at a conference in Egypt; to Aboriginal women from Australia and Canada, when I was in those countries; and to lesbian women and disabled women mostly in different locations in the UK. I spoke also to different women who were involved in the Women's International Sport Movement at two international Women in Sport conferences and at meetings in London, England. I also conducted 'email interviews', which enabled me to 'speak' to other women from all over the world. Communicating by email is like having an extended conversation. Introducing myself and explaining the research to women I had never met was usually fairly formal and informative – but then over a period of time it was typical for the relationship to become more friendly and trusting so that I was able to probe more effectively about sensitive issues. This is not possible in a conventional 'one-off', person-to-person interview. Networking was an essential method of establishing contact in the first place.

The research seeks to give a voice to the women who are under investigation. It is an attempt to acquire an authentic understanding of their needs, desires, opportunities and constraints. The use of biography or life history as a methodological approach (Bertaux 1981; Birrell 1989; Sparkes 1994) can provide unique insights into the meanings that sport has in the lives of women. It is possible to build the analysis around the experiences of the women themselves and hence to understand better the ways in which they construct personal identities and imagined collective identities. Precisely what it means to be an Aboriginal, disabled, lesbian, Muslim or South African sportswoman can only be understood by those particular women. In his discussion about feminism, Victor Seidler (1994: viii) argues that:

> The personal voice is irreducible because it reflects a particular level of experience, a qualitative connection to self. For what is being explored is the ongoing dialectic between what has been experienced and the relationships within which she is living. Here there *is* a space and time for acknowledging differences between women, even celebrating difference.

These women's experiences take place within specific relations of power and subordination. Theory has, in a sense, been extracted from the narrative and expanded upon. The women's personal biographies are placed within a framework of specific social structures and historical circumstances in an effort to understand the ways in which gender relations in sport cohere with cultural, economic, ideological, political and religious patterns specific to the totality of social relations. It is an approach that recognizes the dualism between agency and structure. Culture in this formulation is conceived to be a 'lived dominance and subordination of particular classes' (Williams 1977: 110), constructed and changed through the interaction of men and women who make, resist and transform meanings and values. As Susan Birrell (1990: 195) points out, it is necessary to be 'informed by an explicit theory of structural relations'. She favours cultural studies because 'it has a general framework for understanding relations of dominance and subordination, and insistence on analyzing the particular conditions of those relations, and an array of conceptual tools to advance the analysis'. She argues, however, that 'cultural studies needs to be decentered from class relations and broadened to take into account gender and racial relations' (1990: 199). Birrell argues for combining feminist cultural studies with critical autobiography – which is probably the most accurate description of the perspective of *Heroines of Sport*.

The women I spoke to were without exception open and generous in their responses. However, much of the material was sensitive and controversial and, according their wishes, most subjects remain anonymous. Throughout the book all unreferenced quotations are from personal interviews. Because the original bibliography was huge and unwieldy, I have not listed all Internet sources and newspaper articles separately from the text.

The role of researcher

In the life history method I am both the researcher and the narrator, placing other women's stories into a context and putting my interpretation on them (Sparkes 1994: 165). 'Passionate objectivity' is the term used by some feminists to describe a form of investigation that recognizes that the researcher is firmly inside the political and social context of the period and of the work, and not separate from them (Hargreaves 1992: 165–6); this is the position I have adopted in writing this book. My commitment to the project relates to my committed engagement with issues of inequalities and discrimination in sport.

I am aware of the likely criticisms that will be encountered. The obvious question that will be asked about my authorship is whether it is right for a White, European, middle-class, heterosexual, able-bodied feminist to do research about the experiences of women from other parts of the world, from other social groups, with different cultures and beliefs – in other words, from groups within which I have no organic relationship. My profile positions me as a member of the hegemonic group rightly criticized for producing biased and incomplete accounts of women in sport. Writing specifically about Aboriginal women, Chuckryk and Miller (1996: 6) argue that there are inevitable tensions between academics (usually White) and activist women, and one woman I interviewed asserted that it is not uncommon for 'outsiders' to be the spokespersons for Aboriginal women, who are themselves not represented in sports forums and other venues (see Chapter 4). Julia Emberley (1996: 104) makes the position clear when she says:

> Traditionally, theory has been the reserve of an intellectual vanguard, to the exclusion of 'the voices of the oppressed'. The current swing to the politics of identity in Anglo-American feminisms with subjective authenticity as the code of legitimation has challenged the role of the intellectual as representative in a hegemonic institution of power: academia – particularly when the intellectuals in question are not members of the underprivileged class, indeed, when their very position within academia makes that membership irrevocable, though not indissoluble.

Emberley (1996: 100) also makes the point that 'This is not to say that non-Aboriginal feminist academics do not have a supplementary role to play in supporting the Aboriginal women's movement.'

There is a very powerful argument that the subjects of the research should also be the owners of the research, so there is more potential for the sort of emancipatory research needed by excluded groups. However, bell hooks (1984) has insisted that those of us who are privileged have an obligation to support and facilitate those from minority groups – I believe she is right. Providing research and knowledge is one way to do this. Although responsibility for the finished product is entirely mine – what is put in, what has been left out, and how it is analysed – I have referred (as much as possible) to the work of female researchers and writers who are members of the groups under investigation and/or come from the same country. Most importantly, I have integrated the women's original voices into the analysis. By these means, I have tried to avoid imposing a biased Western view and I hope that, by positioning the women themselves at the centre, the stories are seen as theirs. Deborah Siegel asserts that 'We are sorely in need of more imaginative paradigms for living with difference, for *engaging* – rather than merely dismissing, tolerating, or caricaturing – ideas (and people) that are different from our own (from us)' (Siegel 1997: 73). *Heroines of Sport* is an attempt to shift women from the margins of sport towards the centre.

The other chapters

Chapter 2, 'Race, Politics and Gender: Women's Struggle for Sport in South Africa', is a case study of women in sport during the apartheid and post-apartheid periods. The focus is on Black women (African, Coloured and Indian) who suffered most severely during apartheid and are struggling now with its legacy. The study considers the particular effects on women's sport of decoloniza-tion and globalization, and how gender and 'race' together have militated against women's autonomy in sport. It is also a celebration of the achievements of all South African sportswomen resulting from a creative struggle for unity in the new South Africa.

The position of Muslim women in sport throughout the Muslim diaspora is tied to the relation between politics and Islam. Chapter 3 looks at the effects of the cultural repression of the 'non-Western' in conceptions of female sporting subjectivities specifically in Arab countries. It considers ways in which religious, political and global processes structure personal and cultural consciousness for women in sport, and looks at the ways in which Muslim women consciously and unconsciously manipulate religious beliefs to negotiate their gender roles in sport. It is fundamentally about negotiation and resistance.

For many Aboriginal people in different countries across the world, the quest for recognition and respect has been accompanied by discrimination and pain. This is a problem intrinsic to the effects of European imperialism, to the processes of colonialism, to the dispossession of the livelihoods and cultures of indigenous peoples by colonial powers, to inherited power relations, and to resistance in the contemporary world to power-sharing with historically disadvantaged groups (neo-colonialism). These ideas are explored in Chapter 4, which concerns Aboriginal women in sport – specifically, Australian Aborigines and First Nation women in Canada. It is about the struggles of Aboriginal women in mainstream sport and the significance of the indigenous games movement.

Martina Navratilova has been an unusual figure in women's sport because she has made public the particular problems of homophobia faced by lesbian sportswomen. Unlike Martina, the majority of lesbian sportswomen – especially those in top-level sport – stay closeted, but at the same time, at amateur level, gay and lesbian sport enjoys an unprecedented boom. Chapter 5 examines this paradox and looks at the significance of gay sports events, in particular the Gay Games. It is about the meaning of sexuality and sexual politics in late capitalism The chapter also considers the exaggerated difficulties for lesbian women in sport in developing countries.

Disability is a human rights issue. Michael Oliver points out that 'disabled people, wherever they live, experience conditions of life far worse than their non-disabled counterparts' (1996: 110). 1981 was the International Year of

Disabled Persons, and its motto was 'Full participation and equality'. But it was not until 1992 that the UN adopted a World Wide Programme of Action concerning Disabled Persons, and 1993 when they produced the Standard Rules on the Equalization of Opportunities for Persons with Disabilities. Even so, disabled people, and more so disabled women, have had to struggle so hard to take part in sport and equalize opportunities for themselves with able-bodied competitors and with disabled men. Chapter 6 is about their struggles and successes, and how increasing numbers of women are sucessfully overcoming the double discrimination of gender and disability. It is essentially about the politics of disability.

Women find confidence and courage in their relations with other women, and through the work of organizations and movements can more easily give voice to what they want. But in the final chapter, in an examination of the 'Women's International Sport Movement', it is argued that most of its leaders continue to come from privileged White backgrounds in the developed world and that they have been joined by 'neo-colonial elites' from the developing world. Two key questions are posed in this chapter: whether the Women's International Sports Movement adequately represents women from marginalized groups; and whether its leaders have properly addressed the questions of marginality and representation.

In summary, through its attention to difference and identity *Heroines of Sport* raises important questions about inclusion and exclusion, about power and privilege, and about local–global connections. It opposes the concept of universalism and recognizes the distinctive differences and characteristics of women who have been outsiders in mainstream sport. It is fundamentally to do with relations of power between dominant and subordinate groups within individual nation states, and between nation states from the West and those from the developing world. Most importantly, it is about the affirmation of identity in sport through struggle, negotiation and achievement. It is about everyday heroines of sport.

2 Race, politics and gender

Women's struggles for sport in South Africa[1]

Introduction

South Africa's first multiracial elections were held in April 1994: Nelson Mandela became president, and a uniquely inhumane political system – apartheid – was finally ended. But the process of transition from the old system of White supremacy to a non-racial democracy has been fraught with difficulties and setbacks. There have been huge political and cultural changes embodying pivotal struggles to radicalize both racial relations of power and gender relations of power – changes and struggles which provide a backdrop for looking at the particular strivings of South African women in sport.

The new country has been characterized as the 'non-racial, non-sexist Republic of South Africa' (Haffajee 1995: 11). The African National Congress (ANC) – the voice of the democratically elected Government of National Unity[2] – claimed that its Reconstruction and Development Programme (RDP) would eradicate the inequities of the past by 'directing resources from the misspent wealth of apartheid towards the impoverished majority' (Ransom 1995: 9). Black communities have, therefore, been target groups for development. Because Black women are the most exceptionally deprived social group, part of the government's plan was to achieve gender equality and women's empowerment alongside racial equality and black empowerment – a route, it was argued, that would stimulate the economy as a whole (Ransom 1995: 9). At the start, the new constitution made provision for a Gender Commission, and the ANC committed itself to a Women's Charter of Rights and effective equality between the sexes (Haffajee 1995: 11).

It was these initiatives, together with those of women themselves, which encouraged Margaret Lessing (1994: preface) to claim that:

> Never in the history of South Africa have the women of this country had the opportunities they have today – nor the choices. Never have they been more powerful. Never have they received so much attention. And never have they been more active.

The anti-racist/anti-sexist philosophy of the Government of National Unity was applied to different areas of political, social and cultural life, including sport. Following the example of other African countries, sport in South Africa has been given official sanction because it is seen as a crucial tool for nation-building (Uwechue 1978) – a position made clear by Nelson Mandela who, on the unique occasion of the first ever first-class cricket game in the township of Soweto, between England and South Africa said, 'Sport has a role to play in uniting countries because it speaks a language and has ideals beyond the reach of politicians' (*Evening Standard* 27/10/95). More precisely, it is argued that sport has the potential to unite people from diverse backgrounds after years of enforced separation:

> Apartheid divided us. Through sport we can break down barriers which kept us apart … barriers of race, class and gender. Women, men, boys and girls of all colours can get together and form friendships.
>
> (Roberts 1995b: 13)

The provision of sport for disadvantaged communities was an immediate priority of RDP and the government-funded National Sports Council (NSC) launched an initiative – known as Protea Sport – intended to introduce sports into severely deprived areas. Recognizing the problems of unequal gender divisions, girls were targeted by the NSC as a specially needy group, although the 'women's sport movement' in South Africa had already been initiated in 1992, when a women's desk was established with financial assistance from the Australian Sports Commission. In 1993, an interim committee was formed, which a year later became the Women's Sports Foundation – originally established as an autonomous body. In 1995, the Foundation was transformed into a standing committee of the NSC – which was responsible for spearheading gender equality in sport throughout the country. The Women's Sport Committee was convened for the first time in 1996.

As a result of the demise of apartheid, South Africa had a unique opportunity to break with past traditions and ideas, and to construct a throroughly radical national sports structure that coheres with the philosophy of the new constitution. But, coexisting with the potential for radicalism is the risk that inequalities will again become established and reproduced. Although there is no doubt that in some spheres transformative changes have already occurred, overall, development towards comprehensive equality between the races and the sexes has been worryingly slow. Six years after the elections, in most spheres of life, including cultural activities in general, and sport specifically, resources between different races and sexes remain very uneven. The people of the new South Africa continue to struggle with the effects of past inequalities, and progress is slowed because South Africa has been in the grip of an economic recession and tied to a budget fixed by its apartheid predecessor (Ransom 1995: 9).

This chapter is about women in sport in South Africa – during apartheid and post-apartheid. It is about their struggles and achievements. The story is only a partial one because there are no substantial publications on the topic, and because the issues asociated with sport development are vast, complex and controversial. It tells something about the creative ways in which women overcame the huge restrictions of apartheid and about how, today, in spite of the immense obstacles inherent in post-apartheid South Africa, they are forging new opportunities for themselves. I gathered much of the material for the chapter during a four-week trip to South Africa in 1995, when I travelled to Johannesburg, Durban and Cape Town, and to townships and other locations (including the University of Zululand in Kwazulu Natal). I visited a range of venues – sporting, educational, administrative and informational – and talked to women from diverse backgrounds who were involved in women's sports during and/or post-apartheid.[3]

The legacy of apartheid

The Afrikaner nationalist government came to power in South Africa in 1948, from which time the apartheid laws of racial segregation were thoroughly and forcibly entrenched throughout every segment of society for nearly half a century. And, for nearly a century before that, racial divisions had been inscribed in social practice (Booth 1998: 10). Not surprisingly, the deep structures of life under apartheid have not been easy to shift, and everybody in South Africa today – including those who are involved in the reconstruction of sport – still lives with the legacy of the regime.

Apartheid in South Africa was a pernicious policy of discrimination through the mandatory division of a nation into four racial categories – Whites, Coloureds, Indians and Natives.[4] (Throughout the chapter, the term 'African' replaces the apartheid characterization of 'Native'; and 'Black' refers collectively to all 'non-White' South Africans.) Cornell and Hartmann (1998: 22) explain the origins of 'racial' categories which, in the case of South Africa, reduced the complex physical and cultural differences within and between the colonizer groups and the colonized groups to crude and divisive oppositions between Black and White:[5]

> The persistence of the idea of biologically distinct human races owes more to popular culture and pseudo science than to science, and the idea's pedigree is not scientific but historical. It emerged originally in the extended encounter between European and non-European peoples that began in the late 15th and early 16th centuries. Discovering human beings in Asia, Africa, and the Americas who looked – and often acted – very different from themselves, Europeans concluded that these superficial differences were surely indicators of much more fundamental differences as well. ... Europeans came to believe that races are in fact distinct and identifiable human ... groups; that there are systematic, inherited, biological differences among races; and that non-White races are innately inferior to Whites – that is, to Europeans.

In apartheid South Africa, race was a discursive category which had great cultural, political and symbolic power. Ideological definitions of colour, descent and ethnic origin sustained a particularly violent and repressive form of control by the White minority (approximately 12.5 per cent of the population) which, for the huge majority of South Africans, meant a denial of human rights and fundamental freedoms in political, economic, social and cultural areas of life. It was a system not only socially condoned and sustained by the government's philosophy of 'separate but equal development', but also legally and politically endorsed, and brutally enforced. The mark of elitism and superiority was whiteness, and that of the greatest subjugation and humiliation was blackness. Skin colour was a constant, inescapable and personalized symbol of racial repression and conflict which, as Sivanandan (1981: 300) has pointed out, effectively repressed working-class liaisons across racial lines:

> The racist ideology of South Africa is an explicit, systemic, holistic ideol-ogy of racial superiority – so explicit that it makes clear that the White working class can only maintain its standard of living on the basis of a Black underclass, so systemic as to guarantee that the White working class will continue to remain a race for itself, so holistic as to ensure that the color line is the power line is the poverty line.

The unity of colour, power and poverty here demonstrates clearly the connection between ideology, politics and economics, but at the same time, masks the ways in which inequalities of gender were also embodied in these relations. What is often missed out from discussions about South Africa is that the rule of apartheid was based on 'the ideological construction and consolida-tion of White masculinity as normative and the corresponding racialization and sexualization of colonized peoples' (Mohanty 1991: 15). Although hegemonic masculinity was institutionalized in White as well as Coloured, Indian and African communities, because it was indistinguishable from apartheid the result was that African women were the most deprived group of all.

Diana Russell (1990: 12) writes about the oppressed lives of African women who were dismissively referred to by a prominent Nationalist member of parliament as 'superfluous appendages'. Millions of African women were com-pelled to live in the infertile homelands (bantustans) and, because their husbands and sons were forced to live and work away from home, had the major responsibility for family welfare. Under the law and in customary practice women had few rights and were not included in legislative reforms until 1988. They suffered also, in very personal ways, from uneven and subjugating gender relations of power. It was claimed that:

> The social and political order in South Africa impacts on working-class black men in a way that brings out the worst kinds of chauvinism in them. Black women present the only cushion against their complete powerless-ness, and any suggestion of equality between the sexes is a real threat to

their ego. The oppression they suffer in the wider society acts as a paradigm for their domination of women.

> (Ramphele and Boonzaier 1988, cited in Kadalie 1995: 20)

Women already lived subordinated lives prior to colonialism, but Cammack *et al.* (1993: 213) have argued that 'the development of capitalism in Africa deepened already existing gender divisions and women's subordination'. Throughout South African society, apartheid has merged with traditional and Westernized structures to consolidate the combined effects of race and gender on their lives. South African sport was a site of inequalities between men and women in all groups, but, especially reflected the extraordinary power and privilege of White men.

Sport in White communities was, *par excellence*, a symbol and celebration of racial (and in particular Afrikaans) superiority and White masculinity (Grundlingh 1996). Multiple facilities were available in a huge range of sports to support the ideology. Municipal funds secured at nominal interest rates, or interest-free loans, were acquired for private clubs, 'many of which', Merrett (1986: 4) claims, 'may be described as the racially exclusive bastions of white privilege'. Most of the resources, paid for by all rate-payers, went to support White male sports, although White women were relatively privileged and in many cases had excellent resources. There were, of course, poor Whites who had very limited opportunities, reflecting diversity within each racial group as well as between groups. In Indian and Coloured areas, there were far fewer resources, most of which were used by men. For Africans, facilities in the townships were impoverished, and mostly only for soccer – in rural areas they were virtually nonexistent for both sexes. In any case, sport was an irrelevance for the vast majority of African women, who were struggling for survival and had to contend with traditional and modern manifestations of male domination at the same time (Cammack *et al.* 1993).

Separate education for different groups was a major force for instilling acceptance of institutionalized racism (Merrett 1986: 3); and sport in schools was a major means of instilling sexism. Figures on school sport illustrate the absence of sporting infrastructures in most non-White schools and the huge differences between White and African schools. In 1984 the government spent R9.84 on sports facilities for each White schoolchild and 0.41 cents for every African child. Another pro-government report, carried out in 1982, found that White schools possessed 72 per cent of all sports facilities, including those of the highest quality. Of schools in the sample, 22 per cent had *no facilities at all* (Merrett 1986: 3; SANROC n.d.: 1).[6] Of the sparse resources available in schools for Indians and Coloureds, most were for male sports, but in African schools there were usually none at all, or a piece of rough ground would euphemistically be called 'a pitch'. When asked about sports facilities for girls, a retired teacher from the Cape Town area explained that 'In our coloured schools, the only sport for girls was netball, because it was the cheapest sport.

Most of our schools didn't have hockey, which isn't all that expensive. But in Black schools there was just nothing'.

The absence of facilities for girls in African schools, combined with poverty, travel problems and patriarchal controls, militated effectively against participation. In poor Coloured communities, the situation was similar, graphically described here by a Coloured teacher:

> The child already comes to school hungry, doesn't have a piece of bread for his lunch, no lunch is served at the school. When you saw your children collapsing, falling asleep, how can you tell them, 'Hey, you've got to play hockey this afternoon, or you've got to play netball. The child has to travel miles to get back home, and the child says, I'm not interested in that netball'. In their own environment there is no netball court or tennis court.

Women's sport during apartheid

Robert Archer (1987: 229) argues that, because of the laws and ideology of apartheid, sport was 'distinctly politicized, to a degree rare in Africa or in other societies'. The government had a segregated sport policy and, although there was no official prohibition of mixed-race sport, a wide range of apartheid laws and regulations effectively obstructed people's ability to travel freely, and prevented non-Whites using the only facilities available in White areas (Hain 1982: 243–4; Ramsamy 1982: 21–4).[7] However, in spite of the tremendous problems facing all Black groups, there was a surprisingly active sports movement in all communities throughout the apartheid rule (Archer 1987; Bose 1994; Brickhill 1976; Hain 1971, 1982; Odendaal 1995; Ramsamy 1982). Ironically, it was in part *because* of apartheid that sport became popular, because it could be used as a form of political and cultural resistance to White domination. The involvement of non-White women in the non-racial (anti-apartheid/anti-racist)[8] sport movement paralleled their involvement in the general political struggle against apartheid, and in the women's movement (Manzini 1992: 7). Predictably, in research on the sport/race/politics nexus during the apartheid years, references to women's involvement and to gender are noticeably absent.[9]

The main representative body for non-racial sport was the South African Council on Sport (SACOS), founded in 1973 (Ramsamy 1982: 13–18). Its unifying slogan of opposition to sport under apartheid was 'No normal sport in an abnormal society'. SACOS claimed to have 'forged unbreakable links between the sporting demands of oppressed South Africans and their broader demands for a society in which they can live in freedom and dignity' (SACOS 1988: 7). The link between sport and politics and the anti-apartheid struggle was the *raison d'être* of membership and sports meetings were often arranged as a front for political activities. But, although women were actively involved in the SACOS sports liberation struggle, the actual practice of sport was heavily gendered. In the *SACOSSPORT Festival '88* commemorative volume, an article entitled 'Women and Sport' (SACOS 1988: 89–90) claimed that women were treated as 'sex objects' in South African sport, that in non-racial contexts women's sports were trivialized, and that there was a lack of women's participation in decision-making, except in women-only sports. Most of the resources were available to men, and women had to work with great determination, and in the face of tremendous difficulties, to keep female sport alive in the Black communities. There were a few exceptions, when women received the active support of men. The following two quotations from Coloured women, both of whom struggled throughout the apartheid era to bring sport to girls and young women in their communities, illustrate the unevenness of gender relations. The first woman's experience was the most typical: 'It was bad enough struggling against the system, but we had to struggle against *our so-called men* who wanted everything for themselves.' The second woman remembers that male SACOS members provided some support for women's sports: 'You must know', I was told, 'that male sports dominated the country, but we were very lucky that *our* rugby counterparts saw to it that we would have netball courts on the side, because, the men argued, "What about our women?" "What about our girlfriends?" '

It has been claimed by bell hooks (1989: 43) that 'Oppressed people resist by identifying themselves as subjects, by defining their reality, shaping their new identity, naming their history, telling their story.' The oppressed sportswomen of apartheid South Africa were, in bell hooks' terms, inventing their own realities and identities and creating a history – but one which is only now being told. The most active group were Coloured women with professional backgrounds – mostly teachers – who had a commitment to the philosophy of SACOS and the time and expertise to devote to organizing sports events and competitions. But it was not easy, as a Coloured teacher – who later became vice president of the Women's Softball Federation – explained to me:

> We stuck to our principle of 'no normal sport in an abnormal society'. It was a great struggle. We could get nothing from the sponsors or probable sponsors. Everything had to come from the players, or the administrator. It was real hard work if I look back at the time we were doing the hockey and softball.

During the SACOS era, women were active agents in the sports process, creating for themselves opportunities, conditions and meanings. So that what they now describe as 'so-called' Coloured sport could survive, they took on multiple and complex responsibilities: they were different combinations of players, coaches, umpires, administrators, organizers, selectors and carers, all rolled into one.

Those involved composed a close-knit, dedicated community, who pulled together to make things work. Lack of funds was a major problem and events were run on a shoestring. Women used their own money on a regular basis to provide kit, food and transport for those players who could not afford to contribute. The following recollections give some idea of the sense of dedication and group cohesion inspired by these women. The first speaker, a Coloured teacher, has since become a development officer for the Western Province Hockey Union:

> I spoke to a friend of mine … and she said to me that on the eve of a tourn-ament, they didn't have a bus to go from Bloemfontein to Cape Town. And they had a meeting with two members. 'What is your salary?', they asked each other – and they actually collectively put their salaries together – and that is how people managed to get where they had to be.

The second account, also from a Coloured teacher who, post-apartheid, was appointed vice president of the Women's Softball Federation, tells of the types of living and travel arrangements that were made:

> We didn't live in five-star hotels. We lived in schools. We slept in sleeping bags, we took our own cooks with us and people fed us. We didn't travel by air, we travelled by road. I remember the bus breaking down over an Easter weekend. As women – we women – we had to go to a softball tournament in Johannesburg. Fortunately for us, we decided to go a day earlier. We waited almost 48 hours for another bus, and at the end of the day, when we got to Johannesburg, people were already waiting for us 24 hours. And we all stayed in homes. No five star.

Sports events were family affairs with women-friendly arrangements. For example, it was explained to me that:

> When women took their families with them to sport it became necessary to develop nurseries. It was insisted that each club had a junior section … and on Saturday morning, mum, auntie, cousin, grannie, would be on the field at 8 o'clock in the morning for the first junior fixture, and then after that leave the children, or take the children with them to the same venue in the afternoon for the senior game.

It was as if everyone was part of a large, caring, extended family, providing emotional as well as physical support, particularly to young girls from poor backgrounds:

> If I bring my 12 children from the under-privileged area where we teach, then it meant that I had to feed them. And this is what we did, this is how we carried on. But we got lots of support from other players and so on. You might today make a pot of soup, and you feed the children, because that is the only time you could get them. You can't also have them on the field so early in the morning without any breakfast or anything. And some of them came from places like Silver Glen which was totally sub-economic, so the food was important.

Gender discrimination, combined with racial discrimination, created a massive problem from which stemmed the growth of all Black women's sports. In the first place, there were a tiny number of courts and pitches specifically for female sports in Coloured, Indian and African areas, and men had priority use of shared facilities. Women were usually barred from central venues and often forced to travel long distances to play. They complained, as well, about excessive council charges for the hire of pitches. When a Coloured sportswoman travelled for the first time in 1995 to a previously White facility at Stellenbosch, she was incredulous. 'I counted that day something like 15 netball courts and probably six hockey fields', she said, 'and I just couldn't believe it!' *Her* reality during apartheid was similar to that of her colleague, who tells the following story:

> Facilities I am sorry to say were very, very poor. None existed. Now I stay in an area in Crusset Park which is quite big. I've been fighting since I started hockey in 1978, and up to this day there is no facility for the juniors. We used to take the soccer pitch and make do on the soccer pitch. The women had to take care of the posts. We had to do the lining of the field ourselves. We had to check out the potholes, so in the winter, on Monday and Tuesday, before Saturday, you must go and fill them up. You know, some of us do laugh, because the way we used to do it was very unorthodox. Anyway, this is what women used to do.

These women were courageous and determined. Remarkably, in spite of the numerous practical and ideological constraints facing them, they struggled successfully to keep their sports alive year after year, and in spite of the lack of resources – facilities, sponsorship, skilled coaching, and open competition – some of them reached surprisingly high standards. They organized local leagues and inter-provincial competitions, and in 1988 SACOS held its second sports festival – known as the 'Olympics of the Oppressed' – where 'the cream of non-racial sport was participating'. SACOS had its own heroes and heroines – those who had achieved remarkably high standards within the non-racial structure. For example, in 1985, Cheryl Roberts was honoured with the Sportsperson of the Year award, having won three national championships and nearly 150 table-tennis titles. Cheryl used to play tennis, but turned to table tennis because her working-class parents had no car to transport her to courts that were a long distance from her home, and because she was turned away from a 'Whites-only' club.

There are also life stories of individual women who supported non-racial sport in defiance of the rules of apartheid, sometimes putting their own lives at risk in the process. A remarkable example is Petronella (Nellie) Kleinsmidt, known as the 'Grandmother of karate in Africa' (Jones 2000). She took up karate in 1965, as a young woman, but because she was Coloured there were few facilities in her own community and she was prohibited from travelling to White-designated areas for training. However, in 1973, she met a White karate trainer – Johan Roux. Kleinsmidt's association with Roux became both personal and political – defying the laws of apartheid and risking harassment and arrest, they set up home together in 1978 and ran a non-racial dojo (karate training school).[10] She explained to me the constant danger that they put themselves in:

> Yes, I was on the security list. We had to avoid the guards – they were there all the time to try to trap us. We were all in danger – Johan and me and the students ... we were breaking the law and could get arrested at any time.

Kleinsmidt also described their support for SACOS and its sports boycott, the aim of which was to pressurize the South African government to end apartheid. The boycott effectively stemmed her career. But her priority was always, unselfishly, to resist segregated sport and the principles of apartheid. When I visited her dojo in 1995, there were children in the class who were White, Coloured, Indian and African – a tribute to her life-time philosophy. Kleinsmidt is more familiarly known as Sensei Nellie – a term of respect which also identifies her as a teacher (Jones 2000). Nellie Kleinsmidt's life story exemplifies the connection between race, culture and politics. Her story also illustrates the way in which Black sportswomen in apartheid South Africa were part of the interplay between oppression and activism. They had to negotiate dominant ideas and structures in order to participate in sport – a process which influenced the definition of their own identities.

The experience, consciousness and identity of African, Coloured, Indian and White women have all been crucially shaped by racism and sexism, but the effects are different for women from different groups. In response to the claim that most White women in apartheid South Africa were raised to be racists – itself a process of oppression – most White women in post-apartheid South Africa say that they were socialized into believing that racism did not exist: 'I didn't know what was going on – I just didn't understand.' When, at the age of 17, Zola Budd (now Pieterse) obtained a British passport so that she could compete in the 3000 metres in the 1984 Los Angeles Olympics, she fulfilled the ideological stereotype of the uninformed, innocent young White South African woman, whose love of sport and precocious talent transcended considerations of racism. But Budd was a *beneficiary* of apartheid, and was openly supported by the pro-apartheid system in her own country and in Britain. Her manager was a prominent member of the racist National Party. By comparison, Black South African female runners were the *victims* of apartheid, barred from the possibility of obtaining a British passport or of competing in international athletics. The Zola Budd incident brought into the open the issue of racism in sport both in South Africa and in the host nation, Britain. Budd persistently denied the connection between sport, racism and politics. In contrast, it was claimed in *Sport and Apartheid*, the newsletter of the International Campaign Against Apartheid Sport and the South African Non-Racial Olympic Committee (SANROC), in April 1986, that 'Most British athletes now deplore the way Budd is using her British passport as a flag of convenience. Fear of recrimination by the BAAB (British Amateur Athletic Board) has forced them to remain nameless'. Nevertheless, two top British sportswomen – Tessa Sanderson ([Black Afro-Caribbean] Olympic gold medal winner for the javelin) and Judy Oakes ([White] Commonwealth shot-putt champion) chose to speak out openly and they joined the growing protest against the way in which Budd was providing propaganda for the apartheid regime in South Africa – running as a South African while carrying a British passport.[11] In common with most White sportswomen in South Africa, Budd enjoyed cultural opportunities and choices which were denied to women from other ethnic groups. Also in common with most other White sportswomen from her country, at no time did she make a statement of opposition to the apartheid system, show solidarity with sportswomen from other 'racial' groups, or argue for non-racial sport. There were some White women who, *unlike* Budd, took the difficult and sometimes dangerous choice to be part of the general struggle against apartheid, a handful of whom chose to participate in non-racial sport.

Consciousness and identity were constructed very differently for Black sportswomen during apartheid – in response to the experience of racist and sexist discrimination and the absence of choice. As we have seen, some Coloured women managed to create spaces and opportunities for themselves, but for African women the chances of doing so were minimal. A Coloured woman who was a member of SACOS recalled that:

> It was difficult enough for us, but the Black [African] people were absolutely forgotten. It was often said the Coloured people, we were the stepchildren of the government. So we got that little bit more. But the Black people were absolutely left out of everything, whether it was education, sports, or whatever.

African women were not, therefore, to any significant extent involved in sport during apartheid. Little is known about the handful who were the exception. Little is known, either, about the few Indian women who played sport. There were distinct gender divisions in sport in Indian communities: large numbers of Indian sportsmen were actively engaged in non-racial sport, but culture and religion, as well as race and gender, combined to restrict the participation of Indian women. Leisure and sport experiences were fundamentally restricted by racial and gender divisions, and the 'triple oppression' (Zuma 1992: 14) of being Black, working-class and a woman, limited the choices available to an even greater extent. The diversity of women in apartheid South Africa illustrates the importance of recognizing the interplay of human agency and constraint, and of understanding, in Susan Birrell's (1989: 213) words, 'the complex relations of dominance and subordination simultaneously structured along racial, gender, and class lines'.

Simply because Africans, Coloured women and Indians in South Africa are now equal with Whites under the law, it does not follow that discrimination against them, originating from apartheid, has not continued. The oppression of Blacks was naturalized through everyday experiences, based on the treatment of race and ethnicity as biological categories. Apartheid legislation would have been ineffective without a supporting ideology which was integral to the lives and minds of people of all colours throughout the country. This poses problems for development, because it is difficult to dislodge long-standing ideas and practices based on separateness and inequality, and to replace them with a humane philosophy of unity and tolerance, symbolized in one of the mottos of the new South Africa:

One Nation – Many Cultures: Together We Become

(Wiid 1994: 84)

Problems of development

Development is equated with progress and liberation. It is generally understood to mean a move from a backward, usually agrarian, non-industrialized economy (accompanied by extensive poverty, high infant mortality, and a lack of education and social welfare), to an industrialized economy (with a generally acceptable standard of living for all the population, comprehensive education, and a welfare infrastructure). A comprehensive sport structure is also an index of development. Development is usually seen as a logistical problem, and 'its goal, to make the world modern, i.e. Western, has rarely been in dispute' (Marchand and Parpart 1995: 11).

Although South Africa is viewed as a developing country with huge problems of scarcity and destitution, White supremacy during the apartheid regime established a sophisticated and advanced way of life for the minority White population. Since the ending of apartheid, extremes of poverty and wealth remain (Sanders *et al.* 1994: 139), and the concept of the 'Third World within the First World' (Marchand and Parpart 1995: 17) is therefore directly relevant to present-day South Africa. Because diversity and separateness have been pivotal in South Africa, not surprisingly, sport development is related directly to unification and equity.

The discourse of sport development may seem straightforward, but it hides massive problems, many of which are signalled by South Africa's social demography. The population is estimated to be approximately 42.5 million: Africans comprise 77.4 per cent; Whites 12.5 per cent; Coloureds 7.7 per cent; and Indians 2.4 per cent. African women comprise 72 per cent of all women over 18 years. The urban population, which has been on the increase consistently since the ending of apartheid, is around 48.3 per cent, and the non-urban population is 51.7 per cent. There are more Africans living in rural areas than in towns – women outnumber men in the former; in the latter, the reverse occurs. Most Whites, Indians and Coloureds live in towns. Because almost all sports facilities are in urban areas, location is another factor that militates against African women's participation in sport. Although there is an expanding Black middle class, huge numbers of Africans endure appalling living and health conditions. It is estimated that around 2.3 million Africans suffer from malnutrition, and the infant mortality rate per thousand live births is 46. Only 53 per cent have access to flush toilets, and just 30 per cent have electricity in their homes. Around 30 per cent of Africans overall are illiterate, but in the rural areas the figure can be as high as 50 per cent. Not surprisingly, few Africans have any form of post-secondary education: out of every thousand, the figure for Whites is 51, for Indians 35, for Coloureds 13, and for Africans only 9. Out of every thousand Whites, 34 attend university; but only 6 out of every 1000 Africans (*1995 Beijing Conference Report SA; Centre for Population Studies SA; Guardian 22/3/95; Women's League* 1993).

Ironically, the ending of apartheid has worsened the plight of many African people, and has increased the 'feminization of poverty'. Lack of adequate housing, safe water, sanitation and basic health care – the main causes of preventable disease – are almost exclusive to the African population and mainly to women. Following the relaxation in 1986 of the influx-control legislation, Africans from the homelands have been migrating in huge and growing numbers into the townships in the hope of finding work. Most of them fail to do so (between 40 and 50 per cent of adult South Africans are unemployed) and so become homeless, without money, and hence forced to survive indefinitely in informal settlements or squatter camps on the urban fringes.

I visited Soweto – the largest city in South Africa with a population of four-and-a-half million people. The city stretches over 30 miles and although there are middle-class Sowetans living in comparatively spacious houses, a short distance away are row upon row of basic, tiny brick or concrete homes many of which have wooden or cardboard extensions with corrugated iron roofs. A little further on are the shanty areas – huge and growing numbers of Black people living in utter degradation under plastic, cardboard and corrugated-iron shacks still with evidence of the razor wire put up to fence them in. The conditions of poverty are extreme and life-threatening. I saw a similar vista at Guguletu – a large Black township outside Cape Town with ugly squatter dwellings that reach as far as the eye can see on both sides of the highroad. I also saw squatter camps outside Durban, and again, driving through the rural areas of KwaZulu Natal. There are now more than seven million inhabitants of squatter camps in South Africa. In these conditions, African women and children are the most vulnerable groups (Sanders *et al.* 1994: 140).

It is difficult to comprehend the scale of the problem of survival for African women. There is little hope for them at present of a life of dignity and quality, and the subject of sport development is an absolute irrelevance, illustrated here by the words of a Coloured woman from Khayaleitsha, a township outside Cape Town:

> There's over one million living in these squatter conditions. Now that is a fight to stay alive, nobody thinks about sport. It is quite clear that health, housing, and job creation are the priorities and that sport is very, very low on the ladder.

Political, social and economic conditions have a direct relevance to the issue of sport development in South Africa. Although SACOS has now closed, some members who were active in the movement during apartheid sustain a radical voice. They insist that until there are fundamental changes in the social fabric of South African society which will liberate the population as a whole, sport cannot be developed democratically. They see sport development as an explicitly political issue and are critical of the money spent on existing programmes, on supporting athletes at the Barcelona and Atlanta Olympics, on promotion of the Rugby World Cup, and on sponsorship for the Cape Town bid for the 2004 Olympics. In 1995, a retired teacher and ex-SACOS member living in a Coloured community in Wetton, outside Cape Town, said to me:

> We've got an RDP which hasn't yet worked. There is still a lack of the basic means for every human being to have a house over his head. You'll find squalor – it was raining two days ago – these people are swimming, they have to swim to get to work. So I say that 3.4 million [rands] could have built a block of flats for 70,000 each, rather than send sportspersons who are already privileged to take part in Barcelona.

The impoverished conditions of life posed a dilemma for sport development in the years immediately following the ANC's 1994 election to power. Radical voices argued that if the money spent on sport were invested in housing and other welfare benefits first, it would bring closer the chances of deprived people being able to include sport in their lives. However, agents from outside the government, who for different reasons see sport as a good investment, are unlikely to put money into welfare activities that attract less publicity and kudos. It is also argued that, although survival is a priority of existence for huge numbers of women, it should not exclude programmes which would improve the quality of life for others who are less seriously deprived.

At the second post-apartheid general election on 2 June 1999, the ruling ANC decisively retained power and Thabo Mbeki replaced Nelson Mandela as President. He made the following statement:

> In their millions and without hesitation, the people of South Africa have renewed the mandate of the ANC to govern our country. The poorest of the poor have said they trust the ANC to bring them out of their condi-tions of misery. The women of our country have mandated us to continue with the struggle for their upliftment and emancipation. Our people, both Black and White, have mandated us to remain firm in the pursuit of our vision of a non-racial society and the important goal of reconciliation.
>
> (McGreal, *Guardian* 4/7/99)

The retired teacher cited earlier made the following statement five years later, in 2000, in reponse to Mbeki's promises. She made it very clear that because so little progress had been made in work and welfare reconstruction in five years that in her opinion the hub of sport development should be the building of a sports infrastructure for young people in those deprived areas where a lack of resources reflected a lack of hope:

> Very little has happened in the five years of freedom that we have had to help the really poor people of our country. Even though many Whites left the National Party at the election and Mbeki has said that wealthy Whites should give up some of their money to help those living in wretched poverty, there are no signs that things will change quickly. People really need action *now*. There's so much unemployment and people are still living in terrible conditions and there's crime and violence everywhere. ... You ask me about sport – well, sport is still not that important in the overall scheme, at least not for adults. What they should be doing is putting money into communities – so kids in schools have got proper gyms and pitches. Too much effort – *and money* – is being spent on funding elite athletes to get medals. ... It shouldn't just be piece-meal reforms and showcase reforms. The idea is that this will boost national pride and bring us all together. But we don't want sport as a palliative – we want sport as a way of life.

Gender inequalities

In the same way that piece-meal sport reforms have not gone far enough towards eliminating racial and ethnic inequalities, they also do not go far enough towards implementing the constitution's philosophy of equalizing gender relations of power. The problem is greater in relation to gender. While race and ethnicity have been prioritized in the quest for equality, in spite of the supposed corresponding commitment to gender equivalence, in *practice* it has not received the same attention. Maviva Manzini (1992: 5) argues that it is 'much easier to think of power as a feature of race, caste and class relations than of relations between men and women, particularly those from the same family, race or nation'. Prominent women in South Africa today – for example, Ramphela Mamphele, vice chancellor of Cape Town University – argue that sexism is now a bigger problem than racism (Daley, *Guardian* 13/10/98). Cheryl Carolus, in her role as the South African High Commissioner in London, has voiced her criticisms of the inherent sexism of the Black consciousness movement: 'Black men felt asserting their blackness meant asserting their maleness' (McGregor, *Guardian* 21/9/98). Gender inequalities and sexism have produced an overriding structure of control throughout South African society, which is exaggerated in sport. Women see the chances of restructuring and equalizing relations between men and women in sport slipping away, because in the post-Apartheid period men have successfully re-established dominance both in practical ways and at the level of ideas. 'Contemporary South African sport', Cheryl Roberts (1993: 9) claims, 'is gender biased, male dominated and sexist.'

Spectator sport sets the scene for the production and reproduction of gender differences and for the pre-eminence of men's sport. For example, the tour of the English men's cricket team to South Africa in 1995 brought huge publicity to the men's game. Press and television pictures of the White English players coaching township boys reaffirmed the popular idea that sport has a masculine gender across ethnic lines and that in cricket White men are dominant. Men's rugby also had an extraordinarily high profile during the 1995 World Cup in South Africa, particularly when Nelson Mandela brilliantly appropriated the Springbok emblem and transformed it from a symbol of White superiority to one of national unity.[12] Mandela's gesture was uniquely important for race relations – for one brief time, the nation was symbolically united. The notion of unity was, however, only partial. It was in effect a celebration, *par excellence*, of South African maleness, masking the gendered nature of South African sport and South African society. The sport–masculine alliance is consolidated by sport sponsors, who are encouraged to invest in men's sport and deterred from supporting women's sport – which, in turn, leads to a worsening of discrimination.

Many women – Black and White – opposed the blatant chauvinism associated with Springbok rugby and the World Cup, and were incredulous and irritated that 'a sporting event was considered so important when South Africa had far more pressing matters to worry about' (Drysdale, *Scotland on Sunday* 28/5/95). A university lecturer made this observation at the beginning of the tournament, 'When you realise that the statistics for violence against women will certainly escalate if South Africa are knocked out of the competition early, then you can see this fixation with sport is tied to keeping women firmly in their place' (Drysdale, *Scotland on Sunday* 28/5/95). (South Africa has the highest rate of violence and rape against women in the world [Govender 1992: 38].) But South Africa *did* reach the final against New Zealand and, incredulously, won the Cup. During the live televised recording, I was in the company of a normally rational and gentle man who became uncharacteristically excited and emotional while screaming at the South African team to 'Get Lomu' (the super-fast, 'invincible', 18-stone New Zealand winger). 'Break his legs', he yelled, 'in 10 places, then he can't run. ... Get him down, stamp on him. ... Let him have it ... finish him off.' This White man – previously an anti-apartheid activist – was caught up in the way in which the new nationalism was being played out in World Cup rugby, but was also caught up in the characteristically aggressive masculinity of male sport in South Africa, and in particular of White male sport. Albert Grundlingh (1996: 197) argues that rugby in South Africa is an arena where 'gender relations are influenced and reinforced':

> Rugby, in part at least because of the rough, physical nature of the game, has acquired a reputation of being pre-eminently 'a man's game'. It has been described as the 'ultimate Man-maker', inculcating values such as 'courage, self-control and stamina'. All of these, it is claimed, are the products of the 'man-to-man' element in rugby, for to play rugger well, you must play it fiercely, and at the same time, and all the time, remember while doing so that you are a gentleman.

Rugby in South Africa, in common with other traditional male sports, is a masculinizing practice. While rugby is linked predominantly to the White community, soccer (the major male sport in Black communities) also invokes rigid expressions of chauvinist masculinity. The pre-eminence of all male sports in all communities militates effectively against women's participation having equal status and being equally resourced – a gendered structure of control which is hugely difficult for women to infiltrate and change.

Sport development work in South Africa has, overall, systematically prioritized boys' and men's sports. Large amounts of money have been spent on township development of traditional male sports, including cricket, rugby and soccer. For example, in 1995, Ali Bacher negotiated an eight-million-rand sponsorship deal for cricket in Soweto. Although girls play cricket and soccer, they do so in tiny comparative numbers to the boys, and they see little of the development monies. Netball is the sport that is played by more Black women than any other, but resources for the game in the Black communities are impoverished. In interviews that I carried out in Soweto in 1995, I was told that there were only two properly tarmacked netball courts in the whole city. The story was even worse in Guguletu, where there were also only two courts for the whole city, but they were below the regulation size and the surfaces were uneven. In an interview with a group of African women, I was told: 'The posts are not fixed, so they keep falling over. And we've got no coaches – no *real* coaches – the senior people in the team are our coaches.' The situation in Guguletu is reproduced in Black townships throughout the country. Put simply, facilities are impoverished and there are no campaigns for girls' sports *equivalent* to those for boys and young men. In spite of rhetoric to the opposite, in practice there is little redirection or channelling of resources directly to women.

Male power is related directly to organizational structures and methods of control, as well. Democracy led to Africans being put suddenly into positions of power in order to redress the White dominance of the past. But gender imbalances were not redressed with equal vigour. From the start, most leadership positions in sport were held by men – at national, regional and local levels. The sports minister has always been a man and the National Sports Council has been controlled by men (mostly African).[13] Women have been conspicuously underrepresented in management positions in the NSC: in 1995, there were 11 men on the Executive Committee, but only two women (one African, one Coloured), whereas women had a high profile in service roles. All the heads of committees were men, with the exception of the chair of the Women's Sport Committee. I was told that in the early life of the NSC there was an abortive attempt by women to ensure they had representation:

We did try to suggest back in July 1992, at the big AGM of the NSC, that there should be a percentage of women on the National Executive, and that one of the three vice presidents should be a woman, and that didn't go down terribly well. In fairness I think it was a proposal put in very late and it wasn't properly caucused.

It could be argued that the Women's Sport Committee had the potential to radicalize the gendered nature of the organization. But for those who served on it the task was not easy. (There were eight women on the Committee and two men.) They had limited funds from the NSC, and the logistics of co-ordinating a gender policy throughout the whole country were extraordinarily complex and difficult. In addition, they were full-time employees elsewhere and could only devote limited time to their work for sport. (All full-time NSC administrators were men.) The very existence of the Women's Committee was viewed as controversial – by some it was considered to be a position of strength to have an agenda specifically for gender affairs; others argued that the Committee lacked real power and that gender issues were effectively ghettoized because the committee was outside the mainstream affairs of the NSC.

The general absence of women in decision-making positions reflected the deep-seated power imbalances between men and women in South African sport and, as in the USA, there seemed to be 'very little willingness among powerful men to transform the social institutions within which they construct their power and privilege over others' (Messner 1993: 732). In other words, South African men in sport failed to put into practice the mission statement of the NSC about gender equity, which was in line with the liberation statements and literature (Ngcongo 1993: 7). An African woman from the Soweto Sports Council was critical that the NSC literature 'is always talking about woman empowerment'; 'But ask them what they are doing around that', she went on. 'It is just statements, nothing else.'

Although since 1995 the women's sport movement has developed momentum, sports organizations are still male-dominated.

> There are four (out of ten) women on the National Olympic Committee of South Africa (NOCSA) executive; two (out of eight) elected women members of the NSC; four (out of eight) women members of the NSC Sport Development Committee; one woman (out of nine) provincial minister with responsibility for sport; two female members of parliament who are concerned with the promotion of sport; and, out of 140 Sports Federations, only 65 have women's desks.
>
> (Hargreaves and Jones 2000)

The governing bodies of sport, with the exceptions of single-sex organizations, are also dominated by men. Even in 'modern' sports, women have to struggle for representation and equal treatment. For example, from the start of the relatively new National Triathlon Association, there were no women on the executive and no women on the selection committees. The Foot of Africa Competition is heavily dominated by men, and in 1995 – the first time sponsorship money was brought in – because of the huge discrepancy between men's and women's prize money (1000 rand/100 rand) some female competitors refused to take part.

Part of the difficulty is that even a minimal increase in female participation is taken to be the index of a successful solution to the problem of gender, explained to me as follows by the General Secretary of the NSC in the Western Cape:

> Where there is an understanding of affirmative action it is always in the context of Black and White ... it is not understood in terms of male and female, so there is continued gender discrimination. It is argued that if women are playing sport then they will become coaches and managers and get into the administration of sport. ... I suspect that is the comfort zone – the team going to the All Africa Games was one third female and that makes us look good, so we don't have to change our admin structures in order to accommodate women any more.

In general, then, gender issues are seen in easily quantifiable terms, and there is a marked insensitivity to the more complex aspects of gender relations. Even short-term practical solutions, dealing with the different and particular needs of women, have been neglected. For example, there has been little concern about providing special facilities for women, organizing crèches, dealing with problems of travel and safety, or arranging more suitable times for competitions, and so on (C. Roberts 1993: 13).

But not all sports associations have ignored the need to integrate women and to take affirmative action. In the last few years there have been improved arrangements and opportunities for women's sport throughout South Africa and at different levels. 'All the successful federations', one woman said to me, 'are developing programmes that include women; those that are undeveloped ignore women.' There are, for example, a handful of organizations that have employed quota systems. The new squash constitution, for instance, laid down that a minimum of 4 out of 12 of the National Executive must be women. Exceptionally, the South African Squash Federation has also had the only democratically elected national president of a mixed-sex association. However, there has been substantial female involvement in squash for years, and its apparent radicalism in respect of gender is in part because it has been, and remains, an essentially White sport with sufficient resources for both sexes.

In most sports, however, women perceive themselves as being in direct competition with men, and there has been a tendency to invoke a rigid system of male domination. Women are frustrated that they have far fewer resources than men – in terms of equipment, facilities, funding, coaching, sponsorship, media exposure, access to shared facilities, and so on. A good example is basketball, the sport that Steve Tschwete, the first Minister for Sport, called 'South Africa's "rainbow sport"'. In 1995, the men's basketball association got money to send a team abroad; there was no money to do the same for women. Practical barriers are underpinned by sexist attitudes. The following comments, which illustrate this point, were made to me in 1995 by members of a group of

African women in Guguletu. They were referring to joint use of indoor facilities:

> We don't get the court if the men are there.

> When you are using the hall, the boys are there intimidating you, and then you have to leave. You don't have the power to chase them away. We need peace and for the boys to stay outside.

> The guys take most of the time; the guys get the best practice. There's not much time for girls to raise our standards.

> There are so few facilities and if there are males there, they don't have the decency to give you space. If we could have our own courts, then we could expand.

Women protest about the intensity of male chauvinism, and about the antagonism and ridicule they experience from male members. And they complain that the media allocates most time to men's sports and routinely produces gendered ideas and images. They are also very aware of the problems of men controlling and coaching women's sports; that, because men hold the top positions in almost all organizations, they not only make major decisions that affect the ways in which women can function, but they can also filter information through to women's groups in the amount and form they prefer. Women feel intensely that they lack power; what they are seeking is to share on an equal footing with men in democratic processes and at all levels of decision-making procedures.

The lack of female power reaches from grassroots to top-level sport. The elite sports programme 'Operation Excellence', set in place specifically to secure medals when South Africa returned to international competition, failed hopelessly to result in the equalization of male and female representation in national teams, illustrated by the following figures: South Africa sent 62 men and 25 women to the 1992 Olympics; 80 men and 32 women to the 1994 Commonwealth Games; 259 men and 70 women to the 1995 All-Africa Games; 70 men and 18 women to the 1996 Olympics; and 130 men and 82 women to the 1998 Commonwealth Games. (The predominantly male character of White South African sport during apartheid was also reflected in the low numbers of women in the national teams – for example, at the 1960 Olympics the South African team comprised 56 men and 2 women [Hargreaves and Jones 2000].)

Gender and diversity

However, there is a risk of producing an undifferentiated account of unequal gender relations and male domination in South African sport which masks the diverse realities of women's lives. As bell hooks (1984: 18) has pointed out:

> Women in lower class and poor groups, particularly those who are non-white, would not have defined women's liberation as women gaining social

mobility with men since they are continually reminded in their everyday lives that all women do not share a common social status.

There is extraordinary diversity among South African women, coming as they do from different racial, ethnic, class, cultural, religious and political backgrounds. Such diversity means that gender subordination is not uniform for all women, and there are conflicts between different groups of women, as well as between men and women. The greatest contrast is between White women, who remain relatively privileged in sport, and African women, who are the most seriously deprived. But there is risk of a neo-colonial discourse developing which produces a stark and rigid dichotomy between the two groups, and which essentializes the position of African women by representing them as uniformly backward, generally poor, illiterate, oppressed by cultural, class, gender, tribal and religious ideologies, and powerless. The popular model of development is one of 'civilization' – a process which would enable African women to participate in sport according to the model of the West. Of course, sport development is only applicable to those who are not living in poverty.

The legacy of apartheid has deprived township women of sport infrastructures. They remain seriously underprivileged and underresourced. Even now, new schools are being built with no indoor facilities, and the most that is usually available is some space for soccer and a court of sorts for netball. In addition, the current gender ideologies and harsh forms of male domination in African communities, rooted in traditional and colonial forms of patriarchy, are material forces which subordinate women and prevent them from taking part in sport. I was told that 'Zulu communities are very male dominated and development work must link up with their culture and ways of thinking. Once they are old enough to marry, Zulu girls don't have a chance.' But, in spite of seemingly insurmountable difficulties, township women are active agents in the process of negotiating new relations of power, in the construction of their own sporting identities, and in the creation of a new social practice. They are by no means passive recipients of handout culture, but are engaged in a constant struggle to secure better opportunities for all African women.

I asked an African woman in Guguletu, 'Have things improved for you since the ending of apartheid?' 'No', she replied, and then, unprompted, continued:

> To begin with I was angry – really angry – and wanted retribution. I hated them, and I wanted them to suffer, and I wanted the good things they had. But that would only destroy my soul. Now I just want to work to make things better, to help my children to have a better chance to do good things … like play sport.

This woman was working with young girls in her local community as a voluntary self-taught volleyball coach. She was determined to help her daughter and friends have the opportunities she had missed because of apartheid. The new South Africa has given women who suffered under apartheid the desire to work for a decent life for themselves and their families. Even though they do not expect instant change, they have a vision of a better future and are more confident to make demands. For increasing numbers of African women, sport and exercise are no longer areas of life that they could not possibly aspire to, but activities they feel may be within their grasp.

The following examples of African sportswomen illustrate the ways they are redefining traditional ideas and constructing their own histories. Inspired by Moila Blanche – an African woman who pioneered Black athletics during apartheid – Lydia Mofula became one of South Africa's top 10-kilometre runners. In 1992 she became the first Black woman to win national colours when she ran in Japan. She had no sponsorship, whereas her White teammates did. Every weekend Moila works with young African girls in an athletics development project. Jerminah Sesoai is a teacher in Soweto and a middle-distance runner, who says:

> My success will do the children of Soweto good, because I'm there for them, fighting for their rights. ... The problem is that there's no stability in schools. There's a lot of politics surrounding sport which makes it difficult to work freely with the children, as well as the lack of training facilities.
>
> A major contribution to the lack of Black sportswomen in this country is that we believe myths such as women who take up running won't be able to have children. Stories like this can put women off sport because they know that men won't marry them if they can't give them children. Another thing that annoys me is that Black women give up sport when they have children. I'm out to prove these beliefs wrong!

Moila and Jerminah represent a new generation of Black sportswomen whose visibility makes them symbolic of Black success and empowerment and, by association, they become models and heroines for all Black women. More and more Black women participate in athletics and, in particular, road-running, and some of the most precocious Black female athletic talent is to be found in the townships. For example, in 1993, when she was only 15 years old, Louisa Leballo, from Meadowlands in Soweto, had won every junior athletics championship that she had entered, winning gold medals in middle-distance events including 800 metres, 1500 metres, 3000 metres and cross-country. But Louisa was unable to go to the World Junior Athletics Championships in Korea in 1992 because she had no sponsorship. Her coach paid out of his own pocket for her to attend home meetings and for equipment, and she was also supported by her mother, who is a single parent and a paraplegic. Louisa is a heroine of the Black community and a role model for other Black girls and young women. But there is a tendency for Black athletes to be 'appropriated' as heroines in mainstream consciousness as well and not to be seen as representative of their specific communities and identities. The production of Black heroines boosts nation-building and the ideology of equality. An African woman from Guguletu was critical of the resources being ploughed into top-level sport and of the use of Black athletes as symbols of South African racial unity. She complained that:

> The present focus on the elite athlete is no preparation for the future. We need an infrastructure of development coaches who will work with 9- and 10-year-olds. They're putting so much energy into the South Africa Olympics instead of building sport from the grassroots.

Black women see sport as a channel for self-definition – simultaneously Afrocentric and feminist. Following years of subjugation under apartheid, their struggles in sport today are part of a wider quest for recognition and dignity; their successes reflect a radical independence and autonomy often absent in other areas of life. Sport is an important politico-cultural space for Black people. 'Black' here denotes not simply a political alliance against racism – it operates as a 'profoundly cultural category' (Rattansi 1992: 40), embodying the construction of a 'united' identity around particular experiences and achievements in sport.

The new South Africa is giving non-White sportswomen new opportunities. For example, in 1992, when the separate race-specific karate associations were unified into one, Nellie Kleinsmidt became a trainer and a referee and has since become a 'South African national referee and has earned the status of continental judge with the Union of Africa Karate Federation' (Jones 2000). Most significantly, in 1998 she obtained her sixth Dan black belt at the age of 59: 'Nellie Kleinsmidt is the first and only woman of colour to have been appointed to the Referee's Board of South Africa and the only woman of colour in Africa to have obtained a sixth Dan black belt' (Jones 2000). In the post-apartheid period she continues to work with people from disadvantaged communitites and pushes all the time for female empowerment in the karate culture. For example, she has worked in numerous administrative roles in international and national organizations, is the co-founder – with Sanette Smit, a White woman – of the Women's Karate Forum in the Western Cape province, campaigns for gender equity in the male-dominated karate organizations, and struggles to change sexist and homophobic practices in karate training. Denise Jones (2000: 15) suggests that '*Sensei* Nellie's struggle for empowerment has always taken place within the broader struggles against racism and sexism.' Her life history is inspirational for other Black women.

Referring to Afro-American women in the USA, Patricia Hill Collins (1991: 70) claims that 'Black women have insisted on our right to define our own reality, establish our own identities, and name our own history.' The same is true for Black women in South Africa. Women like Nellie Kleinsmidt appear, not as victims, but as strong, heroic women who are proud of their colour and their culture, who are authentic representatives of Black womanhood and who are active agents in defining their own identities.

Achieving against the odds

In increasing numbers, young women and girls who make up the enormous pool of previously untapped sporting talent in South Africa are achieving remarkable results. Stories of success are the outcome of the determination and energy of individuals from the heterogeneous mix that comprises 'South African women'. Black women in particular have been participating in increasing numbers in soccer, as a direct result of successful township programmes, spearheaded by the Soweto Ladies Football Club. Soweto Ladies secured 50,000-rand sponsorship money from Pasta Romagna. They won the Gothia Cup championships, competing against club teams from all over the world. Influenced by the success of Soweto Ladies, Nowinile 'Winnie' Qhuma, from Guguletu, challenged the conventional attitudes of Black men in her community, who opposed women's sports, when she successfully formed the first women's soccer club in Guguletu in 1993:

> I realised women in Guguletu are not involved in soccer, while in other areas like Soweto they play the game. Most of our young girls are not involved in sport because their parents refuse to let them play sport. They prefer to keep them at home to do the cooking and cleaning.
>
> (*Sportswoman* 1993)

The Women's South African Football Association (WSAFA), which replaced the disbanded South African Women's Football Association – the White apartheid governing body – was affiliated to the men's football association, and has had a successful record in international competition. The national women's football team played in the finals of the 1995 All Africa Women's Football Competition and were beaten by Nigeria. The team was composed of seven Black, three Coloured and one White woman. Several of the national team members are from Soweto Ladies.

The increasing visibility of Black sportswomen and the racial mix, particularly of national teams, sends out an important message that the racial divisions of the past are being overturned. Black women represented South Africa the first time at the 1992 Olympics – Rencia Nasson in fencing; Cheryl Roberts in table tennis; and Marcelle Winkler in track athletics. Development programmes in townships are essential if integration is to continue and equality is to be realized, and elite sportswomen are playing an important role in this process. For example, Cheryl Roberts has fought for better facilities for table tennis in deprived areas and she visits the townships to train young players in her sport.

Although there are still race-specific and class-specific sports, there are also examples of the breaking down of race and social divisions between different groups of women. But unequal gender divisions and practices still remain exceptionally difficult to change. The philosophy that Nellie Kleinsmidt and Johan Roux have put into practice in their karate dojo, which intentionally challenges traditional gender divisions, is unusual. They explained to me that:

We try not to differentiate between whether it is development for boys or development for girls. Whatever projects we arrange are for both sexes. I am proud to say that in the development of karate, the majority are girls, especially in the junior ranks, I think the ratio could be 60 to 40. There is a greater drop-out rate among the girls than the boys – so more boys get through to the senior ranks – there is a dominance of males at senior level – probably one woman for every ten men.

Kleinsmidt and Roux are trying to change the perception that karate is a male-dominated culture and are helping girls and young women to recognize that it is as legitimate an activity for them as it is for boys and men. They have reservations with the quota system because, they argue, 'it addresses the problem immediately, but is not a long-term solution. ... Gender equality', they maintain, 'will only be sustained if it is built into everyday practices.'

The everyday practices of sportswomen in the new South Africa are inextricably linked to sports structures and political processes – which can obstruct (as under apartheid) or facilitate progress. The 'women's sport lobby' has put pressure on the NSC and on regional and local sports bodies to take more positive action with respect to gender issues. The resultant liberal policy changes have gone some way towards spreading women's sport more evenly throughout the country. As we have seen, the NSC has worked with the national and provincial Departments of Sport and Recreation to promote gender equity and has set up women's desks in each of the provinces. The most important recent change has been the establishment of a Women and Sport South Africa (WASSA) initiative in each province, co-ordinated by a WASSA National Committee, with its own steering committee (with representatives from all nine provinces). Such a structure provides a support framework within which individual women can work more productively. It is a means by which a co-operative and representative network of women can be established for different areas, and for the country as a whole. Facilitated by the DSR, the WASSA structures take responsibility for policy development and the implementation of programmes. The mission of the WASSA national strategy (1997–2000) is 'to develop a culture in which women and girls will have equal opportunities, equal access and equal support in sport and recreation at all levels and in all capacities as decision-makers, administrators, coaches, technical officials, and participants'. By the end of 1997 all provinces had an elected WASSA committee. There are a number of innovative developments taking place at provincial level. For example, the Western Cape was pro-active in formulating a democratically produced Gender Equity Policy for sport and recreation, which was completed early in 1997 and launched later in the year. Denise Jones, who drafted the policy, took what she describes as a 'feminist approach to policy writing' by holding workshops to which participants were invited from all over the Western Cape, so that everyone's ideas could be represented in the final document. There are also plans for launching an Active Girls Campaign and a database for women in sport. These initiatives, at national and provincial levels, were guided by the South African Constitution, the Human Rights Bill, and the Brighton Declaration (Denise Jones – correspondence; see Chapter 7 re. Brighton Declaration).

The links between individual initiatives and the wider structures of sport and society are dialectical. In response to structural deficiencies and barriers, women have pushed the policy-makers to take notice of their demands, and the resultant changes have made it easier for women to make further advances. It is too early to comment on the way in which the most recent organizational and personnel changes will affect gender-equity developments in the future: first, a new South Africa Sports Commission was set up at the end of 1999, intended to rationalize policy structures by taking the place of the National Sports Council and co-ordinating work with the Department of Sport and Recreation, and second, at the same time, Mr Ngconde Balfour was appointed as the new Minister of Sport and Recreation. Although in 1994, with the formation of the new post-apartheid sport apparatus, the great potential to radicalize gender relations in South African sport was not realized, after six years of struggle, women are more demanding, better organized and are gaining ground.

Speaking out

We have seen that there is constant tension between agency and constraint in the sporting lives of women of all ethnicities. Black women are particularly conscious that they face difficulties and opposition ahead. 'It is good you are talking to the Black women separately', a woman from Soweto said, 'because they will give you a true picture, they will not be intimidated.' She continued:

> We have had a unification of all sports in South Africa, but it's a question of people in the First World still holding onto positions. In the Third World these people are struggling to get positions. In the Third World they know what the situations are in the townships and what is needed to develop women. First world people are not aware.

Most importantly, African women want to be integral to the development process, but reject imposed structures and manipulative and unsustainable practices. For example, in some organizations Black women are given token positions but, it was put to me, 'It only symbolizes unity, but is not a reality.' The implication is that racial inequalities are still distinct. The tendency for courses to be set up in the townships, and for coaches to be brought in, but for a limited period only so that there is no continuity, is also seen as a publicity stunt. An African woman in Guguletu argued that:

> The situation now demands that the so-called Whites should allow us in sports, and what they are doing is to help some people – to get some people just to pose. They are not really dealing with our problem, you see, it's just a

pose just to get brown faces in their teams, and then making it as if they're developing, they're expanding and then it ends there. For example, if we get clinics – OK – everybody's invited to the clinics – they take a picture and they send it to their sponsors, I suppose, and they say, 'This is what we are doing'. And it ends there. There is no actual development in ... our communities. That is the problem we are experiencing. The management of these sporting codes, everything is still in their [the Whites'] hands, it's difficult to get to them.

It is usually assumed that Black South Africans are the beneficiaries of liberation, but because of their economic power the reality is that at present White people are more easily able to take advantage of the new openings in communications, trading and travel. As Beresford (*Guardian* 22/3/95) has pointed out, 'The fruits of liberation are still a long way off for the country's majority population.' This is the reason why there is uneasiness in some sports where it is known that, during apartheid, those who were then, and are now still, in positions of power, did nothing to oppose the system, ignored the sports boycott, and sent teams abroad. Racism is seen by many African women to have originated and to be perpetuated by White people, who still benefit from their supremacy during apartheid, and who tend now to want to 'let bygones be bygones', to distance themselves from the past and adopt new identities.

Among all Black women's sports groups, there is a strong feeling that a pro-active approach is needed, and that in order for women of all ethnicities to be able to work productively together, White women must be prepared to speak out and initiate change. There is concern about the abundance of untapped Black female talent, and about the absence of adequate programmes that will unleash it. The necessity to address actively the effects of apartheid was put to me in this way:

> We need more women to come into the country to play and to coach. Not world rugby in this fantastic stadium where we paid an exorbitant amount of money to see an event. I didn't go because I'm not interested unless they remove that animal – to me it's still an apartheid symbol, the springbok. I want them to come into my culture, to ordinary clubs, and to junior sport for girls. Everybody seems to think, 'Oh, Elana [Meyer]!' But what about the other Elanas?[14]

As well as asking for improved resources, Black women are making a number of requests that could relatively easily be implemented: for example, that the townships be used as venues for events, that priority be given to Black groups in coaching and training schemes, that a quota system be practised to enable Black women to take part in the decision-making procedures, and that there be a representative number of players from different racial groups in competition squads.[15] These requests cohere with the agreement reached at the World University Service-South Africa (WUS-SA: 1) meeting, held in Johannesburg in 1992, that there is a need to 'facilitate visibility and direct participation of the South African women who suffer most oppression'.[16] African women do not want to be represented by men, be they Black or White, or by White women. They want a direct say in their fate.

But the solutions to sport development are not straightforward and do not relate only to the most commonly posed dichotomy – Black means deprived/White means privileged. Because the official politics of women's sports now is to give priority to Blacks – which, in practice, means Africans – in some cases White women have been made to feel that *they* are now being discriminated against; and in other situations they feel the effects of reverse racism. There is a problem also for Indian and Coloured women who, during apartheid, were part of the sport liberation struggle, and who feel now that they are being marginalized. Divisions within the Indian community, based on religion and culture, also produce additional diversities and needs that tend to be overlooked in sport development. There are divisions, too, amongst Africans – for example, the Zululand Sports Development Project (ZSDP) has been opposed to the NSC because 'it is ANC controlled' and for that reason are working independently to get Zulu sport leaders in the communities. An added complexity is posed by class, which is said by some to be the greatest divisive force in South Africa today – more important now than race (Ransom 1995: 10). Because the National Party had a policy of separate development, acknowledgement of difference has tended to be limited to racial rather than class or other grounds (Sunde and Bozalek 1993: 31). For example, there is a growing Black middle class who are benefiting directly from the new opportunities provided by the increased international commercialization of sport, some of whom are becoming separated from the communities of their roots. But there are also poor, uneducated Coloured, Indian and White women whose needs tend to be left out of the practical and theoretical strategies for women's sport. The needs of disabled females in sport also receive little attention, although their numbers have been growing, in part because women and girls, as well as men, are victims of intertribal war (Annecke 1990: 14); and the particular problems of compulsory heterosexuality and homophobia in women's sport, which affect lesbian participation, have also been neglected.

bell hooks (1984: 6) argues that women must learn to accept responsibility for fighting oppressions that may not directly affect them as individuals and, referring specifically to South Africa, Jane Flax (1992: 460) urges feminists 'to learn to make claims on our own and others' behalf and to listen to those which differ from ours'. These are challenges to all women who are working in sport in South Africa, increasing numbers of whom are taking them up. Many White women acknowledge their advantages in relation to Black women and are working with them to increase opportunities for sport in deprived areas. Black women in general have fewer management and coaching skills and less experience of dealing with gender issues, and White women are taking initiatives by organizing training courses for them. Solidarity between different groups of women was symbolized by the Foundation of the Women's Sport

Foundation in 1993, and by the publication of a journal exclusively about women's sport, entitled *Sportswoman*. The significance of sport in the lives of women has also been given attention in organizations which are concerned with women's issues in general. For example, the Women's Bureau of South Africa has a sport sub-committee and a policy for a girls' sport development programme. In a number of different provinces there have been initiatives to introduce and raise consciousness about the values of community sport and exercise programmes,[17] and there has been greater integration of girls and women of different ethnicities into sports clubs.

Theories of development

So how do we make sense of the unique diversities embodied in women's sport development in South Africa? There have been debates between women about the best way forward – some believe that remaining in the political mainstream is the most productive, whereas others argue that 'trying to forge national unity among women in a country with schisms of race and class like South Africa is doomed' (Haffajee 1995: 13). In sport, there has been a growing women's movement of co-operation and inclusion, which puts the interests of women first, trying to include those of women from *all ethnic and social backgrounds*. This approach embodies the reality that different women can and do work in different ways. Haffajee (1995: 13) argues that the voices of South African women need to 'boom out' so that they can 'seize the moment and reap the benefits that their newly-won democracy has to offer'. Since the ending of apartheid in South Africa, more women in sport are finding their voices, negotiating for improvements, and making demands in order to improve the opportunities for *all* South African women in sport.

Characterized here as South African sport feminists, they have been part of more general feminist activities in the wider South African society and in other parts of the developing world. Feminism in South Africa did not spring up in the post-apartheid period but had been established earlier when, for example, African women were trying to make their voices heard under the harsh tribal laws which disempowered them (or when Afrikaner women were negotiating the patriarchal teaching of the Dutch Reformed Church). In post-apartheid South Africa, in spite of the liberal constitution and its emphasis on equality, there has been continued resistance to radical changes to improve the status of women. We have seen that sport development programmes affect men and women differently, and that the particular needs of women have not been taken into account adequately by those in positions of power. This has been a general problem in the conceptualization of development projects and in development theories, and was the impetus for the growth of different women- and gender-centred approaches.

The initial concern that arose in the 1960s was to make women visible and to work for greater equality between men and women. This approach was known as Women in Development (WID), and has been characterized as a typically liberal perspective that did little to question Westernized methods or to change gender relations and ideologies (Elsdon 1995: 262–7; Moser 1993: 2–6). Then, in the 1970s, an approach associated with radical feminism – labelled Women and Development (WAD) – arose in opposition to male power and male-dominated institutions. The focus was very much on women's culture and women-only projects (Marchand and Parpart 1995: 13). In the 1980s, a socialist feminist approach emerged that embodied concerns about the terrible poverty facing increasing numbers of women, and the effects of global patriarchy (Elsdon 1995: 2; Marchand and Parpart 1995: 14; Moser 1993: 3–6). This approach became known as Gender and Development (GAD). It focused on gender-sensitive rather than women-only strategies. A more recent and potentially transformative approach is the Third World Women's (TWW), or the empowerment, perspective. Because it is articulated by Third World women themselves and connected to their particular experiences through collective action, it avoids the criticism of being inspired by Western feminisms. Women's oppression is seen not only as a result of gender relations of power, but also as a feature of colonial and neo-colonial oppression, experienced differently by different women according to their 'race, class, colonial history and current position in the international economic order' (Moser 1993: 74; Chowdhry 1995: 36; Elsdon 1995: 266). Linked closely to the experience of trying to improve the lives of women in a country of extreme diversities, the idea of empowerment raises the question of alternative, as opposed to existing, patterns of development (*DAWN* 1985, cited in Elsdon 1995: 26). The central philosophy of this perspective is the right to determine choices in life and to influence the direction of change, in resistance to the domination of oppressors.

The first three approaches to women's development in the Third World parallel (broadly speaking) the variants of mainstream Western feminism – liberal, radical and socialist. Black women in the West perceived the focus of these perspectives – the two systems of discrimination, sex and class – as racist and ethnocentric and their critique induced a shift to 'a more micro-level of analysis that lent itself better to the complex interplay of different aspects of inequality'. There arose, as a result, a tendency 'to theorize the so-called "triple oppressions" of gender, race and class in a more cultural and symbolic mode' and to stress the diversities of women's experiences (Barret and Phillips 1992: 4). Then came postmodern versions of Western feminism proposing the fracturing of experience (Coole 1993; Walby 1992) and the loss of validity of the structures of patriarchy, racism and capitalism. Postmodernist feminism argues that patriarchy, racism and capitalism should not be used as essentialist, unitary concepts because, in reality, *because of diversity*, they are complex and incoherent. However, in South Africa, the three systems of gender, race and class clearly remain potent social forces – relational and mutually determining – signalling that the notion of causality should not be abandoned in the face of complexity (Walby 1992: 32–3, 40).

These theoretical positions are linked to practice. Maria Nzomo (1995: 136) explains the position of African feminists:

> While postmodernist discourse would emphasize *difference* and *diversity* among women, African feminists are emphasizing *unity in diversity* as a necessary strategy for strengthening the women's movement, their solidarity and their empowerment.

But these two positions are not necessarily incompatible. If feminists acknowledge differences, it neither forces a false universalism nor leads to fragmentation, but, it is suggested, 'allows for both autonomous organizations and actions, as well as coordinated programmes based on agreed issues and areas of cooperation'. This process should produce a supportive and creative 'feminist politics of difference' (Meintjes 1993: 39).

Identity politics, however, is a contentious issue in the South African context. Because the National Party had a divisive policy of separate development, many feminists have been hesitant to explore the question of difference: 'If acknowleged at all, it has primarily been limited to difference on racial rather than class or other grounds. As a result, the South African women's movement has rested on a very tenuous notion of "collective identity as women" ' (Sunde and Bozalek 1993: 31). But there is also the problem of White women theorizing about Black women, because it is argued that racism (and other forms of oppression) fundamentally alters a woman's identity, and for that reason Black women have a clearer perspective on oppression than White women, who appropriate other women's experiences when they carry out research (Sunde and Bozalek 1993: 32–3). The privileging of oppression and difference is described by Stanley and Wise (1992: 357, cited in Sunde and Bozalek 1993) as the 'epistomological privilege of the oppressed'. However, it has also been argued that experience alone cannot provide a theory of gender relations:

> Linked to this is an awareness that the categories of subject/object, insider/outsider, margin/centre are continually shifting and are not fixed in themselves. The postmodern position is that there is a need to acknowledge the contradictions and contextual nature of all women's varied identities.
>
> (Sunde and Bozalek 1993: 33)

This leads to the sense that it is impossible to reach a position of commonality around the question of gender. In different ways, feminists have been trying to find a way out of the impasse. One step in the right direction is for White women to make explicit their position of power in relation to Black women, and to make their work explicitly political. Such a position would open the way for sport feminists in South Africa to work collectively to explore diversity. The problem, of course, is that in the present political climate many women want to distance themselves from the past and adopt new identities. Meintjes (1993: 39) argues that, if feminists acknowledge differences,

> this neither forces a false universalism upon the women's movement, nor does it lead to political fragmentation of such a movement. Instead, it allows for both autonomous organizations and actions, as well as coordinated programmes based on agreed issues and areas of cooperation. This process allows for the development of a much more supportive and creative feminist politics of difference.

In addition, Meintjes insists that such a feminist approach must be based on the experiences of South African women specifically and not of women from the north. There is a tendency among some women to avoid discussing race because of the new ideology of non-racialism; but, she argues, 'to get to a comfortable non-racial situation, we have got to correct the racial divide that has occurred because there is so much hostility and anger. We need to overcome this discomfort with a discussion of race' (Meintjes 1993: 41–2).

It may be that sport, more than other areas of life and culture, can remove the fear that if differences are exposed there will not be sufficient common ground on which to build a women's movement. bell hooks (1982: 152) maintains that 'Racism is the barrier that prevents positive communication and it is not eliminated or challenged by separation.' Women who take part in sport do so because of their love of it, which may help to override some of the stark divisions of the past. Although there are still many areas of conflict between the distinctive groups of women in South African sport, there is also a strong sense that they can work collectively to challenge gender inequalities and other forms of discrimination. Everyone I spoke to believes that women-centred policies are needed and that sport developers must pay greater attention to the particular problems, needs and desires of different groups of women.

A significant point of consensus among women in South Africa is that sport is liberating and enriching. Ransom tells us that 'Liberation and freedom are invisible; they reside in the human spirit. Though liberation from apartheid has come, the freedom to live by different values has yet to be established' (1995: 10). Race, ethnicity and gender are unstable social constructions, which impact on women in sport, and through which they are forging new values and meanings. There is a growing incentive for women of all racial groups – African, Coloured, Indian and White – to work *together* to challenge gendered and sexist practices in South African sport and to improve opportunities in all communities. There is no doubt that, in increasing numbers, women in sport in the new 'Rainbow Republic' are finding ways to celebrate *unity out of diversity*.

3 The Muslim female heroic

Shorts or veils?

Introduction: sport, politics and religion

When Nawal El Moutawakel from Morocco took the 400-metre hurdles title at the 1984 Los Angeles Olympics, hers was the first gold medal to be won by a woman from the African continent. Nawal had made history. Her achievement was especially remarkable because she was simultaneously the first Arab woman *and* the first Muslim woman to win a gold medal. For different reasons, and in different contexts, Nawal El Moutawakel was hailed as heroic. Disregarding the reality that the category 'Muslim' is heterogeneous and that attitudes to women's involvement in public sport vary from country to country, she was reported in the Western media to have triumphed over a unified, restricted 'way of life' that normally excludes women from sport. Her success was celebrated as a fundamental break with tradition, a signal of courage, new possibilities, changing attitudes and newfound freedoms. In Morocco, she was a figure of national triumph and Arabic pride, a sign of radical womanhood made possible by forward-looking government. It was unprecedented for a Muslim woman to be conspicuous in 'global' sport and in the global sports media and, more broadly, Moutawakel's gold medal signalled a momentous symbolic victory for Muslim women across the world.

But eight years later, in 1992, when Hassiba Boulmerka from Algeria arrived home for a heroine's welcome after her victory in the 1500 metres at the Barcelona Olympic Games, she was booed and jeered by a section of the population commonly referred to as Islamic fundamentalists (Mackay, *Guardian* 8/5/98). Although Hassiba's success was also a significant landmark in the history of Muslim women in sport, it symbolized poignantly the struggles over women's bodies throughout the Muslim world and the powerful links between sport, politics and religion.

Nawal El Moutawakel's story is unusual. In contrast to most other girls and young women in Morocco and across the Arab world, her parents were keen to encourage her athletic ambition. Although she trained in the United States for eight months before the Olympics, the bulk of her training had taken place at home in Morocco, and she also received sponsorship and public acclamation from King Hassan II. In an interview with me in 1994, she pointed out that, 'Although it is much easier in Morocco than in a country like Algeria, there is still a lot of conservatism. After all these years since I won the gold medal, there is no Moroccan woman to follow in my footsteps.'

Moutawakel comes from a comparatively liberal, secular Arab state that gave her psychological and financial backing and nurtured her as a symbol of nationhood and progress. Most importantly, Morocco is keen to present an image of vibrant womanhood suited to the global world of the new century. This is a stance which takes issue with the popular Western perception of the backwardness of Islam and its discrimination against women. But Moutawakel is still exceptional. In all Muslim countries, the issue of female participation in sport is tied to strongly held beliefs about the female body embraced by culture, tradition, religion and politics. For women's bodies in sport, as in other areas of life and culture, the Qur'an has become the measure of right and wrong.[1] But the words of the Qur'an are understood in different ways by different groups – by the ulema,[2] politicians, 'ordinary' men and women, and athletes themselves. Hassiba Boulmerka explains how, as a result, the woman's body – *her* body – is the site of power and struggle: 'For Muslim women I symbolise freedom but, believe me, many people think it's not appropriate for women to take part in sport dressed in clothes that show parts of our bodies' (Mackay, *Guardian* 8/5/98). An Algerian sports journalist explains more fully:[3]

> For democrats, women's sport is one way of furthering equality between men and women, as well as manifesting a degree of tolerance. For the conservative and religious leaders, sporting women become the first targets in the fight to halt progress, and that is symbolic of all that is bad in Algerian society.
>
> (Butcher, *Guardian* 11/1/92)

The tiny number of successful, pioneering Muslim sportswomen, such as Nawal El Moutawakel and Hassiba Boulmerka, are perceived in Western thinking and by liberal Muslims as heroines who offer promise and possibility for their sex; or, conversely, in more traditional Muslim communities they are branded as sinful and decadent women who are distorting the truth of Islam. The struggles over their bodies have local and global dimensions relating to specific national, religious and political discourses, to global Islamic issues, and to the nexus between Islam and the West. This chapter explores the complexities of these struggles. While much of the discussion has relevance to Muslim women all over the world, its chief focus is the Middle East and North Africa – the 'heart' of the 'Muslim world'.

The Muslim world

It has been estimated that there are around 1.3 billion Muslims in the world (Colvin, *Sunday Times* 30/8/98), and that 'Islam today is the official religion of twenty-four world states and the religion of over 90 per cent of the population of Saudi Arabia, Egypt, Iraq, Iran, Pakistan and Bangladesh and the dominant faith in offically secular Indonesia and Turkey' (Nagata 1994: 65). Most Muslim people live either in nation states which emerged when Muslim nationalists fought for independence from Western powers and where the official religion is Islam, or in multiethnic and multireligious countries in which Muslims are numerically dominant. But with population mobility there are sizeable Muslim communities in countries with other major religions – in predominantly Hindu India, for example, there are 112 million Muslims, and in dominantly Christian states throughout the whole of the West there are large Muslim populations. In Western Europe there are between six and eight million Muslims:[4] in France and England, Islam is the second most important religion and it is predicted that a similar situation will soon prevail in several other European countries (Gerholm 1994: 190). Altogether there are Muslim populations in about 50 countries in the world, extending to communities as far-flung as Argentina, the Balkan States, Indonesia, the Philippines and South Africa. Islam is the world's fastest-growing religion, with a genuinely global character (Gerholm 1994: 2; Ahmed and Donnan 1994b: 1).

'The World of Islam' describes a vision of unity connecting all Muslim people across the world. It includes 'transnations' of diasporic communities which have been constructed through the desire to maintain links with the land of birth and/or origin and with other diasporized people with similar roots in other countries of migration. Diasporic communities are essentially hybrid ones, existing marginally 'between cultures', and embodying instabilities of cultural identity. Muslims who find themselves in often hostile 'host' environments choose to practise cultural and religious traditions linked to their countries of origin. They do so as a way of 'centring marginality' and actively constructing meaningful identities for themselves. Bromley (1998: 2) mentions the 'connectivities and deterritorializations made possible by the new technologies of the so-called global age in which identities can be simultaneously local, national, and transnational'. So, although the influence of Islam varies from country to country, and within countries, Muslim culture tends to be treated as homogeneous, as normative Islam, as absolute truth.

Islamism

In Western analyses, it is argued that Muslim culture has become a legitimation of Arab racial pride and that it has increasingly taken a fundamentalist form (Gellner 1994: xii), associated with the desire to possess and practise a unique, uncompromising religious truth and tradition (Gellner 1992). The development of Muslim women's sport in countries all over the world is inextricably linked to the discourses surrounding Islamic fundamentalism or 'Islamism' in different parts of Africa, Europe and the Middle East (Halliday 1994: 93). Although relatively few Muslim women throughout the world live directly under the umbrella of Islamic fundamentalism, they are all influenced in the ways they think and feel and in the ways they live their lives and use their bodies by its global effects, described here by Nagata (1994: 64):

> Islam as an ideology of renewal has been gathering momentum in the Middle East and North Africa since the mid-nineteeth century, but the Islam that strikes chords in the world today is associated with the so-called 'resurgence' which moved to centre stage in the 1960s and 1970s. This marks the point at which contemporary Islam seriously became a player in the international political domain, seeking power both as an end in itself and as the means of spreading an Islamic way of life.

Since the advent to power of Ayatollah Khomeini in Iran in February 1979, his condemnation to death of Salman Rushdie in 1989 after the publication of *The Satanic Verses*, and the Gulf War in 1991, the Muslim world has been shaken and transformed.[5] Fundamentalist movements have grown, notably in Afghanistan, Algeria, Egypt and Jordan, and millions of Muslims living in the West have been more outspoken and organized about their Islamic identity. Modern Islamization arose in opposition to European colonialism, and has condemned 'Westernization' and the effects of modernization and secularization. For Muslims across the world there is a conflict in the way in which they live their lives between the Islamic tradition and the pervasive influence of Western culture. Since sport insinuates Westernization, it presents women with particular cultural and bodily uncertainties.

Islam is claimed to be 'as strong now as it was a century ago' and, in some ways, 'probably stronger' (Gellner 1992: 5). Islamic faith is rooted in the idea of 'divine command', based on Allah's revelations to the Prophet Mohammad in the seventh century and recorded in the Qur'an (Gellner 1992: 6). The Qur'an provides a basis for a moral order and way of life which has become both doctrine and divine law. Gellner (1992: 7) argues that, because the religious current is predominant in Islam, theologians have become the 'monitors of political rectitude – whether or not they have the power to enforce their verdicts'. The strong Muslim concept and practice of community facilitates the translation of Qur'anic ideals and commands into social life.

Although there are different Islamic sects, existing alongside different sectarian and cultural traditions (Ahmed and Donnan 1994b: 6), there is a common focus (for or against) arguments for doctrinaire, 'high' and 'correct' interpretations of the Divine message – a supposed return to early Islam (Gellner 1992: 15). Discourses around fundamentalism are tied to the quest for identity, itself a response to social and political processes – notably, urbanization, political centralization, wider markets, labour migration and other global influences. Whereas the postmodern Western world promotes a culture of change, youth and consumerism, embracing noise, movement and speed, traditional Islam discourages change and emphasizes calmness and stability (Ahmed and Donnan 1994b: 12–13). Fundamentalists express fierce concerns about the likelihood of Western-style changes causing a shift in, or even a replacement of, everything that is worthwhile and pure in Islamic culture and traditions. Although relatively few Muslims in the world zealously adhere to doctrinaire forms of Islam, at a political level anti-American ideologies have strengthened in recent times and the beliefs of Islam have been selectively interpreted and transformed into politics. According to Colvin, there is little open opposition from the moderate face of Islam, and the Qur'an is being used increasingly to challenge Western capitalism in the absence of Marxist alternatives (*Sunday Times* 30/8/98).

In its fundamentalist forms, Islam has become a total system enabling religious control over culture and life, propagating the belief that Islam is a superior alternative to the perceived corruption of capitalism and the obvious failure of communism. Islamism today plays a dominant role in political and social life through the twinning of secular power and religious truth; it transcends social divisions and national cultures, appealing to different classes and sectors of different communities. Halliday (1994: 94–5) argues that control of the state is the central concern of Islamist movements, expressed through revolt against secular trends of the state; the use of Islam as an instrument of state power; and the use of Islamism in a multiethnic and multireligious context to articulate their interests and identities. Islamist sympathizers of all persuasions create networks that work *with* and *through* the apparatuses of the state (Karam 1998: 74), effectively influencing personal and cultural consciousness. The Islamization of political discourse reflects a general and growing conservatism and anti-secularism, based increasingly on aggressive and violent means of control (Colvin, *Sunday Times* 30/8/98).

The sense of being a Muslim in both Islamic and multiethnic states is tied, as well, to images of the East in the West and the West in the East, and to local and global tensions between Muslims and non-Muslims. With the rise of the extreme Right in Europe there is growing Islamaphobia and demonizing of 'The Muslim' (Mahl 1995: 14; Runnymede Trust 1997), which poses a dilemma for liberal Muslims who oppose the fundamentalist line but do not support Western antagonisms. Mahl (an Algerian woman, here using a pseudonym for safety) explains that:

> Fundamentalists promote not only their version of 'Muslimness', but also impose on us all a single forced identity at a time in history when we would rather stand for our multiple identities and gender, class, race, nationality, politics, and so on. In the same way many in the Western Left fail to acknowledge that a significant percentage of people born in Muslim countries and communities may not accept religion to be an essential marker of their identity.
>
> (1995: 14)

Women and Islam

Women occupy a special place in Islam, and the alignment of politics with religion has had a marked and often negative effect on their lives. It has been alleged that in places where Islamic jurisprudence (Shari'ah) is practised, women's rights have been reduced (Weiss 1994: 129; Whitehorn, *Observer* 19/6/94) and that the influence of Islamic fundamentalists, even when not in political control, has resulted in coercive forms of control and made women fearful of victimization (Mahl 1995; Tohidi 1991). Mahl (1995: 14) argues that the control of women is essential to fundamentalist politics, because of 'the focus on identity and subsequently on women who are seen as the guardians of identity, of cultural and religious values, of the purity of the blood'. Separate development for men and women is crucial to the fundamentalist credo tying women to their homes, discriminating against them in law, education, health, and employment, and idealizing their reproductive and moral roles (Mahl 1995: 15). Separatism is an ideology which has had crucial consequences for women's sport.

Akber Ahmed (1992: 33) argues that there is a huge distinction between the 'noble Islamic ideal' and the continuing oppression of Muslim women. He goes on: 'Where their [women's] lot is miserable and they have no rights, as is certain in tribal areas, it is to be attributed to male tyranny, not Islamic advice and is in need of urgent redress' (1992: 43). In common with Hassiba Boulmerka, some Muslim feminists argue that harsh treatment of women is not supported by the Qur'an and that Mohammed offered far more to women than present-day implacable fundamentalists. Halliday (1994: 96) describes Islam as like all great religions:

> a reserve of values, symbols, and ideas from which it is possible to derive a contemporary and social code: the answer as to why this or that inter-pretation was put upon Islam resides therefore, not in the religion and its texts itself, but in the contemporary needs of those articulating an Islamic politics.

Put bluntly by Ahmed and Donnan (1994b: 14), 'Muslim women in particular seem to be squeezed between Islamic fundamentalism and modernity, and between modernity and postmodernity'.

Although Muslim fundamentalism has a global constituency, and Muslim women throughout the world are influenced by it, the types and levels of constraint they experience and the opportunities they have to negotiate for changes and freedoms, vary greatly according to the countries and communities they live in. As we have seen in relation to sport, struggles are greater for women in Algeria than for those in Morocco. At one extreme are women in Afghanistan, who are ruthlessly controlled by the Taliban in every aspect of their lives, where girls' schools have been forcibly closed, and where women's sports have been prohibited (O'Kane 1998: 37); in Iran, women are challenging barriers and negotiating new opportunities in sport within a theocracy; in Egypt, women have choices within the laws of the secular state, although many Egyptian feminists argue that, when it comes to 'the women's issue', the ideas of the state vary very little from those of Islamists and, in practice, the governing ideology is Islamist (Karam 1998: 78, 127); in East Africa, where over 30 per cent of the population is Muslim, the traditionally liberal character of Islam has begun to change, closely influenced by and in part funded by fundamentalist movements from other Muslim countries (Anderson 1998: 33), reducing opportunities for women's sport; in Malaysia, there is growing polarization between Muslim and non-Muslim, the officially secular state is Islamicizing, and women's sports are tied more and more to religious prescriptions (Nagata 1994); in Syria, there is a greater separation between Islam and the state, women have more opportunities in sport than in other Muslim countries, real attempts have been made to take account of women's demands, and it is mandatory for women to be represented in all sports organizations.

Islam and the female body

The social construction of women in Islam is linked to the power of symbol and control over the body. This lies at the heart of attitudes to women's sport in the Muslim world. Hijab (religious modesty) is fundamental and precious to all Muslims but, under the influence of fundamentalism, very narrow and rigid interpretations of modesty are being applied and fostered more and more. Helen Watson (1994: 143) explains that

> The [Qur'anic] concept of modesty, sitr al-'aura (literally 'covering one's nakedness'), provides the basis for regulation of behaviour, the segregation of sexes, and proper dress. The Qur'an speaks of being 'modest in thy bearing' (verse 31; 19) and mentions Allah's reward for men and women who 'guard their modesty. ... Specific instructions for women are set out in verses 24; 30–1: 'Tell the believing women to lower their gaze and be modest, and to display of their ornaments only that which is apparent, and to draw their veils over their bosoms and not to reveal their adornments save to their husbands and fathers.'

Although the Qur'anic concept of modesty applies equally to men and women, in practice it has been used almost exclusively to regulate the attitudes to, and usages of, women's bodies – as a result, the emphasis on traditional female dress has become a pivotal feature of the recent resurgence of Islam (Watson 1994: 144, 151). All styles of dress relate to hijab, but it is the veil that has become the most potent signifier of Muslim womanhood and, arguably, 'a basic requirement of Islam' (Karam 1998: 135). The most extreme fundamentalist interpretation of the Qur'an demands that the entire female body, including the face, be concealed from public gaze. In this case, the purdah or curtain, literally as well as symbolically, separates the spaces, the lived worlds, of men and women. More typically strict versions require uniform black cloaks and veils, which cover the body, with the exception of the face; less strict interpretations, but which also require veiling, can in some cases allow women to wear trousers or skirts, blouses with long sleeves, and a headscarf; and liberal interpretations tolerate 'decent', non-provocative Western dress with no veil.[6]

The veil is a symbol of cultural difference. For non-Muslims it conveys the idea that Western women are liberated and Muslim women, by comparison, are oppressed. The veil represents the 'Otherness' of Islam and is condemned in the West as a constricting mode of dress, a form of social control, and a religious sanctioning of women's invisibility and subordinate sociopolitical status. In the eyes of a Western, liberal critic, allowing women to take part in sport freely and in modern sportswear is, in contrast to veiling, liberating and empowering. But, although many Muslim women who are forced to wear the veil feel angry, repressed and resistant, and are often fearful of showing opposition, they are also troubled that anti-fundamentalist sentiments will be interpreted as anti-Islamic ones and will be used to fuel Islamaphobia (Mahl 1995: 14).

Other Muslim women hold a positive view of hijab – for them, wearing the veil is a deliberate choice, a politicized act, rather than a reaction to male power – what Watson (1994: 152) describes as 'a sort of feminism in reverse'. For them, exposing the female body in sport is immoral and the veil signals a rejection of arguably provocative and public displays of the body. Veiling has been revived by Muslim women living in Britain, France and Egypt, for example, 'as a way of coping with the challenges of contemporary life in those countries, and of emphasizing Islamic identity' (Ahmed and Donnan 1994b: 14). 'Unveiling' and taking part in sport is interpreted as a new form of imperial control (Kanneh 1995).

Although Muslim women's subjectivities are constructed within a context of Islamic traditions and values which places the body in a focal position, the anxieties experienced by Muslim women about their bodies arise from the coupling of Islam and politics. Women's attitudes to sport – to ideas about participation or non-participation or about different modes of participation – are all responses to these anxieties. The pursuit of economic modernization and the inevitable shift towards secularization (which has occurred in different Arab states, for example) has provoked Islamist ideologues to use the control of women's bodies, especially by means of veiling, as a visible and tangible symbol of success. In stark contrast, athletic images of Nawal El Moutawakel and Hassiba Boulmerka running in the Olympics in vests and shorts symbolize a loss of control and a failure of belief. The female body in Islam is at the centre of cultural contest, scrutiny and meaning (Kanneh 1995: 347), and Muslim women in sport encapsulate this contest. They consciously and unconsciously manipulate religious beliefs to negotiate their gender roles and the contradictions between tradition and modernity in sport. The way they do so varies according to the context.

The case of Iran: background and politics

Iran provides a clear example of the way in which the regulation of women's bodies has been tied to changing politics and to the relationship between the powerful and the powerless. During the 1930s, under the secularist ruler Shah Reza Khan Pahlavi (in power from 1925 to 1941), the compulsory wearing of the veil was abolished (Roberts 1980: 875). Iranian women remember the sense of release and joy that they felt: 'There was singing and dancing because we were free; the black shroud had been removed from our heads'; 'We were athletic and joined sports clubs. We wore bikinis on the beach. There were no exceptions – men, women, brothers, sisters' (*People's Century* BBC 2, 4/9/98). After Reza Khan was forced to abdicate in 1941, and his son, Mohammed Reza Pahlavi became shah, the secularist state philosophy continued. Many middle-class and university-educated women adopted Western dress and enjoyed sports and exercise. But under the developing capitalist system the shah was seen as a symbol of the tyranny of Western imperialism and censured for neglecting the needs of the majority of Iranian people. There was limited legislation in favour of women's rights, but it did nothing to counteract the consequences of capitalist development which, for the majority of women, brought continuing or worsening exploitation. Women from poor and traditional families were prevented from entering school, college or employment, many becoming the subjects of cheap female labour, sexual harassment and degraded status at work and at home. As a result, there was a general feeling among women that Western dominant culture had nothing to offer, and there was increased alienation from commodified images of femininity and a return to more traditional ones (Tohidi 1991: 256–7). The end result was 'resentment, distrust, and hidden hostility toward unveiled "modern" women' (1991: 257). Sport therefore never touched the lives of most Iranian women, and in traditional communities Western-style sportswomen were decried as decadent.

At the same time, the shah was systematically and ruthlessly repressing democratic and leftist organizations, and there were no popular women's groups. Fundamentalists were left to 'gain control by channeling people's frustration and anger into a familiar language, ideology and value system' (Tohidi 1991: 258) – that of Islam.[7] Islamic discourse motivated more and more women to wear the veil,[8] which became a critical symbol of a shift towards fundamentalism and opposition to the shah.[9] These two popular drives enabled Khomeini to take leadership of the revolution and then, only days after the shah's defeat, he announced restrictive measures against women based on Islamic laws (Tohidi 1991: 252). Opposition was coercively aborted. Together with 'members of national ethnic minorities, popular and progressive organizations, workers and newly formed labour councils, intellectuals, journalists, publishers', women 'became victims of the waves of terror imposed by a theocracy that showed itself to be more and more regressive' (Tohidi 1991: 252).

From a modernizing Islamic state, Iran became a backward-looking Islamic republic, governed by ancient religious laws which were, according to some interpretations, deployed to subjugate women in ways that were worse than during the Pahlavi regime (Tohidi 1991: 253). The civil code in Iran required all women, including non-Muslims and foreigners, 'to wear the veil and observe Islamic hijab'. The Ayatollah Khomeini commanded that 'no part of a woman's body may be seen except her face and the part of her hand between the wrist to the tip of her fingers' (Tohidi 1991: 253).[10] Step by step, all areas of Iranian society became resegregated by sex, including schools and universities. Laws and restrictions were implemented, supported by an ideological climate of fear, which inhibited freedom and independence for women. This was the set of social and gender relations of power within which Iranian women have struggled through the 1980s and 1990s for opportunities for girls and women to take part in sport.

Islam and women's sport

In common with women in other Islamic countries, the support of Iranian women for female sport is based on the idea that Islam is a religion of 'balance and equilibrium' (Abdelrahman 1991: 10), which embodies a reverence and concern for the healthy female body. They argue that physical education should be an integral part of Islamic education and that Muslim women have a responsibility to exercise their bodies in order to fulfil their roles as wives and mothers. Although most women who are involved in female sport tend to operate outside any explicit political framework or intention, the work of other feminists who are politically aware and affiliated has helped their cause (Karam 1998).[11] Since the 1979 revolution, women have been challenging gender discrimination in such areas as the family, education, culture, work and law (Tohidi 1991).

Muslim women in sport tend to work within the parameters of Islamic thinking. If they were given a feminist label, they would be characterized as either Islamic or Muslim feminists (Karam 1998: 9–12): both groups use the Qur'an in order to show that – *within Islam* – equity between men and women is valid (Karam 1998: 10). Muslim feminists support the individual's right to interpret the readings of the Qur'an, but are less pedantic than Islamic feminists, who believe that 'women are oppressed precisely because they try to be "equal" to men and are therefore being placed in unnatural settings and unfair situations, which denigrate them and take away their integrity and dignity as women' (Karam 1998: 9). At the UN's Fourth Women's World Conference (FWWC, Beijing 1995), Islamists supported the use of the term 'equity' as a replacement for 'equality', which, Karam (1998: 6) argues, 'seems to centre on affirming women's access to rights which do not necessarily equal those of men, as well as women's rights to differ from those of men without being subjected to any form of hierarchy'. The philosophy of equity is in general promoted by women activists in Muslim countries, and the provision of sporting facilities in single-sex contexts sanctions the idea of 'equivalent to', though not 'identical with', opportunities for men. The theory of equity provides spaces for female exercise *and* female modesty – an essential fundamental for women's sport to advance under Islam.

Although traditionalist clerics have been consistently dogmatic about their desire to 'Islamicize' Iran in every way (Hirst, *Guardian* 5/1/98) and have opposed all forms of sport for women as 'un-Islamic', over the years 'sport feminists' have worked quietly and persistently, in separate spheres from men, to improve opportunities for girls and women in sport. But it has only been since the 1997 election, when Mohammed Khatami became President, that there has been a discernible easing of the strict controls on women's lives and greater potential for sport development for women. The activism of huge numbers of women has made it clear to all political candidates that the support of women is more important than ever before, and when Khatami promised to address questions about individual freedom, the intrusiveness of Islam, and the rights of women, more than 80 per cent of women voted for him (Shahid, *Detroit News* 26/5/97; Macleod 1998: 29). Characterized as a 'modernist' pitted against the traditionalist clergy, Khatami was expected to create change. Cautiously he encouraged a more open, tolerant atmosphere and the popular push for a more secular, liberal society gained momentum (Hirst, *Guardian* 5/1/98). The position of women was high on Khatami's agenda: in 1997 he appointed the country's first ever female vice president and the first ever Director for Women's Affairs; had women in his cabinet; increased the budget for women's affairs; fostered the opening of a full debate on women's rights; took several steps to upgrade the cultural status of women in Iranian society, including creating a special fund for women's sport; and hosted an international women's sporting competition (*Islamic Republic News Agency* [IRA] 3/8/98; Macleod 1998: 29). Since his inauguration, more and more women disgarded the long black chuddar and wore instead brightly coloured raincoats and headscarves (MacLeod 1998: 29). Women were able to enter university, secure more senior positions at work, do work that was previously exclusive to men, achieve some power in politics, and increase their visibility in sport. Not surprisingly, the reformist policies of Khatami have been very popular among women and young people (more than half Iran's population is under 25) and, as predicted, he retained power at the election in February 2000.

Women's sport has been a popular feature of the reformist movement in Iran. The most well-known advocate of sport for women is Faezeh Hashemi, daughter of Akbar Hashemi Rafsanjani, Khatami's predecessor. She is one of 14 women members of the Iranian parliament and Vice President of the Iranian Olympic Committee. As one of the most powerful women in the country, Faezeh Hashemi uses her position to lobby for advances for women in sport. She is a vociferous critic of the policies of Islamic hardliners, campaigns for women's rights, including improved rights under the law, argues that interpretations of the Qur'an have both political as well as personal meanings, and claims that the clerics who argue that sports for women are forbidden in the Qur'an do so for 'narrow-minded political reasons' (Macleod 1998: 29). She has also campaigned for women to be allowed to bicycle in public (Longman, *New York Times*

26/5/98). Faezeh Hashemi points to the connection between sport and personal politics when she argues that 'It [sport] gives us more confidence and improves our social skills. If we push against tradition in sports, it will pave the way for reform in other areas' (Theodoulou, *Times* 29/8/98).

Since Khatami came to power, women's sport has become a significant symbol of greater opportunities for women in all areas of social and cultural life and is now an explicit feature of domestic policy, illustrated here in this government statement:

> The Islamic government has initiated strong measures to bring women's sport into the mainstream of national development planning. The first step was taken by the establishment of a Sport Research Committee, in 1988, to study women's athletic needs nationwide. This committee provides a strong basis for planning women's sport activities ... The next significant measure was the appointment of a woman as 'deputy director' of the National Committee of Olympics ... Such steps brought women's sport into light. In 1991, the first Islamic Countries Congress for Women's Sport was held to provide the ground for women's participation in regional and international contests. ... During recent years, Iranian women, including the handicapped, have taken part in many national and international contests, and proved their endurance and high potential.
>
> (*http://salamiran.org/Women/General/Women And Sports.html*)

Faezeh Hashemi argues that in many ways women are better off since the revolution than before, because 'the freedom that existed applied only to ... maybe two per cent of the women in Iran. ... Now we have the headscarf, but all women can comfortably take part in all social activities' (Amanpour, *CNN World News* 19/3/96). She stated in 1998 that roughly two million Iranian women participated in some form of sport, compared with 400,000 two years earlier and 10,000 before the Islamic Revolution (Longman, *New York Times* 26/5/98). In 1996 she accompanied her father, who was president at that time, on a six-nation African tour, and took the opportunity to promote Muslim women's sports. When she was in Sudan, she claimed that in Iran there were over 6000 women coaches and referees, 200 of whom had international certificates. Iran, she said, was willing to send coaches to train Muslim women in other Muslim countries and also to grant scholarships to Muslim women to study at the Iranian Sports University at Bachelor's, Master's and Ph.D. levels. Such advances for women in sport are used as reasons for Iran to proclaim itself as being a model of revolutionary Islam.

Sport for women in Iran, as in other Muslim countries, represents an important cultural reform. There are obvious signs of changes and advances. More women are participating than ever before; they can now take part and compete in the same sports as Iranian men; and, so long as they are using indoor facilities where there are no men, they can wear shorts and T-shirts. Schoolgirls play soccer – a sport that was banned for women during the revolution, and there are clinics for women to train as soccer coaches and referees; there are mixed recreational sports in the parks, such as aerobics, jogging, table tennis, in-line skating and soccer; and, exceptionally, in some private clubs, men and women sometimes swim together (Longman, *New York Times* 26/5/98). Although the law still requires that in mixed and public activities women must be clothed so that only their hands and faces are revealed, they can gain a sense of freedom and movement which, however limited in Western thinking, is a radical advance from the strict revolutionary female body disciplines of twenty years ago.

Individual sportswomen are presented as symbols of radical Islam. Lida Fariman is an example. When she took part in the 1996 Atlanta Olympics, she became the first Iranian woman to participate in a summer Olympics since the revolution. A few Iranian women had taken part in regional competitions as well, such as the 11th Asian Games held in Beijing in 1990 when, as at the Olympics, they were only permitted to do so because their events (shooting) enabled them to be fully clothed (Pourhaddadi 1998: 12).[12] But Lida's participation was also significant because she became the first woman ever to carry the Iranian flag during an Olympic opening ceremony (Longman, *New York Times* 26/5/98).[13] She said she was 'honoured to show to all the peoples of the world that a woman was chosen as the representative of Iran to carry the flag of my homeland', and to act 'as a representative of the Muslim women of my country with full consideration of Islamic attire'. As a target shooter, Lida can wear a scarf and coat in competition. Although she was the only woman in Iran's Olympic squad of 18, and she only came 46th out of a field of 49 competitors, she hopes to be selected to go to the 2000 Olympics in Sydney, Australia, and to be, again, a symbol of what's possible for women in Iran (Longman, *New York Times* 26/5/98).

But Lida's vision of the possible is a limited one. She has elite connections and takes part in a sport in which she can wear traditional dress. The same is true for Elmira Mostajaboldaveh, who has to wear a scarf under her riding hat and a thigh-length coat over her jodhpurs in order to train with the national equestrian squad and compete against men in open competition. In 1996 in France, Lida finished second out of 84 riders. Kayaking, table tennis, mountaineering[14] and skiing are other sports that Iranian women can compete in without compromising Islamic rules, but in popular sports – such as basketball, swimming, track and field, and volleyball – they are disallowed from entering mixed events, such as the Olympics, and can only take part in female-only competitions, like the Muslim Women's Games, where there are no men present. In national events, such as the annual 'Olympic Run', 'a distance race held in Tehran in the summer, when temperatures routinely top 100 degrees' (Longman, *New York Times* 26/5/98), women must wear coats, long trousers and scarves; and, in aquatic and winter sport events, they are prohibited from wearing what are characterized as 'provocative' skin-tight aerodynamically efficient suits. It is obligatory for schoolgirls playing soccer and basketball outdoors to wear full Islamic dress. Islamic militants are strongly opposed to greater freedoms for women in sport – for example, in 1996, 20 of them attacked female cyclists in a park. Two years earlier, militants had been critical of Faezeh Hashemi for pressing for women to cycle in public for the first time, even although the cycling paths are segregated, so fathers and sons go by one route and mothers and daughters go by another (Longman, *New York Times* 26/5/98). However, there are signs that the influence of the Islamic hardliners is fading and that a further separation of religion and the state is taking place.[15]

Issues of difference

The advances that women have achieved and the difficulties they still face point to the complexities surrounding the development of sport for Muslim women. Muslim women are not a homogeneous group and different women in different contexts are struggling for different outcomes. Faezeh Hashemi, for example, challenges the system from within and has been described as an 'Islamic feminist'. She is both popular and despised – supported by most women who believe the only way forward is to work with respect for the traditions and beliefs of Islam, but criticized by secular feminists (Karam 1998: 13), who believe that because she wears the black chuddar and supports segregation, any reforms are piecemeal and inadequate. She is also criticized by fundamentalists who want a return to stark gender divisions based on religious laws. Longman (*New York Times* 26/5/98) explains that

> [Hashemi] favors clothing that covers everything but the hands and feet of female Iranian athletes who compete outdoors, and she criticized the 'nudity' of women who competed in brief uniforms at Atlanta. She does not believe women should attend soccer matches until the 'moral behavior' of men at the stadiums can be improved.

But other women have more radical views and are taking more radical action. Although the Ayatollah Khomeini had banned women from attending men's sports matches, even fully covered, when Iran got through to the World Cup Soccer Final in 1997, around 5000 women defied public segregation legislation, forced their way into Tehran's Azado stadium, and joined in the welcome-home celebrations for the national squad (Hughes, *Times* 20/6/98; Longman, *New York Times* 26/5/98; Macleod 1998: 29). It was reported that 'Women tore off their black headscarves and danced alongside men in the street. In some towns, the Revolutionary Guard joined in the celebrations' (Borger, *Guardian* 20/6/98). In 1998, Iranian women were permitted to attend the World Wrestling Championships in Tehran, when a special viewing section was allocated to them.[16]

But, although there is an increasing radicalism among women, there is also fear of vicious reactions. A young handball player complained: 'We must play in these coats that tie up our feet and are very hot. And we are not allowed to freely associate with the soccer players. The morals police will arrest us and beat us with whips' (Longman, *New York Times* 26/5/98). Mahboobeh Soufaf, who has been an exile from her country since the revolution and is on the National Council of the Resistance, managed to get a ticket for the 1998 Soccer World Cup match between Iran and the USA. She claimed that all the 3000 tickets that FIFA allocated to the Iranian Football Association were in the hands of the country's Revolutionary Guard and in the crowd there were high-ranking officers of its intelligence wing (Hughes, *The Times* 20/6/98). 'We must show our anger', she said.

> It is why we must go to the stadium. I know people say sport and politics are separate, but sport is becoming more and more important to women and to the youth. It is a way of showing that we belong, that we care, and that we are angry with the mullahs.
>
> (quoted in Hughes, *The Times* 20/6/98)

Breaking into stadia to support men's sport is still a huge step away from participating openly in sport. But it is a symbolic step of defiance, which has led to other reforms – for example, women's soccer is now allowed, the training of women coaches and referees began in early 1998, and permanent women's sections in major stadia have been set up. Also in 1998, Mahin Gorji, a 19-year-old reporter, became the first woman to cover a live football match (Borger, *Guardian* 20/6/98). Sport has become a metaphor for social change in Iran and it has been argued that the popularity of football has been a more powerful force than the ideas and censures of Iran's clergy (Bhatia, *Observer* 21/6/98).

After the 1979 revolution, large numbers of Iranians emigrated to the USA, and particularly to Los Angeles, which became nicknamed 'Irangeles'. In the USA and other host countries, Muslim women with roots in Iran have a choice about whether or not, or in what manner, they take part in sport. Secular feminists are those who want similar choices – more complete modernization of sport, the opportunity to take part in mixed activities, and personal freedom about how they present their bodies. A woman who runs a gym in North Tehran voices her frustration to a visiting male journalist about the coercive constraints she faces as a woman : 'I'd like to be able to jog in the streets in my shorts and not to wear this', she says, tugging at her headscarf. And, because men are forbidden access, she adds, 'Wouldn't it be nice if I were allowed to invite you in to see my friends working out?' (quoted in Theodoulou, *The Times* 29/8/98).

Although the participation rates for women in sport are rising, it is still the case that those from poor and traditional communities can (should they want to) do little to combat the laws and ideological constraints of their country, whereas women from privileged backgrounds can more easily forge opportunities for themselves. Western-style activities which focus on bodily images of perfection and sexuality are part of a growing leisure industry, popular among wealthy middle-class Iranian women. These women work out on the latest hi-tech Californian-style machinery in body-clinging Lycra leisure wear. When they are in private or all-women settings, they wear their hair free and put on tight-fitting jeans. In public, they wear designer scarves and colourful raincoats. They reveal preoccupations with appearance by wearing nail polish and crimson lipstick, coloured contact lenses, and undergoing cosmetic surgery. In common with women in the West, their bodies represent commodification and desire (Hargreaves 1993), in stark contrast to those of Muslim women in head-to-toe black chuddars. They are 'hidden' symbols of rebellion against the mullahs' vehement opposition to the freeing of women's bodies for sport.[17]

The situation in Iran illustrates how Muslim women's bodies in sport are always vulnerable, always 'in process' at the heart of the contest between Islamism and modernization. Many of the dilemmas, contradictions and complexities facing women in sport in Iran are also apparent in other Arab states, but vary in character and intensity with the political climate. While Iranian women have been freeing themselves *for* sport, Algerian women are facing harsher discrimination to keep them *out* of sport. The history and achievements of Hassiba Boulmerka illustrate poignantly the connection between Muslim women's bodies and the nexus of personal, political and religious ideologies.

Hassiba Boulmerka and Algeria

Hassiba Boulmerka grew up in Algeria during a relatively pluralist and secular period of its history. Algeria had gained independence from France in 1962, and for nearly 30 years afterwards moderate Muslim politics enabled many women to challenge religious laws and cultural traditions that they found restricting and discriminatory (Morgan 1998: 347). In this climate, Boulmerka was able to develop her love and talent for running (Layden 1997: 37), although with increasing difficulty because of the growing power of Islamic ideologues, reflected in an attempt in parliament to abolish schoolgirl sport (Hornblower 1992: 91).[18] In the 1988 All-Africa Games, Boulmerka won both the 800- and 1500-metre races, and she became the first Algerian woman to win a World Athletic Championships title when she took the 1500 metres in Tokyo in 1991. Together with fellow Algerian Noureddine Morceli, the men's 1500 gold medal winner, she was welcomed home as a national heroine – fêted at the airport by a cheering crowd, carried on a motorcade through Algiers, and presented with La Medaille du Mérite, the country's highest honour, never before awarded to civilians. The Algerian sports minister, who at the time was a woman – Madame Leila Aslaoui – declared that both victories were 'applauded by every single Algerian' (Butcher, *Guardian* 11/1/92). She was wrong. Unlike Morceli, Boulmerka quickly became a target of condemnation for militant Muslims (characterized as the 'more faithful'), who were encouraged by a strengthening of Islamism (Morgan 1998: 347). In mosques throughout the country, fundamentalist imams who were affiliated to the Front Islamique du Salut (FIS)[19] pronounced a kofr – a public disavowal of Boulmerka (Butcher, *Guardian* 11/1/92). 1992). The object of their condemnation was her body – they argued that because she ran in shorts and vest in public, she had broken the rules of the Qu'ran.

Algeria had been one of the most liberal Muslim countries in the world, but the FIS had become a powerful force in the country taking an aggressive stand against the secular, modernizing, and allegedly corrupt ruling Front de la Libération Nationale (FLN). Opposition to new opportunities and freedoms for women was central to FIS philosophy. By the time that Boulmerka went on to win the 1500-metre gold medal at the 1992 Olympics, she had become thoroughly caught up in the growing opposition between state and society. After winning her World Athletic Championships title, she had described her cry of joy as, 'A cry from the heart for every Algerian woman, every Arabic woman' (Butcher, *Guardian* 11/1/92); by the time she had won her Olympic gold, she had taken an explicit stance against fundamentalism,[20] talked openly about her suffering and forced residence in Italy in order to escape the threats on her life, and was appealing to other young Algerians to take a similar stance (Morgan 1998: 347). 'I'm a danger to the fundamentalists', she is recorded as saying. 'I am a symbol to the young that women don't have to hide behind their chadors' (Hornblower 1992). In 1992, when she was 16, Miriam Hemdane, an aspiring athlete, claimed that 'Hassiba is our idol. We are in a hostile environment, but she gives us hope' (Hornblower 1992: 91).[21]

The growing tide of Islamist power, and the inability of the secular state to deal with it, has made it impossible for girls and young women to take part in mixed competitions or train in public in Western-style sportswear, or to participate in sport after marriage or even past the age of puberty – if at all. Women who defy tradition and Islamism are, quite literally, in fear of their lives. Through ideological propaganda and terrorism, the armed dissident wing of the Islamist opposition, the GIA, impels the mainstream Islamist organization, the relatively moderate FIS, to keep up its doctrinaire battle against secular tendencies. It is reported that, since 1992, around 75,000 people have lost their lives during Algeria's seven-year civil war, and that Islamist extremists have carried out unimaginable atrocious massacres (Hirst, *Guardian* 5/1/98). Although terrorist violence may seem unrelated to female sport, it has bred a culture of fear in Algeria, propped up by dogmatic adherence to (and unbending interpretations of) Islam, which influence relations of power between men and women and public attitudes to women's bodies. Those who are working for improved opportunities for women's sport know that it is 'a particularly sensitive subject, given the political, social and economic crisis that the country is in', and they are often 'fearful about having anything they say misconstrued and seen as anti-Islamic' (personal interview 1996). It is claimed that 'the freedom and legitimate right of women to play sports in Algeria has been impeded by various social, cultural, political, and economic obstacles, the result of which is a lack of women in competitive sports – only 3,000 during the course of 1994' (Mechti and Sayad 1994).

There has been a notable drop in the numbers of girls and women taking part in sport in Algeria during the 1990s, especially in competitive and elite events, following a previous steady increase in the number of female athletes during approximately a decade and a half from the second part of the 1970s. For example, in 1978 several female athletes took part in the All-Africa Games in Algiers and the women's handball and basketball teams won gold medals. It was during this period that Sakina Boutamine became the first Algerian woman to take part in an Olympic Games – in Moscow in 1980. From the end of the 1980s onwards, there was a rapid decline in participation as girls and young women were discouraged or forbidden from participating, and punished for disobeying. The increase in numbers of female athletes during the 1970s and 1980s followed legislation to encourage female participation in schools and colleges; the decrease during the 1990s coincided with anti-secular pressures, the rise of fundamentalism and reversed legislation. Figures for school-level volleyball illustrate the trend – in 1986–7, there were 1607 players; by 1990–1, grants and sponsorship were withdrawn and the figure had dropped to 918 (Mechti and Sayad 1994). The changed political climate has been used by men to justify grossly uneven resourcing in sport between men and women, and sportswomen themselves face hostility, prejudice and censure – for example, Salma Souakhri, who showed great promise at the Barcelona Olympic Games, was thrown out of school and forbidden to finish her Baccalauréat[22] and Yasmina Azzizi, who came fifth in the 1992 Olympic heptathlon, has had shouts of 'Whore' aimed at her during training. Obstacles for female athletes in Algeria have become formidable – some give up, others leave the country because of threats to their safety (Mechti and Sayad 1994).

Boulmerka has become a spokeswoman and an ideologue, most specifically for Algerian women in sport, but also for Muslim women throughout the world. But her position is untypical and controversial. She has resisted the popular idea that there has to be a choice between the East and the West, between Islam and rational capitalism, arguing that it is possible to take the best from Islamic and Western philosophies and still be a good Muslim. Morgan (1998: 347) argues that she uses a curious cultural language, steeped in disparate cultural traditions which blends 'Western individual initiative and Eastern community-inspired discipline'. Certainly, Boulmerka claims to have acquired, through her personal struggles and achievements in sport, a deeper love of her country and an enduring belief in Islam. She wants people in the East and the West to believe with her that 'Islamic culture is not the hotbed of fanaticism it is often made out to be and that it is not necessarily hostile either to individual effort or to the plight of women' (Morgan 1998: 348).

Boulmerka's vision of a radical female Muslim identity is fundamentally political and unquestionably heroic because she has spoken out in the face of oppression and threats to her life. Exceptionally, she is targeting those she calls fascists who, she says, 'hide behind the veil of Islam in order to impose their political will' (Moore 1992: 53, cited in Morgan 1998: 348). She is not taking issue with what she believes to be the essence of Islam, but with its extreme and politicized versions. Morgan (1998: 348) describes how Boulmerka has infused 'the vocabulary of equal rights and women's sports into the cultural vocabulary of

Islam'. She knows that by doing so she offends the 'more faithful' Muslims, but she is adamant that her position is not un-Islamic and does not go against the grain of what it means to be a Muslim woman (Morgan 1998: 348). Boulmerka believes that her faith alone, and not blind obedience to moral dictates, is necessary for godliness and salvation. She is concerned with the same question that preoccupies other radical Muslim women – whether or not it is possible to build a form of Muslim feminism on affirmative readings of the Qu'ran that will enable women to develop their interests in the modern world without rejecting their Muslim faith. Radical/secular feminists argue that Islam *can* be a tool for women's liberation, that the Qur'an does not direct that society be frozen in the seventh-century Arabian mould, but that it should be adaptable to the needs of changing times and circumstances (Nagata 1994: 80; Van der Gaag 1997: 31).

Boulmerka has been labelled both victim and heroine, a courageous individual who, in reality, can do little to effect real change in a country in the grip of extremists. However, her struggles are especially significant in the international context, where the debate about modesty has gained momentum. In some countries, Muslim women who have confined themselves to female-only participation according to conservative interpretations of Islam have made significant advances, but those who want to take part in mixed international events and who are secular Muslims face far greater hurdles and antagonisms. For these women, Boulmerka is a powerful symbol of resistance and change. Influenced by Boulmerka, and following in her footsteps, remarkably, Nouria Merah-Benida of Algeria won the 1500 metres at the 2000 Sydney Olympics. Referring to her gold medal, she said, 'It's for the Arab women so that they can develop like the other women of the world' (Williams, *Guardian* 2/10/2000). In her new position as a full member of the International Olympic Committee (IOC), Boulmerka will be in a unique position to argue in support of Muslim women in sport and to put some pressure on Muslim countries to change their policies about women in sport. In the year 2000 she was one of the first ten athletes to be honoured in this way as part of the IOC's latest radical reforms.

Gaining power is necessary for those who seek change, and power comes from organization. With this in mind, Muslim women in sport have set up organizations, held meetings and congresses, instigated competitions, and lobbied for their cause, at both national and international levels. The internationalization of the discourse around Muslim women in sport assists in the creation and legitimation of a power base.

Islamic solidarity and internationalism

In order to enable Muslim women to take part in international competition, efforts were made during the 1990s to establish special all-female events. The initiative came from Iran, where the first Islamic Countries' Sports Solidarity Congress (ICSSC) for Women was held in 1991 in Tehran. There were invited representatives from twenty Islamic countries, men and women, all of whom were associated with state sport apparatuses, supportive of sport for women under Islam, but opposed to Western-style sport for women. From the start, the relationship between women's sport, the State and Islamism was obvious. The opening address was given by the president of the Islamic Republic of Iran at the time, Akbar Hashemi Rafsanjani, who explained that the purpose of the Congress was to establish the true status of women's sports in Islamic countries and to set up a suitable framework for competitions according to the principles of Islam. Referring to mixed international events, he argued that 'The problem for Muslim women in sport lies in the current manner of the practice of sport in World and Regional Competitions.' He went on to explain that 'Muslims should be careful that women do not get involved and suffer undesirable consequences from such sports' and that, by bringing to the Congress experts from Islamic countries who believe in preserving the purity of women and in the teachings of Islam, it should be possible 'to prevent the corruption which may result from the simultaneous presence of men and women athletes in one and the same arena'. He suggested that there were 50 countries who would organize their sport so that women were sheltered from 'decadent Western Culture'.

A year later, at the third Congress on the same topic, the Islamic Countries Women's Sport Solidarity Council (ICWSSC) was founded (presided over by Faezeh Hashemi) and the Islamic Countries' Women's Sports Solidarity Games (ICWSSG – known as the Solidarity Games) were planned to take place in Tehran the following year. The object of the 1993 Games was to show that 'sport for women who are Muslim can be organized within the context of their religious beliefs and that women in Islamic countries are not excluded from sport but are encouraged to participate'. There were 407 athletes taking part from countries including Azerbaijan, Bahrain, Bangladesh, Islamic Republic of Iran, Kyrgyzstan, Libya, Malaysia, the Maldives, Pakistan, Syria, Tadjikistan and Turkmenistan. The teams from Kyrgyzstan, Islamic Republic of Iran and Azerbaijan took first, second and third places respectively.

At the opening ceremony there were 13,000 male and female spectators, but men were excluded at all times from venues so that competitors could wear sports gear. Women from Azerbaijan, Libya, the Maldives, Pakistan, Syria, Tajikistan and Turkmenistan competed in full-length Islamic dress and veils. The opening speech at the Games was made by Faezeh Hashemi, who confirmed the Games' Islamist philosophy and appealed to solidarity between Muslim women from different countries when she said:

> In order to prove our rightfulness with regard to our participation in social and sports activities, we Muslim women have no intention whatsoever to resemble men. We practise sport because it guarantees our health and grants us joy and strength, but not at the cost of damaging reverence and sanctities. ... Having regard to the divine nobility and greatness, we – Muslim women – value our unification and shall always endeavour to strengthen our solidarity. ... I hope that you will help develop and promote physical education and sport amongst women of the Islamic Countries.
>
> (publicity pamphlet)

The speech that was delivered by Dr Ghafouri Fard, head of the Physical Education Organization of Iran, openly blames the Western ideologues and organizers of sport for depriving Muslim women of international competition at World and Olympic levels. He pinpointed the dilemma that Muslim women face in international sport:

> The circumstances under which women's sports are practised internationally prevents Muslim women from taking part in the respective competitions by virtue of their Islamic nobility and religious criterion. They are indeed placed in a position to have to select either 'Sports' or 'Islam'. The restriction alluded to in the preceding lines is not caused by their feminine physical condition ... but rather it is a cruel imposition enacted by the leaders of World Sport.

However, he claimed that the Games were not a challenge to World and Olympic competitions, but a way of implementing the sacred instructions of Islam which recognizes the value of sport to Islamic culture and to physical and mental well-being.

The opening ceremony of the second Solidarity Games in 1997, also held in Tehran, was spectacular, and followed the practice of an Olympic Games, with an Iranian athlete carrying a torch and lighting a ceremonial flame.[23] All competitors, including foreign competitors, wore the hijab. Ninel Kopysova, an official with the Turkmenistan team, many of whom were wearing head-covering for the first time, said, 'It is important for women from Muslim countries to show solidarity.' The opening ceremony was televised, but cameras were again excluded from the competitive events, so that men could not see any relaxation of the strict Islamic dress code (*BBC News Southwest Asia* 16/12/97). The politico-religious ideology of Muslim women's sport had by this time become thoroughly entrenched throughout the Islamic world. The only opportunities for the majority of Muslim sportswomen to compete internationally is at Islamic events, where men's and women's competitions are strictly separated. These events have become showpieces for the development of women's sport in member states and are celebrated as a signal to the West that Islam is a forward-looking community that protects and nurtures its women. Although in 1997 there were a limited number of competing countries from different parts of the Islamic diaspora, new nation states (such as those of the former Soviet Union) were among them. They were able to express their reinvented Islamism through their female athletes, who only a few years previously had been taking part in open mainstream international competitions. Muslim women's bodies in sport have become firmly established in the international arena and the very fact that they were hidden from sight enables them to be used as a potent sign of the unity of the world state of Islam. The First West Asian Games were also held in 1997 in Tehran, when all ten competing countries – Iran, Jordan, Kuwait, Kyrgyzstan, Lebanon, Cadre, Syria,

Tajikistan, Turkmenistan and Yemen – agreed that women should not participate in public view.

Women's sport organizations

Because the momentum for Muslim women's sport has taken place within Islamic codes and conditions, and because there is condemnation of secularism in Islamic countries where women's sport is being authorized, any chance for women to take greater control of the process has to occur under the same conditions. It has been argued that relationships between the state, Islamists and women's organizations form important axes within the complex interplay of power and hegemony (Karam 1998: 3). In 1991 in Egypt, for example, the government banned a secular and openly feminist political organization, sequestered its assets and transfered them to an *Islamic* women's organization (Karam 1998: 2), making it obligatory for women in sport in Egypt to work within an Islamic framework. In all Islamic countries, the 'official' voices of women's sport are those of women who work in official capacities in sports organizations, government agencies, or schools and universities. They cannot suggest radical, secular changes, for fear of losing their jobs. Even in liberal Islamic states, such as Syria, where women are not obliged to wear the veil, it is difficult for them to speak out against Islamic codes. The more oppressive the conditions, the more important it has been for Muslim women in sport to create their own (women-only) associations which provide them with opportunities to bond together and show organizational strength, explained here by one of the leaders: 'Organisations give us some autonomy. On the one hand we may appear to be subservient, but within our own spaces, we are in control and can make some impact.' Muslim women in many countries – for example, Bahrain, Bosnia, Egypt, Iran, Iraq, Kuwait, Jordan, Lagos, Lebanon, Malaysia, Morocco, Pakistan, Palestine, the Philippines, Qatar, Nigeria, Syria, Turkey, Ukraine – are seeking empowerment through organizations at both national, regional and international levels. While cross-cultural unity supports Islam and confirms Muslim identity which transcends nation states, it also provides some potential for women to negotiate new gender relations of power within their individual nation states, to enhance the general position of Muslim women in sport, and to secure better funding for women's sport. Regional and international conferences and organizations 'strengthen the ties between women working to promote women's sports in different countries'.

Professor Nabila Abdelrahman, from Egypt, has played a pioneering role in establishing organizations for Muslim women in sport. In 1995, she planned an International Scientific Conference for Arab Women and Sport (Abdelrahman 1998) in Alexandria.[24] The conference resulted directly in the endorsement of the Brighton Declaration (see Chapter 7) and the establishment of the Arab Women and Sport Association and the Egyptian Women and Sport Association (IWG 1998: 2). The Arab Women and Sport Association aims 'to enhance women's participation in sport, prepare women for roles in sport leadership and

ensure Arab women are represented in all sports organisations at all levels'
(IWG 1998: 3). Following the conference, national sports associations for women were established in twelve Arab countries, who then affiliated themselves
to the international group. The chance to belong to a growing movement,
encouraged by a sense of promise, has led to the foundation of women's sports
organizations in other countries as well. In 1997 and then 1999, Professor
Abdelrahman organized the Second and Third International Conferences for
Arab women in sport, with the aim of further improving opportunities for
Muslim women in sport.[25] Her position as the only woman on the Egyptian
Supreme Council of Youth and Sport helped her to secure sponsorship for all
three conferences and to attract delegates from all over the Arab world, and to
have international guest speakers. The conferences, organized originally for
women from Arab countries, have included Muslim women from other areas as
well, who have been inspired to set up meetings and events in their own
communities. There is a progressive sense of global Islam in the international
Muslim women's sports movement, which grows in strength and effectiveness.

Muslim women and mainstream sport

For most Muslim women in sport the division between the secular and the
sacred is blurred and the issue of sports participation is confined to the insular
world of Islam. But Muslim women in sport are drawn into the modern, global
world of 'mainstream' international sport – which encroaches on Muslim values
– through the advances that women in sport are making globally, through
connections with women in sport in the Western world, and through the
visibility and seductive pull of commodified sport, exemplified by the Olympic
Games. As Muslim women create for themselves more opportunities within the
confines of Islam, and as standards of training, coaching and performances
improve, they find it more and more difficult to manage their religion and their
identity while still pursuing sport. The issue focuses primarily on whether
interpretations of the Qur'an can allow Muslim women to compete in global
mainstream sport against athletes from countries all over the world, or whether
mainstream events should be organized in single-sex competitions with no men
present, so that Muslim women can be included. The issue, as we have seen, is
not simply an Islam–Western conflict. There are Muslim women, like Nawal El
Moutawakel and Hassiba Boulmerka, who believe that it is possible to be a good
Muslim in secular contexts, and there are liberal Muslim states which support
such a view. For example, in Marrakech, in 1998 (the International Amateur
Athletic Federation [IAAF] Year of Women in Athletics), Hassan II, King of
Morocco, spoke about the growing role of women in sport and praised the
performance of the Moroccan women's team at the 26th World Cross Country
Championships. Referring to the link between sport and women's emancipa-
tion, he insisted that the sports movement for Muslim women 'is taking place
within the framework of the cultural and religious traditions of the Arab world'.
This very same pronouncement could easily be made in other Islamic states,

which (in contrast to relatively liberal Morocco) are strongly influenced by fundamentalism, and where women are denied the option of taking part in public meetings. One such country is Qatar in the Persian Gulf where, until 1998, women were also forbidden from spectating men's events.

The local and the global

Mixed athletics took place for the first time in Qatar in May 1998. The event was a second-division IAAF Grand Prix meeting in Doha, the capital. Mikaela Ingberg, of Finland, bronze medal winner of the javelin at the 1995 World Athletic Championships, opened the competition and became the first woman ever to throw the javelin in Qatar and the first female athlete to be watched by men in that country. Indeed, it was the first mixed athletic meeting in an Arab country. The meeting was given Grand Prix status on the condition that women could participate. There were five events for women – the 100 metres, 400 metres, 100 metres hurdles, discus and javelin. It was, said Primo Nebiolo, President of the IAAF, 'emblematic' of the IAAF Year of Women in Athletics when the organization wanted 'to strengthen the concept of sexual equality within our sport, which has been of primary concern for many years' (Powell, *The Times* 8/5/98).

Qatar is a Muslim state where 'a strict allegiance to the fundamentalist Wahabi Muslim faith and to local custom has for more than 15 centuries required that women be largely invisible outside the home' (Mackay, *Guardian* 8/5/98). Marriages in Qatar are arranged, women do not have the vote and are not allowed to drive, and they can only play sport in sports halls, schools and universities where there are no men.[26] It would have been inconceivable to imagine a mixed sports meeting in Qatar – or any of the Gulf States – even one year earlier. The Grand Prix was, therefore, heralded as a critical symbol of change.

The Grand Prix was made possible in large part because of the negotiating skills of Nawal El Moutawakel who, since giving up competitive athletics, has become a spokesperson for Muslim women in sport and has been appointed to membership of the IAAF Council and the executive board of the IOC. In these roles, she approached the Qatari royal family, speaking first to progressive-thinking Sheika Moza bint Nasser al-Misned, one of Sheikh Hamad Bon Khalifa Al-Thani's three wives.[27] In spite of opposition from religious leaders, Moutawakel secured an agreement that a mixed meeting could take place, pointing out that 'It is a giant step forward just to be talking about these issues in Qatar ... but we must take things gently and understand the culture we are dealing with' (Mackay, *Guardian* 8/5/98). John Nubani, the Qatar International tournament co-ordinator, was sensitive to both the 'Qatar government's position and image in the world' and to the fact that the inclusion of women in spectator sport in Qatar was crucial in the country's bid to host the 2006 Asian Games (*AOL Sports Newsletter* 3/5/98).

The Qatar government insisted that all female athletes should be dressed 'respectably' in consideration of the Muslim tradition. There were therefore no body-hugging or two-piece outfits showing bare midriffs – Ingberg, for example, wore cycling shorts, a T-shirt and a bandanna to cover her hair (Mackay, *Guardian* 8/5/98). But none of the female competitors were from Qatar. The only Qatari women in the stadium were spectators wearing full-length, traditional black apaa dress and there were very few of them – most women were prevented by their husbands or fathers from attending. This was, however, a marked advance from the previous year, when a few Western women went to watch the IAAF's first athletics meeting to be held in the Gulf, which was for men only, and were reportedly spat at and stoned (*Athletics Weekly* 13/5/98: 3; Mackay, *Guardian* 8/5/98; Powell, *The Times* 8/10/98). At a seminar that preceded the Grand Prix, the event was described as 'sport's equivalent of the fall of the Berlin Wall' (Powell, *The Times* 8/10/98).

The seminar, organized by the IAAF, in co-operation with the Qatari royal family and the Qatar Athletic Federation, was entitled, 'Towards the Third Millennium – The Growing Role of Women in Sport and Society'. Primo Nebiolo claimed that the decision to stage a mixed Grand Prix in a country where gender equality has never before been taken into consideration constitutes a 'real social influence' to which international sport organizations should aspire (*IAAF Press Release* 7/5/98). The meeting attracted 100 female physical education teachers and lecturers. The mood was one of caution – that if too much is demanded too soon, it will lead to reactionary measures and reverse the slow advances that are being made. None of the conference delegates, all of whom work in schools and colleges promoting physical education and sport for girls and young women, went to the Grand Prix meeting because, they explained, 'Our husbands or brothers would not like us attending' (Mackay, *Guardian* 8/5/98).

The Qatar Grand Prix throws into stark relief the relation between the global and the local, symbolized by contrasting images of women – those on the track, some of the best female athletes in the world pitted against one another in running, jumping and throwing competitions, using their well-muscled bodies to win money in the commercialized world of sport; and those covered from head to toe in black, restricted in their movements by heavy clothing and politico-religious imperatives. There is at one level a sense of consciousness of the world as a whole, a coming-together of different traditions and cultures (Robertson 1992), but at the same time a powerful sense of difference, far removed from the notion of a 'global community' of women. But even though no Qatari women took part in the Grand Prix, it nevertheless illustrates the prominence of culture in the processes of globalization, the idea that cultural experiences are becoming increasingly delocalized and homogenized (Ahmed and Donnan 1994b: 3) and that we are in a period when culture has become more explicitly politicized than ever before. At the Qatar Grand Prix, women were at the heart of the interaction between the particular (Islam) and the universal (the West), between 'nationalism' and internationalism, between the cultural and the political (Albrow 1996). The desire of the Gulf states to host international events has projected women's bodies in sport into public view for the first time in those countries, presenting a radical image of progress and possibility in contrast to one of women trapped in the past.[28] For Muslim women, the conjunction of different forms of culture is experienced 'in the body' and it is this deeply personal level which, for them, is central to any future construction of identity in sport.

Muslim women and the Olympics

The nexus of Muslim women's bodies, culture and politics is incorporated in negotiations surrounding participation at the Olympic Games. In her role as president of the ICWSSC, Faezeh Hashemi has urged the IOC to do more to promote sports for Muslim women, and in doing so to be sensitive to their specific needs. Hashemi points out that there are 500 million Muslim women in the world – one quarter of the world's female population – who cannot take part in Olympic competitions in existing conditions, causing the absence of female athletes from the national teams of several Muslim countries at the 1992 and 1996 Olympics. At the IOC International Conference on Women and Sports, held in Lausanne in 1996, she petitioned the IOC to authorize single-sex venues to enable the participation of Muslim women in Olympic competition. She also negotiated with Juan Antonio Samaranch, president of the IOC, to allow Muslim women, when possible, to take part in the Olympics in 'Islamic dress'. As an Islamic feminist, she bases her arguments on close readings of the Qu'ran and its satellite texts.[29]

In contrast, there are lobbyists who link the issue of Muslim women in the Olympics to human rights and who are pressing the IOC to ban countries who enter male-only teams. Speaking about the politics of sport at a conference in 1994 in Australia, Marlene Goldsmith (1995: 14) pointed out that 'South Africa and Rhodesia are the only countries that have been expelled from international sport because of human rights violations in their countries', and that 'it is difficult to explain why racism should be singled out for special treatment as the only human rights issue of sufficient importance to warrant a boycott'. She details some of the horrific human rights violations which are inflicted upon females, including genital mutilation; she points out that, in many countries in the developing world, women have fewer rights and opportunities in many areas of life, including education, health, the law and work; she cites Pakistan as one of the most oppressive societies in relation to women where cultural practices, including eating, health care and dress codes, seriously discriminate against women and are detrimental to their health – where women suffer from health problems such as osteomalacia, eczema and ulcers resulting from lack of exposure to sunlight, and osteoporosis from poor diet and little exercise (1995: 17–18). Goldsmith argues that the most oppressed group in relation to international sports participation is women, yet those who suffer some of the worst deprivations and atrocities 'remain without defenders in international sporting conclaves ... because they are represented at such conclaves by governments that repress them' (1995: 18).

The pro-boycott position has been made official through a women's rights activist body, Atlanta (Atlanta Plus), set up originally by three women – two from France, a human rights lawyer and a scientist (the former, Linda Weil-Curiel, is the co-ordinator), and one from Belgium, who is the past Secretary of State for European Affairs.[30] The idea was a response to commentaries at the opening ceremony of the 1992 Barcelona Olympics, which celebrated the ending of apartheid and the re-entry of South Africa into the Olympics but were silent about the 35 delegations that had no female competitors (because religion is misused to serve political ends; because of a lack of top-calibre women athletes; or because countries were poor and devoted their limited sports budgets mostly to men).[31] The main concern of Atlanta is that by permitting countries that disallow women from taking part in sport to participate in the Games, the IOC is contravening its own Olympic Charter.[32] Atlanta is therefore demanding an Olympic ban on those countries.[33]

The IOC has been antagonistic to Atlanta, and only made its reasons clear in 1995, leading up to the Atlanta Olympic Games. The IOC argue that the position of Atlanta on 'gender apartheid' is 'an insult to Nelson Mandela, the South African people, and black people as a whole'; that they cannot agree to waging war against religion; that there is no global consensus for punishing such nations; and that they cannot make policy because the UN had taken no stance on the issue.

Atlanta's response is that the IOC is autonomous in this matter, that the rules of the Olympic Charter are their own and therefore can be enforced against goverments that flaunt them. Furthermore, they point out that in the past the IOC has given support to male demands – for example, when the Iranians campaigned for 'men only' to present medals and refused to walk behind a Spanish woman holding their country's placard. Atlanta also decry the IOC's support of the Women's Solidarity Games which, they claim, Iran used as part of a political campaign to extol their way of life and beliefs.[34] Atlanta have received cross-party support from the German and French parliaments, from the Parliamentary Council of Europe, and from the UN.[35] The original French publicity material has been translated into Arabic, English and Spanish, and has been sent to hundreds of organizations around the world and the movement has gathered support from women and men in different parts of the world fighting gender discrimination.[36] The objectives of Atlanta were approved at the annual meeting of the (US) Women's Sports Foundation in 1995 and, in the same year, at the 'First World-Wide Forum on Physical Activity and Sport', which was organized under the auspices of the United Nations Educational, Scientific and Cultural Organization (UNESCO), the IOC (ironically), the World Health Organization (WHO) and the World Federation of the Sport Gear Industry (WFSGI).

At the 1996 Atlanta Olympics, 26 countries sent all-male delegations.[37] An Atlanta delegation – from Belgium, France, Germany, Greece, Iran, Kenya and the USA – held a press conference and met with members of the IOC Executive Commission.[38] In 1996, an open letter was sent to Juan Antonio Samaranch, president of the IOC, repeating the boycott demand and proposing that 1 per cent of Olympic ticket money should go to fund women's sport in poor countries (where women do not participate for financial reasons).[39]

In spite of the IOC's hostility, Atlanta maintain that its action has had some success:

- The IOC has added a provision to its Charter concerning gender.
- Iran sent one woman to the Atlanta Olympics and she held the national flag.
- Their support is growing daily – among political bodies, sports organizations, and individuals.

Ironically, however, support is not forthcoming from some leading figures in international women's sports groups, who argue that segregation in sport does not necessarily imply discrimination and that Atlanta should show greater sensitivity to the cultural conditions of each country and to those women trying to secure advances for themselves while facing huge constraints.[40]

Historically, there has been a tendency for religious beliefs and cultural practices to remain private affairs, but in recent times there has been a marked shift so that these subjects are now public concerns. Atlanta has used the effects of globalization to 'expose' and politicize a previously insular, religious and private matter. Although Islamic sport feminists are opposed to the Atlanta initiative because they argue it is politically inspired and proposes an image of Muslim countries as backward and non-democratic, more radical feminists believe that their assertive stance is forcing the IOC to look seriously at the question of female participation in the Olympics and has opened the door for other groups or organizations to lobby in different ways. Cultural relativism suggests that one has to be sensitive to the cultural conditions of each country and that it is wrong for predominantly White, Western, non-Muslim women to interfere in the traditions and values of cultures other than their own. But Atlanta has never claimed to speak for all Muslim women and does not wish to take issue with Islamic culture in general, or the way in which sport is practised in Islamic countries. Their argument is that the IOC supports discrimination because it allows those countries who refuse to comply with the Olympic Charter to take part in the Games. Importantly, Atlanta does give a voice – albeit a surrogate one – to those women from Islamic states who would otherwise have no voice because gender relations of power are desperately uneven (personal interview). Although the 'official' women's voice of sport in Islamic states is supportive of the Islamist position, those women who want free access to international competitions, and who endorse a boycott, cannot state this so publicly, for fear of reprisals. Women in sport from Islamic countries who desire change but lack power need support of 'outsiders'. It is also argued that a characteristic of feminist work in other fields is making demands that have relevance to women from disparate backgrounds and places across the world, and therefore it is illogical and dishonourable to refrain from intervening on behalf of women in the Muslim world. Because the right to sport has never been as high on the agenda of feminist action as rights to health and work, for example, and because the vested interests in keeping Muslim women out of sport are highly politicized and emotive, it has been especially difficult and complex to counter opposition to advances for them.

The next target for Atlanta was Sydney 2000. The organization was renamed 'Atlanta-Sydney Plus'. It maintained pressure in order to attain equal access for men and women in respect of the Olympic Ideal, regardless of religion or tradition. Atlanta-Sydney called on the IOC to ban twenty-five countries from the Sydney Olympics including Afghanistan, Botswana, Iraq, Haiti, Kuwait, Libya, Oman, Palestine, Qatar, Rwanda, Saudi Arabia, Senegal, Somalia, Sudan, United Arab Emirates and Yemen. Action was focused on two levels:

- *Economic*: the IOC should attribute a specific share of the Olympic Solidarity funds which it contributes to the National Olympic Committees for the formation of women athletes. Thus it will be possible to distinguish the hard-core countries which refuse the participation of women from the Games for exclusively ideological reasons and not for economic ones.
- *Political*: the IOC should condemn and sanction, without any ambiguity, all national sports politics founded on segregation of women (separate games, banning women from certain disciplines, prohibiting women and men from practising sports together). This is the sense of the UN Human Rights Commission, of the Council of Europe, and the European Parliament.

Although Atlanta-Sydney Plus had a growing base of support, it also faced vigorous opposition. The IOC refused to change its policy for the Sydney Olympics but, nevertheless, the Atlanta-Sydney initiative highlighted ways in which external forces – specifically what Weiss (1994) describes as the 'global superstructure' – are influencing the participation of Muslim women in sport more than ever before.

Conclusion

There are three key questions that arise from this investigation of Muslim women in sport: Is the Muslim women's body in sport subject or object? Can only those women who have lived experience of a culture represent or speak about it? Are the heroines of Muslim women's sport those who are working within the Islamic framework or those who struggle for secularized sport?

The predominant Western representation of Muslim women is that they are objects of oppression, subordinated within starkly uneven gender relations of power, and that, whether or not they take part in sport and what form the participation might take, is determined by tradition, religion and politics. The contrary view is that the West misunderstands Islamic culture and that Muslim women are active subjects, redefining their roles, setting their own agendas, and working for improved opportunities in different fields of life and culture, including sport. In this view, sport is just one of the increasing numbers of women-oriented and women-run movements, reflecting a rise in women's social power and changes in gender attitudes among men and women (Weiss 1994: 129–30).

However, the Western/Islam solution to the subject/object question sets up false oppositions which fail to take account of the great divergences within Islam (and also among Western interpretations of Islam) – 'between Muslims who are profoundly critical of the human rights records of certain Muslim countries and those who maintain that such criticisms are merely symptoms of Islamophobia'; 'between different interpretations of specific terminology, doctrines and injunctions in the Qur'an and Islamic traditions'; 'between the perceptions and experiences of women and men' (Runnymede Trust 1997: 6). Between women, as well, there are huge differences in ideas and practices. Muslim women in sport are not a homogeneous group and Muslim women's sport is not unitary: some Muslim women quest for freedom but have none; others have been able to manipulate structures and relations of power to advance their cause. Muslim women's bodies are, therefore, both subject *and* object, unstable and in process, tied as they are to political struggle – not just at the level of the personal, but linked to state and religious ideologies which depend for their credibility on discourses about women and their bodies. Muslim women's sport is thus merged with identity and difference, reflected in the varied ways in which women speak about it, argue about it and analyse it.

As we have seen, the leaders of women's sport in Muslim countries are Islamic feminists – they reject the stereotype of subjugated woman, embrace Islam, and use sport as a means through which they can express a specifically Islamic gender identity. Fatma Al-Hashimy, president of the Iraqi National Women's Sport Federation, established in 1992, and a member of the Iraqi National Olympic Committee, exemplifies the position. Under her presidency, the Iraqi Women's Sport Federation has worked to establish women's sports clubs and to increase participation of women in sport activities, and she was instrumental in the opening, in 1994, of the first College of Physical Education for Women in Iraq. She makes the link between women's sport and Islamic ethics clear when she says:

> We have in our Islamic religion the best ideal, Islam has respected the Woman and encouraged her to take her responsibilities towards her husband, her children and herself; taking care also of the house and the responsibility of employment requires her participation in sport activities.
> (Al-Hashimy 1997: 38)

The functional fit between traditional gender roles and support of female sport for health in the discourse of Islamic feminists makes it relatively easy for them to work within an Islamic framework to advance the cause of women's sport.

Their movement gets further legitimacy because women's rights in Islamic countries has become one of the most emotive of political issues, and there has been a spread of interest through the Arab world in the specific question of women's sport.

The position for secular feminists is very different. They 'firmly believe in grounding their discourse outside the realm of religion … and placing it, instead, within the international human rights discourse', viewing religion as a private matter for individual women (Karam 1998: 13). As a result, they are characterized as 'clones of the West, implementers of imperialist agendas, and – the ultimate deligitimizer – non-believers', and there is no point of contact whatsoever with Islamic feminists (Karam 1998: 13). Women in sport with secular views – those who are angry at having to wear the veil and who want to take part in open events – have no voice, no legitimacy and, therefore, no power in official women's sport in Islamic countries, so we face the question about representation, about whether outsiders to Islamic culture can speak on their behalf or, more specifically, whether Western feminists can be representative in any way of their needs and desires (Karam 1998: 7).

There is no straightforward answer. Chow (1993: 93) claims that it is untenable if 'Western feminism imposes its own interests and methodologies on those who do not inhabit the same sociohistorical spaces, thus reducing the latter to a state of reified silence and otherness.' But it can also be argued that Muslim women in sport who are forced to be silent in their own cultures should be able to secure some form of representation and support from outside without being reduced to 'the Other'. Muslim women who are opposed to the melding of sport and politics – however subtly this may occur – believe that Islamic feminists in sport are part of a dominant structure of power and control which is fundamentally oppressive. At the moment, the diverse views of Muslim women in sport are not openly expressed and debated and many Muslim women have no chance to determine their own sporting futures. Atlanta-Sydney (n.d.) argue that 'Demanding, through sports, an end to segregation or discrimination of which women are victims is exemplary for several reasons, and it is probably the most effective means of getting around the notion of national sovereignty and cultural differences.'

The last question about Muslim heroines of sport is therefore also complex. The extent of diversity and the range of different opinions and practices suggests that the sum total of the struggles of Muslim women who are working, albeit in very different ways, for advances in women's sport has been surprisingly effective and that individual struggle has been heroic. There is more openness about women's sport than ever before and there have been achievements which would have been inconceivable a short time ago, often linked to the energy and determination of individual women. For example, Sahar El-Hawary formed and funded an Egyptian women's national indoor soccer team, kitted the players out in cycling shorts under their football strip to avoid criticism from Islamists, struggled to developed a club infrastructure so that she could go on to form a full 11-a-side team that qualified for the African Nations Cup in Nigeria in

1998, after which the Egyptian Football Federation gave them some funding. Sahar El-Hawary's aim was for the team to take part in the Women's Soccer World Cup in America in 1999. She has spent most of her own fortune on women's soccer in Egypt; has wooed and won over bureaucrats who argued that women's soccer was a waste of government resources; travelled throughout Egypt staging games in the most rural areas to convince everyone that women play soccer well; and obtained official sanction from the Ministry of Sport for the first women's soccer league and national team of Egypt and to promote soccer to girls in school. She is the first African Egyptian Arabic woman on the FIFA committee.

Sahar El-Hawary is just one of the women who are leading the movement for change in sport in Islamic countries. They do so in different ways and in different circumstances but, together, they are making it easier for the next generation to redefine more completely the uses of the female Muslim body. By doing so, they are changing public opinion – with which, Bhatia (*Observer* 21/6/98) contends, lies the greatest chance for change.

4　Aboriginal sportswomen

Heroines of difference or objects of assimilation?

Introduction

Australia and Canada are both diverse nations embodying assorted peoples, cultures and geographies. Both are countries where the identities of different ethnic groups – and in particular those of indigenous peoples – have become tied to cultural politics, as have the increasingly urgent quests for national Australian and Canadian identities. Through an investigation of Aboriginal women in sport, this chapter points to ways in which culture in general, and sport specifically, embody the politics of exclusion, of difference, of recognition and of identity. It focuses in particular on the coupling of race and gender, on examples of racism and on ways in which Aboriginal women struggle to secure identities and meanings through indigenous sports movements and in mainstream sport. Avtar Brah (1991: 168) asks the question, 'What does it mean to be a Native American or Native Australian woman whose land rights have been appropriated and whose cultures have been systematically denigrated by the state as well as by the dominant ideologies and practices within civil society?' This chapter asks further questions: What does it mean to be a Native Canadian or Native Australian woman who takes part in sport? Can Aboriginal sportswomen be heroines of difference, or is taking part in sport inevitably an act of assimilation?

The term 'Aboriginal' is a generic term used to describe indigenous peoples (those born in a place or region) of settler-invader colonies. Settler-invader colonies refer to those colonies 'where, over time, the invading Europeans (or their descendants) annihilated, displaced and/or marginalized the indigenes to become a non-indigenous population' (Ashcroft *et al.* 1998: 211). North American Aborigines generated new twentieth-century terms such as 'First Peoples', 'First Nations', 'Native Americans' and 'Amerindians', which symbolized their territorial antecedence and distinguished them from the offspring of early settlers and from immigrants (Ashcroft *et al.* 1998: 4–5; Salee 1995: 306).[1] The focus of this chapter is Australian Aboriginal peoples (for example, the koori from southeastern Australia, the murri from Queensland, the Nyoongar from Western Australia, and Torres Strait Islanders) and Canada's First Peoples (characterized according to language – for example, all the tribes from the Great Plains, the Great Lake areas and most of the Maritime region, which are collectively known as the Algonquian peoples and who constitute well over half of Canada's Indian population; the Athapascans of the north and west (the second largest group), which include the Na-Dene communities; the Iroquoians of the Eastern Woodlands who make up Canada's third largest native division; and the Inuit of the Arctic Maritimes (MacDonald 1978).[2] Aboriginal tribes claim to be nations in their own right, distinct from each other and from the rest of Australian and Canadian society. Collectively, they are characterized as Fourth World peoples who have been colonized and dominated.

Australian and Canadian Aborigines were fully self-sufficient, independent peoples before the invasion and appropriation of their lands by White Europeans, a process which started as early as the 1500s (Cheska 1988: 85; Cornell and Hartmann 1998; Littlewood 1982). Nancy Struna (1993: 114) argues that early in seventeenth-century America, 'hegemonic English culture was constructed at the expense of native Americans':

> Long before any Europeans arrived, there were hundreds of thousands of indigenous people in central America. Organized by nations, tribes, and clans, these native Americans were as diverse as were any people on any continent. Language, religion, political arrangements, economies, and labour and leisure patterns varied from nation to nation and tribe to tribe. Some of these people were hunters and aggressors, while others raised crops and traded and were content to defend themselves.

But Europeans generally did not recognize the validity of indigenous civilizations, classing Aborigines in terms of genetics and ancestry as 'different', 'inferior', 'uncivilized' and 'savage'. 'Aborigine' became a racialized description underpinned by spurious biological arguments used to justify domination by the colonizers. Referring to the British Empire, Avtar Brah (1996: 190–1) describes the transformation of the colonized from native peoples into 'the Native', which, she argues,

> implicated a variety of structural, political and cultural processes of domination, with the effect that the word Native became a code for subordination [and] the term 'British' assumed a positionality of superiority with respect to the Native. The Native became the Other. In the colonies, the Natives were excluded from 'Britishness' by being subjected as natives.

Victoria Paraschak (1997: 3) points out that the establishment of Canada as a separate nation state in 1876 was based on the premise that 'native peoples had an "uncivilized nature" which was to be altered before they could enjoy full civil rights'. Race and colour thus became clear markers of social inequalities, of White (European) superiority, 'insiderness' and cultural preservation in contrast to Black (Aboriginal) inferiority, 'otherness' and cultural eradication.

Writing about Australia, Rodney Hall describes the 'near destruction of the 300 Aboriginal nations that flourished before white colonisation began in 1788. The population at the time of the British arrival was about three million. Within 200 years about a tenth of this number remained – it was in effect genocide' (*Observer* 6/10/98). Following the systematic seizure of their lands, especially during the nineteenth century, Australian Aborigines were forced to relocate to designated White-run areas, and then in later years during the twentieth century they were tragically dispossessed of their children (Pilger, *Observer* 22/3/98). Communities were eliminated and families fractured. There are many parallels with Canada, where early European settlers encountered a complex, rich society composed of 55 individual nations – the Native peoples of Canada (Dickason 1992). At first, there was co-operation between the indigenous peoples and the Europeans, but as they opened up the West for fur and gold, and later commercially exploited the resources of the north, the colonizers forced the Native peoples from their lands, tribes were liquidated, and most of those remaining were confined to reservation areas. The War of 1812 (between the United States and Great Britain), the last of the colonial wars, firmly established British imperial power (Dickason 1992). Canadian Aboriginal children were also seized from their homes and 'forcibly placed in sterile, military-like, hostile institutions called residential schools' (Armstrong 1996: x). Prejudice against, and dehumanizing mistreatment of, native peoples were endemic as both Australia and Canada developed into modern societies in which, from the mid-nineteenth century, white Euro-Australians and -Canadians established themselves in positions of power politically, economically and culturally. The breaking up of tribes left indigenous peoples without protection and without the means of self-government (Littlewood 1982). The European colonizers were responsible for the near destruction of indigenous cultures and for the enforced acculturalization of native peoples into 'White society' (Churchill 1999: 34–5), where they found themselves without status.

Traditional sports and games

Sports and games were integral to indigenous cultures. We know very little about them, but enough to deduce that they were organic elements of ethnic communities and identities. Indigenous sports and games were, in a very real sense, part of a 'whole way of life' – a 'lived system of meanings and values' (Williams 1977: 110). Although there were male- and female-only sports and games, in both Australia and Canada there were also many activities in which divisions of gender were blurred and girls and young women joined in with the boys and young men. For example, in reports of his travels in North America, Captain John Smith from England observed that the Native Indians held festivals involving 'dauncing and singing, ... Musique', and 'sprorts [sports] much like ours heare in England'. He observed that football was popular with 'women and young boyes', who 'make their Gooles [goals] as ours only they never fight nor pull one another doune' (cited in Struna 1993: 115–16). Ball games were major recreational activities in Native American cultures and sometimes carried religious significance, when the ball symbolized the Earth, the Sun or the Moon (Greenberg 1997: 20; Oxendine 1995: 25). Alyce Taylor Cheska describes shinny, a game resembling field hockey or ice hockey, which was played mostly by women and children in almost all the regions of North America; and double ball, a game resembling lacrosse, was also considered to be a woman's game (Cheska 1976: 43), as were football, juggling and tossed ball. Women played all types of ball games that were regarded as men's games, too – hand ball, hand-and-fott ball, racket ball, lacrosse, and kick ball race (Cheska 1976: 39). They also played, sometimes together with men, a game that resembled modern basketball, and they were known to play at keeping a small ball in the air by hitting it with their hands (Greenberg 1997: 20). Writing about sports and leisure in the nineteenth-century fur trade in the Canadian northwest, Greg Thomas (1990: 15) describes how women from the Cree tribe played a ball game called 'tishesvy's' – translated as 'a pair of stones' or 'testicles':

> Two stuffed leather balls, attached together by a thong about six to ten inches long, were tossed from person to person and caught by means of sticks thirty or more inches in length. The object of the game was to carry these balls or throw them through the opposition's goal (similar to lacrosse). As these goals could be as far as one mile apart, it produced 'a fine, robust class of women'.

Sports and the learning of lifestyle skills frequently occurred simultaneously. All Plains Indians, girls and boys, were able to ride by the age of 5. Pakes (1990: 27–8) tells us that:

> Children could ride bareback or double as the need arose, all based upon real life necessities that sometimes occurred. Games were devised on horseback all of which had to do with skill and maneuvering at all seasons in warfare. This is where such actions as the 'overhang', in which a rider hung under the neck of his galloping horse and shot at the enemy, were taught and practised.

For Canadian Indians and Inuits, there was no organized separation of life, work and play. Activities were linked to the seasons, to nature, outside life and everyday existence. For example, the object of a game called 'snow snakes', common on the Alberta plains, which was usually played by women, was to see how far they could throw willow sticks across the ice. The sticks were often tipped with the horns of buffalo calves (Pakes 1990: 30). Running races and canoe races were popular among Native Canadian women and in the winter, girls and boys played sliding games and would toboggan together. Pakes (1990: 31) explains that, 'Besides simply riding downhill on sleds, the boys often followed or chased the girls on theirs. The girls were the "buffalo", and the boys

were the hunters. When the boys caught them, they counted their "kill" '.
According to Joseph Oxendine (1995: 24), 'Most reports emphasised the high
status and seriousness of women's sports' in American Indian nations.

In Australia, Aboriginal girls and young women also took part in a range of
recreative activities that could loosely speaking be called games and sports.
They, too, were linked to lifestyle: to nature, the seasons, symbol and religion.
For example, 'Young Aboriginal women ... skipped with vines, climbed trees
and played "purru purru", a ball game based on the principle of keepins-off. The
ball was made from kangaroo skin stuffed with grass' (Stell 1991: 3). For years,
swimming was a popular recreation among coastal and river-dwelling
Aboriginal women – they were observed by early settlers to be very proficient
in the water, and in recent years a woman living in rural New South Wales
remembers swimming with Aboriginal women who could swim underwater for
'quite a distance' and who 'would find baby platypuses in their nests' (Stell
1991: 153). In the nineteenth century, Aboriginal women were exploited for
their skills in the water – for example, in Western Australia they were
kidnapped and used as divers for pearl shell in Broome's pearling industry. Stell
(1991: 4) describes how 'the pearlers chose them in preference to men because
of their proficient swimming and superior underwater lung capacity'. But many
of them were sexually exploited, continually raped, and there were high
incidences of deaths, resulting in 1871 in legislation prohibiting the use of
Aboriginal women on the pearling boats (Stell 1991: 4).

It has also been recorded that in many remote communities in Western
Australia an Aboriginal form of hockey was played. Tatz (1995: 284) explains
that 'Hockey sticks were made by holding branches of a jam tree in a fire and
then bending them to shape. Balls were made from knobs in tree trunks.' He
goes on to describe how women played in teams made up from traditional
groups, and the game was so popular that they would travel great distances to
play.

Although women's traditional sports and games in Australia and Canada
have to a large extent been hidden from history, the limited evidence available
points to the premise that, prior to colonialism, they were numerous and
flourishing features of indigenous history. Indigenous women's sports and games
give meaning to the ideas of culture as everyday life, of ethnicity as lived
experience, and of the importance of sport in the production and reproduction
of communities. Women's traditional sports and games were integral to individual and group identities and to ideologies about harmony with Nature and
the environment upon which Australian and Canadian indigenous nationhoods
were built. However, colonialism reduced indigenous sports in general to
residual status and in most cases rendered indigenous women's sports completely
obsolete. In contrast, European sport was considered to be a channel for
'civilization' and 'acculturation' of native peoples, but although in late nineteenth century and early twentieth-century Australia and North America
increasing numbers of indigenous males played European sports, there was very
limited female involvement. Sports from Europe were patriarchal as well as

imperialist in character. The traditional way of life, which had embodied female sports participation as 'natural', spontaneous and authentic had been completely ruptured and replaced by imposed, contrived and 'foreign' forms of sport embodying chauvinist male supremacy as well as White cultural supremacy.

Sport has been one channel in the decolonization process through which Aboriginal groups have tried to free themselves from the damaging psychological effects of colonial subordination (Fanon 1986, 1993). The struggle of Australian and Canadian indigenous peoples for autonomy and self-determination, however, has generally been told as if it has been a common process for males and females. In some ways it has been. Most Australian and Canadian Aboriginal women live with the sense of having less in common with White women than with Aboriginal men, and the starting point in the struggle for autonomy for Aborigines of both sexes has been sensitivity to difference and the quest for Aboriginal identity. But unequal gender relations of power make the process more difficult for Aboriginal women than for Aboriginal men. The race/gender nexus and the connectedness of Aboriginal women's racialized and gendered identities (Paraschak 1996a) makes the analysis of Aboriginal women's sport very complex.

Cornell and Hartmann (1998: 111) point out that 'It was not until World War II and the following decades that a supratribal consciousness began to emerge on a large scale as a common basis of identity and action among the larger part of the Native American population.' The position was similar for Australian Aborigines. In both countries, a migration of native peoples into industries and to the cities resulted in the emergence of multitribal communities and supratribal politics. The postwar migration of other non-Whites to Australia and Canada – in particular, those from the continents of Africa and Asia – consolidated and strengthened policies and practices of discrimination in both countries, which, together with the global anti-racist movements of the 1960s and 1970s, consolidated and accelerated the development of a politics of difference and identity.

Black politics and Aboriginality

The emergence of Black politics and the civil rights movement in the USA in the 1960s led to a global focus on the oppression of minorities, and validated separatist politics and the quest for identity (Mitchell 1971: 175). By the end of the decade, in both Australia and Canada, indigenous peoples were engaging in activist politics (Churchill 1999: 39), and Aboriginal ideas and sensitivities were embodied in the political rhetoric and ideologies of 'multiculturalism'. In Australia, the definition of Aborigine that was accepted by Aborigines themselves was a 'person of Aboriginal descent who identifies as an Aborigine and is accepted as such by the community with which he or she is associated' (Ashcroft *et al.* 1998: 211). Morton (1998: 358) points out that 'Being Black and being traditional became the marks of authentic Aboriginality, thus bolstering the mutually interpenetrating images of "an ancient race" and a

"50,000-year-old culture", cliches that have retained their force to the present day, particularly in Australia.'

Aboriginality is a relational concept – it has meaning only in terms of 'White ethnocentrism'. The quest for recognition and respect, for identity and pride in Aboriginality, continue to be expressions of resistance to a long history of racism and subordination, especially pressing because, out of all the diverse ethnic groups composing Australian and Canadian societies, Aborigines have experienced – and continue to experience – extreme forms of oppression and suffering. In both Australia and Canada today, now largely immigrant, multicultural societies, Aboriginal peoples have become small minorities. The population of Australia is 18.5 million; approximately 1 per cent are Aborigines. The population of Canada is over 30 million; approximately 2–3 per cent are Aborigines (Donnelly 1997: 317; Le Clair 1992: 136; Paraschak 1997: 3). Although the histories and cultures of Aboriginal peoples vary from nation to nation, from region to region and, indeed, from tribe to tribe, there are basic commonalities between them. Australian and Canadian Aborigines are recognized citizens, counted in the census, with a vote and with limited powers to run their own affairs; but in both countries they suffer from health, employment, social welfare and educational deficiences, and face overt and subtle forms of racism. The majority of Aborigines live in rural or remote communities, although they are increasing in numbers in urban and semi-urban areas. Those living in outlying regions are most severely disadvantaged and socially marginalized (Le Clair 1992: 136; Tonkinson 1998: 297). In Australia the child mortality rate for Aborigines is 25 per cent higher than the national average (Kizilos, *Australian* 6/8/98) and 'Australia is the only First World country on an international "shame list" of countries that still have endemic trachoma in children – which causes blindness' (Pilger, *ITV Network* 31/8/99). Aboriginal communities generally suffer higher rates of suicide, child molesta-tion, rape and domestic violence; the indigenous population is overrepresented in the unemployment statistics and at every stage of the criminal justice system (Brooks, *Guardian* 16/1/99). Tatz (1995: 11) describes graphically the picture in Western Australia, where, he claims that:

> Aborigines remain the poorest, sickest, most homeless, least literate and hungriest of people. Generally they are the most oppressed, repressed and depressed community. In a country that takes pride in its 'multiculturalism', Aborigines are often relegated as a subspecies of ethnicity, as a subset of the migrant population.

In a similar vein, Churchill (1999: 18) makes the point that 'the material conditions to which indigenous peoples in the United States and Canada are subjected remain abysmal'. In Canada, specifically, 'Aboriginal women on average live ten to twelve fewer years than non-Native Canadian women' (Chuchryk and Miller 1996: 3), infant mortality is higher, earnings are lower, and 'Aboriginal people are not receiving the health, educational and physical or recreational services most Canadians are getting' (Le Clair 1992: 136). 'The suicide rate is seven times higher, and the average age at which suicide occurs is fifteen years lower. Aboriginal women are also more likely than non-Native Canadian women to live at or below the poverty line. Current Canadian government figures indicate that, where one in ten of non-Native Canadian women is the victim of domestic violence, six in ten Aboriginal women are victimized' (Chuchryk and Miller 1996: 3–4).

The suffering of Aboriginal peoples has been intrinsic to the effects of European imperialism, to the processes of colonialism, to the dispossession of the livelihoods and cultures of indigenous peoples by colonial powers, to inherited power relations, and to resistance in the contemporary world to power-sharing with historically disadvantaged groups (neo-colonialism) (Ashcroft *et al.* 1998: 2; S. Hall 1996b). The suffering of Aboriginal women, has, in addition, been linked to patriarchal structures and forms of discrimination. All these features of Aboriginal history are tied into the struggles that individual Aboriginal women and groups of women have faced in order to take part in sport – to their failures, and to their successes. For Australian and Canadian Aboriginal women, success in sport has been a heroic symbol of 'achievement in the face of adversity', linked to the politics of racial and ethnic exclusion, to the politics of Australian and Canadian Aborginal nationalisms, and to the politics of gender.

Aboriginal women and sport

Native men and women have worked in two broad ways to secure advances in sports: first, through representation in mainstream sport (i.e. modern 'Olympic-style'/Western/Eurosport/'White' sport) and, second, by forging opportunities through specifically indigenous sports organizations and competitions. In the first case, Aborigines have the opportunity to make a mark in mainstream society, to be accepted alongside non-Native sportsmen and women according to the ideologies of equality of opportunity and inclusion. In this liberal-pluralist perspective, it can be argued that there is freedom from ethnocentrism and a sense of belonging resulting from interaction with wider Australian and Canadian society. The second case is a response to hostile, racist ideas and practices endemic in White ethnocentric society. It results in organizations and competitions that are run by Aborigines for Aborigines – either for participation in Western-style sports or as a way of re/creating forms of culture that include traditional elements and have an authentic connection to pre-colonial history and identity – in common with what Frantz Fanon (1995: 153) describes as a 'passionate search for a national culture which existed before the colonial era'. Aborigines are part of two worlds: part of the complex interaction between two forms of sport (defined as imperial culture and indigenous culture) and two kinds of nation-building (that of the nation as a 'whole' and that of indigenous 'nations' within the nation state) (Tonkinson 1998: 287).

Liberal democracies have at the core of their ideology the assumption of equal rights and opportunities for individuals and minority communities, but for Aborigines the realities of living in multicultural societies are linked to practices of exclusivity, rather than inclusivity. Aboriginal children were prevented from entering public swimming pools all over Australia until, in 1966, 'Charlie Perkins, who became the first Aboriginal university graduate, chained himself to the turnstile of the municipal pool at Moree in Western New South Wales and withstood threats of violence until the first black kids were allowed in' (Pilger, *Observer* 22/3/98). But even after doors were opened legally, the struggle for Aboriginal girls and women to get into sport has been especially harsh, and although in Canada their involvement has been considerable in both traditional games and festivals and mainstream Eurocanadian sport (Paraschak 1995b: 71), in most cases it has been hidden from history. With reference to mainstream sport, Marion Stell (1991: 236) asserts that, 'In the cultural pecking order of Australian sport, white males have always placed themselves at the top. They determine the order of those who follow: second are race horses, third aboriginal males, fourth white women and fifth and last black women.' According to Colin Tatz, 'Aboriginal women have received less in the way of sports encouragement, facilities and access that any other single sector of the Australian community' (Tatz 1995: 6). In Canada, too, far fewer Native women than White women, and far fewer Native women than Native men, have access to sports resources.

Tatz (1995: 269) argues that, because of its complexity, the interplay between racism and sexism in sport – what he decribes as 'racist-sexism' – is exceptionally difficult to write about:

> Some aboriginal women's experiences are unique, such as removal from parents or decades-long confinement in girls' homes and in mission and settlement dormitories. Many aboriginal women's experiences, though seemingly similar to those of white women, are much more extreme in their poverty, physical and legal restrictions, and in their assigned status within tribal tradition. ... The crucial question is whether their access and participation are hampered more because they are black than because they are women. The answer is yes. They are black, they are women and they have either historical, social, cultural and tribal prescriptions confronting them: together these realities form the highest possible hurdles.

During the early years of the twentieth century, in Australia and Canada institutionalized racist-linked forms of discrimination restricted the sports participation of Aborigines of both sexes, and patriarchal arrangements and ideologies compounded the problems for women (Tatz 1995: 271; Paraschak 1997). According to Tatz (1995: 6), most Australian Aboriginal girls

> were raised on isolated, remote government settlements or Christian missions, where sport was ignored, deplored, prohibited or bereft of facilities. Many were forcibly removed from their parents and raised in 'assimilation

homes' because as 'half-castes' they were thought to be salvageable for a life in white Australia.

Exceptionally, some Aboriginal girls and young women had exposure to Western education and sport and had enthusiastic teachers and coaches, some had help from white patrons, and others moved to urban locations where there were greater opportunities. In most cases, participation was the result of chance meetings, coincidences and unusual social situations.

Pioneer Aboriginal sportswomen

Cricket was the first modern sport that Aboriginal women broke into in Australia. During the 1930s, a team from Queensland included two Aborigines: Edna Crouch and Mabel Campbell. In the 1940s, Edna's niece Thelma also represented Queensland and played for the Australian junior team (Tatz 1995: 271–2). Later, in the mid-1950s, Faith (Coulthard) Thomas represented South Australia against England and New Zealand and was selected for the national team in 1958 (Tatz 1995: 272). She was the first, and still in 1995 remained the only, Aboriginal woman to play cricket for Australia (Stell 1991: 237–8; Tatz 1995: 273). In the 1970s, May Chalker became the first Aboriginal golf champion (Stell 1991: 237; Tatz 1995: 278).

Most of these pioneer women were poor, and through sport they made contacts with people from different class and ethnic backgrounds. Faith Thomas was taken as a baby to a remote mission in South Australia, but she did well at school and went to university for a year – and that was where she first played cricket. May Chalker, who lived in remote wheat country in Western Australia, was one of ten children, and she took up golf 'because there was no other sport for women in the Wialki district' (Tatz 1995: 278). Success in mainstream sport was often the result of unusual and supportive relationships with White patrons. In the 1960s in rural Victoria, Dick Hine, who was a badminton-loving dairy farmer, coached several of the twelve Mullett children who lived in a nearby tumbledown shack and 'transported them, clothed them and became the family mentor' (Tatz 1995: 274). Cheryl Mullett became the most outstanding badminton player of the family, winning several national titles at junior and senior levels, representing Australia in different competitions, and winning innumerable state titles. Other sisters in the family – namely Sandra, Linda and Pauline – between them won national and state titles. Tatz (1995: 275) describes how the Mullett sisters 'gave up badminton because of the lack of money rewards and the enormous costs for the rural amateur, in travel, equipment and clothing'. But all the family went on to successful careers in government service, agricultural research, hospital work and education. 'The ladder to these things', says Pauline, 'was sport: we met people, got to know people. Without sport we wouldn't have the confidence' (cited in Tatz 1995: 275). Sharon Firebrace, a senior volleyball player for Victoria and Australia in 1968, was from a family of seven children, with a mother 'unable to cope'. She

'was sent to a home at the age of six – and, in her words, "was pushed out at 16" '
(cited in Tatz 1995: 281). But she herself became a qualified teacher and is now
an influential leader of the Aboriginal community (Kizilos, *Australian* 6/8/98).
Tania Dalton, who played volleyball for her state and the country, also came
from 'a large family with limited means [which] meant that travel to Melbourne
for training and competition had to be done the hard way: through small
donations, "chook" raffles and the like' (Tatz 1995: 281).

Tatz (1995: 273) links the successes of these Aboriginal sportswomen to
political changes, arguing that the year 1957 provided greater freedom for them
with new citizen rights and the end of exclusion from social and sports clubs.[3]
From this time, they were able to take part in a wider range of sports and very
often played more than one sport to quite a high level.

There seem to be fewer records of successful First Nation Canadian sportswomen. Two of the best known – identical twins Sharon and Shirley Firth,
Dene Indians from Ivunik in the Northwest Territories (NWT) – were highly
successful international skiers. They came from a family with twelve children.
Sharon records how the family was poor and sometimes they were hungry; how
they lived first in the bush, where they snared rabbits and went ice fishing; how
they could cut and clean their own fish by the time they were five years old
while their brothers were off hunting with their father; how they moved to
Ivunik and lived in a shack with three rooms for everybody to sleep in and one
room for the kitchen and living room; and how the windows were covered with
ice in the winter. She writes of her love of the world of Nature that they were so
close to – walking with their mother down by the riverbanks, seeing figures in
the ice crystals and hearing the ice crystals chime (Zeman 1988: 102–4). But,
because of their hard life, sport was an attraction for Sharon and Shirley and
they first started Nordic skiing in 1967, when they entered one of many sport
development programmes that were opening up for First Nation peoples. Sport
was an important feature of assimilationist policies that were being pursued at
the time by national and local governments, as part of a 'civilizing' strategy and
in order to salve the conscience of 'the nation' for mistreatment of its
indigenous peoples. The skiing programme was supported by the Department of
National Health and Welfare, the Northwest Territories Council and the
Canadian Amateur Ski Association. Sharon and Shirley were both members of
the 1972 Canadian Olympic Team, when Sharon was the overall winner of the
Trans-Am (twelve-event) Series. Shirley achieved the best time ever by a
Canadian woman at the 1972 Olympics; Sharon went on to represent Canada
again at the 1976 Olympics; and both sisters were in the Canadian Olympic
Team in 1980 and again in 1984. One or other of them made their mark at
different times in the World Cup circuit and the World Nordic Championships,
and in 1985 Sharon was the overall winner in the Great American Ski Chase.
In 1987, both sisters were honoured as Members of the Order of Canada
(Zeman 1988: 99–120).

But the Firth sisters had a problem trying to straddle the gap between
tradition and modernity, between the local and the global – a problem that is

commonplace for sportswomen from Aboriginal communities. Snowshoeing and other indigenous activities, which are traditional sports and take place in the community, create an authentic sense of belonging and identity, whereas international competitive skiing is a Westernized and globalized sport culture which pulls participants away from their communities. Once Sharon and Shirley had retired from competitive skiing, they both had difficulties adjusting to new lives – for Sharon going back 'home' to the NWT to live and work was traumatic and upsetting, and Shirley felt alienated living in a European culture. They were both distressed about their identities – having spent years away from home skiing, they had had their links to the past ruptured and their attachments to the NWT weakened. Shirley described what 'home' really means for her: 'The snow, the thousands of lakes and ponds. ... I'm always homesick for the land, not to mention the people' (Zeman 1988: 117). The production of troubled and complex identities was directly related to the cultural repression of the non-Western and the sense of threat to Aboriginality.

The characteristics of modern sport help to reaffirm difference, and Aboriginal peoples (in particular) are faced with the distinction between the local (their families, communities, traditions, way of life) and the global (modern travel and communications, competitive, commercialized, 'homogenized' sport). Many Aboriginal sportswomen experience a very real sense of loss of, and displacement from, local culture, at the same time as they are seduced by, but also alienated from, mainstream sport because they are the racialized 'Others'. They adhere to the particular (the sense of roots and organic identities in Aboriginal culture) *and* assimilate into the universal (the sense of being part of a bigger agenda that unites everyone into a single nation state or global community) (Wallerstein 1984: 8).

Negotiating between cultures is linked to issues of race and racism in the wider society. The link between ethnic consciousness and racism in personal life and throughout society leads some Aboriginal sportswomen to return to their communities after they have finished competing, in order to work on all-Aboriginal sport projects in coaching, sport development and administration. In this way they are building opportunities for young women in Aboriginal communities, giving them new visions, enriching their lives, and helping them to transcend discrimination. A number of Aboriginal women have linked their love of sport to their interest in politics, Aboriginal identity and anti-racism. One of these people was Faith Thomas. She explains that she was not conscious of being an Adnyamathenha person when she was young, but as a successful sportswoman she came to understand the politics of race and difference. She refused an exemption certificate, without which she was denied privileges (such as access to White sport clubs) *because* she was Aboriginal, and she remembers racist abuse. Faith became an active member of the Australian Aboriginal Sports Foundation, which she co-founded in order 'to help the up and coming sports kids who had nothing' (Tatz 1995: 273). Also in Australia, Karlene Dwyer-Brown retired from a fine basketball career and then became the administrator of sport and leisure for the Aborigines Advancement League, and

Angie Ahkee has used her role as an organizer of Aboriginal and Islander sports carnivals to combat racism in sport (Tatz 1995: 291).

But, with very few exceptions, Aboriginal women are not making significant inroads into the higher levels of sports coaching and sports administration in mainstream sport. Those who take part in all-Aboriginal sports do so in 'racialized spaces' (Paraschak 1996b). These are contradictory spaces, margin-alized from mainstream society, but which facilitate the construction and reproduction of ethnic communities and identities, and which sustain self-determination, and community and cultural revitalization. But, because the Aboriginal talent that is nurtured feeds into the mainstream sport system, these spaces also help to sustain the ideology of equality of opportunity and to mask the structural constraints facing all Aboriginal sporting females.

In spite of adversity, Aboriginal women are making their mark in sport in different ways – through mainstream channels, and through all-Aboriginal sport, which feeds into mainstream competition or which is part of the indigenous sport movement. They are increasingly active in both competitive sport and social sport, in an expanding number of events, and at state, national and international levels. Through these channels, Aboriginal sportswomen are actively reversing the image of Aborigines as victims. Sharon Firebrace believes that it is fatal for Blacks to look too long at their hardships: 'Don't portray me as a victim,' she says, 'I am not a victim but a victor' (Kizilos, *Australian* 6/8/98). Although so few Aboriginal women have been prominent in sport, nevertheless they have influenced the representation of Aboriginal sportswomen and the psyches of Aboriginal communities and of the nation as a whole. Those who have acquired the status of sporting heroine have contributed significantly to the shaping and reshaping of Aboriginal and national identity. In Australia, there have been three particular Aboriginal sportswomen – Evonne Goolagong, Cathy Freeman and Nova Peris-Kneebone – who have acquired fame at national and international levels. Their personal biographies highlight issues and controversies surrounding Aboriginal women in sport.

Evonne, Cathy and Nova: sporting heroines

Evonne Goolagong was the first Aborigine to play top-class tennis and, before Cathy Freeman became famous, was characterized by Colin Tatz (1987: 62) as the best-known and most acclaimed Aboriginal sportsperson in the world. She fits the 'success from poverty' stereotype: she was from the outback, the third of eight children, her father was a sheepshearer, and her mother made her first tennis dresses out of sheets; as one of thousands of children who attended a visiting country tennis school, she 'showed such promise that she was taken to Sydney to live with the family of her coach, Vic Edwards' (Stell 1991: 237); she was the winner of four Australian singles titles, the Italian, French and South African Opens, and she was the Wimbledon singles champion in 1971 and 1980 (Vamplew *et al.* 1994: 6). In 1971, she was named Female Athlete and Australian of the Year and was awarded an MBE. Following her marriage, she is known today as Evonne Goolagong-Cawley and is the chief Aboriginal representative for the 2000 Sydney Olympic Games.

Nova Peris-Kneebone, also from a poor Aboriginal family, had shown promise as a sprinter when she was a child being brought up in the outback Northern Territory. She achieved sporting glory as the first indigenous Australian to win an Olympic gold medal, which she did in 1996 as a member of the victorious Australian women's hockey team. Nova was the product of an Aboriginal sport development scheme. She was playing hockey at top level from the age of sixteen, became a mother at nineteen, but continued to play afterwards. In 1992 Nova was named three times in the Northern Territory Sports Awards (Tatz 1995: 285), then she transfered to athletics and won gold medals in the 200 metres and the 100-metres relay at the 16th Commonwealth Games in Kuala Lumpur, Malaysia, in 1998.

Cathy Freeman is another outstanding athlete – at the age of sixteen she became the first Aborigine (man or woman) to win a Commonwealth gold medal in track and field: she was running in the Australian 4 x 100-metres sprint relay team at the 1990 Commonwealth Games in Auckland, New Zealand. The following year she was named Young Australian of the Year. Then, at the 1994 Commonwealth Games in Victoria, Canada, she won the 200 metres and the 400 metres. Cathy's mother was born on a reserve on Palm Island, in Queens-land, was one of a family of ten, who depended on food distributed by government agents, and left school when she was twelve years old. Following the forced removal of the family to southern Queensland, for many years Cathy's mother was a single parent raising a family of five. When she remarried, she and her husband encouraged and supported Cathy's talent. From poor beginnings, Cathy Freeman has become the most famous Aboriginal sportswoman of today, winning an athletic gold medal for the 400 metres at the 2000 Sydney Olympics (Jeffreys, *Sunday Telegraph* 16/07/00; Smith, *Courier-Mail* 2/3/96; Tatz 1995: 292–5).

Evonne, Nova and Cathy are all sporting heroines. But their identities as heroines are complex and changeable, bringing to the surface and magnifying questions of difference and identity. Each is the 'property' of different groups with different world-views – her own, very personal, home and tribal community; a supratribal Aboriginal population that includes all the indigenous peoples of Australia; a multicultural Australia, the nation as a 'whole'; and black anti-racist international groups. They have, therefore, to negotiate the nature of their own identities and ownership of them, and the media have a part to play in these processes.

Each of them has been consistently classified in the (White) media as 'Black', 'Coloured' or 'Aboriginal'; for each one of them, the media have constructed a story of 'victory over adversity'; and they have all been portrayed as a role model for other Aboriginal girls and young women. Racialized accounts of Aboriginal superstars – treating them as the 'Other' – appear to be commonplace. But the athletes themselves manage such representations in different ways, relating specifically to their political position on Aboriginality. For example, during her playing years Evonne Goolagong remained resolutely outside Aboriginal affairs and politics. When she was continually bombarded by reporters' questions about her race – 'what was it like they wanted to know to be the first Aborigine at Wimbledon, on Centre Court, playing tennis at a high level? Had I been discriminated against? How did I relate to Arthur Ashe?' – she said that she wanted desperately to be treated as a promising tennis player, not as a tennis player with black skin (Goolagong 1975: 122). Although, in common with Nova Peris-Kneebone and Cathy Freeman, Evonne Goolagong experienced racism (for example, when she was sixteen she was referred to as a 'little nigger' by an opponent, an Australian premier had said he hoped that in the 1980 Wimbledon final she 'wouldn't go walkabout like some old Boong' (Tatz 1987: 64) and she has commented that 'All tennis players lose concentration, but since I'm an Aborigine, it's brought up constantly – except when I'm winning!' (Stell 1991: 238)) she claimed never to have had any racial problems (Goolagong 1975: 98). In comparison, Nova and Cathy relate their personal experiences to the more general problem of racism throughout Australian society. For example, Cathy has a strong sense that her family was part of the 'stolen generation'. She explains that 'My grandmother was taken away from her mother because she had fair skin. She didn't know her birthday, so we didn't even know how old she was when she died. ... I'll never know who my grandfather was, I didn't know who my great-grandmother was, and that can never be replaced.' She goes on to point out: 'You have to understand that when you have a government that is so insensitive to the issues that are close to people's hearts, that have affected so many lives for the worse, people are going to be really angry and emotional' (Jeffreys, *Sunday Telegraph* 16/07/00). Cathy Freeman's sense of self, although tied in this way to the past, is at the same time grounded in present-day racism. Before she was well-known she was pointedly ignored at shop counters, was the object of racist language [called 'nigger' and 'coon'], and experienced physical abuse (*Koori Mail* 14/8/96; Smith, *Courier-Mail* 2/3/96).

In 1971 Evonne Goolagong was granted a visa to travel to apartheid South Africa and became the first non-White to play against Whites in a tennis tournament there, and the first non-White to win a South African Championship (Goolagong 1975: 67). She travelled again to South Africa in 1972. Aboriginal leaders condemned her for insulting her own people by entertaining racists with her tennis. She was also denounced by American black activists for going to South Africa after Arthur Ashe had been refused a visa. When she was there, she received preferential treatment as if she was White, and was wined and dined in otherwise 'all-White' hotels and restaurants at a time when Black, Indian and Coloured South Africans were banned from high-level competitive tennis and from the places and lifestyles enjoyed by Whites. On her return from South Africa, she received a cable from the Australian prime minister, William McMahon, in the multicultural language of national unity, thanking her for being an 'ambassadress' for all peoples of Australia (Goolagong 1975: 132). Goolagong was sufficiently integrated into mainstream (White) Australian society to incite those with strong Aboriginal identities to claim that 'Living with "the Edwardeses" made her more White than Aboriginal' and was 'paternalism at its worst' (Goolagong 1975: 24–5). She became the 'uncomfortable subject of a national debate' (1975: 131), caught between the discourse of the powerful, colonial elites and those of the national and international Aboriginal communities, who continued to criticize her for doing nothing about Aboriginal affairs, for failing to speak out on land rights and racial issues, and for being insulated from the problems of most Aboriginal women (Littlewood 1982: 36; Stell 1991: 238; Tatz 1995: 276).

From the start of their sporting careers, Nova Peris-Kneebone and Cathy Freeman have both had strong Aboriginal identities, although not without contradictions and ambivalences. Their awareness that Aboriginality is linked to discrimination co-exists with the knowledge that Australia as a nation has taken them to its heart and that the global world offers them new opportunities and visions which seduce them away from their Aboriginal roots. In 1993 Nova joined a Western Australian schools programme that seeks to improve Aboriginal self-esteem, and she was 'very aware of the significance of [her] achievements in the Year of the Indigenous People' (Tatz 1995: 285). She has a strong sense of responsibility about being a role model and is 'determined to alter the attitude that young Aboriginal mothers are not a sporting "investment" ' (Tatz 1995: 285–6). Her sense of family and community and her links with indigenous peoples are very strong; indeed, she dedicated her 1996 Olympic hockey gold medal to the Aboriginal people of Australia. She has particular concern that Aboriginal girls face greater hurdles because of their backgrounds and attitudes, and her motto for life for them is, 'You can achieve if you really believe.' Immediately following her Commonwealth Games athletics gold medal wins in Malaysia, she referred to her family at home and to her ancestral tribal lands: 'In Darwin and out at Kakadu, I'm sure they'll be rocking tonight. Far out. This is unbelievable' (*Sunday* – Malaysia 20/10/98; *Deadly Vibe* 20: 9).

Cathy Freeman also links her success in athletics to her Aboriginal identity, and she has done so in a most public and dramatic fashion. After winning the 400 metres at the 1994 Commonwealth Games in Victoria, Canada, she ran around the track on a lap of honour holding aloft both the Aboriginal flag and the Australian flag. She did the same after victories at the world championships in 1997 and 1999 and, again, when she won the 400 metres in Sydney (Jeffreys, *Sunday Telegraph* 16/07/00). She explained her reasons for doing this in Victoria:

> I did it because I knew how proud it would make a whole race of people. I'm proud to be Aboriginal and I guess I really wanted to have an effect on the self-respect of all Aborigines. It wasn't myself I was representing.
>
> (Smith, *Courier-Mail* 2/3/96)

But Mosely (1997: 24) points out that:

> Freeman's flag-bearing went far beyond the issue of the rights of indigenous Australians. In placing the Aboriginal and Australian flags back to back

during her post-race triumph, Freeman flashed subliminal messages to all Australians that spoke not simply of pride in her Aboriginal culture and heritage but, by inference, of the pride of all those cultures which have come to make Australia a pluralist society. Cathy Freeman's simple act raised the national gaze. Australians were afforded a vision of themselves as a multi-racial society. It was a fresh rather than a new view but the ensuing public debate testified to a nation grappling with issues of race, ethnicity, cultural pluralism and national identity.

Cathy Freeman received acclaim *and* criticism for her action. To grasp the Aboriginal and national flags *together* was interpreted by liberals as a symbol of unity and reconciliation, a new 'constructive nationalism'; some White conservatives insisted that the Australian flag was the only legitimate one; some Aborigines viewed her act as a sign of tokenism, of assimilation into the White world, and of alienation from her roots; but the majority of Aborigines claimed her as *their* heroine, *their* champion (Tatz 1995: 293). Pat O'Shane, an Aboriginal magistrate, expresses the popular view: 'She showed she is very proud of her race and a proud member of the Australian team' (*Australian Morning Herald* 25/8/94). Cathy Freeman has become a hero to Aboriginal children; for some of them, replacing basketball's Michael Jordan. However, Glenn Brennan, who works in the indigenous unit of the Australian Sports Commission, claims that she has had the greatest effect on older people: 'There are people who were once very embarrassed about their culture and heritage, but her pride has trickled down into the community.' He goes on to say: 'That Freeman can parade with the Aboriginal flag is a major step forward for Australia. Evonne Cawley could never have done it. They would have thrown her out of tennis. Freeman has given Australia more confidence' (Overington, *Sydney Morning Herald* 9/8/97).

The discourses of Aboriginality and of Australianness have been combined by both Aboriginal leaders and white politicians, and Cathy Freeman's symbolic act has highlighted the relation between the two. She has pricked the consciousness of all Australians about indigenous peoples – including those in power. By such a public act, she has symbolically thrown off the cloak of oppression and marginalization for all Australia's Aborigines and she has shown how sports superstars can use their status to highlight issues of difference and discrimination. But, ironically, Cathy Freeman has not freed herself from the difficulties of having an identity which is constructed across different, and sometimes antagonistic, discourses (S. Hall 1996a: 4). Even before winning at Sydney, she had made a fortune from circuit winnings, advertising and sponsorship and had travelled all over the world mixing with the global-sporting-entertainment elites. She has admitted feeling estranged from her culture 'even to the extent of enrolling in university courses to enable her to answer questions about Aboriginality' (Tatz 1995: 294). The twin senses of being an Aboriginal athlete *and* an Australian, of belonging *and* feeling alienated, is a problem for all Aboriginal sportswomen. It has been highlighted by Cathy Freeman, and is accentuated in the context of international competitions such as the Commonwealth Games and the Sydney 2000 Olympics.

Aborigines, politics and major sporting events

The Commonwealth Games and the Olympic Games are global stages for the playing out of identity politics, and elite sportswomen can be key people in the processes. For example, at the 1994 Commonwealth Games, which took place in Victoria, Canada, Angela Chalmers – the best-known Canadian female athlete of native heritage at the time – carried the national flag at the opening ceremony (Paraschak 1995a: 1). Whether or not it was intentional, popular culture – via the personage of Chalmers – produced a public image of inclusiveness, togetherness, oneness. It was symbolically significant that she was the key representative of the Canadian nation – out in front, holding the flag, leading the rest of the 'team' (country) behind her – at a time when Native Canadians were making demands for self-determination. In this way, the host country could communicate to the rest of the world the idea that its indigenous peoples are integrated into Canadian society, and that they have equal opportunities to reach the highest levels of achievement. This, in turn, implies national progress. The high visibility of one individual athlete is thus a powerful symbolic force. The fact that Angela Chalmers went on to win a gold medal in the 3000 metres consolidated the effect.

But positions of sports stars within the discourses of nationhood are highly complex. Public statements made by elite sportswomen, such as Angela Chalmers, about their Aboriginal identity are, overtly or covertly, always political. At the very least, they signal the presence of Aborigines, their self-respect and their problems. For example, in a feature article in the *Vancouver Sun* newspaper (23/8/99), it was reported that Angela Chalmers, whose native name, Dusmanwe, meaning 'Walk Fast Woman', is proud of her native ancestry and Sioux roots. The article goes on:

> She was touched deeply by a letter a teenage girl from a Sioux reserve in Manitoba recently sent her, extolling Chalmers for her achievements and telling her about herself. 'I thought, I have to write to this girl and I have to make a difference to one of these young aboriginal youths', Chalmers said, 'I have to somehow do that. If I can do that, I'll have accomplished much more than winning medals'.

Although the indigenous populations of both Canada and Australia are tiny minorities of the total populations, they have become highly visible and vociferous – through sport and other forms of culture and politics – forcing the governments to acknowledge that the condition of their indigenous minorities is a crucial aspect of any redefinition of nationhood (Tonkinson 1998: 287).

There are, then, differing interpretations of the role of elite indigenous athletes. On the one hand, it can be argued that the discourses of 'Canadianness'

– and also of 'Australianness' – subsume the countries' internal differences and that Aboriginal communities are thus appropriated by 'the nation', co-opted through sport into state apparatuses, and sports stars are used as symbols of this process. At work here are hierarchies of power and legitimacy. What Victoria Paraschak (1995a: 2) describes as 'images of Canada for world-wide consumption' mask the fact that 'there has been a lack of federal government support for native participation in sport, including for the Native Sport and Recreation Program; the Northern Games; and the North American Indigenous Games' (Paraschak 1995a: 13).[4] In this last perspective, Western sport is viewed as a colonizing culture which has asserted its identity and authority on the colonized 'Other'.

An alternative analysis is that sports stars are active agents in representations of difference and identity, involved in what Avtar Brah (1996: 192) calls 'political and personal struggles over the social regulation of "belonging" '. As we have already seen, at the same time as they are celebrated as heroines of the whole nation, they are also embraced by Aboriginal groups as belonging specifically to them, and therefore as cause for Aboriginal pride. Glowczewski (1998: 351) claims that 'The recent fame of some Aboriginal champions promote[s] a cultural respect which erects them as symbols of a new political force.' Littlewood (1982: 130) argues that, 'Unlike the assimilationist position with its emphasis on the importance of individual achievement in modern society, the pluralist position emphasises the persistence of and the need for the preservation of cultural heritage.'

In major sports events in both Australia and Canada, the contest over identity also takes place through the use of Aboriginal imagery in sport – a way of invoking a sense of 'Otherness', a feeling of an ethnic unit, and a vision of the past. Staurowsky (1998a: 304), among others, has investigated the racist implications of the use of Native American imagery in sport, as 'an outgrowth of literal economic, political, and ideological ownership'. She argues that the symbols have 'an Indian façade but a racialized-ethnocentric value structure and meaning', and that 'the accumulated effect is the delivery of limiting impressions of Native peoples as fictional, near-mythic fighting figures or exotics whose customs and practices are viewed as comical or quaint rather than deserving of reverence'. She is describing the creation of essentialist images of indigenous societies as colonial inventions.

In major sports competitions hosted in Canada (and Australia), such representations are commonplace. For example, at the closing ceremony of the 1976 Montreal Olympics, members of diverse tribes, brought together for the first time in 200 years (Paraschak 1995a: 13), were juxtaposed to the athletes in a colourful parade with all the paraphernalia of an imagined Amerindian lifestyle, including drums and wigwams and feathered flags; the 1983 World University Games in Edmonton included native performers in a ten-day cultural event; the opening ceremony of the 1988 Winter Olympics in Calgary had a strong native presence as well; and at the 1994 Commonwealth Games in Victoria, British Columbia, Native images also implied acceptance and celebration of difference and multiculturalism (Paraschak 1995a: 3–7). A common and gendered feature of native representation is that most of the strong images are of males (Staurowsky 1998a: 304). Although the federal government and festival organizers, rather than Native people themselves, produce these images for both national and global consumption (Paraschak 1995a: 7), high-profile Aboriginal athletes – by implication – are identified with their production. So, when Angela Chalmers was featured as the flag-bearer of her country, she was implicitly condoning the official representations of her 'own' peoples and the implications of ethnic assimilation and harmony. Aboriginal activists use major events of this sort to try to get other messages across – in particular, that nativist stereotypes and discourses are a damaging denial of the disharmony and discrimination that permeate society (Staurowsky 1998a: 309). For example, prior to the 1988 Winter Olympics, the Lubicon Lake Indian Band launched a protest asking museums worldwide to boycott the Glenbow Museum's Olympic project (a display of rare Indian and Inuit art objects from all over the world) unless the Canadian government addressed the issue of land rights (Paraschak 1995a: 5). Elite Aboriginal sportswomen have a choice – implicitly or explicitly to support the establishment's multicultural vision, which embodies mythical ideas of tradition but which may help to provide a sense of belonging for Aborigines from different tribes, different areas, and from country and urban settings – or to identify openly with those who are lobbying for political and public recognition of the wrongs done to Aboriginal peoples. Elite Aboriginal sportswomen are unavoidably caught up in the politics of Aboriginality and the dilemma of identity – a problem particularly significant for those involved in the Sydney Olympics.

The successful Australian campaign for the 2000 Olympics (organized by the Sydney 2000 Bid Company) presented to the selectors an image of a united society which had resolved its human rights problems and reconciled differences. Although Charles Perkins[5] was the only indigenous member of the Bid Committee, he was joined by Evonne Goolagong-Cawley and Aboriginal performers to join the team presenting the case for Australia to the IOC in Monte Carlo in September 1993 (Godwell 2000: 4). Evonne Goolagong had rediscovered and reinterpreted her Aboriginal identity shortly after she had retired from competition in the mid-1970s. At that time, when apartheid was still intact, she referred to her South Africa visits, describing herself as 'the guinea pig' and explaining her behaviour in terms of youth and naivety (Goolagong 1975: 130):

> I'd heard of apartheid, but I guess I didn't realise how historic my entry into the tournament would be. I had supposed non-whites could play tennis in South Africa, which they can and do; I had also thought the best could rise to the top as I had in the white sphere of Australian tennis, which they cannot. I learned that the best aren't given the same opportunities as the whites and that they have been barred from the tournaments necessary for improvement.

> (Goolagong 1975: 131)

Goolagong's late awareness of the politics of race in apartheid South Africa encouraged her to look into her own Aboriginal history and to discover that discrimination against her family had been far greater than she had been told (Tatz 1987: 277). She went on to promote a book on Aboriginal oral history because, she claimed, 'I'm just sort of proud that I am Aboriginal, and this is the first book I've seen that has Aborigines speaking out for themselves' (Tatz 1995: 277). The fact that she was a founder member, with Faith Thomas, of the National Aboriginal Sports Foundation (NASF; later replaced by the National Aboriginal Sports Council) (Tatz 1987: 64), and has become open about her own Aboriginality, established her credibility – for the White organizers and some Aboriginal groups – to be a figurehead for unity and for the Australian pan-Aboriginal community during the Sydney 2000 proceedings. But she remained silent about the ways in which Sydney 2000 became a platform for Aboriginal protest and politics aimed to embarrass and stir to action the provincial and national governments.

During the bid period, the IOC ignored a letter from the Aboriginal Legal Service detailing human rights abuses against Aborigines, which should have disqualified Australia from hosting the Games (Tatz 1995: 347), and following the success of the Australian bid there was a deterioration of race relations, causing Aboriginal leaders of different political persuasions to predict a call for a Black boycott, mass protests and demonstrations at the Sydney Olympics (Godwell 2000: 2). Although Charles Perkins originally supported the Australian bid because he believed it would bring the races together, he subsequently changed his position and called for an international boycott in protest at what he called the 'worsening racist treatment of his people' (Lynch, *Independent* 8/12/98). He claimed that 'health facilities for Aborigines [were] "atrocious", housing conditions "terrible" ' and that his people were 'dying on average twenty years earlier than white Australians'. He went on: 'Unless these things change before the Olympics, then I would suggest that the European people, especially the British people, don't bother coming over. They would be dancing on our graves.'

Colin Tatz (1995: 13) suggests that Paul Keating, the Labour prime minister during the early 1990s, became the first political leader to acknowledge the huge prejudices that Aborigines face – 'the "devastation and demoralisation", the injustice, the murders, the "discrimination and exclusion" '. But in 1996, when the Conservative coalition government was in power, more than 400 million Australian dollars were slashed from the Aboriginal affairs budget, and the Equal Opportunities Commission, 'whose responsibility is to protect minorities and raise awareness about racism', was also impoverished (Pilger, *Observer* 22/3/98). The prime minister, John Howard's, idea of 'a new spirit of freedom' conceals racist sentiments in a country that is experiencing unprecedented economic difficulties that are affecting most acutely its indigenous population. The worst blow is the failed attempts by the Aboriginal people to use the Native Title Act, passed by the Federal Parliament in 1993, to claim entitlement to land that was stolen from them. In 1998, amendments to the Native Title Act, restricting future Aboriginal claims to land and sea areas which they believed had finally been returned to them, were passed in the Senate in the face of fierce opposition from Aboriginal leaders (Milliken, *Independent* 9/7/98; Zinn, *Guardian* 15/6/98, 7/7/98). The legislation transfers land to rich White Australians, including Kerry Packer and Rupert Murdoch, and protects the interests of White farmers and miners. John Pilger (*Observer* 22/3/98) describes it as an Australian version of apartheid, bringing racism into the centre of Australian politics.[6]

Support for the 1998 bill was made easier by the success earlier in the year in the Queensland state elections of the One Nation Party, with its overt anti-Black, anti-Asian, anti-immigration politics. Although at the following general election the One Nation Party secured no seats at all, its earlier success had exposed the depth of racism in Queensland (resulting from rural decline and discontent) and the profound problems for race relations throughout the nation (Milliken, *Independent* 9/7/98; Woollacott, *Guardian* 2/7/98; Zinn, *Guardian* 15/6/98). With a marked rise in the number of attacks on Aboriginal youths, the moves made by Paul Keating, the former Labour prime minister, for reconciliation between Whites and Aborigines have been seriously set back.

Racism is at the heart of Aboriginal identity politics, and the attempts to produce an image of 'Australianness' through sport implicates everyone in-volved (administrators, athletes and politicians from every ethnic group and political persuasion) in wider political issues and discourses. For Aboriginal sportswomen to be silent about the polemics surrounding Aboriginality can be interpreted, implicitly, as support for those in positions of power. The opposition between White political leaders and Aboriginal activists came to a head in 1988 – 'Australia's' bicentenary year – when 200 years of settlement were celebrated 'in the face of considerable Aboriginal outrage' (C. Hall 1996: 68). 'Having declared an oppositional "year of mourning", Aborigines adopted the neatly ambiguous slogan, "White Australia has a Black History" ' (Tonkinson 1998: 292). The Sydney Olympics marked another 'moment' when debates were focused on nationalism and cultural identity; followed, in 2001 (the date of the centenary of Australian federation) by debates about the future of Australia as a republic and the associated demise of the links with colonial Britain and the monarchy. At play in those debates are definitions of citizenship, of nation, of community (C. Hall 1996: 68), but also, as Tonkinson (1998: 288) points out, 'the encapsulated "World" status of Aboriginal people is fundamentally significant' (Tonkinson 1998: 288). Sport is part of a wider political climate and succession of events in which Aboriginal sportswomen are unavoidably implicated.

Additional antagonisms over indigenous/non-indigenous control and power at the 2000 Olympics arose because of the refusal to appoint an Aboriginal member of the Sydney Organizing Committee for the Olympic Games (SOCOG), set up to replace the original Bid Committee when Sydney was chosen as the host city. Charles Perkins claimed that Aboriginal people were frozen out of the planning procedures and their recommendations were ignored. The National Indigenous Advisory Committee (specifically set up to improve relations between the indigenous and non-indigenous communities, and with a specific mandate to report to SOCOG) had no representative on the Olympic Organizing Committee (Godwell 2000: 10), a decision which the chairperson, Lowitja O'Donoghue, described as a 'slap in the face' (Zinn, *Guardian* 28/11/98). In 1998, she predicted that indigenous people would call Black athletes to boycott the Games if governments failed to change their position on race relations (Lynch, *Independent* 8/12/98). International sport facilitates solidarity between indigenous groups from different countries – a form of political pan-Aboriginality – and Aboriginal athletes were unable to insulate themselves from the boycott appeal even when they remained silent about it. Depending on their stance, they became subjects or objects in the discourse of global race relations surrounding the Sydney Olympics. Reacting to the huge pressure of being a potential gold medal winner, Cathy Freeman openly dissociated herself from the Aboriginal boycott. Her position was that a boycott prevents White–Aboriginal co-operation and that if she succeeded, she would be a powerful symbol of Aboriginality and what is possible for her people.

There was also controversy over the way in which indigenous peoples were represented in the publicity for the Sydney Bid and the forthcoming Olympics. The Olympic organizers appropriated Aboriginal symbols, using the boomerang for the Games' logo and launching the torch relay from the Aborigines' most sacred site, Uluru. Aborigines asserted that 'They've stolen something and they're using it on the international scene' (Lynch, *Independent* 8/12/998). There were objections from some Aboriginal people about such show-casing of their culture, including the appropriation of their 'motifs and artistic representations' (Godwell 2000: 16) and the characterization of performers as 'tourist curios – like koalas and kangaroos' (Godwell 2000: 5). Synthia Slowikowski (1993: 181) argues that 'the labels "primitive" and "civilized" are not innocent or naive', but are used as opposites, the 'primitive' taken to mean ' "other", "exotic", "ancient", "foreign", "pure", etc.' and that 'sometimes the primitive is performed as an "authentic" tradition that is actually recently selected or invented'. Aborigines are aware that public images at major international sports events, such as the Sydney Olympics, are produced within unequal, White-dominated relations of power and conditions of display, that there is a manipulation of tradition, and the Aboriginal is set in the context of modern culture. With the question 'Who owns the past?' in mind, critical Aborigines reject Western hegemonic representations and appropriation of Aboriginality by White Australians and want, instead, control over their own cultural symbols.

The controversies over the Sydney Olympics posed particular problems for elite Aboriginal athletes. Understandably, they want to compete because it will probably be their only chance in Olympic competition, but they are made to feel like pawns in a struggle for ownership of their identities. The push towards identification with the powerful bureaucrats of the Sydney Olympics, and the sense of assimilation as an Aboriginal into Australianness, were probably more complete for Evonne Goolagong than for Cathy Freeman and Nova Peris-Kneebone. As the Sydney Olympics approached, Goolagong remained one of the leading actors, comfortable with her ethnicity and heritage in the context of multiculturalism. Cathy Freeman's athletic brilliance and global media pop-ularity also made her particularly useful for White Australia and she, too, became integrated into the official image of national unity manufactured for the international community. She was young, she was personable, and she was an Olympic hopeful – not surprisingly, therefore, she became 'the face' of the host nation for the Sydney Olympics. Although Cathy opposed the Olympic boycott, she openly identified herself with the Aboriginal community and, like Nova Peris-Kneebone, became a role model for her own people (Smith, *Courier-Mail* 2/3/96). She writes a regular column in the Aboriginal magazine, *Deadly Vibe*,[7] encouraging young Aborigines to take up sport, and she is positive about her influence:

> I like the fact that I have the chance to change the course of someone's life, just by giving them a word of encouragement or just by being myself. I believe I could be a good leader. In fact, I think I am a good leader already in my own way. I think I am a good person
>
> (Smith, *Courier-Mail* 2/3/96)

Cathy recognizes and negotiates skilfully her dual identity and shared ownership, which she explains very simply: 'When I run at home, I'm always "Cathy Freeman, the Aboriginal athlete". Yet when I run overseas, it's always "Cathy Freeman, the Australian" ' (Smith, *Courier-Mail* 2/3/96).

Darren Godwell (2000: 5) states with clarity that,

> At a fundamental level, the association of Australia's Aboriginal and Torres Strait Islander peoples with the Olympic Games is about politics. The politics of identity – both Australian and Indigenous, Australian race politics, and the politics of power – both structural and individual.

Mainstream inter-ethnic sport poses particular and complex problems for Aboriginal sportswomen relating to the polemical discourses of political and ethnic identities but, in contrast, all-Aboriginal sports events and competitions present opportunities for a shared culture of values and understanding.

All-Aboriginal sport – traditional and modern

From the beginning of colonization, and during the forging of the countries' original constitutions, Aborigines were excluded from nation-building activi-ties. Since they have been full citizens,[8] their experiences of oppression and racism have led them to search for meaning and to seek to create their own identities or 'nations' (Salee 1995; Tonkinson 1998: 293). Nation-building is usually assumed to be the creation of a 'common culture', an 'abstract commu-nity' which is more recent and different from the culture of earlier kinship-based communities – a process described as 'ethnogenesis'. Referring to Australia – and this is equally true for Canada – Tonkinson (1998: 293) points out that 'The challenge for Aboriginal nation-builders has been to overcome problems of distance and cultural diversity, and to present a unified front and a positive self-image.' Aboriginal peoples from both countries are spread across huge geographical areas and come from distinct tribes and clans, and there are large numbers of mixed-race Aborigines, especially in the urban areas (Littlewood 1982: 3). There are, therefore, huge differences between those Aboriginals living in remote areas of central and northern Australia who retain an authentic connection with past tradition, and those of mixed descent living in Southern Australia, many of whom are urbanized and 'Westernized' (Tonkinson 1998: 294). Similarly, in Canada, there are immense differences between, for example, the Inuit and Dene peoples living in the Northwest Territories, Native peoples living in reservations, and those living in urban areas across the country. Nevertheless, because of systematic racist discrimination, there is, at the same time, a notion of common Aboriginal identity based on a shared sense of difference from and opposition to the non-Aboriginal (specifically White) population. Littlewood (1982: 4) argues that, 'Given that Aborigines are subordinate to non-Aborigines in political, economic and social spheres, any distinction between tribal and non-tribal Aborigines becomes irrelevant.' Tonkinson (1998: 294–5) goes as far as to suggest that Aborigines themselves invoke the colonial-imposed notion of Aboriginal ethnicity and use essentialist ideas about an Aboriginal 'essence'. However, he goes on to argue that the process of identity politics has become increasingly 'culture-centred, emphasizing commonalities, continuity and survival' and 'has less to say about oppression than about Aboriginal culture as enduring and empowering' (Tonkinson 1998: 302).

In recent years, cultural reconstruction and ideological nation-building work have taken place through the establishment of indigenous sports organizations and events. Colin Tatz argues that *'sport can, and does, have more important functions in Aboriginal societies than it does in the lives of other Australians'* [emphasis in original], including helping with some of the serious social problems that are endemic in Aboriginal communities (1995: 315–23). All forms of all-Aboriginal sports activities are attempts to grasp power, to reverse the privileging of European culture over traditional culture, to revalue local culture, and to recreate and redefine ethnic Australian and Canadian communities and identities. They also provide a channel for Aboriginal men and women to get into mainstream sport and mainstream organizations with the potential to break them into the structures of power in those institutions.

Reinventing the traditional

The renaissance of old sports and games signifies resistance to the colonization of indigenous cultures and to the seductive pull to abandon Aboriginal culture for Australian/Canadian White culture. For example, the Yuendumu Games, often called 'The Black Olympics', are a four-day celebration of sports, dance and play which have taken place in the Northern Territory of Australia every year since 1962.[9] Although the programme includes modern events (including

Australian Rules football, softball, basketball, athletics events, visits by past Aboriginal sporting celebrities, and popular contemporary music) as well as traditional ones (such as spear-throwing, tug-of-war, traditional dancing and corroborees) (Australian Broadcasting Corporation VHS 1982, 1984; Tatz 1995: 326–8), the Yuendumu Games, nevertheless, have a specifically 'indigenous character'. Organized by Aborigines for Aborigines, they are unique in Aboriginal cultural life and have been the inspiration for the creation of other Aboriginal sports and cultural festivals.[10] The link between past and present is fundamental; whole communities travel for hundreds of kilometres to join in and everyone sleeps under the stars in a friendly, family atmosphere. A traditional holistic approach to sport and recreation is fostered, encouraging the participation of everyone in the community, regardless of age, sex or skill level, de-emphasizing winning, and celebrating culture and religion (Horn 1999: 26). Even when playing modern sports (Australian Rules football is the main interest, and other modern sports, for men and for women, are key events), it has been observed that Aborigines play *against* one another and *with* one another, in a spirit of fun, sharing and freedom (Tatz 1995: 328). Women play a key role in traditional events. They keep in touch with the past by stripping to the waist and decorating their bodies with ochre for the corroboree and dancing. Robson (*Australian Magazine* n.d.) describes how 'Dancing begins just before sunset [and] the women move in unison across the crumbling red earth.' The link between past and present is embodied by the oldest performer, 'a tiny crumpled figure said to be well past 100', who 'wears a khaki beanie and numbered college-style T-shirt'.

The Black Olympics are a symbol of homogeneous Aboriginality, attracting participants and spectators from different indigenous communities and of all ages and both sexes. A tangible sense of cultural pride supports the motto of identity politics: 'Cultural revival is survival.' Because in local Aboriginal communities very few women, especially older women, take part regularly in sport or physical recreation, indigenous festivals have important symbolic significance for Aboriginal womanhood. For example, the Black Olympics exemplify the way in which Aboriginal sport provides an important context where women from rural areas can come together to celebrate their ethnic identities through traditional games, customs and shared experiences, and where they can engage with modern sports in ways that suit their lifestyles and beliefs in resistance to 'the real deculturation process that has been taking place since the first European contact' (Salee 1995: 293). Referring to Canada, Salee (1995: 293) points out that in globalizing cultures, the radicalization of Aboriginal discourse and the revitalization of Aboriginal culture and practices is fundamental to identity. All-Aboriginal festivals give women and men the opportunity to transcend the racism which affects their access to mainstream sport. In addition, for women, they provide a brief time and space each year in which they can escape from their unequally gendered relationships with Aboriginal men and enjoy sports from which they are normally excluded.

In common with Aborigines from remote areas of Australia, those from the north of Canada have in general had greater autonomy to develop their own native-derived cultures than Aborigines from other areas.[11] The Northern Games – which took place for the first time in 1970 – could be described as Canada's equivalent to the Australian Black Olympics. They are described by Paraschak as 'a weekend of "traditional" games and activities', 'a flow of experiences, a "happening" ' (Paraschak 1997: 11, 1991: 85). Inuit games and some Indian events formed the basis of the festival. The Good Woman Contest – 'a variety of activities which simulated traditional living skills, such as bannock making, tea boiling, seal skinning, muskrat skinning, and fish cutting' (Paraschak 1991: 82) – was a way of testing and celebrating the everyday activities of women by reaching back to past times, linking today's women to their mothers and grandmothers before them. The nature of the activities (essentially 'non-sporting') and the ethos of the festival (prioritizing ethnic identification through participation) are in plain contrast to the aggressive competitive structures of Eurocanadian sport and for that reason originally had to struggle to secure official funding (Paraschak 1991: 82). But, in line with the Canadian government's recognition of difference and multi-ethnicities and their response to the 'Aboriginal problem' (Salee 1995), the Northern Games now have government support, allowing Inuit and Dene peoples to retain control, although with some pressure from government officials to structure the Games 'more in keeping with a Eurocanadian-derived, meritocratic style of sport' (Paraschak 1991: 91). Although the programme continues to include traditional games events for both men and women, Paraschak (1997: 14) points out that 'Several changes were recommended, including the division of events by age and sex, the development of community trials to choose participants, the standardization of rules, and the improved scheduling of events.' An interesting development has been the introduction of categories for men as well as for women in the Good Woman Contest (Paraschak 1991: 89).

The concern to 'be traditional' is mediated by the seductive pull of mainstream sport and this is the dilemma that Aboriginal peoples face all the time. Both the Northern Games and the Black Olympics retain an authentic Aboriginal character at the same time as they include modern features. Salee (1995: 293) argues that such a mix does not, however, necessarily devalue the pull of 'tradition'. He points out that

> The ancestral customs and practices, however thin they may wear in some cases, serve as an ideological mooring where the collective imagination can anchor and elaborate a concrete identity. This identity, even if invented, even if tainted by borrowings from the very culture it claims to oppose politically, constitutes the impregnable rock on which Aboriginals lay their territorial claims, mobilize themselves, and express their desire to gain autonomous control of their collective destiny. Present day Aboriginal identity is, in fact, undergoing a process of reconstruction which brings it to define itself against non-Aboriginal society. In asserting itself, it may resort

to the very cultural, intellectual and institutional categories from which it claims to take its distance, but it does not make it less legitimate or less cogent; it does not make its opposition to mainstream values and discourse less real or less valid.

The key element is power – the power to control activities and influence the common psyche. All-Aboriginal events, like the Black Olympics and the Northern Games, that prioritize traditional components, are uniquely significant ways of inspiring identity. There are also all-Aboriginal programmes composed only, or mostly, of modern Western-style sports. For example, Victoria Paraschak (1997: 16) writes that

> southern Canadian native peoples, who have interfaced with Eurocanadians for much of this century and have increasingly adopted a customary Eurocanadian way of life, have ... developed a self-funded all-Indian sport system, largely comparable to mainstream Eurocanadian-derived sporting practices.

Both these types of all-Aboriginal sports organizations – those that focus on traditional elements and those that focus on mainstream events – are important to Aboriginal identification. The absence of racism helps to generate feelings of togetherness, commonality and belonging. In the case of women, the specific sense of being an Aborigine is combined with the shared experience of having a *female* Aboriginal identity.

Women are involved in all types of all-Aboriginal sports activities – as performers and as organizers – although in much smaller numbers than men. For example, when the Australian National Aboriginal Sports Foundation (NASF), an all-Aboriginal body, was founded in 1969, twelve well-known Aboriginal sportspeople were invited to become original members, but only two were women – Faith Thomas and Evonne Goolagong. NASF was set up with government funding with objectives to provide Aborigines with 'access to sporting and recreational amenities in order to help them to overcome any social and cultural difficulties they may encounter in the general community through sport' (Littlewood 1982: 35–6). Radical Aboriginal critics viewed the NASF as a government-inspired assimilationist project and its members as puppets of White Australia. However, those Aborigines who were involved in the work of the NASF believed that, in spite of government money, all-Aboriginal organizations can confer power and revitalize the cultures and narratives of dominated groups. Although officially non-political, the NASF acted in the interests of the Aboriginal community, for example, and ironically, by protesting about Evonne Goolagong playing in the otherwise all-White South African tennis tournament during the apartheid regime, mentioned above (Littlewood 1982: 36). The NASF was replaced by the National Aboriginal Sports Council (Tatz 1995: 315) and the link between sport and

Aboriginality was validated and symbolized through the creation of Aboriginal Sports Awards (Tatz 1995: 109).

Gender relations in Aboriginal sport

In 1972, the Canadian federal government set up the Native Sport and Recreation Program with the specific aim to integrate native participants into mainstream sport. The scheme lasted only until 1981 (Paraschak 1997: 6) because Canadian Indians rejected the logic of assimilation into predominantly White sport with its unequal race and ethnic relations of power and control. In contrast, the discourses and practices of All-Indian sport prioritize self-determination. Victoria Paraschak (1997: 7) explains that

> Indian leadership is ensured because the tournaments are run by native peoples, and Indian champions are identified through their own system based on Indian regions and Indian (through descent) membership criteria. There is consultation with people at local level, and no limitations are placed on the level of skill needed to compete.

But there is less potential for autonomy for women in All-Indian sport than for men. The focus on Eurocanadian events and methods favours male participation, and the majority of those in administrative positions of power and decision-making are men. Paraschak (1995b: 71) points out that, although the All-Indian Sports System includes sports for both sexes, those for males are favoured and 'aspects of Aboriginal women's involvement in sport are shaped by the same patriarchal relations which underlie mainstream sport' (Paraschak 1995b: 71). Over the years Aboriginal women have struggled to increase opportunities and resourcing for their sex and, although the philosophy of gender equality is in general accepted, in many situations it has been hard to put into practice. The unusual example of the National Aboriginal Coaching School illustrates how a radical gender equity ideology and practice can effect a speedy shift in traditional patterns of male domination. Since its inception in 1994, the Aboriginal Coaching School has been committed to a 50 per cent gender balance in the numbers of coaches trained, and one of its aims is to improve communications between males and females. It is claimed to be 'the only program offering Aboriginal women meaningful participation in the Canadian sport system' (*Action* spring 1998: 4).

Although there continues to be gender bias in favour of males in Aboriginal sports leadership, a few exceptional women have infiltrated the top administrative levels from where they can work for the benefit of all Aboriginal women. For example, Cara Currie plays a prominent role in Aboriginal sport. She is the vice chair of the Aboriginal Sport Circle (ASC), a national collective of regional Aboriginal Sport Organizations, and the International Vice President of WIN (World Indigenous Nations) Sport (a co-ordinating body for Aboriginal people in sport across the world). The Aboriginal Sport Circle is working to build a sport system which, together with other equity issues, treats women as equals and provides them with the same opportunities as young men (*Action* autumn 1997: 15). Thomas, who is also a member of ASC, points out that:

> Issues surrounding women across the country are coming to the fore, not just in sport, but in all walks of life. Its equality; everybody has the right to participate in anything they want, and sport is one of those rights. In Aboriginal communities, equality is a big issue, too, and women deserve to have equal accessibility to sport.
>
> (*Action* autumn 1995)

There has been an expansion of Aboriginal sport at local, national and international levels during the last decade, and Aboriginal women have been proactive in securing representation at all these levels. Competitions between teams and regions in Canada and the USA predated the first North American Indigenous Games (NAIG), which took place in 1990 in Edmonton, Canada. The publicity material explains that:

> The Mission of the North American Indigenous Games is to improve the quality of life for indigenous peoples by supporting self-determined sport and cultural activities which encourage equal access to participation in the social and cultural fabric of the community they reside in and which respects indigenous distinctiveness.

The first NAIG Games attracted nearly 3000 participants from Canada and the United States; in 1993, at the second Games, there were over 8000 participants; in 1995, at the third Games, the number was over 10,000. The fourth NAIG Games – which took place in 1997 during one week in August in Victoria, Canada – were a mixture of sport competitions and Aboriginal cultural festivities. There were 4500 Aboriginal youth and 500 senior athletes (over 21) competing in 17 different sports, with '800 coaches and managers, and 2500 Aboriginal singers, dancers, musicians, and paddlers' (*Action* summer 1997). The programme included cultural events representing a way of life symbolized in the NAIG motto, 'True, strong and brave', starting with more than 60 traditional Aboriginal ocean-going canoes arriving in Victoria's Inner Harbour – the culmination of a 500-kilometre Tribal Journey, followed by a traditional Salish Welcome Ceremony, where Tribal Journey participants were welcomed by local chiefs. There were demonstrations of traditional activities, such as war canoe races, arctic sports, hoop dancing, and lahal (Aboriginal stick games). Although more males than females have participated in each of the NAIG games, women are involved in a full range of traditional events and modern sports and the programme for women is expanding – for example, soccer (and its five-a-side indoor version, Futsal) is popular with First Nation women in Canada and the women's game has become an important feature of the NAIG festival. Most significantly, NAIG has a gender equity philosophy, requiring equal numbers of women and men on the coaching, management and chaperone staff teams (*Action* summer 1997).

An increasing number of all-Aboriginal international competitions between different countries are taking place, and the numbers of events for women is increasing proportionately as well. For example, in 1990 a women's component was added to the International Aboriginal Cup between indigenous Australians and Canadians (Tatz 1995: 283). There have also been recent initiatives to expand the horizons of international Aboriginal sport to become fully global in character. Indigenous groups from Australia, New Zealand and Japan attended the last NAIG games (*Action* summer 1997), signalling this effect. The idea of a World Indigenous Nations Games was first presented to a meeting of the World Council of Indigenous Peoples in 1977 by J. Wilton (Willie) Littlechild, the founder of NAIG, but it was not until 1990, at a meeting of the Indigenous Parliament in Guatemala, that the concept of the WIN Games was given official support. In 1994 in Mexico City, organizing for the first WIN Games in 2000 started. WIN provides a supranational arena for the universalizing of problems of indigenous peoples and a mechanism for resisting the destruction of their culture and ways of life. The WIN Games will also provide a venue for shared experiences, the opportunity for women from different tribes and countries to talk to each other, and scope to address gender inequalities and issues affecting Aboriginal women from different parts of the world – in other words, to make the voices of indigenous women accessible.

It could be argued that the authentic Aboriginal sporting heroines are those who reject the values of mainstream sport and take part only in specifically Aboriginal sports and culture in order to keep community traditions and consciousness alive. But ASC and NAIG make an explicit link between all-Aboriginal sport and mainstream sport, which is reflected in the creation of the Canadian National Aboriginal Sports Awards (ASA). A major aim of these awards is to celebrate Aboriginality through the successes of athletes and by so doing to create role models for future generations. Thomas (*Action* autumn 1995) explains the ASA rationale:

> The idea of this program is to showcase our women athletes. It's like anything else, in sport – you've got to start somewhere. And for our athletes to finally realize, 'Yes, if I can do it in the Aboriginal community, why not go for the national team?' that's the vision shared by our organization, the Aboriginal Sport Circle, and the North American Indigenous Games. More Angela Chalmers', more Alwyn Morris' competing at the Olympic Games would create role models for our young people.

In Australia, too, there are efforts to make visible and to celebrate successful Aboriginal sportswomen. In Australia in 1986, the annual National Aboriginal Sports Awards were inaugurated, and in 1994 a photographic exhibition (the Aboriginal and Islander Hall of Fame) was set up, depicting Aboriginal sportsmen and women 'who represented Australia, or their State or Territory, or held a national record or title, or who achieved a notable "first" or some distinguished performance. ... A further criterion was the person's contribution to Aboriginality' (Vamplew *et al.* 1994: 2). For Aboriginal women in particular, the creation of an image of female health, power, achievement and choice was in stark contrast to the more usual one of victim pushed into regular child-bearing, often from the age of 15, in order to secure welfare benefits, and with no time for sport (Tatz 1995: 271). Sports awards and photographs generate a vision of the possible, a sense of personal and Aboriginal self-esteem. The attempt is to encourage Aboriginal women to be subjects not objects of their own history and, specifically, to empower themselves through sports and physical culture. Unlike those radical Aborigines who oppose involvement in mainstream sport, the majority of those running the all-Aboriginal sports system want their successful athletes to move on to take part in global competitions, such as the mainstream Olympics. As they get drawn into the wider global discourses of sport, Aboriginal athletes can become visible symbols of Aboriginality to the world at large, as well as icons within their own communities.

Internationalism and the quest for medals have become significant features of Aboriginal sport and gained momentum as the Sydney 2000 Olympics drew near. In Australia, the Olympic Training Centre for Aborigines and Torres Strait Islanders (OTCATSI) was set up in 1998 and scholarships were inaugurated with the specific aim to get more Aborigines into the Olympics. There was, however, a gender imbalance in this process – for example, in South Australia out of eighteen Aboriginal Sports Talent Scholarships, only six were awarded to females – and the scheme as a whole led to controversy. Those who opposed a system of awards argued that it was a cynical shop-window display of opportunity for the Olympics and a form of reverse discrimination – favouring Aborigines and prejudicing other ethnic groups, including Whites. 'Some non-Aborigines claim that Aborigines develop a racism against them' (Glowczewski 1998: 347) and maintain that everyone should be treated equally. Aborigines defend programmes of positive discrimination in their favour, as a right not a privilege, in readjustment of the 'gross inequality of chances, choices and facilities' (Vamplew *et al.* 1994: 3) experienced by their peoples in the past. When applied to the distribution of cultural resources, the liberal paradigm has failed to find practical solutions that acknowledge equality and difference. Such distinctions are linked to human agency and structures of power.

Through their work in Aboriginal communities, Aboriginal women – although in smaller numbers than men – have been active agents in forging for themselves opportunities and identities through the indigenous sports movement *and* in modern sports. Their involvement in traditional activities signals authentic, organic connections with Aboriginal lifestyle; and their participation in modern sports, such as basketball and softball, reveals their interest in Western culture. As Daniel Salee (1995: 293) points out, 'Exposure of so-called traditional societies to western social and economic ways inevitably implies the fact and process of their acculturation to western values and discourse.'

However, there is a clear tension between Aboriginal and mainstream philosophies but also between Aborigines themselves, based on the rural/urban divide. Some Aboriginal women will only play in Black-only competitions in rejection of aggressive European-style competition and its inherent racism. Aborigines who have consistently believed in and lived through their sense of an Aboriginal 'essence' accuse others of using their Aboriginality as a convenience, of being assimilated into Australian state-bureacratic mainstream sport, of making bad alliances with non-Aborigines ('black outside but white inside'), and of only recently 'coming out' as Aborigines ('instant coffees') (Glowczewski 1998: 347; Tonkinson 1998: 298) in order to get sports scholarships. I interviewed some young Australian Aboriginal sportswomen who were confused and unhappy about criticism from other Aborigines. Some I interviewed had lived all their lives in urban Australia and had never taken part in (or even heard about) all-Aboriginal sports events, including the Black Olympics. They therefore feel alienated *from* indigenous events because they are urban livers, and alienated *in* mainstream sport because of their experiences of racism. Other young sportswomen who had moved from rural communities to live in towns were also alienated from both contexts. One successful hockey player told me that when she returned to visit her family in the outback, they condemned her for 'turning White' and so she felt that she belonged nowhere. She had suffered a loss of identity and was painfully searching for and trying to reconstruct a sense of selfhood and personal value. All the athletes I spoke to experience a 'hyphenated' sense of belonging – they search for identity relating to their roots and also for identity in the country as a whole. They are searching for full access to Aboriginal-Australianness or -Canadianness.

Life histories and narrative identities

We know very little about how individual Aboriginal women struggle for identity in sport, about their problems and aspirations, their politics and affiliations, or how they make sense of and articulate their personal situations. Writing about North America, Victoria Paraschak, points out that there is a scarcity of research about Aboriginal athletes in general, and much less is known about women than about men. The same is true in Australia. Paraschak's case study of the Six Nations Reserve in southwestern Ontario – the largest Indian community in Canada – is an exception. Although Six Nation women's involvement in sport is long-standing, Paraschak focused on the years 1968–1980, during which time she found there was extensive involvement of women in a variety of sports, including, in varying amounts, badminton, basketball, baton twirling, billiards, bowling (both five- and ten-pin), broom-ball, cross-country running, figure skating, golf, hockey, horseback riding, karate, lacrosse, softball/fastball, speed skating, tennis, track and field, and volleyball (1996a: 88). But, interestingly, she discovered from informal interviews that, at different times, women from the reserve also took part in archery, barrel racing, harness racing, professional ballet, roller derby and professional wrestling. Her research revealed that women were involved as coaches, administrators and executives, as well as active participants, and she produced sporting biographies of five women who had outstanding careers in sport, competing in a variety of events in both Euro-American leagues and all-Indian tournaments. Their careers, she claims (1996a: 89), 'lay to rest the myth that Aboriginal female athletes are not worthy of recognition'. Also through interviews, Paraschak revealed other previously unknown information – for example, that Indian girls who came from traditional longhouse backgrounds got more support from their families to take part in sport than Christianized girls, who were dissuaded from participating. She was also told that some Aboriginal people internalized the biologist assumption that, as a race, they were predisposed to be 'natural' athletes. Through these methods, Paraschak has exposed evidence of formerly 'invisible' Aboriginal girls and women, and has been able to identify certain trends, levels of consciousness and cultural traditions that affected their participation in sport.

In the final section of this chapter, I am also letting Australian and Canadian Aboriginal women speak for themselves. Their stories generate insights into their lived experiences, identities and cultures. Although they come from different countries and different communities, Australian and Canadian Aboriginal women share experiences and feelings both as Aborigines and as women, and their narratives relate to the political, social and cultural dimensions discussed earlier in the chapter. The following quotations – from a tiny selection of the women I interviewed or with whom I exchanged emails – give power to their voices and comments by foregrounding them and minimizing the commentary. I have worked to make the venture collaborative, with a 'reciprocal quest for understanding' (Sparkes 1994: 173). The final words in this chapter come from the subjects themselves; they are fragments of their life stories, their thoughts and their concerns.

Economy and culture

The starting point for understanding the voices of Aboriginal women in sport is to look at their accounts of social background, cultures and lifestyles. Several of the women are from urban areas and, although they come originally from poor families, they have done well at school and in higher education, and are now middle class, sharing experiences and aspects of lifestyle with urban Whites. However, without exception they talked about their roots and about the social problems faced by Aboriginal women, with a sense of connection to them.

> In the rural communities people have it worst. The health rate is one of the worst in the world and so women can't take part in sport even if they wanted to. It's being compared to Third World countries, particularly in remote Australia. Education is very poor. (Subject A [Aus])

There are huge distances from remote areas to facilities – remote communities don't have facilities. They do have sports officers, but because Australia is such a vast area, they can't get out to those areas very often. There are financial restraints. (Subject B [Aus])

It is more difficult for Aboriginal women than White women. Some sports are out of the pockets of Aboriginal women … For Aboriginal women, part of their culture is looking after the kids. In the low socio-economic families – there may be up to, say, eight children – there are one-parent families, so their ability to pay is diminished. It's such a big deal for them to get out of the house and get involved in some organized competition – that means they've got to be responsible to turn up for every game, every training session. In our lifestyle so many things happen in a week, that it's difficult to make that long-term commitment which is what organized sport's all about. (Subject B [Aus])

[Referring to all-Aboriginal sports events] The costs are kept to a minimum so that people can pay … But it's all to do with their way of life – you know, they just don't have a history – and experience – of sports. That's the older ones. Lots of them were separated from their families when they were kids – it's like they don't belong anywhere. … And now they're living in towns, they don't know where to go, they've got no contacts, it's [sports] not part of their lives. (Subject A [Aus])

Because in Aboriginal society, women have the sole responsibility for bringing up the family – sometimes sisters and brothers give their kids to you – and you bring them up as your own child – and that practice still goes on today – in rural, urban and remote areas of Australia. We still practise the extended family. The time available for women to play organized sport is minimal and it's not a priority. The priority is to rear the children and keep the home in order. The father figure may not be present in an Aboriginal family, so it's much more difficult for the woman to have that time away. Women can't be more involved in their children's sport because of those issues and also the issue of leaving children in a crèche is just not culturally appropriate. (Subject B [Aus])

The majority live in cities, but not out of choice. I was forced to move to the city, there's no prospect of paid work in rural areas, only voluntary. … Maintaining identity, racism, land rights and native title are an increasing battle. I go back to try to help with sport, but it's difficult and in the team I'm in here [city], I don't feel welcome, I don't feel good. I may leave. (Subject C [Aus])

My biggest concern is that we still tend to community sport and recreation because we have a huge problem with youth suicide in our Northwest

Aboriginal communities and towns and also health problems that can be alleviated by people participating in physical activities. (Subject B [Aus])

I went to the National Aboriginal Sports Conference where a lot of questions about the link between education, health, and sport came up. It's all very well to have a few role models, but you need to give kids access to healthy lifestyles and an alternative to drugs, alcohol, etc. through sport. You need to get to the community at grass roots levels to help them to have a different focus and aim. We opened a can of worms that the government was not prepared to tackle. (Subject F [Aus])

I host a radio programme which has a sports segment. I try to get across sporting events – Aboriginal events. But it's hard to hear about them. I also want to promote Aboriginal sport in urban as well as community rural areas. People in urban areas get lost. (Subject E [Aus])

There's a lot of poverty and neglect and abuse on the reservations – and that's where most Native people live. Sports schemes are good for morale and good for the community. ... I don't know about equality with the guys – I didn't experience negativity or sexism. I played lots of sport on the reservation and got lots of help – from my Mum and from my family. I think I only had problems when I left. (Subject J [Can])

One of the biggest drawbacks is money. You can't build a proper sports infrastructure with the the sort of funding that's made available. ... It's not that there's *no* money filtering in – there's just not enough. For the sort of investment that's really needed, the Native groups just don't have enough, and the government won't give what's needed. It's like you're in a deprived area – you can't travel – it's too far and too expensive – it's not practical, so all you've got is some people working to the bone with very limited resources. ... It's hard, I'm telling you it's hard. And it's harder for women. There's lots of drinking and violence against women. The men take out their hate on women. Really they're frustrated, they've got no hope ... Women are the target. And women have to work to keep the family together. (Subject K [Can])

All-Aboriginal sport

Chuckryk and Miller (1996: 7) argue that 'the impact of environmental, economic, and political pressures on the lives and work of Aboriginal women in contemporary tribal colonialist economies has mitigated the abilities of Aboriginal women to pursue traditional activities'. Nevertheless, Aboriginal women have used sport in all-Aboriginal contexts to reinvent the past as well as to take part in modern, colonial-style sport. There are clear divides between traditional and modern sport, but in both forms, so long as they take place in all-Aboriginal settings, women talked about a sense of organic Aboriginal identity and culture, of common ways of behaving and relating, of feeling 'at home'. They also mentioned different styles of play, and antagonisms from non-Aboriginal players and teams which relate to notions of difference and 'natural ability' – the very essence of racist, biologist ideology.

> All-Aboriginal teams are often preferred. They usually make a team with their family, their relatives. But when they go to play competitions, non-Aborigines fear them because they're an all-Black team. (Subject B [Aus])

> Sporting events such as local sports days are great social events which bring families and people together as an identifiable group of Aborigines. (Subject C [Aus])

> They like that feeling of being in a team; they like the need for sharing, co-operation, helping each other. Each a team effort, they're all striving for the one thing. In my research, I found that for Aboriginal girls, team sports was part of their self concept – they evaluated themselves much more highly when they played team sports than most other activities at school. What attracted them was the feeling of being cohesive, close – the ability to help each other, share, co-operate – direct themselves towards a team goal rather than an individual goal. (Subject B [Aus])

> National Aboriginal week is across the country. Some of the activities of celebrating our Aboriginality are all-Aboriginal sports carnivals – they are the biggest deal. We play team sports – for women, netball and basketball. (Subject B [Aus])

> Aboriginal sports events are much more comfortable to play in – you've got your own people there – brothers and sisters, cousins, nieces, nephews. ... all playing together in the same team. When you go to a non-Aboriginal event, it's hard to bring your own children there because kids run amuck, but it happens in our lives all the time. In an Aboriginal carnival, we stay who we are, we don't change who we are because of who we're playing with. We're more comfortable with our own people because they know what it's like to be Aboriginal and part of being Aboriginal is having a lot of kids hanging around you all the time. They might run on the court – in all-Aboriginal sports events, because we're used to it, it's not a big deal. If that happened in a non-Aboriginal sports event, the house would be on fire, they'd get upset, they'd pull your team out, they'd react in a really negative way. The comfort of playing within our own people is much better. (Subject B [Aus])

> We also have 'Aboriginal time' – we are more relaxed about time and responsibilities and issues regarding sport – our priorities are looking after

kids. Non-Aboriginal sport rules are real strict. The way that the carnivals are organized from an Aboriginal point of view are much more culturally appropriate because those things are taken into account. The women actually organize the carnivals to take an account of Aboriginal customs and culture. If you've got two teams and they've got no uniform, it's not important. (Subject B [Aus])

Also teams have a perception that they're not treated equally on the court – cos their skills are quite good compared to most non-Aboriginal people, but we have a different style of play with regards to basketball. For example, players might steal the ball off the opposition team more often than a non-Aboriginal person; there's more fast breaks; there's more lay-ups; there's more 3-point shooting. The game is a really fast, very assertive form of play. My own experience is that they fear that, they don't like to lose to Aboriginal people. (Subject B [Aus])

The way we play, it's labelled as aggressive by non-Aborigines. They say we play different because *we're* different – you know, physically. They find excuses when we beat them – so instead of saying we're better players – stronger, faster, more skilful, better teamwork – you know, all the things they say about White teams – it's like we're at fault – we've been too rough. They don't say it, but it's like we're cheating, not playing fair, when it's just we're better. We're a really good team. You know, we're a *really* good team. (Subject A [Aus])

Indigenous carnivals bring together people from different states. They're social, interactive events which bring communities together, and provide a sense of identity. (Subject G [Aus])

International forums and sports meetings for indigenous peoples are important for the exchange of ideas, especially women's issues. Women have to deal with race *and* gender issues – we need support from one another about women's problems in indigenous sport. (Subject J [Can])

Most young Aboriginal people aspire to compete in mainstream sport – most of them aren't so interested in all-Aboriginal sport. But then they get into difficulties – there's always racism – and, like me, my family don't accept what I'm doing, they don't want me joining with Whites. ... I don't know where I belong, I don't know what I want. (Subject H [Aus])

I, myself, am Aboriginal (Plains Cree) and all of my family, with the exception of my mother and I (we live in Northern Ontario), still live on our Reserve in Fisher River, Manitoba. My interest in Native sport began early in my athletic career when I noticed how few Aboriginal people participated in the mainstream sport system. They were absent at every level of

competitive sport. My interest in Native sport peaked in 1995 when Kelly
Bull, the organizer for the Ontario Aboriginal Recreation Circle, called me
(I had no idea who he was or that such an organization even existed) and
asked if I would compete for Ontario at the 1995 North American Indigenous Games in track and field. I accepted and it was one of the most memo-
rable times of my life. I was supposed to compete again at the 1997 Games,
however, Native sport in Canada, particularly in Ontario, is always in
turmoil and I declined the offer for practical reasons. ... Anyway, I am
devoted to trying to develop Native sport in Canada in any way possible
including writing the history of the North American Indigenous Games
from its genesis to its evolution as one of the most powerful sport organizations in the world. (Subject I [Can])

Basically, the indigenous sport organizations that have developed across
Canada were created as an alternative to the mainstream sport system
which discriminated against reservation athletes. Most First Nations do not
have the financial or personal resources needed to compete in the mainstream sport system (e.g. most First Nations are in isolated areas so that
travel costs are far too high to compete in the mainstream sport; as well,
many areas do not even have basic facilities needed for basic training –
gymnasiums). As such, the alternative sport system was designed for two
reasons: (1) to provide Native athletes (disadvantaged athletes) with a
training ground in which to develop as elite athletes (although there are
many problems with this system of sport as well) and (2) sport is viewed as a
positive outlet to combat the oppressive conditions that exists in many
Native communities. The latter reason is more recognized than the other –
most Native reserves can hardly justify putting money into developing athletes when basic health care on their reserves is on par with Third World
countries. Thus, many Native leaders view sport as a positive alternative to
the alcohol and drug problem that affects their communities. Most of the
indigenous sport organizations in southern Canada view this as the main
reason for promoting the alternative sport system to their people, the general public, and to the governments and private agencies that help fund
their activities. (Subject I [Can])

WIN ranks as one of the largest and most powerful, but least known, of all
the sport movements in the world. When I went to see Littlechild about
NAIG I was totally taken by surprise about WIN – I had some idea that
World Games were planned, but I had no idea about the overwhelming
nature of this project. The Games are planned for sometime early in next
millennium ... The WIN Games are supposed to rival the Olympic Games
in both size and grandeur. The idea behind the Games is to help create
unity through sport for Native Peoples across the world. This is why the
United Nations is a big player in the Games. Unlike the Olympic Games,
whose organizers once professed that politics was separate from sport, WIN

organizers openly admit that politics has *everything* to do with sport – and WIN will be proof of this statement. (Subject I [Can])

Like the Six Nations Reserve, the Kahnawake Reserve is unique among Canadian Reserves ... Kahnawake has a well-developed sport program. This is because Alwyn Morris lives on the Reserve and works closely with Wilton Littlechild and Carra Currie in trying to develop a stable national Native sport organization – it's called the Aboriginal Sport Circle. As far as I can tell, if you're Native and you want to be an athlete the best places in Canada to live are on the Kahnawake Reserve, Quebec, and the Hobbema Reserve, Alberta – where Littlechild and Currie reside. (Subject I [Can])

Racism and associated problems

All the women I interviewed had experienced racism in personal ways. They expressed poignantly their feelings of hurt and mistrust of non-Aborigines – feelings that lived with them over the years. Many of the women were highly politicized, describing examples of institutionalized racism, differences between urban and rural Aborigines, and the particular problems resulting from living in remote areas and on reservations.

Racism in country towns is rife. It's exacerbated by Native Title and the reconciliation process. There's also Aboriginal deaths in custody, with the finger pointing at police. Living with those problems – sport's not important. (Subject A [Aus])

In rural communities there are marked divisions between Black and White. ... For example, racism in basketball – non-Aboriginal kids won't play on the same court as Aboriginal kids – they say that they're too rough, etc. – they won't mix with Aboriginal kids. It's very widespread ... (Subject B [Aus])

Most non-Aboriginal people have never met an Aboriginal person in their life – what they see on TV is it – and there's still fear in them. They don't know us unless they meet us and know who we are and what we're about and then they find they've got a friend for life. (Subject B [Aus])

When I first played basketball for my state I played mostly with girls who had two parents who were quite well off and lived in the wealthy suburbs of Perth. I was the only Aboriginal person in the team and I'd come from a poor family in a low socio-economic area and I grew up with a stepfamily. There were 14 or 15 of us at one time in one household ... I remember being called 'Little Black Duck'. And I'm not very dark at all. The reason I was called the black duck was because I played for my district team which was called Swan District. Being a swan they called me the duck and because

I was Aboriginal, they called me the black duck. This was never said in front of my face – this was banded around by parents and I could hear parents sniggering behind my back. And as a child I did not know how to handle that. … To go to state training, because my mum had all the kids behind her she couldn't take time out to drive me 45 minutes across town, then stay there for three hours and then drive me all the way home because training was every Saturday and Sunday for three hours for four months leading up to the Australian trials. So I used to catch a bus and then a train and then another bus. So that would take me an hour and a half to two hours to get to training. I had to leave at six o'clock in the morning to get to training by 8.30am. It would be a whole day trip for me by the time I got home. So Mum couldn't take the time out to do that for me because she had all the other children to look after. I did this all the time and I used to get home from training – and I was only 15 or 16. And I used to bawl my eyes out, I used to cry like crazy because I knew the girls didn't accept me. They had never met an Aboriginal person in their life and they didn't want to. I had to put up with their sniggering and their remarks. The worst feeling that I've ever had is for someone not to include you in their group. In basketball – in order to create a team, the team feeling is created off the field, so the acts you do socially as a group gel you and make you cohesive as a team on the court. But I never felt like a member of the team because they never accepted me off the court, so on the team I rarely got the ball thrown to me and I always felt as if I was being ill treated by the players. Not all the players were like that, but the majority were. I can only remember one person being quite decent to me. I never got on with the coach at all – I never felt he played me enough because I was different. I was different to everybody and they made sure I knew I was different. I never had my mum and dad come and watch me train and support me like the non-Aboriginal parents. I always felt that was unfair. But, anyhow, I ended up playing state basketball. I was in the under-16s, the under-18s and the under-20s sides and then I made it into the state women's team and we have a national basketball team in Perth that plays against other states and I got selected for that team as well which was called The Breakers. And the same girls that I grew up with were in that team as well – the majority of them – and the same thing happened all the time – and I never had the courage to say anything to anybody because all I wanted to do was fit in. I thought I was just a person, and I treat people exactly how I think I want to be treated, not how they're treating me. I wasn't brought up that way. I finished basketball at that level when I was 26 just before I had my first child. It should have been a happy time in my life but I can tell you it really wasn't, it was a very testing time. I remember a girl saying the only reason I got where I was was because I was Aboriginal. What a load of garbage! When people treat you like that it gives you the strength to prove them wrong and say 'I can do this' and it motivates you. But you don't find out that kind of information until you get wiser and older. I didn't have the social skills to handle the ringer I was being put through by my non-Aboriginal team-mates. (Subject B [Aus])

Living on a reservation insulates you from the racism you get when you travel out to matches and to different areas. (Subject J [Can])

I didn't have any Native friends in high school – though I tried to talk to a few. I was an urban Indian and they were reserve students bussed in each week from distant areas and boarded, only to return to their reserves on Friday. Some students had to stay for the entire semester because their reserves were fly-in areas and it was too expensive for them to go home each week. It must have been tremendously hard for the students to leave home at such an early age. This system still continues (most Northern reserves have no schools) and is akin to the 'Boarding School Era'. Regardless of their intelligence, these students were streamlined into the general, and most often, basic level classes with the belief that most of them would not finish high school and would not go into post-secondary education. Our educators thought most would return to the lifeless reserves and get drunk and live off the government for the rest of their lives. And the children, too young to fight for themselves, fell into this trap. This is what I saw. And this is what lives in my memory. I hated it and I vowed to do as much as I could for my people. (Subject K [Can])

I still do not tell people outright of my Native heritage. I've found that being Native is both a privilege and an obstacle. I've been hired specifically because of my Native heritage (employment equity) and have been told by some vicious people that I could not get the job on my own merits. I receive money from my Band to go to school and am criticized for wasting government money. ... And when I do tell people I am Native, and that I do have full Native status, they are always surprised. Their reaction always stings a little because it means to me that even the people I know and trust the most, who I feel are most open-minded, still harbour racist attitudes and beliefs about Native. It means to me they think all Native people are drunk and lazy and living off the government on their reserves. Then when I am introduced to other people, one of the first things that is often said about me is that I am Native – like I have no other attributes that are worth mentioning. ... I don't mean to rage on – I am not actually militant about Native rights – I am for equality of all peoples. I just like to express my views when people are willing to listen. Otherwise I stay quiet. Many Canadians are fed up with Native rights issues so I pick my audiences very carefully. ... My experiences don't even compare to some of my friends (I now am friends with other Native people). Some restaurants won't serve Native people. (Subject K [Can])

There's inverted racism within the Aboriginal community. There's rejection on the basis of light skin colour. There's no strong sense of belonging outside of the family unit and people feel threatened by those who leave the flock and take part in White mainstream sport and resent that they can fit into both worlds and that they have a choice. It's as if this weakens the community. (Subject D [Aus])

Some non-Aborigines consider giving grants specifically to Aboriginal women is unfair, that it's a form of discrimination. There are so few grants given, it's just a bit of a joke. There are so many other scholarships provided for other selected groups, why not to Aborigines? (Subject C [Aus])

I started playing field hockey at about 9 or 10. I grew up in Riverland, a country area. I was probably the only Aborigine in a school of 2–300, then virtually *the* only Aborigine at high school with 400–500 kids. It made it more difficult, there was no one else to relate to, to share things with in terms of cultural identity. It was a burden being the token representative of Aboriginality. ... When I became successful in sport I got most funding from the Aboriginal Sports and Recreation Fund. I got the cost of training, uniforms, equipment, travel. Money came from a fund set up to benefit *only* Aboriginal people. But there was resentment from ... non-Aborigines because I got funding and not them. I got no encouragement or support. (Subject E [Aus])

When I was a teenager there was mainly name calling – 'coon', 'abo', 'boon'. Although I am lightskinned, if it's known I'm an Aborigine then I come in for the same treatment. So I never told anyone. Sport was one of the ways I could regain self-esteem and get on in life, doing something I am good at. (Subject E [Aus])

Racism has mostly been from other Aborigines – 'the dark people'. I've had resentments from them about getting a scholarship.(Subject F [Aus])

Women suffer both discrimination *and* racism being Aboriginal *and* female in sport. We get abuse more often than support, from other Aboriginal women as well as White ones. It's very difficult not being accepted by your own people. You get tagged as a tomboy or lesbian if you show an interest, you're not supposed to be good at sports. Then you get criticized – 'You only got there *because* you're Aboriginal.' 'You're only good at sport *because* you're Aboriginal.' 'You only got funding *because* you're Aboriginal.' You have to have a strong personality to pull through. It's a really hard fight. (Subject E [Aus])

My main interest is softball – I work in the South Australia Softball Association. ... One incident is very vivid. I was invited to try out for the State

Softball side in 1979/80, at the peak of my performance. I made it to the final selection, but then I was omitted from the team. At the time I didn't want to believe it was because of racism, but everyone was surprised I hadn't made the team. Two years later I was asked to try out again and was told then that I hadn't been chosen because I was Aboriginal. They'd felt it was not a good image, and that I was overweight. I feel it could be a disadvantage being Aboriginal in sport if the selection is between an Aboriginal and a non-Aboriginal. I've been in World Masters softball – in Junior (over 35) and senior (over 45) levels. I am the *only* Aboriginal female to participate. But my position is threatened because I'm Aboriginal. I have to fight to keep in even if my ability is very presentable. (Subject G [Aus])

My father is Aboriginal and my mother is White and I've inherited her fair-skin. ... It took me a long time feeling comfortable saying I was an Aboriginal. Some Aborigines do not have the skin colour and phenotype normally recognized as Aboriginal and they often live their lives as non-Aborigines. ... I'm from Southern Australia. My father was Aboriginal and a recognized sports person. When I moved to Adelaide I became more involved in racial issues. My experience of racism as not being very dark – people assume I'm not Aboriginal and make racist remarks against Aborigines in front of me. 'Second rate' is what they say. I suffered from a lack of self-confidence and never said anything. ... But it empowers me to learn more about my culture, so when people make derogatory remarks I can defend with an informed opinion. ... I play hockey and I find it easier to be accepted because I've got a light skin. I don't say anything and people think I'm not Aboriginal. I don't find my Aboriginality works against me in sport, more in social life. (Subject H [Aus])

Gender relations of power in Aboriginal groups

There was a general sense among the Aboriginal women that I spoke to that gender relations were more unequal for them than for their non-Aboriginal counterparts. Without exception, there was resistance to inequalities of gender.

Men have greater access to sport than women – it's cultural and economic – and because White men control most sports. (Subject G [Aus])

[Referring to sports scholarships] I do think they are really good because they give women the encouragement to go ahead and pursue a sport which they would otherwise be unable to take part in because of finances. Finances are the biggest problem. But there are no scholarships available specifically for girls and women. The men run the programme and may use their power to make them available. They don't have a quota policy. (Subject B [Aus])

At the Institute there are over 600 scholarship holders, only two of them have identified themselves as being Aboriginal, and they are both male. They have a 'most outstanding Aborigine' category for their sports awards. The Australian Sports Commission have a funding programme – currently myself and two other boys receive grants. There's about $4.5 thousand over 2 or 3 years, to cover competition expenses, training and medical. The idea is to get as many Aborigines to the Olympics as possible, to find the talent to make Australia sucessful at the Games. (Subject H [Aus])

[Referring to the Aboriginal Training Centre] It may alleviate the sort of problems I had. Trains athletes, coaches, managers and sports administrators. Can be empowering. If we are going to empower ourselves, we have to be in positions where we can make decisions about our own sports and recreation for our own people and also to get women in there so we can have (gender) equity and equality. (Subject B [Aus])

I feel there are more successful Aboriginal women who play an important role in society than Aboriginal men. ... Nova Peris-Kneebone is the artistic director of the Festival of the Dreaming – the artistic programme leading up to the 2000 Games. Rachael Perkins is the first Aboriginal woman director. There are actresses, many writers. ... But in sport it's more difficult. We should show them in sport, like in other things, that men *think* they're singing the music and the women are dancing to it, but it's really the other way round! (Subject E [Aus])

Yes, it is more difficult for Aboriginal women/girls to take part in sport. ... There are many reasons for non-participation and each varies according to the Band Council that directs the activities on each Reserve. ... Paraschak's study (of Aboriginal females on the Six Nations Reserve in Ontario) is the only one I know of that documents some of the barriers that limit Native female participation in sport and her word by no means covers all the barriers that are out there. For example, I know of several Native Reserves in Northern Ontario where sport is totally banned from the communities. The Chiefs there claim that sport *causes* the alcohol, drug and violence that runs rampant in other communities. In other areas where sport is allowed, Native women are rarely given the opportunity to fundraise for their sport teams – they are either not given time slots in Bingo or their fundraising ideas are not approved by the Band Council. *Everything* that goes on Native Reserves *must* be approved by the Band Council, which is typically run by men. (Subject I [Can])

[With reference to the National Aboriginal Achievement Awards or NAAA] Take a look at the number of men vs women nominated for sport – you can easily see that there is no gender equity in sport – at least in the awards given for sport. As well, it appears as though female athletes have to have far more accomplishments than male athletes in order to receive the award for sport – similar to the Tom Longboat Award [sport award for Native Canadians only]. ... I do know that Angela [Chalmers] hoped her winning the 1995 NAAA would inspire more Native females participation in sport – at all levels. (Subject I [Can])

Yes, it is more difficult for indigenous girls and women to particpate in sport. ... Indigenous women have children at a much younger age than non-indigenous women, therefore there's the problem of who would care for the children while the mother participates. ... Indigenous communities are very family oriented and it is semi-traditional that women and children spectated, not participated. This is beginning to change because there are a lot more female indigenous role models and it is more acceptable for girls to participate. I have been fortunate because my whole family were very sporty, we were all given the opportunity to succeed. I was able to reach national-level competition, while my sisters competed at regional and state level. Women in urban areas have more opportunity to access sport facilities and programmes. (Subject B [Aus])

Representation of sports stars

Without exception, the Australian women I spoke to were proud of their top-level athletes. Cathy Freeman has become a household name and Nova Peris-Kneebone and Evonne Goolagong are also well-known and much loved in Aboriginal communities. The responsibilities that role models have to their communities was also talked about by several women. There appear to be no equivalent Native Canadian superstars – Angela Chalmers was seldom mentioned by Canadian Indians – but they did identify with Cathy Freeman because she was Aboriginal.

[Referring to Evonne Goolagong-Cawley] She suppressed her Aboriginal identity when she was playing at Wimbledon. Now she's come out and as a consequence she's the representative for Aboriginal people at the Sydney Olympic Games. Someone of her high profile is good for us as Aboriginal people – same as Cathy Freeman and Nova Peris-Kneebone. I'm really proud of them and I'm glad that they're women in those positions – it's taken them a lot to get there. But because they're sports people they're expected to have an opinion about everything and because they're sports people, they may not have sensible opinions. Because of their sports status, they're put into positions of power. It's good because they're Aborigines *and* women, but they may not have the right skills and knowledge to be representative of all Aboriginal people. (Subject B [Aus])

Seeing other indigenous sportswomen is always encouraging. They break down the barriers and make it easier every time. 'We need more of them.' (Subject F [Aus])

[Referring to Cathy Freeman wrapping herself in the Aboriginal and Australian flags] We were all very excited. It brought Aboriginal people together on the issues of national identity. Important things like language are being lost, and sport can restore feelings. Historically we've always done well in sport. It's a way a marginalized group can feel acceptance and equality in mainstream society – by joining clubs etc. But this can also turn into a stereotype that Aborigines are only good at sports and not credited for their intellectual abilities. (Subject D [Aus])

Cathy Freeman's action was *fantastic*. She thought she was uniting Australia, but I feel she might have divided people, bringing up the issue of whether you should have one flag or both. Aborigines *do* have a different culture and flag and it's only right, even if she was competing for Australia, that she could also fly her own flag, to make Aboriginal culture recognized. There can never be enough Aboriginal role models. Especially as a woman, as the odds are stacked even more heavily against her. Any person from a minority group who achieves something outstanding gives others hope that they can do so also. (Subject H [Aus])

I am opposed to the way Aboriginal people are being used for the Sydney Olympic Games. Although Aborigines are treated badly, they're used to promote *Australia*. It's a pretence. (Subject G [Aus])

Successful Aborigines are given a label of having assimilated, which involves denying your national identity to an extent. They have to move away from the Aboriginal community to train in non-Aboriginal communities. They are seen by many as having deserted, and as identifying with White mainstream qualities. You can't have both. High achievers are forced to make a sacrifice. But they should keep in touch with their communities. Make statements like Cathy Freeman did. To do this is a conscious choice. Evonne Goolagong did not link back to the grass roots in the same way. But 20 to 30 years ago the opportunity and possibility of doing this did not exist. You were literally just ripped out of your culture and forced to comply to another set of circumstances and to get on in the best way you could. Now you can feed back into the community. That's what I've chosen to do. I go back into the community and visit schools and clubs. I connect back to them. This applies to big sportstars as well. (Subject C [Aus])

Sport is a useful tool for helping Aboriginal communities to help face existing problems – health, lifestyle, identity – to be strong enough to face racism and feel that you can accomplish something, have something to aim for. Cathy Freeman was the first *woman* to politicize Aboriginal sport. When she won I felt an incredible sense of patriotism. ... Talking about sponsorship, when they want to push someone it's almost always men cho- sen – usually football players – so it's good for it to be a *woman*. (Subject E [Aus])

Being a good sportswoman is firstly for yourself. It enhances your self-esteem. But Aboriginal women have to do 110 per cent in order even to be looked at. Sportswomen like Cathy Freeman – their achievements are so high that they could not be ignored. They're judged on the merit of their ability rather than their cultural identity. Freeman's flag episode was a declaration of how proud she is of her heritage, but taken out of context it is seen as a purely political statement. (Subject G [Aus])

We don't have 'a Cathy Freeman' in Canada and we could do with athletes like her. It was great that she was open about her Aboriginal roots and I know that I was rooting for her to win and was jumping up and down and even crying. Maybe Angela Chalmers will make a comeback and be *our* Cathy Freeman at the Sydney Olympics. You know, when you never see a Native women on the rostrum – like the world stage – it's really depressing – it's like we don't exist. (Subject K [Can]).

There is Waneek Horn-Miller who is captain of the women's water polo team which has earned a berth in the 2000 Olympic Games – they'll go if they can find sponsors to fund the trip. Although Waneek has been in sport for a few years, it is only recently with her team's win at the Pan-Am Games [water polo] that she has been in the news. She is Mohawk from the Kahnawake Reserve in Quebec. ... I believe that her mother is Continenta Horn ... an ardent political activist for Native women's rights in Canada in the late 1960s and 1970s. (Subject I [Can])

Postscript: 'Cathy Freeman's Games'

Even before Cathy Freeman won her Olympic gold medal for the 400 metres at the age of 27 in 49.11 seconds – the first-ever gold medal won for track athletics by an indigenous Australian – the Sydney Olympics had been dubbed 'Cathy Freeman's Games'. For months preceding the Games her face was on billboards throughout urban Australia endorsing mobile telephones, running shoes and airline companies (Mackay, *Guardian* 'Guide to the Olympics' n.d.). But the most impressive image of all was the giant poster advertising the Sydney Olympics with the caption, 'The Spirit of Australia'. Cathy's face had become a popularised symbol of a multicultural Australia and of reconciliation between Black and White. The sense that White Australia had taken her to its heart and Black Australia was overflowing with ethnic pride at her success reached a dramatic peak when she ran the race of her life in Sydney – and won.

With a background of continuous and thunderous applause, crying and shouting from the record-breaking crowd of 112,574 spectators, Cathy sat down on the track, head lowered, taking stock of the enormity of her achievement. Slowly she took off her shoes and got up for the victory lap, barefoot. As she had promised, she held both the Australian and Aboriginal flags but this time, she had tied them together in a knot, reinforcing the impression of oneness and stability. Again, Cathy had made a gesture of goodwill and not defiance.

Cathy's win consolidated the key themes of multiculturalism, reconciliation and unity which had saturated the ceremonies preceding the Games. In acknowledgement of Aboriginality, Nova Peris-Kneebone was chosen to carry the Olympic torch from the sacred Aboriginal site at Uluru. She was the first of 11,000 Australian torch-bearers, and also ran her leg in bare feet, 'Out of respect', she said, 'for my people'. She handed over the flame to Evonne Goolagong-Cawley (*Turkish Daily News* 9/6/2000). Aboriginal culture was then given theatrical treatment at the opening ceremony of the Games, and integration and oneness were depicted in the song, 'World of Harmony'. Hugh MacIlvanney maintains that, 'Everybody apparently welcomed the respectful recognition of an indigenous people so long neglected and abused' (*Sunday Times* 17/9/2000). To authenticate the effect, it was kept as a tightly-guarded secret that Cathy Freeman was to be given the honour of taking the Olympic torch on the last lap of its journey to light the cauldron on the rim of the stadium which was to stay burning throughout the Games. The effect was dramatic and emotive as she stood slimly silhouetted in a shiny-metallic body suit against the night sky, cascading water, and the Olympic flame. Cathy Freeman was being immortalized.

But through this uniquely stark, public and global imagery, in reality Cathy Freeman has embodied the complexities of Aboriginal politics and identity. This complexity is apparent even at the level of her body. At the top of her right arm Cathy has a tattoo, "cos I'm free', which has frequently been shown in newspaper and magazine photographs. But in the final of the 400 metres she wore a 'Nike swift suit', a streamlined symbol of 'ultra' modernity which encased her whole body, including her head, and hid the message of the tattoo. The impression was contrived and futuristic, in contradiction to the Aboriginal essence of closeness to Nature and its imagery of a free-running body, bare-footed, with wind-blown hair. The all-in-one body suit is specially designed to lower air resistance, but it is also a symbol of the commodification and corporate appropriation of a hugely talented sportswoman.

Another contradiction is at the level of the political. Aboriginal sporting accomplishments are still rare and Cathy Freeman's Olympic gold has high-lighted ethnic difference as well as transcending ethnic difference. Waneek Horn-Miller (see p. 125) failed to secure a medal playing water polo for Canada, and it was her sense of Aboriginality which transcended her sense of Canadian-ness when she jumped up and down and shouted and cried in celebration of Cathy's spectacular win. Like Waneek, it seems that most Aborigines from all over the world have identified with Cathy Freeman and claimed her as their own, elevating her to the status of rare and remarkable Aboriginal heroine. However, outside the stadium, Aboriginal activists, in opposition to the Sydney Olympics and to the use of Aboriginal imagery and Black involvement, were continuing their protests. On the day of the opening ceremony, around 500 Aborigines gathered around Sydney Harbour demonstrating about the human rights abuses against their peoples. Three of them canoed out to Fort Denison in the middle of the harbour and raised an enormous Aboriginal flag from the main tower, 'demanding a treaty, an apology, and amendments to land rights legislation' (*The Australian* 16/09/2000). Other groups disrupted traffic in different places in the city protesting against a range of issues including land rights, mandatory sentencing and deaths in custody. Their repeated chanting, 'Who owns this land? We do' and 'Who stole this land? They did', was in direct contradiction to the cheering and clapping surrounding Cathy Freeman's race (*The Australian* 16/09/2000; *The Age* 16/09/2000). The Australian and international media embellished Cathy's success and joined the world together in celebration of a popular version of Australianness, but they downplayed and in many cases ignored the other sense of a ruptured nation of difference and inequalities. Cathy's refusal to consider a boycott, explained earlier, embodied the contradiction of her position as an Aboriginal athlete.

Cathy Freeman has said that she is not political, but has also said that she is aware of her heritage and the importance of an Olympic Gold to her people. Shortly before the Olympics she spoke out 'to the effect that it was high time all the pious talk about reconciliation in her home land produced action' (McIlvanney, *Sunday Times* 17/9/2000). At the 2000 Sydney Olympics she became, unequivocally, the most famous, most impressive Aboriginal athletic heroine with global distinction. Her popularity and position have given her greater credibility and potential to influence a tide of change in race relations in Australia. Aware of her potential, in interviews following her victory she asserted, 'I'm proud of who I am; of my race and my country' and 'I'm sure what has happened and what I symbolize will make a lot of difference to people's attitudes. It will change attitudes in the street and in the political forum' (BBC 1 *Olympic Grandstand* 9/10/2000; Sullivan, *Time* 9/10/2000).

Conclusion

Writing as a Canadian Aborigine, Emma LaRocque (1996: 11) argues that:

> Colonization has taken its toll on all Native peoples, but perhaps it has taken its greatest toll on women. While all Natives experience racism, Native women suffer from sexism as well. Racism and sexism found in the colonial processes have served dramatically to undermine the place and value of women in Aboriginal cultures, leaving us vulnerable to both within and outside our communities.

The struggles of Australian and Canadian Aboriginal women in sport have emerged out of their understanding of and experiences as the 'colonized' and in order to gain representation in sport they have had to confront the racial and gender exploitation endemic in both societies. In a chapter entitled 'Aboriginal Women's Writing and the Cultural Politics of Representation', Julia Emberley (1996: 102) points to the way forward for Aboriginal women in cultural politics and resistance when she claims that 'An articulation between anti-imperialist and women's movements necessitates a theory of gender subordination in post-colonial criticism – criticism directed toward surpassing the colonizer/colonized opposition – which cannot be insisted on too forcefully.' But, although the most usual representation of Aboriginal women is as victims, Patricia Chuchryk and Christine Miller (1996: 4) point out that, in spite of the huge obstacles they face, they are 'actively participating in improving the quality of life in their/our communities'.

Aboriginal women are forging opportunities for themselves in sport in both all-Aboriginal and mainstream situations. Running their own sports festivals, organizations and clubs avoids the inherent racism of mainstream sport – the 'scars of assimilation' – and reinventing traditional sports and activities is a special statement of community, belonging and identity. As Julia Emberley (1996: 108) points out:

> Cultural autonomy allows for the emergence of a tradition that would in turn provide the necessary space for Aboriginal people to think their own insertion, as subjects, into history. The formation of a historical tradition is part of the ongoing cultural and political struggle in and for representation. And it is through the formation of a historical tradition that a politics of 'identity' can emerge with cultural and political implications for action made possible.

Aboriginal women in mainstream sport are also immersed in a politics of difference and identity. They are challenged by institutional and personal forms of racism, but they can grasp power through the creation of public images of identity and possibility. In Australia and Canada, increasing numbers of Aboriginal women are taking part in sport in different circumstances and in different ways. Their struggles and successes are evidence of critical praxis. They are both agents of change and authentic sporting heroines of their communities.

5 Sporting lesbians

Heroic symbols of sexual liberation

Introduction

In spite of the force of social taboo which marginalized and obscured the significance of homosexuality in society throughout the twentieth century, being homosexual – lesbian or gay – is being part of a 'social world' that is primarily visible in the urban centres of all geographical areas, and reaches to every socioeconomic stratum in society, both in the developed and developing worlds (Herdt 1998: 279; Leznoff and Westley 1998: 5). But the public discourse of homosexuality – created in the nineteenth century – has been confined almost exclusively to the West where, up until the late 1960s, essentialist and medicalized definitions of homosexuality predominated (L. Hall 1997) and are still today taken for granted by many people outside academia. The idea that heterosexuality is 'natural' and that homosexuality is 'unnatural', pathological and socially damaging remains engrained in commonsense thinking and is materialized through the processes of law and in everyday behaviour and discourse. In all countries in the world lesbians and gay men face discrimination; in most countries they experience physical violence; and in some countries their lives are threatened by government policy and ideology. Although in the West, lesbians and gay men continue to be stigmatized and devalued, there have been significant liberalizing trends and scope for contestation – for example, in the USA, lesbian and gay organizations are able to challenge the recent backlash against gay rights and same-sex marriages. But outside the West, excessively harsh and uncompromising discrimination against homosexuality prevails and many homosexuals are forced to live in silence and so become forgotten victims. It is not unusual for attacks on sexual minorities to be condoned by governments and supported by the police 'in the name of religion, ideology, public morality or national sovereignty'. Saiz (1998: 23) points out that:

> Although international treaties aimed at eliminating racial and gender discrimination were adopted by the United Nations in the 1960s and 1970s, discrimination on the basis of sexual orientation is not yet explicitly prohibited or even mentioned in any international standard. ... Inaction

has also been justified in the name of cultural relativism: asserting universal gay and lesbian rights is seen by some as imposing Western values on cultures who construct sexual and social relationships differently.

In the West, during the 1960s and 1970s, the term 'gay' was used as an alternative to homosexual in order to reflect a more positive attitude (Pronger 1990: 120–1) and the gay liberation movement transformed thinking about rights and possibilities for lesbians and gay men. The movement made possible the rapid development of gay cultural activities, and over the past two decades there has been an explosion of lesbian and gay sport. Outside the West, however, opportunities have been minimal. It was not until the 1990s that there was an emergence of organizations in Africa, Asia, Latin America and the Middle East, working 'to combat discrimination and violence against sexual minorities' (Saiz 1998: 23), and there are still very few state or municipal cultural opportunities for homosexuals living in those areas. Sport is absolutely marginal to the overall struggle for recognition. Nevertheless, small numbers of lesbian and gay sportswomen and sportsmen from the developing world are forging opportunities for themselves, and the increased global visibility of sporting homosexuals from the West has helped to strengthen international lesbian and gay solidarity in sport.

This chapter examines the particular struggles and achievements of lesbian women in sport. Although the focus is on countries in the West, developments there have implications for lesbian women throughout the world. Over the years, lesbians have suffered systematically from oppression and exclusion in sport, and to avoid discrimination they have mostly kept their sexuality hidden. 'Coming out' in sport is for them a heroic quest.

Setting the scene: gay liberation/women's liberation

Although by the end of the nineteenth century male homosexuality was beginning to find a voice, Jeffrey Weeks (1990: 87) points out that 'it was to be another generation before female homosexuality reached a corresponding level of articulateness'. Lesbians were isolated and most of them fitted into the general world of women linked to the social roles of marriage, childcare and family care. It was only after the First World War – and especially following the public ridicule of lesbians – that there was greater political awareness of female homosexuality and the beginnings of a collective consciousness (1990: 95). Weeks (1990: 89) argues that attitudes to lesbianism are linked to the 'general' position of women, based on supposed 'natural' differences between males and females. Lesbian struggles for identity in sport have been inextricably linked to 'gay liberation' *and* 'women's liberation'. The gay liberation movement became, arguably, one of the most successful of the new social movements that sprang up during the 1960s in North America[1] and played a major role in the emergence of identity politics (Plummer 1998a: 609). Gay liberation was spearheaded by the Stonewall riots[2] in New York in 1969, when lesbians and gay men were resisting police harassment. Stonewall has been described as the single most important event in the history of gay rights – when lesbian and gay identities became more open and political, which led to the rapid spread of a new movement across all Western capitals (Segal 1997: 206). Bawer (*Guardian* 14/6/94) points out that:

> Though it wasn't the first time anyone had contested the right of the state to punish citizens for being gay, that riot marked a pivotal moment because news of it spread in every direction and sparked the imaginations of countless gay men and lesbians around the world. It made them examine, and reject, the silence, shame and reflexive compliance with prejudice to which most of them had never conceived a realistic alternative.

Sally Munt (1998: 14) claims that 'the Stonewall Riots became the principal heroic symbol of the foundation of modern lesbian and gay existence'. Stonewall was the beginning of a revolution in thinking about homosexuality, a spark for a collective consciousness, and the origin of a social movement for the rights of homosexual men and women – all essential components for political power. Because in the past lesbians were individualized, treated as 'unnatural', 'abnormal', and therefore unmentionable, they have had a limited collective social history. Before Stonewall many lesbians had remained hidden in a 'heterosexist', 'homophobic'[3] culture; following Stonewall, many lesbians felt less isolated and self-consciously identified themselves as a legitimate minority group (Segal 1997: 207).[4] The politics of identity created a climate of openness, and matters that used to be kept 'personal' and 'private' were presented as 'community' and 'public' affairs – a development that had a particular link to culture.

Visibility has had a profound effect on gay leisure culture. In North America and Western Europe, 'the gay and lesbian population, in hitherto unforeseen ways and in greater numbers, has claimed attention in politics and the media, culture and the arts' (Herdt 1998: 279). Since 1969 there has been a marked increase in the impact that lesbians have made on a whole range of cultural activities, and their presence and advances in sport have been notable. The Gay Games, discussed later in the chapter, are an open celebration of homosexual sporting identity and community that lesbians and gay men have created and claimed as their own. Munt (1998: 6) sees political possibilities in the creation of lesbian space of this sort, and views as a heroic project the embodying of space with desires. She argues that:

> Our resistance to a homophobic culture is a relentless demand for presence, an occupation of space which we have colonized in the name of a configuration of desires we call 'lesbian'. The more reflective we can become about these tactics – the more effective becomes our rhetoric of resistance. Lesbian desire, then, is that which is productive, excessive, expansive, a pleasure-machine which can open up new spaces in which we can live.

But because in the late 1960s and 1970s the gay liberation movement, in common with the Black consciousness movement in the USA, was dominated by men, most lesbian interventions took place within the Women's Liberation Movement. As well as challenging the relations of power embodied in compulsory heterosexuality and homophobia, lesbian women were also resisting discriminatory distinctions of gender between men and women. Opposition to men and patriarchy became common ground between lesbianism and second wave feminism (Stein 1998: 558). 'Freedom' and 'tolerance' for lesbians was an important feminist demand, and Adrienne Rich's article 'Compulsory Heterosexuality and Lesbian Existence' (1980) was important in the development of a radical lesbian perspective (Zaretsky 1995: 255). Rich argued that lesbianism is not a matter of sexual preference (which is an issue of *individual* rights), but is a question of *identity* (comprising *shared* experiences and consciousness). She described a 'lesbian continuum' (1980: 648) into which *all* women – not exclusively those who desire genital sexual experiences with other women – can be placed, in opposition to male power and compulsory heterosexuality. She views gender as the primary form of social difference, patriarchy as the overarching discriminatory structure, and lesbianism as a broad and inclusive conceptualization of female bonding.

In the early 1970s, lesbian feminism emerged out of the most radical sectors of the women's movement. Arlene Stein (1998: 553) describes how the definition of lesbianism was broadened and transformed 'from a medical condition, or at best, a sexual "preference", into a collective identity which transcended rampant individualism and its excesses as well as compulsory gender and sex roles'. Influenced by this more general lesbian feminist discourse, numbers of sport feminists in the West, many of whom were lesbians *and* radical feminists, have argued that sexuality, specifically in the form of compulsory heterosexuality, lies at the heart of women's oppression in sport. They have sought to assert their identities in sport by means of a 'Woman-centred' philosophy in opposition to male-dominated and male-defined sport (M.A. Hall 1996: 91; Hargreaves 1994: 29–32; Lenskyj 1986). Women-only sports activities, clubs, teams and organizations that sprung up were influenced by, and sensitive to, feminist ideals of gender equity *and* to the particular position of lesbians. Some had a predominantly- or all-lesbian membership.

Queerying gender

But although a collective 'Woman' identity was constructed, inside and outside sport it was in reality a veneer of unity. There had been a misleading tendency to generalize to all women from the perspective of the White, middle-class, heterosexual, able-bodied, Western woman. In mainstream feminism, and then sport feminism, Black feminists led the way in exposing the myths of 'equality of opportunity' and pointing to the failures to address comprehensively the different sites of oppression based on, for example, race, ethnicity, age, class and disability, as well as sexuality (for example, Birrell 1989; Guess 1997: 157;

Edwards and Hargreaves 2000). Equal-rights discourse had shifted through radical separatist discourse, to a new discourse of difference and diversity. The work of Michel Foucault became particularly influential in lesbian theorizing and practice – notably his insistence on anti-essentialism and his view of power as constituting, not simply repressing, sexuality (Foucault 1980a, 1980b). His ideas encouraged recognition of the variability and plasticity of sexuality. The term 'queer', which reflected this thinking, was associated with Queer Nation, which was started in the USA in 1990 as a challenge to the popular politics of sexuality, originally by people involved in AIDS activism and the hostility to homosexuality. 'Queer' foregrounded the deconstruction of identity and opened the doors to the multiplicities of sexuality – to difference and individual rights. Most significantly, it has been applied to developments in theories and practices around sexuality to suggest that lesbians share with gay men a 'non-normative sexuality which transcends the binary distinction homosexual/heterosexual to include all who feel disenfranchised by dominant sexual norms – lesbians and gay men, as well as bisexuals and transsexuals' (Stein 1998: 561).

Judith Butler (1990, 1993) has taken the decentring of lesbian identities a step further by reappraising the binary oppositions of sex and gender, 'denaturalizing' gendered and sexed identities, and encouraging them to be seen as performances (Martindale 1995: 88). The most common assumption about gender suggests that it is pre-social, pre-linguistic, the very essence of our being, based on natural differences between male and female. Butler suggests that popular ideas about male and female produce identity boundaries which determine the kinds of gender identities we are permitted to have (gender norms), and those that we are not (Butler 1990: 148). But Butler develops the discussion by placing the body once more as central to an understanding of gender and introduces the term 'gender performativity' to explain that gender is not the expression of what we are, but, rather, is something we 'do' – that we enact gender, repetitively, and non-voluntaristically, over time. Repetition, for Butler, is central to performativity, ensuring that gender identity is not a fixed category, but is open and fluid, even although 'bodily gestures, movements and styles of various kinds constitute the *illusion* of an abiding, gendered self' (Butler 1990: 140). So, according to Judith Butler, we 'do' heterosexuality and lesbianism, straightness and queerness – they are cultural practices – which, she contends, through performance, can produce gendered norms *and* can displace them (Butler 1990, 1993). She argues that bodies themselves (sex) are materialized within the regulatory framework of normative heterosexuality (Butler 1993).

In recent years, claims that homosexuality is socially and culturally constructed ('constructionist' thinking), and is linked to fluid, lifestyle-based models, have gained ground (Plummer 1998a, 1998b). The notion of identity, the politics of identity and the categories of identity have, as a result, all been called into question (Guess 1997: 156). In the 1980s and 1990s, queer theory shifted practice away from collective civil rights-style movements towards 'a politics of carnival, transgression, and parody' (Stein and Plummer 1994: 181).

Importantly, it embraces the diversity of sexuality and sexual styles, affirming that 'lesbian culture is not homogenous but heterogenous' (Munt 1998: 7). It is argued that in the new urban image of 'queerness' the alliance between fem-inism and lesbianism has become somewhat tenuous, that there is less interest in gay activism, less exclusivity between heterosexual and homosexual, and a marked emphasis on conspicuous lifestyle statements. The attraction of some homosexual women to 'lifestyle' sport, together with their appropriation of the queer label and an explicit and flamboyant expression of self, appears to illustrate this postmodern trend. Sport for them is part of a more general celebration of gay culture, which extends to the media, fashion and lifestyle – depicted later, in the section on the Gay Games (see pp. 157–63).

But there is no consensus about what is meant by the social construction of sexuality or how it should be analysed (Jackson 1995/6: 31). For example, in the quest for identity, Carol Guess (1997), in common with other young third wave feminists, wants to reclaim the lesbian label that preceded contemporary queer poststructuralism. Although she distances herself from the legacy of separatism, her view of the world, which recognizes the existence of structures of power and forms of oppression, is one she shares with other women. But she also acknowledges shifts and changes, instabilities and differences, which make lesbianism for her a *process* of identification and not a fixed state. This sense of community and the processes of identification explored by third wave feminists are particularly relevant to women in all-lesbian or lesbian-positive sport activities. Although it is acknowledged that lesbian women in sport are not a homogeneous group with differences and complexities in their experiences, sport can provide for them a refuge from structured discrimination in mainstream (heterosexual) sport or in wider society, providing a logic for the lesbian label and lesbian consciousness. Writing about queer-feminist theory in physical education, Heather Sykes (1998: 155) asserts that in previous research that documents the experiences of lesbian physical education teachers, 'however nuanced and rigorous the intersections with other identities/subjectivities, this research maintains the "lesbian" as the marginalized Other to heterosexuality'. In order to avoid reproducing the privileging of heterosexuality and the marginalized otherness of lesbianism, she attempts to combine queer and feminist theories of sexuality in order to 'examine the relations between lesbian sexuality and heterosexualities' (1998: 155).

Lesbians in sport in history

Heterosexism is an oppressive system of dominance based on the pivotal idea that heterosexuality is the only 'natural' and valid sexual orientation and that homosexuality, in contrast, is 'abnormal', 'unnatural', 'deviant' and 'sinful'. Heterosexism is entrenched in all social institutions – in the family, the school, legal apparatuses, the media and popular culture. It has been endemic in modern sport and since the 1950s there has been persistent intolerance of sexual diversity and insidious discrimination against lesbians (Cahn 1994;

Griffin 1998; Lenskyj 1986). Writing about women's sport in the USA, Susan Cahn (1994: 165) explains that 'What began as a vague suggestion of lesbianism emerged as a full-blown stereotype of the "mannish lesbian athlete" in the years after World War II.'

Brian Pronger (1990) argues that homosexuality is fundamentally an issue of gender. 'Being homosexual', he writes, 'is the expression of a deep paradoxical, psychic relationship to the myths of gender' (Pronger 1990: 121):

> Homosexuality undermines, in a positive way, the most important myth of our culture. This is a myth upon which all human relations are based. In many respects, this myth determines the way one lives, by giving power and prestige to half the members of our society and denying the same to the other half. This myth permeates not only the most important institutions of our society, such as religion, medicine, law, history, the arts, and athletics, but it is also deeply imprinted on the psyche of every human being in our culture. This myth has been responsible for many centuries of subjugation, oppression, and exploitation. It is, of course, the myth of gender, a sociocultural form that divides power between men and women. The gender myth endows the relatively minor biological differences between males and females with major social significance. Homosexuality, though it by no means relinquishes this myth, subverts it.
>
> (Pronger 1990: 2)

Because the muscularity and power invested in female sporting bodies inverts the myth of gender by rendering women apparently less 'feminine' and more 'masculine', sportswomen have feared being labelled as lesbians.[5] Cahn (1994: 183) suggests that, in the USA, 'By the 1950s all female athletes and physical educators operated under the cloud of sexual suspicion.' The stereotype of the mannish lesbian athlete pressured women to display the characteristics and insignia of heterosexuality – to display to the world that they were 'real' women – to wear make-up, nail polish, pretty clothes, jewellery, and to show off boyfriends and husbands. The pressure to display heterosexual signs – defined as 'compulsory heterosexuality' – was most powerfully applied in traditional male sports, where women most dreaded the stigma of muscularity and implied lesbianism. The fear or irrational hatred and hostility towards women who were perceived to be homosexual – known as homophobia – led to the systematic oppression of lesbian women in sport. There was an unexamined assumption that the huge majority of women were naturally heterosexual and the few remaining 'others' were sexually degenerate and dangerous. Homosexual openness was thus repressed and lesbian sportswomen stayed hidden and remained silent. In the following quotation, Cahn (1994: 184) describes the way in which compulsory heterosexuality was normalized and how homophobia became a material controlling force over the sporting lives and thinking of women in the college system in the United States:

Although women's sport advocates did their best to 'prove' heterosexuality and to suppress 'mannishness', in the end this strategy did little to diminish the lesbian stigma of women's sport. Hostile observers perpetuated lesbian athletic stereotypes through their unrelenting ridicule of skilled athletes as 'grotesque', 'ugly', 'masculine', or 'unnatural'. Leaders of women's sport unwittingly contributed to the homophobic climate when they began to orient their programs toward a new feminine heterosexual ideal.

Cahn (1994: 162) also writes specifically about how the All-American Girls Baseball League was negatively affected by the spread of homophobia throughout society after World War II:

Police raids on gay bars, military purges, and the firing of homosexual government employees under Cold War security policies added to the homosexual panic of the 1950s. In an era of political, legal, and media attacks on homosexuals, the association of women's sport with 'mannishness', often a coded reference to lesbianism, jeopardized any attempt to market women's baseball as mass entertainment.

But in spite of the climate of fear, it is also claimed that during the years between the late 1930s and the early 1960s, 'a significant number of lesbians found sport to be a receptive site for forming relationships and creating a shared culture' (Cahn 1994: 162). Writing about lesbian life in twentieth-century America, Lillian Faderman observes that 'softball teams during the 1950s and 1960s succeeded in providing legends and heroes for the lesbian subculture, as well as offering participants and viewers some possibilities for making lesbian contacts in outside bars'. Softball networks were also used to 'spread the word about military witch-hunts against homosexuals' (Festle 1996: 303). There are oral accounts of British female athletes (assumed to be lesbians) attending the 1936 Olympic Games who had close and supportive relationships. Other sporadic examples from 1940s and 1950s England support the premise that all-female sport was a special space that provided sanctuary for lesbian women, and where they bonded together and created a small, caring community (personal interviews). Festle (1996: 45) suggests that, although it was too dangerous for lesbian athletes to be open about their sexuality, 'nevertheless, they articulated a growing collective culture through action, style and unspoken understandings'. However, the unrelenting heterosexism, homophobia and fear of stigma facing lesbian women meant that, with few exceptions, they remained firmly closeted. The result has been the failure to record a proper history of lesbians in sport.

Knowledge about and visibility of lesbian women in sport is much greater today. In recent years sport feminists have been influenced by the opening up of debates around the politics of sexuality and, more specifically, by the development from the 1980s of feminist theories and critiques of the politics and culture of lesbianism (Butler 1990, 1993; Heywood and Drake 1997; Martindale

1995; Munt 1998; Nardi and Schneider 1998). During the 1990s there has been a considerable flow of research specifically about lesbian women in sport and physical education (for example, Burton Nelson 1994; Cahn 1994; Clarke 1995, 1998; Festle 1996; Griffin 1998; Lenskyj 1991, 1997). Sportswomen today are more prepared to talk about being a lesbian, even although they usually ask for anonymity. Their stories provide a better sense of the extent of homophobic prejudice (also termed 'lesbophobia' when hatred is directed specifically at women), the forms it takes, its effects on lesbian women, and their coping strategies. Because in general there is more openness about sexuality, and more lesbians and gay men (although still in very small numbers) have made the decision to 'come out', there has also been a rapid and remarkable development of a new, explicitly gay sporting culture.

Experiencing homophobia

Sport constitutes a social practice in which there is systematic, institutionalized discrimination against lesbian women according to gendered and sexualized systems and structures of power. Discrimination affects them as individuals in different places and in different ways – for example, during day-to-day sporting activities, in the changing room, in the lecture theatre, on the pitch, or travelling to a match; and as a result of prejudice which negatively affects their sporting careers – for example, through team selections or professional earnings. Writing in 1996 about the USA, Festle (1996: 267) asserted that homophobia and lesbian-bating constituted 'a sort of 1990s version of McCarthyism in the athletic subculture'.

Homophobia is deeply rooted in fear and is sustained by stereotypes of lesbians, myths about them, and abuse directed at them. The practice of labelling sportswomen – especially those playing team sports – as mannish, butch, dykes, lesbians, freaks or sickos, is a popular way of conjuring up the idea that lesbians colonize sport, and of deriding and pathologizing them. The abuse is insidious. It puts pressure on heterosexual women to disclaim such labels and send out heterosexual signals. Lesbians are therefore trapped in a mythical culture of heterosexuality where the assumption is made that everyone is 'straight' or 'normal' unless explicitly stated otherwise. So, although sexuality for most people is intensely personal, lesbians are forced either to 'make a statement' about their sexual preference or to assume a heterosexual identity. The process is also insidious because, although heterosexist discourse can be deeply offensive to lesbians, it is usually passed off 'innocently' as a 'harmless' joke or innuendo, as a part of the after-match banter in the locker room or during a long coach trip to an away fixture. There is nothing lighthearted either about the ostracism that lesbian athletes suffer when they are 'outed' or choose to 'come out'. Heterosexual athletes are known to dissociate themselves from lesbian teammates and to end long friendships with them. Homophobic harassment of known lesbians also occurs and is more likely to be sexually explicit. For example, members of a UK predominantly lesbian soccer team gave the following examples of abusive remarks and chanting that they had experienced: 'You're disgusting'; 'Perverted sluts'; 'Weirdos'; 'Fags'; 'Black dyke, Black dyke, Black dyke'; 'What's she like in bed, then?' 'Go on, tackle, get at her – that's what she wants.'

Homophobic and heterosexist attitudes – and, specifically, hostility to lesbianism – are also prevalent in Australia where cricket, tennis and hockey have been labelled 'dyke sports' (Burroughs *et al.* 1995: 268, 276, 279) and where it is claimed that 'The media's preoccupation with lesbianism within women's cricket serves only to titillate the public, trivialize the game itself, and denigrate women's sport in general' (1995: 272). When the Australian women's cricket team was on tour in America, team members were 'hounded' by the media and, according to one of them, were 'treated like freaks' on their return home (1995: 272).

Homophobic-induced fear runs very deep. It has led to increasing numbers of allegations that lesbians have not only 'infiltrated' sports, but that in some cases they have taken them over or 'colonized' them, that they have become predators and obsessed by power, resulting in reversed discrimination against heterosexual women. In 1995 in Australia, Denise Annetts lodged a complaint to the Anti-Discrimination Board alleging that she had been dropped from the Australian cricket team because she was heterosexual and married. Disregarding the evidence, the Australian media produced biased and homophobic reports of the incident and a media anti-homosexual backlash followed (Burroughs *et al.* 1995: 272). In situations where it is known that there is a sizeable number of lesbians, there is always verbal abuse, innuendo and suspicion. For example, the all-women's tennis Eastbourne Tournament, scheduled to take place each year before Wimbledon, is characterized pejoratively as 'The Dyke's Delight'. It attracts lesbians who are comfortable and relaxed in each other's company which, without justification, raises the spectre of them being predatory, 'contagious' and dangerous. Lesbians go to tennis tournaments primarily to watch the game and to give their support to lesbian players (in the past, primarily to Martina Navratilova). There is no evidence that they dominate the event or intimidate non-homosexuals. The same is true for women's golf, where it is 'common knowledge' that there are numbers of lesbian players and followers. However, the idea that lesbians are tyrannical is not substantiated by evidence. In fact, the opposite is more likely to be the case. Lesbian sportswomen tend consciously to practise inclusiveness, rather than exclusiveness (Hargreaves 1994: 253–4).

Homophobic harassment combines with other forms of abuse to consolidate compulsory heterosexuality and reproduce unequal relations of sexual power between hetersexual women and lesbian women. The effects are dehumanizing and always inflict personal pain, a process explained here by Plummer: 'The notion of homophobia individualizes the entire problem of homosexual hostility, making it a problem of personalities rather than societies' (1998b: 90).

According to Pat Griffin (1998: 57–9), much of the prejudice and discrimination against lesbians in sport arises from the fear that they are predators who will seduce and corrupt girls and young women which, she suggests, taps into 'the deepest fears of parents and heterosexual athletes and coaches'. Griffin explains further that, 'According to this stereotype, lesbians coerce innocent, young, weak, and unwilling heterosexual women into unnatural sexual liaisons' (1998: 58). She claims that it is 'one of the most enduring, pervasive, and destructive aspects of the lesbian stereotype in sport' (1998: 57), making commonplace such remarks as, 'Lesbians in the sport hurt women's golf' – attributed to US golf commentator Ben Wright, in 1995 (Festle 1996: 265). The evidence points instead to the fact that it is heterosexual males who sexually harass and abuse girls and young women in numbers that constitutes a serious social problem (Benedict 1997; Burton Nelson 1994). Ironically, and worryingly, Helen Lenskyj (1992: 21) suggests that 'Allegations of lesbianism directed at female athletes deter many women from rejecting unwanted sexual attention or complaining about sexual harassment (from men), since they fear that such actions will confirm that they are not sexually interested in men, and hence, lesbian.' The unwarranted fear of lesbianism and the unsubstantiated claims about the predatory nature of lesbians in sport causes far greater anxiety and resistance than the very real threat of abuse from heterosexual men. Ironically, the (probably small, but recognizable) shift of sportswomen into lesbianism could be interpreted as a reaction to power relations with men that are starkly uneven and often based on serious and violent instances of sexual harassment and abuse.

Homophobic discrimination can wreck sporting careers in very concrete ways. There is considerable evidence that lesbian athletes are passed over by selectors, lose scholarships and sponsorship, lack media support, and fail to secure promotion or to get positions as coaches and administrators. Referring to North America, Helen Lenskyj claims that

> there is ample evidence that the women in sport and physical education who are lesbian have to survive in a most inhospitable climate because of the pervasiveness of homophobia, which often takes the form of discriminatory hiring and firing practices.
>
> (1992: 28)

Lesbians who are professional sportswomen have the particular fear of losing their livelihood and their chosen way of life as a direct result of disclosure of their sexual orientation. Although it is now known that there are professional golfers who are lesbians and for the first time a top golfer has come out, it is still the case that the vast majority of lesbian professional players remain closeted in order to protect their income and reputations.[6] The situation in 1996 described below has not fundamentally changed:

> Asked why *not one* of the LPGA's [Ladies Professional Golf Association] golfers have admitted to being lesbian, an anonymous pro explained

impatiently, 'Because it would be suicide. Because you'd get cut off from every endorsement possible. Because there's money and careers at stake'.

(Festle 1996: 267)

Mariah Burton Nelson was fired from the US Women's Professional Basketball League for being a lesbian. Her coach on the San Francisco Pioneers was a man who claimed the team uniforms were made by a 'bunch of faggots' and called the players 'girls'. Understandably, Nelson had remained closeted. When the coach fired her, he first said, 'You're not tall enough' (she was the tallest woman on the team), and then 'You're not quick enough'. The real reason was because a reporter had told the owner of the club that he had seen her at a Gay Day celebration (Burton Nelson 1994: 106–7). A similar situation occurred in 1982, when Betty Baxter – previously one of Canada's top Olympic volleyballers – was fired from her position as the head coach of Canada's national women's volleyball team. She was fired for no obvious reason, except that it had become known that she was a lesbian (*West*, November 1990: 36).

Hiding, passing and denial

The effects of hatred and fear directed against lesbians in sport is deeply divisive. As we have seen, heterosexual women fear being labelled as lesbians and lesbian women are driven to 'pass' as straight for fear of victimization. But there is also a division between those lesbians who *do* disclose their sexuality and those lesbians who *do not* disclose their sexuality. The definition of homosexuality as 'the love that dare not speak its name' (Pronger 1990: 220) is a poignant reminder of the reasons why the majority of lesbian sportswomen keep their sexuality concealed. Whereas gender and race are 'inscribed on the body', are always visible, sexual identities generally are not and can, therefore, be hidden. As Fraser (1999: 109) puts it, 'Unlike the "ineradicable" visible marks which declare one's gender and race, the signs of sexuality can be "separated" from the self.'

It has been recorded that 'most lesbians, whether athletes, coaches, administrators or faculty, remain invisible for reasons of simple survival' (Lenskyj 1992: 27). When being interviewed by a journalist from *The Advocate* (the US national gay and lesbian news magazine), a professional golfer anonymously admitted:

I'd like to be able to come out, and I know a couple of other women who would. But to do it takes a kind of maverick quality that I just don't have. I'm afraid – I'll admit it. I'm afraid even to be talking to *The Advocate*. What if you decide to print my name? Or what if someone figures out who I am? This is my job, this is who I am, this is where I want to be, where I've worked all my life to be. I'm just not willing to be a martyr and give it all up. It's painful, it makes me unhappy, but it's the way things are. Period'

(*Unity '94* 1991: 10)

Writing about the British context, Gill Clarke (1995) and Andrew Sparkes (1994) have examined the ways in which the widespread social, cultural and political forms of heterosexism and homophobia force physical education teachers to live two lives – to conceal their lesbian identities at school and to risk coming out, but only discretely, outside their place of work. To hide one's homosexuality and pass as heterosexual are repressions of sexuality, denials of self, and misconstructions of identity. They are actions which result from the social distinctions between heterosexuality and homosexuality which, in turn, are products of power relations, and not biology. Lesbian sportswomen have to negotiate their roles in the context of power relations – for instance, between a young closeted athlete with a fiercely heterosexual, homophobic, chauvinist male coach; or between a games player and other members of the team who have husbands and boyfriends and children. Lesbian identities are repeatedly reproduced or reformed within such relations of power.

In a life-history study of lesbian *and* heterosexual women, Sykes (1998: 158) describes how the women 'accepted and resisted discourses of the closet' (1998: 157). She explores how the idea of ' "the lesbian closet" has been essential to the foundational status of heterosexuality as the normal sexuality' in physical education, how heteronormative speech strengthens the heteronormativity/lesbian sexuality boundary, specifically, 'how our silences and everyday talk about heterosexuality sustained "the closet" keeping lesbian sexuality inside and heterosexuality outside' (1998: 171).

There is a huge pressure on lesbian women in sport to conform to heterosexual norms and pass as heterosexuals. Heteronormativity is a key concept in queer theory which makes clear how 'heterosexist "normalcy" normalizes itself through making homosexuality "deviant" ' (Martindale 1995: 68). The way for lesbians to acquire normalcy and avoid deviancy is to present an image of acceptable feminine behaviour. Some lesbian sportswomen go to extreme lengths pretending to be heterosexual. In denial of their own sexualities, they purposefully present a public image of heterosexual femininity – or, more precisely, emphasized femininity or 'hyperfemininity' – that which is the most culturally valued expression of heterosexual femininity, considered to be of the greatest appeal to heterosexual men (Connell 1987: 183–8). 'Passing' as heterosexual is a device employed by lesbians to take attention away from their real sexual identities. It is a process of 'apologetic behaviour' resulting from the domination of one sexuality over another.

Babe Didrikson's transformation 'from butch to lady' during the 1940s is a famous example of apologetic behaviour. Media reports were never explicit about the 'lesbian look', but innuendos that she was loud, arrogant and 'mannish' were enough to drive her to change into a softer, more feminine 'lady'. She substituted trousers for skirts, cropped hair for long hair, and a plain face for make-up. And she denied her boisterous, tomboy past and married. Another golfer on the tour recalled: 'By the time I met Babe, she was not tough or manly. ... Sometimes she overdressed a little – she'd wear frilly blouses that didn't look right' (Festle 1996: 46). Whether or not Babe Didrikson was actually a lesbian or bisexual is unimportant. The observation that matters, and that reflects the imperatives of hegemonic heterosexuality, is that she was originally criticized for being 'unfeminine', then later celebrated for her newly 'feminized' appearance.

At the end of the 1980s, the Ladies Professional Golf Association (LPGA), which had been steadily growing in previous years, lost sponsorship, cancelled a tournament, settled for a smaller purse in another competition, and suffered from less corporate funding and television exposure than in previous years. Festle (1996: 266) argues that this was in large part because the sponsors believed that a number of players were lesbians. To overcome the image problem, the LPGA hired a fashion consultant to promote heterosexual femininity, with such success that it was claimed a few years later that 'The lesbians these days look more femme than the straight players!' (Reed 1994b: 92). Marketing heterosexual attractiveness in women's sport has now become commonplace. Another example comes from Australia, where kits for the women's cricket, netball and basketball national teams were selected specifically in order to construct an image of emphasized femininity and to reduce the chance of lesbian labelling (Burroughs *et al.* 1995: 267).

Throughout elite women's sport, the general behaviour of players as well as their appearance is carefully monitored, and rules governing homosexual behaviour are stringently applied. A lesbian member of the LPGA tour explains the situation in women's golf:

> There was a mandatory players' meeting once. One of the top players, a dyke, led the meeting. She told us, 'ladies, we do not care what goes on inside your bedroom door. But keep it there'. The message was loud and clear: For the women's golf tour to succeed, we need to rid ourselves of the lesbian stigma.
>
> (Reed 1994a: 92)

Denial is an additional and complementary strategy for securing heterosexual hegemony and controlling homosexuality (Griffin 1998: 66–8). Most sport organizations, administrators, promoters and coaches either deny the existence of lesbians in their sport or deny that there is homophobia of any sort. By doing so they create the myth of a heterosexual consensus and implicitly condone heterosexism and homophobia. Pronger (1990: 375) explains the power of the homophobic culture of denial:

> The homophobia of women's competitive sport finds its expression in the repeated renunciation by athletes, coaches, and sport administrators that there is a significant lesbian presence in women's sport. That homophobic culture of denial often ends in public purges of lesbian athletes and coaches

and functions to prevent the implicit homoeroticism of women's sport from becoming an explicit, indeed celebrated practice.

We have seen how various sporting discourses position lesbian sportswomen as 'different', and how that difference is confirmed in everyday social practices, even through silence and denial. Lesbian women *and* heterosexual women in sport are in a constant process of learning and practising sexual meanings and confirming or challenging dominant constructions of sexuality. The institu-tion of heterosexuality is inherently gendered, depending on the discursive/symbolic dominance of men over women and, more specifically, on heterosexual (hegemonic) masculinity 'which is constructed in relation to various subordinated masculinities as well as in relation to women' (Connell 1987: 183). The examples we have seen in sport illustrate clearly that the further division between, and dominance of, 'emphasized' heterosexual fem-ininity over non-heterosexual femininity, supports hegemonic masculinity. Sporting discourses of sexuality assume the normativity of heterosexual social and sexual relations between women and men and 'performing' hegemonic heterosexuality in sport helps to perpetuate patriarchal relations and the wielding of power over 'other' sexualities. Sexuality is not, however, static. Jackson points out that 'Sexuality is constantly in the process of being constructed and recon-structed, enacted and re-enacted, within specific contexts and relationships. Sexuality is thus constructed by what individuals actually *do*' (1999: 5).

Transcending divisions

We have seen how sportswomen of all sexual orientations 'practise' heterosexu-ality and by doing so separate themselves from each other which, according to Helen Lenskyj (1991: 62; 1995: 51), inhibits 'collective political consciousness and action'. In sport there is a general unwillingness to challenge heterosexism or to stand against homophobia. Administrators will typically say, 'In "our" sport there is no problem', and athletes are caught up in a system which is likely to discriminate against them if they say anything. Although the official rhetoric of Western state sport apparatuses supports equality of opportunity for different and minority groups, the problem of subtle and institutionalized forms of discrimination based on sexuality is seldom addressed.[7] Because lesbian women and gay men are invisible, unlike Black or disabled athletes, and most elite homosexual athletes stay closeted, it is easy for sports leaders and organizations to do nothing. In the top levels of the sport establishments of Western countries, there are few progressive voices about the politics of sexuality and so changing the climate of homophobia and discrimination against lesbian women rests with women themselves.

In 1990, Birgit Palzkill urged that:

It would be in the interests of all sportswomen to declare solidarity against the discrimination of lesbian women. For here the issue is by no means a specific problem of lesbians but is about breaking away from a degrading form of 'femininity' for all women.

(Palzkill 1990: 230)

Eight years later, in a similar vein, Pat Griffin (1998: xi) made the following plea:

> It is in the interests of heterosexual women to stand with their lesbian and bisexual teammates and colleagues to challenge anti-lesbian discrimination. In doing so, they also free themselves to achieve their potential as athletes, coaches, and women in the world without the tyranny of compulsory femininity, heterosexuality, and fear of being called a lesbian.

But in spite of nearly a decade of concern for the rights of lesbians in sport, it is hard to find examples of any radical 'mixed-sexuality' initiatives intended to address and eliminate heterosexism and homophobia. The Canadian Association for the Advancement of Women and Sport (CAAWS – see M.A. Hall 1996: 96–9), set up in 1981, is an unusual example of an association that originally had a radical feminist mission (probably inspired by the Second Wave women's movement in Canada), which it failed to realize. M.A. Hall (1996: 98) documents that the CAAWS 'made a serious effort to be both antihomophobic and lesbian-positive':

> In the mid-1980s, the following resolutions were passed at various annual general meetings: 'CAAWS endorses the inclusion of sexual orientation in the Canadian Human Rights Code'; 'CAAWS is opposed to discrimination against lesbians in sport and physical activity, and that CAAWS undertakes to support advocacy efforts to ensure lesbian equality of rights'; and 'Given that there are lesbians within CAAWS, and homophobia within CAAWS, the Association needs to address these internal concerns'.

Possibly in part because of the 1990s backlash against feminism, and also in order to sustain funding, CAAWS shifted to a less controversial and more typical liberal gender-equity perspective. Ideological differences between liberal and radical feminists that revolved around sexual politics made it difficult for lesbians to keep issues of visibility and homophobia alive. M.A. Hall (1996: 98) argues that 'The membership and leadership have always been split between those who see sexuality as a private and personal concern and those who see it as a political issue.' There is a tendency among liberal sport feminists to argue that no particular group of women deserves special treatment, and that lesbians should not be in the limelight but should be arguing for equality for *all* women, regardless of sexuality. In contrast, radical sport feminists want to politicize sexuality and to debate fully and openly the problems facing lesbians in sport. In the last few years, the liberal position has gained the ascendancy in CAAWS, which sees itself now as 'part of the Canadian sport community and much less as a feminist organization linked to the women's movement' (M.A. Hall 1996: 98). In common with other Western countries, the liberal sport feminist position in Canada has been strengthened and the radical lesbian position weakened by government legislation that prohibits initiatives perceived to promote homosexuality.[8] The strengthening of right-wing politics in, for example, North America, Britain and Australia, has resulted in anti-feminist and anti-gay-rights backlashes that exacerbate the problems faced by lesbian sportswomen. Throughout mainstream sport, throughout the West, there is in general a markedly conservative and cautious approach to the politics of sexuality.

Political structures of control, combined with ideological and practical structures of control, can seriously limit the autonomy of lesbian women in sport. But there are some women – lesbian, bisexual, heterosexual – who work actively to combat homophobia and who resist discrimination and intolerance. For example, Jody Conradt, women's athletic director at the University of Texas, refused to respond to allegations and slurs about lesbians in her teams, declaring that 'The best team I ever had had diversity. When our society learns to embrace diversity, we'll be a lot better society' (Festle 1996: xxvi–xxvii). But still, in the year 2000, there is ignorance and prejudice and those who want change lack power. The contention that power comes with knowledge supports the case made here by Lenskyj (1991: 67) for open debate:

> Public discussions and educational projects on homophobia in sport represent an important step toward politicizing lesbian issues among nonpolitical lesbians, and equally important, among heterosexual women and men. ... Moreover, the related acts of giving voice to one's sexual identity and naming one's experiences of oppression are individually and politically empowering for lesbians. ... From their position of relative privilege, white heterosexual men and women can more readily challenge the homophobia that silences and immobilizes many lesbians.

Although it is particularly difficult for lesbians to talk openly about the painful effects of discrimination, Clarke (1995: 53) also argues vigorously for an end to silence and apology:

> But whilst we remain silent, I would argue that we continue to perpetuate and reinforce myths, stereotypes and fears about lesbian women in sport. Through these practices we deny them the right to participate openly and fully in sport. This right to participate should be a basic human right and not something reserved for the heterosexual majority.

By speaking out, lesbians in sport and their supporters are openly transgressing traditional cultural limits and regulations. They are resisting compulsory heterosexuality and patriarchal relations of power which are intrinsic to it, combating stereotypes about homosexuals, and celebrating difference and inclusiveness. Speaking out is an essential start for any change in people's perceptions of lesbian women in sport.

Visibility and power: lesbian sporting heroes

Munt reminds us that 'Claiming a lesbian self remains an heroic performance for all who inhabit an intransigently homophobic culture' (1998: 4). For lesbians in sport to 'come out', to make their presence felt, and to claim personal and group space *as* lesbians, is a challenging act of resistance to homophobia and a refusal to be reduced to an absence. Sexual (lesbian) categories of difference and identity that operate in sport are usually private; coming out makes them visible and public. Coming out is, therefore, a reflection of greater confidence, a more assured sense of identity and of self, and an act of personal politics. Griffin (1998: 162) argues that:

> One of the most effective tools in counteracting homophobia is increased lesbian and gay visibility. Stereotypes and the fear and hatred they perpetuate will lose their power as more lesbian and gay people in sport disclose their identities. Although some people will never accept diversity of sexual identity in sport or in the general population, research indicates that, for most people, contact with 'out' lesbian and gay people who embrace their sexual identities reduces prejudice.

Liberal reforms do little to change public attitudes; taking part openly as a lesbian in sport can do a lot more. The huge popularity of sport makes it one of the most public channels through which lesbian women can resist stereotypes and harassment. Elite athletes can play a special role in this respect by creating positive images of lesbian women for worldwide consumption. Because most elite lesbian athletes remain closeted, the exceptional one who does disclose her sexuality becomes a special symbol of resistance and promise. From the first moment she comes out, she is appropriated by the lesbian community (and rather differently by the media) and portrayed as having a shared identity with all other lesbians. As Munt (1998: 102) explains, 'In lesbian culture there are a few lesbian warriors who distil the desires of the many; they are the folk heroes, fantasy figures who carry a multi-symbolic load of inspiration.' More than any other lesbian elite athlete, Martina Navratilova has been an inspirational figure, invoking an exceptional image of sporting womanhood for lesbian culture. She is described, as if in homage, by other lesbian sportswomen, as follows:

She's our idol.

She's great – she's so political, so honest.

It takes guts to do what she's done.

It's good for all of us. It makes us feel good and it gives us courage.

It was monumental that an elite athlete of her caliber had the courage to come out, to declare that she is gay. She is an 'icon' for all the positive things in sport.

Martina is such a gay icon. She has been put on a pedestal. Because she is the only person to have 'come out' in world class sport, in the gay world she is the movie star, she is the hero.

(personal interviews)

In the eyes of other lesbians, Martina Navratilova is redefining the stereotypes of mainstream sport and transforming victimization into triumph. She fulfils the vision of lesbian hero characterized below by Munt (who explains that because heroine 'can only be a heterosexist qualifier to the ordinate hero', she uses the latter description):

In the interests of defending a range of cultural strategies which evangelize lesbian life, one particular format seems to me to stride out onto the page: the hero. Heroes offer a metaphor of the self in movement, change and process. She is a radical myth, a lesbian success story, an icon of struggle, and both we and 'mainstream' culture need her versatility. Normalization is resisted by the public discourse of lesbianism – if our lesbianism is kept secret, then our private desires become domesticated – hence the importance of images like the heroic, which exist in the popular, public realm. To live as a lesbian today, even after twenty-five years of attempted liberation, is still an heroic act.

(1998: 2)

But Navratilova's rise to heroic status has not been without setbacks and prejudice. She has experienced homophobia and discrimination – experiences she shares with the few other elite sportswomen who are known to be lesbian or bisexual. When Billie Jean King was 'outed' in the media in 1981, following a lesbian affair with a woman who was filing a suit against her for lifetime support, she adopted an 'apologetic' stance. She held a press conference, and with her husband and parents beside her she described her seven-year relationship with her lesbian lover as 'a mistake'. She later insisted that she hated being called 'homosexual' and that her marriage had survived her 'irregularity' and become stronger (*The Times* 2/5/81). Although King remained a popular tennis star throughout her career, after it was known that she was bisexual she was called upon to 'resign from her post as president of the Women's Tennis Association because of her "sexual perversion"' (Festle 1996: 238), and she lost a conservative estimate of $1,500,000 (£1,000,000) in sponsorship, advertising and endorsements during the three years following the revelation and millions of dollars after that in lost deals. What was described as 'a lesbian witch hunt' followed (Festle 1996: 241).

Later that year Navratilova became one of the victims of the witch hunt after her relationship with writer and lesbian activist, Rita Mae Brown, was also made public in a newspaper report (Griffin 1998: 44–5). Navratilova's sexual life was examined in the media and she became the butt of abusive chants and letters (although it is recorded that for every letter to *World Tennis* 'complaining that a story about an "avowed lesbian ... makes me sick", there were two applauding her honesty, courage, grace, and ability'; Festle 1996: 241). Although she was a hugely talented tennis player, she lost millions of dollars in endorsements after her sexuality was disclosed, and although she continued to be a remarkably popular tennis star, she also faced hostility – hisses, boos, jeers and hate mail – from homophobes. Nevertheless, Navratilova understands and uses the power of her position to advocate lesbian and gay rights and to oppose discrimination. She is unreservedly politicized, 'speaking at a national rally in Washington, helping to raise funds for the Gay Games, and joining the lawsuit against Colorado's antihomosexual rights bill' (Festle 1996: 274). Her popularity was evident at a Gay Games fundraising event – 'A Tribute to Martina' – held in Madison Square Garden in 1994. She attended the occasion, which raised over $250,000 (£160,000). She has also espoused the rights of 'women, children, the elderly, and animals' (Festle 1996: 27). Martina Navratilova has secured heroic stature less as a result of her amazing sporting talent than because she has shown to the world a political and ethical conscience – she has made the personal political.

King, by comparison with Navratilova, has been more cautious and aware of the personal cost of resistance. Some years after her court case, King admitted her bisexuality (Blue 1994: 173) and has since spoken out against homophobia and has attended Gay Games fundraisers (Kort 1994: 136). Both King and Navratilova have subverted gendered norms through their enactments of bisexuality and lesbianism, and through their challenges to heterosexism and homophobia. Their actions encourage other non-heterosexual women to share in the construction of a specifically lesbian self-consciousness. As Munt (1998: 4) argues, ' "Lesbian" continues to be a powerful and strategic sign, an identity.' These two elite lesbian sporting heroes have encouraged the construction of a lesbian identity, a sense of belonging to a 'community', a sense of 'we'. They have paved the way for other top athletes to join the quest to replace negative images of lesbianism with positive ones. But those who have done so are tiny in number. In 1996, at the age of 42, Muffin Spencer-Devlin became the first player in the 46-year history of the LPGA tour to come out (in a *Sports Illustrated* article) (Griffin 1998: 47). She had spent many years carefully masking her lesbian identity and working to become a financially successful international golfer before she had the confidence to make a statement. She said at the time, 'It is like an incredibly huge weight being lifted from my shoulders' (*Guardian* 14/3/96). In 1999, Amelie Mauresmo, a rising young and thriving tennis professional, who reached the final of the Australian Open championship, became the first French athlete – male or female – to admit publicly her homosexuality.

Those elite athletes who are known to be lesbians or bisexual, and who survive the experience, usually do so because they are sufficiently successful not to be financially ruined as a result of the inevitable loss of sponsorship, etc. The public may disrespect non-normative sexuality, but they appreciate precocious sporting talent and so brilliant lesbian sportswomen are torn between abuse and praise, between dismissal and reverence. The inevitable harassment comes from other players, as well as from the media. Young lesbian sportswomen need to be well adjusted and confident with their sexual identities to survive. Taunts of masculinization are the most common forms of abuse. For example, during the 1999 Australian Open, Martina Hingis was alluding to Mauresmo when she said, 'She's here with her girlfriend; she's half a man', and Lindsey Davenport is reported as saying, 'She has a guy's shoulders, and looks better suited to the shot putt.' Drysdale, in *Scotland on Sunday* (23/5/99), reported on the French media's reaction to Mauresmo's revelation:

> When the nineteen-year-old, bicep-bulging marvel that is Mauresmo marked her arrival on the international tennis stage by reaching the final of the Australian Open, and promptly declared that she was madly in love with Mademoiselle Sylvie Bourdon, a St Tropez bar-owning sophisticate, the Gallic television equivalent of *Spitting Image* commemorated her achievement by featuring a puppet with a woman's head attached to Arnold Schwarzenegger's body, accompanied by the sarcastic voice-over: 'Here is the first time in the history of French sport that a man has come out as a lesbian'.

Speaking as if on behalf of the whole French nation, more derision came from a sports commentator on a Paris radio show: 'We have waited patiently for a girl to come along and beat Graf, Seles, Sanchez-Vicario and Hingis and now, my God, we have produced a player that makes Martina Navratilova look like Catherine Deneuve' (Drysdale, *Scotland on Sunday* 23/5/99).

He went on to describe Mauresmo as 'bi and butch' and his remarks were greeted with approval and jeering during the ensuing phone-in programme. Mauresmo has had to face a barrage of abusive language with mannish caricaturing and persistent implications of lesbianism. In an interview, she referred to the decision to reveal her sexuality:

> The decision was even more terrifying for me than playing in the Australian final, but I didn't want months or even years of mindless speculation about my sexuality. So I took a deep breath, told the truth, and I only hope that I will be treated fairly for what I am because I love Sylvie, and I don't care who knows it. We are very happy together, and being with her makes me feel good both in the head and in the heart. Let's be honest, it has led

to me performing the best tennis of my life, so that has to be a good thing, doesn't it?

(Drysdale, *Scotland on Sunday* 23/5/99)

Lesbian sporting heroes find themselves exposed in the spotlight of the normalized binary division of heterosexual/homosexual and are caught up in a process of struggle in their quest for legitimation. By speaking out they are making a symbolic statement of resistance to a homophobic culture; they are facing head-on the popularized, negative label of ridicule and are transforming it into an assertion of positive identity. Navratilova and Mauresmo are both muscular and powerful; each has been characterized as 'the masculine woman', 'the butch' – abusive descriptions among homophobes, but re-coded by lesbians. Munt (1998: 54) points out that:

> Butch is *the* recognizable public form of lesbianism; despite the media hype of chic femme in the early 1990s, it communicates a singular verity, to dykes and homophobes alike. Butch – despite the evidence of butch hetero-sexual women and the passion of femmes for women – is the gospel of lesbianism, inevitably interpreted as the true revelation of female homo-sexuality.

In lesbian imagery, muscularity bestows eroticism on the lesbian body; the butch body is constructed as 'a sexual agent, something that *does* rather than *is*' (Munt 1998: 54). But the butch body is flexible – it can be read as sexual and political at the same time. Navratilova, and now Mauresmo, are both contemporary icons of sexual and political butchness, turning the shame of social ostracism inside out and reproducing it as heroic pride (Munt 1998: 55). Although butch is only one category of lesbian gender, because it is the most easily read, it is the most easy to use as a symbol of opposition. It is not surprising that outstanding ability in sport has become a signal of homosexuality. Developing power in the body by working out, building muscle and winning tennis championships is an embodied sign of an opposite to emphasized femininity, a way of appropriating masculinity and foregrounding butch lesbianism. In her discussion of the advent of postmodernism and queer theory, 'which challenged the idea that gender was "extra" to the body', Munt (1998: 71–2) asserts that

> Butch bodies themselves became stylistically fashioned. The ur-model[9] here was Martina Navratilova; media coverage of her body-building into the 1980s synchronized the desires of a new generation of lesbians nurtured by ideologies of personal achievement, individualism and commodity fetish-ism. This new butch body was a very American phenomenon: think, for example, of the dumping of Czech Martina for the re-built, honed and blonde Martina; the vitality and fitness of the American body was being idealized. The new body culture of the 1980s drew dykes to the gym in droves. Butch aesthetics became muscle-bound, nouveau macho replacing

the finesse of 1950s romanticism. The ethic of chivalry which had enveloped sexual liaisons in previous decades became satirized. In the new performativity an adjectival hardness became intrinsic to the reconstruction of butch.

Munt's analysis endorses the idea that there is no clear division between sexuality and gender – neither is a static or essentialized condition, each shifts and changes and is acted out and understood according to specific circumstances. The social construction of the butch body has changed historically – it has been pathologized, sexologized, romanticized, and fused to discourses of pride and shame (Munt 1998: 54–94). Jayne Caudwell (1999: 393–4) has pointed out that there is a new celebration of the butch lesbian in line with queer politics. The contemporary, queer butch 'can be seen as a form of subversion, one that destabilizes dominant notions surrounding heterosexuality' (Caudwell 1999: 395). Within this construction, butch is not a homogeneous characterization, but includes multiplicity. The specific butch type in discussion here is the athletic butch.

There is another dimension to the analysis. Today's 'out', elite sporting butch body is connected to the politics of difference and identity affecting all minority groups but, more specifically, to the popular 1980s ideology of individualism, and to the commodification and sexualization of the female body in late capitalist sport (Hargreaves 1994: 145–73). The athletic, muscularized butch body has been routinely constructed in opposition to the ultra-feminized one, but 'current representations of the female sporting body show some collapse of conventional points of reference, some acceptance of values that have previously been marginalized, and the emergence of new, radicalized images of female physicality' (Hargreaves 1994: 173). Elite lesbian athletes are not outsiders to the general widening of definitions of femininity in sport or to the postmodern, lifestyle-fracturing of sporting identities. But, although today muscularity in the female body is valued and admired, appropriated by women as physical capital, to become accepted it is conditional upon publicly avowed heterosexuality. When heterosexism is accentuated, elite lesbian athletes become alienated, separated as 'others' from heterosexual sportswomen, and drawn into the 'lesbian community'. Because they are defined and trapped by hegemonic heterosexuality, elite lesbian sportswomen can become emblems of agency, power and possibility for other lesbians. They both elicit *and* refuse homophobia; they reflect shame *and* heroic idealization.

Gay sport: belonging and identity

There are reasons why lesbians, in common with heterosexual women, choose to participate in sport: the investment of muscle, speed, strength and stamina in the body and pride in its achievements are physically and psychologically empowering; and sport provides the opportunity for women to spend time together and to bond with other women. But the social stigma associated with homosexuality means that in mainstream sport relationships between lesbians and heterosexual women, and between lesbians and other lesbians, exist artificially, regulated through the 'doing' of heterosexuality. Lesbians therefore tend to prefer open and inclusive athletic environments where they can meet other same-sex women and where 'it is recognized that homophobia and discrimination against lesbians is the problem, not lesbians' (M.A. Hall 1999). Referring to lesbian sportswomen from the USA during the mid-twentieth century, Festle (1996: 44) explains that

> Team sports like softball and basketball gave them a chance to achieve, have control over their own bodies, be aggressive as well as cooperative and self-sacrificing; and it gave them a chance to meet, work with and play with other women who shared the same interests and values.

'It should be no surprise', Griffin (1998: 182) suggests, 'that lesbian athletes and coaches find love and community among other women who share a love of sport.' She goes on:

> Industrial sport leagues, professional touring teams, community recreation teams, college teams, and other sport events have provided a place where lesbian athletes can share their common passion for sports and women in a community that shared their need for secrecy and discretion in a hostile society.

Sport has provided a unique space for lesbian women where they can be together; it may be that there is a greater percentage of lesbian women in sport than in the rest of society. Lesbians may have more leisure flexibility than most heterosexual women, and it is possible that because butch lesbians have appropriated the codes of masculinity sporting lesbians are attracted to activities which are associated with powerful, muscular physicality and traditional images of masculinity. However, because of the enforced secrecy around sexuality, we do not have comprehensive evidence to show patterns of lesbian participation in sport and, of the research there is, most has been sited in North America (for example, Cahn 1994; Festle 1996; Griffin 1998; Lenskyj 1986).

We do know that fighting for lesbian space in sport has resulted in the establishment and growth of all- (or predominantly) lesbian/gay sport. (However, gay sport is not yet a realistic option for sportswomen hoping to advance into mainstream elite sport.) 'Gay sport' is a relatively recent phenomenon, originating from the 1970s (Pronger 1990: 219). Since that time there has been an explosive growth of lesbian sports clubs, organizations and competitions throughout the urban Western world, at local, national and international levels, and there are also enthusiastic lesbian sport fans and well-established lesbian fan clubs (Griffin 1998: 186-7). For example, the Dinah Shore Golf Tournament in the USA has become a landmark of lesbian subculture, described as 'Dyke's Heaven'. Each year over 5000 lesbians converge on Palm Springs for the tournament, described as the hottest ticket on the lesbian calendar (Reed 1994a: 23; 1994b: 95). According to gay columnist Deb Price, lesbians also pack galleries at LPGA events: 'She says the LPGA ought to denounce homophobia out of respect to its loyal fans' (Festle 1996: 358, n. 2).

The gay sports phenomenon is a symbol of the growing demand for homosexual cultural activities, the need to experience greater visibility and solidarity, and the quest for an 'imagined community'. Gay sport creates space to be an 'insider' (rather than an 'outsider' in mainstream sport), to enjoy sport in a friendly and inclusive atmosphere, and to escape from the heterosexism and homophobia of mainstream sport. In short, 'Gay sports clubs and competitions offer lesbians and gay men the opportunity to express themselves not only athletically but also culturally' (Pronger 1990: 270). Pronger makes it very clear that 'Gay culture is one that is *not* orthodox. ... Joining/belonging to gay culture is an act of resistance to the oppressiveness of orthodox culture. Gay culture is a response to homosexual oppression (1990: 217, 219).

Gay sport enables lesbians to come out without the labelling and repercussions and discrimination that accompany coming out in mainstream sport. It challenges stereotypes, gives lesbians a higher profile, creates positive images for other lesbians, and provides a safe women-only space and a sense of comfort and belonging – explained here by a lesbian woman who has been a competitive athlete for years in mainstream *and* gay sport, and now, as a veteran, avoids possible discrimination and harassment:

> I wouldn't dream now of being a member of a club or team where I couldn't be open about my sexuality. I don't any longer want to be a target or get involved in the process of trying to change bigoted attitudes. ... It's all a question of choice. Most of us operate in a heterosexual world and if I want to be amongst other lesbians and feel very comfortable, that's my choice and I should be able to do that. It can be likened to the needs of disabled or black sportwomen. They should be able to organise a network or a structure for themselves, and so should we. Sport is still a very hostile environment. We are still in a situation where most lesbian sportswomen are closeted.

Other lesbian women turn to sport for similar reasons. They have expressed their feelings to me in interviews as follows: 'I don't feel on my own any more, I don't have to pretend, and I don't have to face the bigots'; 'Sport has helped me to identify ... now I know other women who have the same problems'; 'I've learned so much about myself through gay sport – most importantly, I've been able to enjoy sport *and* enjoy being with other women. I have learned to value my physicality without shame. I was always worried about being strong and muscular before, now I enjoy my body.'

A lesbian woman at the Gay Games expressed the personal and particular value to her of taking part in same-sex sport: 'To see the kind of celebration that was happening, people able to be open about their lifestyle, was really a wonderful kind of healing process for me' (*West* November 1990).

The relationship of sexual politics with human rights politics is also important to many lesbian sportswomen, who find gay sport a haven of escape from right-wing, judgemental and socially conservative sportsmen and women. The following quotations from interviews suggest that these women were driven away from mainstream sport because they believe that it encourages aggressive competitiveness and selfish individualism:

> The other important aspect is my politics. All the lesbian women I know care about the things I care about – they are left wing, I'd say – but often don't even know it! They care about human rights, about discrimination, about racism. ... You know, they're just *decent* people. ... I've known some really reactionary people in mainstream sport – not just homophobic – you know, real chauvinists, mysogynists, even fascists – but not in gay sport.

> I hate a lot of elements about elite sport. There's this fierce aggression and some nasty behaviour. Because I'm Black, I get a lot of racism fired at me ... in gay sport there's none of that.

> Because I don't look butch – in some ways I was lucky. But it meant I was always having to fend off these disgusting guys – always making suggestions – or just winking or knocking into me so-called 'accidentally' – you know. ... Lesbians aren't like that – not the ones I know. Not the ones at my club. It's not the same pressure. ... And we do things in the community – we want to win, but we care about other things as well – *important* things. Like we collect for cancer because one of my mate's mum's got breast cancer, so we go on this special run. A lot of the other girls just cared about winning – they'd sleep with anyone if they thought he'd help. ... I know I won't get into the England squad now, but I don't care.

Gay sport has become a widespread cultural phenomenon, giving lesbians and gay men much greater visibility and pushing forward the growing public acceptability of homosexuality. It provides sport-loving lesbians and gay men with a prejudice-free space – something that mainstream sport has failed abysmally to do. The growing popularity of gay sport is a significant expression of gay and lesbian identity politics. 'Open' participation by increasing numbers of lesbians reflects an assertive individual stance signifying community pride and group identity. There is no stable, fixed state of lesbianism; rather it is lived on a day-to-day basis, and 'doing' gender by 'doing' sport constructs new and positive images of lesbianism. Such images have political power through their visibility in dominant culture. Gay sport signals 'a move beyond demands for the tolerance of private sexual preferences to the thematization of public group identities and the construction of alternative lifstyles' (Featherstone *et al.* 1995: 10). A focus on culture has been central to this new identity politics. Zaretsky (1995: 244) argues that identity politics have normally been understood to be a repudiation of universalizing philosophies, such as liberalism and Marxism, which recognized not only that 'the local or particular community of identity, such as lesbianism or the African-American community, can be the central point of identification for the self', but also emphasized that human 'rights' and the larger interests of class and social justice (respectively) prevail. But the newer politics can be seen to have some continuity with these traditions through a consideration of psychoanalysis. Zaretsky (1995: 248) argues that 'Freud demonstrated that everything social and interpersonal dissolves and is remade within individuals to take a personal form.' Freud's concept of identification can be used to explain how lesbians, for example, restructure social meanings about sexual preference. The recent impetus to define lesbian identity in terms of culture – our example of which is gay sport – has challenged the established coupling of sexuality with the 'private' realm and the hegemony of the private/public split (Zaretsky 1995: 245).

The breakdown between private and public is very marked in Western urban contexts, where there has been some liberal increase of tolerance of a person's right to be gay, mixed with escalating right-wing intolerance. This tension between freedom and constraint highlights the significance of the growth of gay sport, events and organizations. The greater the number of lesbians and gay men that participate in sport openly as homosexuals, the greater is the cultural and political effect and the greater is the sense of a new embodied politics. Gay sport in the West – the pinnacle of which is the Gay Games – has become immensely popular to the extent that it can be characterized as a 'new movement' with politico-personal implications.

Gay sport incorporates a huge range of activities from recreational sport to international single-event and multi-sport competitions. There are lesbian or women-only events, and gay competitions which include events for men and women of all sexualities. Local-level gay sport incorporates a plethora of clubs for different sports, for example women's football teams, Hackney Amazons and Clapham Wildcats, and women's volleyball teams, Dynamo Dykes – all from London, England; Nobody's Rib, from North Carolina, USA; city-based teams, such as Team Las Vegas, USA, and Team Sydney, Australia. Examples of regional events are the Northwest Gay/Lesbian Sports Festival (North America), the Key West (USA) Women's Flag Football League, and the southern hemisphere women's fast-pitch softball team, ANZAF (i.e. Australia, New Zealand and Friends). National sports organizations and events have been set up in all countries in the West – for example, Gay Integration through Sports and Arts Holland (GISAH) and the British Gay and Lesbian Sport Federation (BGLSF). National associations are slowly developing in other parts of the world as well.

The BGLSF reflects the unprecedented boom currently enjoyed by amateur-level gay sport throughout the West and is a good example of the widespread advances made generally by umbrella national organizations. The BGLSF was founded in 1994 as a co-ordinating body for lesbian and gay sports clubs throughout the UK (Clarke 1998: 155) and is now one of the fastest-growing sections of the gay community with more than 2000 members. The next European level is also flourishing. The European Gay and Lesbian Sports Federation (EGLSF) describes itself in its 1994 annual report as 'a fast growing network of gay, lesbian and mixed sportsgroups from Europe'. In 1995, there were 260 affiliated clubs and it is estimated that by the end of the century more than another 100 should be added to the list (*Axiom News 54*, 29/11/99–15/12/99). EGLSF is a lobbying body as well as an organizing body. For example, it conducted an investigation into discrimination against gays and lesbians in member countries resulting in the publication in 1994 of the EGLSF European Blackbook which was presented to the president of the European Non-Government Sport Organizations (ENGSO) and to delegates from the UK, Norway and Sweden at a symposium (against discrimination in society) of the Council of Europe (*EGLSF 1994 Year Report*). EGLSF also organizes the EuroGames – a lesbian–gay multisport festival started in 1992 'to promote the self-respect of European lesbian and gay athletes and to foster the network between lesbian and gay sportgroups' (*EuroGames III Official Programme 1995*). After a few years, EuroGames was described as the largest event of the gay community in Europe.

The final level of participation is global international – between athletes and teams from countries around the world. It follows from the increase in participation and events at local, national and regional levels that global competitions are also thriving. For example, the Gay and Lesbian Soccer World Cup was first held in 1995 between teams from Europe and North America and has grown to become a bigger competition and gradually more inclusive of teams from outside the West. Similarly, the Gay Games, first held in 1982, was originally a predominantly North American affair, then incorporated Western European countries, then other Western countries, such as Australia and New Zealand, and is now spreading to include some competitors from the developing world. Liaisons between lesbians and gays from different countries across the world is facilitated by advances in communication technology, especially email. There are newsletters and organizations for different sports and different groups – for example, *Pacelines* is an international newsletter for lesbian and gay cyclists. There are also powerful lesbian and gay sports lobbies that work together with other lesbian and gay pressure groups. For example, in 1996 in Atlanta, 'for the first time in Olympic history lesbians and gay men had a dedicated visitor's centre to provide and promote "a highly visible presence to the world's gay and lesbian community during the summer of 1996" ' (promotional leaflet, cited in Clarke 1998: 154–5). At the 1997 annual Lesbian and Gay Pride Festival in England, also for the first time, BGLSF had a tent. Gay athletes also network together to enter mainstream events – for example, in 1991, 75 gay athletes competed in the Chicago Sun-Times Triathlon, and there are lesbian and gay groups that take part and support participants in the London Marathon.

Gay sport is an offspring of the lesbian and gay liberation movement, part of the post-Stonewall Pride movement. Munt (1998: 15) maintains that 'The heroic gesture of Stonewall has been crystallized in the individual gesture of "coming out", which is also a motion of "coming in" – to the lesbian and gay community.' Gay sport thus ties the individual lesbian into an heroic community of resistance, confering selfhood through identification. This is a process consolidated and popularized most of all at the Gay Games – the biggest event on the gay cultural calendar. The Games attract representatives from all sections of the lesbian and gay community – lesbians, gay men, bisexuals, transsexuals, young, old, able-bodied and disabled, those from different countries and from different ethnic and social groups. For all of them, to take part in gay sport is to come out, to make a political statement through belonging.

Gay Games: radical philosophy and practice

The Gay Games, first held in San Francisco in 1982, were founded by Tom Waddell, an ex-Olympic decathlete. Some 1350 athletes from 12 countries took part in 17 different sports and there were 400 cultural participants.[10] The Games have been held every four years since then. In 1986, they were again in San Francisco – this time there were 3482 athletes and, most significantly, 40 per cent of them were women. Vancouver was the host city for Gay Games III. The sports programme was extended to 23 sports, there were 7500 athletes and 1200 cultural participants. Gay Games IV took place in New York in 1994 and was combined with the 25th anniversary celebrations of the Stonewall Riots. A record number of athletes (11,000), for any sports event, were competing in 35 sports. There were 15,000 cultural participants and people came from 45 different countries. 1998 marked the fifth Gay Games, held in Amsterdam – the first time the venue was in Europe. This was claimed to be 'the biggest lesbian and gay event of the century ... the biggest lesbian and gay event ever held in the world!' (*Gay Games Amsterdam 1998*: 4). There were over 15,000 participants from over 60 countries and five continents, with 2500 cultural participants, together with 200,000 spectators (*Gay Games Amsterdam 1998*: 4). There were 30 competition sports, six demonstration sports, and an extensive cultural programme; 25,000 Gay Games Amsterdam 1998 medals, etched with the Gay Games motto, 'Friendship Through Culture and Sports', were presented to each participant 'in true Gay Games spirit'. The organizers made it clear in the official publicity material that 'The old Olympic adage, "Participating is more important than winning", was at the heart of our motto for the Gay Games Amsterdam 1998: "Friendship Through Culture and Sports" ' (*Gay Games Amsterdam 1998*: 18).

The philosophy and practice of Gay Games, inspired by Tom Waddell, is fundamentally different from the aggressive competitive ideology and divisive conventions of mainstream sport. Inclusiveness, involvement and experience replace the exclusiveness, elitism and achievement-orientation of orthodox events. The description 'Gay Olympic Games', the original choice of title, had to be changed to 'Gay Games' following the United States Olympic Committee's (USOC) insistence that they had a legal monopoly of the term 'Olympics'. It was argued in court that 'Gay Games' did not convey the same message as 'Gay Olympics' would have done: ' "Gay Games" is not an adequate translation for the "Gay Olympics"; "Olympics" conveys an image of excellence and wholesomeness, of "normalcy", that "Games" cannot begin to convey' (*Cincinnati Law Review* 56, 1988: 1518).

But the USOC won the battle and the 'Olympic' description was dropped. However, Tom Waddell was encouraged to challenge the implied 'unwholesomeness' and 'abnormality' of Gay 'non-Olympic' Games and to distance himself from the Olympic label. He explained:

> We were using it [Olympics] initially to describe our Games, but let's look at the Olympics. The Olympics are racist, the Olympics are exclusive, they're nationalistic, they pit one group of people against another, and [are] only for the best athletes. That doesn't describe our Games.
>
> (Pronger 1990: 252)

The Gay Games ideology of inclusiveness and doing one's best was confirmed and the Federation of Gay Games was set up. Its mission statement reads as follows:

> The Federation of Gay Games is the international governing body for Gay Games and is composed of individual and organizational members from around the world. The purpose of the Federation is to foster and augment the self respect, dignity and pride of gay men and lesbians throughout the world and to engender the respect and understanding of the non-gay world. The Federation ensures that Gay Games continue to exist according to the founding principles of participation, inclusion and personal best. And as such, all activities conducted under its auspices are inclusive in nature, with no individuals excluded from participating on the basis of sexual orientation, gender, race, religion, nationality, ethnic origin, political belief(s), athletic/artistic, physical challenge or HIV status. Gay Games provide participants with the opportunity to express themselves openly, in a safe and accepting environment. The experience of participating in Gay Games has proven to be the highlight of a lifetime for many. By allowing individual participants the opportunity to celebrate the diversity and scope of the gay and lesbian community, stereotypes are challenged and barriers are broken down both within the gay community and between our community and the non-gay world. The Federation continues to spread the core message that 'Games can change the world'.
>
> (*Gay Games Amsterdam 1998*: 14)

Complexities of inclusiveness

In the official handbook of Gay Games II (1986), Tom Waddell wrote:

> The message of these games goes beyond validating our culture. The Gay Games were conceived as a new idea in sport based on inclusion rather than exclusion. Since anyone from anywhere is welcome to participate in this event, we transcend the traditional problems of ageism, sexism, and racism, and just as importantly, nationalism. There are no competing world ideologies in these games. ... Inclusiveness is the central philosophy of the Gay Games.
>
> (Pronger 1990: 254, 256)

Tom Waddell's reference to 'our culture' signifies 'gay and lesbian culture'. 'Our culture' is an expression of a collective gay and lesbian identity and consciousness. The fact that the Gay Games have escalated to become the biggest cultural event on the gay calendar is because thousands and thousands of lesbian women and gay men (sports participants/cultural participants/spectators) descend on Gay Games' host cities and create a sense of solidarity and belonging. While the ideology of 'sport for all' is also important, and it has been estimated that there are as many as 5 per cent heterosexual participants, the Games are part of a whole festival of events with an overwhelmingly gay/lesbian sensibility. Inclusiveness refers in the main to inclusiveness of 'difference' regarding lesbians and gay men. Gay Games philosophy decentres identity politics principally by recognizing multiple lesbian and gay oppressions and identities. This occurs firstly with regard to different (homo)sexualities. The discourses of gender blurring, gender ambiguity, 'dev-iant' sexuality, indeterminate sexuality, etc. are rendered unimportant because *all* forms of sexuality are made both visible and acceptable. There is no admission test, although competitors are asked to sign a declaration that they are competing 'in the gender in which they live their daily life' (in an attempt to avoid problematizing the status of 'transgendered' competitors; Engels *Guardian* 24/6/94). So, at the Gay Games there are bisexuals, transsexuals, transgendered people, gay men, and lesbians, etc., all with different sexual preferences and lifestyles – such as, butch, butch-femme, dyke, designer dyke, lipstick lesbian, lesbian chic, androgynous style, 'camp' lesbian, and some who identify themselves as 'queer' ... all of whom are embraced into the 'Gay Games family'.

Second, inclusiveness relates to lesbians whose identities intersect with other social divisions, such as race, disability and age. The organizers have tried to attract participants from a wide variety of social groups, including Black, disabled and elderly lesbians. Although no research has been done to substantiate such a claim, there are, for example, arguably a higher representative percentage of Black, Asian and Latina lesbians from the USA in the Gay Games than there are Black, Asian and Latina women in the mainstream Olympics. At Gay Games V in Amsterdam, there were events with 'Caribbean and Blacks in America' themes, and events for elderly gays ('Gay Greys [55]'),

Christian gays, Jewish gays, disabled gays, deaf gays ... (*Gay Games Amsterdam 1998*: 8). Most venues were wheelchair-accessible and sign-language translation was provided at several finals. There were also special arrangements for childcare. The facilitation and valuing of open participation and 'doing one's best', in preference to the elitism of high-level performance, encouraged large numbers of lesbians to take part who had been alienated from mainstream sport. The marathon was the largest event of the Amsterdam Games because it had unlimited registration. Unusually, there were also unconventional activities on the programme aimed at encouraging participation and enjoyment. The following account of 1994's Gay Games IV (in New York) creates the sense of inclusiveness and essential non-discrimination that is characteristic of the participatory culture of the festival. Participants included:

> a slow, chunky, novice runner (applauded by thousands for her effort), a bisexual tennis player, a golfer with AIDS, a blind skier and distance runner, an African-American lesbian grandmother in wrestling, and a multi-cultural co-gender in-line skating team.
>
> (Festle 1996: 268)

The following, more detailed account of Donna – the novice runner depicted above – illustrates how principles of inclusiveness and supportive enthusiasm can have a profound psychic effect on individual performers. Donna, who wore thick glasses to avoid being classified as legally blind, had shied away from sport in the past for fear of being ridiculed:

> It was warm but windy on the day of Donna's five kilometer race. Once the gun went off, she began shuffling along, her eyes focused on the white lines of her lane. After the first three of 12.5 laps she dropped near the back of the pack, moving slowly but with determination. At lap five she moved from the inside to the outside lane to allow Sue Foster, our teammate and the eventual winner, to whiz past her. Several other women lapped her as she continued to slug along, concentrating on each step. Donna still had a lap and a half to go as the second-to-last woman crossed the line. ... Donna seemed oblivious to the fact that she was running by herself. As she moved into the final lap, all of Team New York was on its feet, screaming encouragement to her, and soon everyone in the stadium was chanting and shouting for Donna. Buoyed up, with about 300 meters to go, Donna lifted her head toward the finish and began pumping her arms and legs harder than ever. As the crowd continued to roar, she crossed the line, flinging her arms in the air.
>
> (Villarosa 1994: 91)

Donna reacted: 'It was really exciting ... There is nowhere else in the world where someone like me could run a race and have everyone in the stands clapping and cheering for me' (Villarosa 1994: 91). Donna's experience was emotional and special, but not exceptional. All performers gain a feeling of friendship and togetherness, of support and personal achievement. The title of the official Gay Games newspaper, the *Daily Friendship*, symbolizes the importance to individual lesbians of the community ideology and practice.

The third level of inclusiveness relates to the global characteristic of the Gay Games. The Gay Games IV logo was composed of three elements – the three interlocking circles of the Federation of Gay Games logo; the torch, a symbol of athletic achievement since ancient Greece; and the triangle, a unifying symbol denoting the struggles of lesbian and gay people the world over. The intention to open the doors to people from countries across the world has been part of the strategy of the Gay Games since their foundation, although for political, logistical and financial reasons success has been limited. In many countries in the world, homosexuality is illegal and can be punishable by execution (for example, in some African [including North Africa] and Gulf states); by imprisonment of between ten years to life (as in the Indian subcontinent and some African states); by imprisonment of between three and ten years (like in parts of Eastern Europe, South America and Southeast Asia); and by imprisonment of up to three years (like in various African states [including North Africa]). Though not normally punished by imprisonment, homosexuality is also illegal in several other countries (for example, in Africa, South America, Southeast Asia, new nation states from the 'old' USSR); and, although in most parts of the West homosexuality has been decriminalized or not mentioned in law, it remains illegal in some states in the USA and Australia (*Gay Games 1998 Official Souvenir Programme*: 30–1). The criminalization of homosexuality effectively bars large numbers of lesbians and gay men from around the world from taking part in the Gay Games. These are people who can live repressed, secretive and endangered lives in their own countries. Others risk attending the Games, but avoid publicity for fear of being 'outed' on their return home. Even for those who come from countries where homosexuality is no longer a crime, for many lesbians and gay men who attend the Games it is the only time they can 'be themselves' because of the cultural stigma of homosexuality in their own homes and countries. For large numbers of lesbian and gay men, the Gay Games are an escape from the hegemonic heterosexuality and homophobia that permeate their cultures and everyday relationships. For example, Charity Mohlamme from Cape Town, South Africa, went to the Amsterdam Gay Games to perform traditional dances. In spite of the anti-discrimination clauses in the new constitution of South Africa, she reported that 'Gay Games is amazing. It's incredible to see so many gay people. Young, old, black and white. In South Africa, there are no visible older lesbians' (*Daily Friendship* 2/8/99: 2). Kunda, from Harare in Zimbabwe, says, 'It's a good opportunity to show who I am, as it is illegal to be gay in my country' (*Daily Friendship* 2/8/99: 2).

The themes of human rights and international solidarity were important features of the 1998 Gay Games. An outreach programme was put in place in order to open the doors to lesbians and gay men from the developing world who would otherwise be unable to attend. Co-operation with organizations including

Amnesty International, HIVOS (Humanists Institute for Development Cooperation Foundation), NOVIB, FNV, CNV, ILGA, XminY, COC and Levi-Strauss, as well as the Dutch Ministry of Foreign Affairs was sought, and the UN inserted a message in the official programme: 'The joint United Nations Programme on HIV/AIDS (UNAIDS [incorporates UNICEF; UNDP; UNFPA; UNESCO; WHO; World Bank]) supports the efforts of the gay and lesbian community to foster friendship and understanding through culture and sports (*Official Programme*). The organizers invited men and women connected to local gay rights movements in Africa, Asia, Latin America, and Central and Eastern Europe – in all, over 300 people were sponsored from different countries, including Namibia, Mexico, South Africa, India, Brazil, Kazakhstan and Lebanon (*Gay Games Amsterdam 1998*: 7; *Official Programme*). Gay Games VI, scheduled to take place in Sydney in 2002, is committed to extending the outreach programme, giving special attention to Asia and making new networks in the southern hemisphere.

The Gay Games forge crucial links between the local and the global. Lesbians from both the developing and the developed worlds can exchange ideas about ways to cope with homophobia and prejudice. Patricia Sekaule from South Africa says, 'Gay Games gives me a chance to learn how people from other cultures live' (*Daily Friendship* 2/8/99: 2). But there is no consensus among lesbians from across the world about politics or agency. At the Queer Games conference, which took place during the week preceding the official programme, there were 'reports from communities which eschew the "western" model of "outness" ', suggesting that confrontation and demands for equal rights are not the best strategies for integration. They 'prefer to promote harmony with family traditions and maintain invisibility, whether that invisibility is dictated by social constraints and political persecution, or simply serves those who, while engaging in homosex, do not consider themselves homosexual' (*Daily Friendship* 2/8/99: 15).

However, homosexuality is one of the unifying themes of the Gay Games, attracting women from far-flung places across the globe. But Gay Games identification represents a shift from the identity politics of the 1970s which was Western-based and suggestive of homogeneity. Lesbian women at the Gay Games bring with them distinctive experiences resulting from disparate social, cultural, religious and political conditions. They signify a non-essentialist position with multiple identities that are fluid and shifting in line with different cultural and political conditions (Weeks 1994). For example, women who travel to the Gay Games from countries in the developing world with oppressive regimes can experience a sense of tranformation of identity. They can come from harsh and dangerous situations where their sexual identities are hidden, to a relatively 'safe' place of non-discrimination where sexual identity is fore-grounded and celebrated. But, although there is no transhistorical, totalizing global lesbianism, which subsumes differences, there is a sense in which local identities relating to place are part of a bigger transnational community consciousness through which women's desire and love of other women is positively reinforced. Part of the process of constructing a Gay Games lesbian identity is that the personal problems that individual women experience as a direct result of being a lesbian in a secretive setting become publically affirmed.

The Gay Games have to some extent tried to resolve the tension between identity and difference. Although still a predominantly White, middle-class movement, they are democratized in philosophy and intentionally inclusive of lesbians who are Black, disabled, of different ages, and from different places. The Gay Games have embodied the idea of 'multiple allegiances' in theory and to some extent in practice (although participation is dependent on personal capital, outreach programmes and sponsorship).

Sexual politics

The success of the Gay Games rests on political and financial backing. New York 1994 was something of a turning point in these respects:

> President Clinton sent a warm message of support; the city's mayor was at the opening ceremony; the State Governor, Mario Cuomo, joined in an early basketball session; immigrant officials relaxed the usual rules and admitted people who [were] HIV positive; mainstream companies like the Miller Brewery were advertised in the programme; and the organisers claimed that the Games would bring $200 million of business into the city, at least as much as the World Cup.
>
> (Engels 1994)

Mayor Dinkins stated proudly that 'It is so fitting that these games are conducted here in New York City where we recognize diversity as a critical component of civic strength' (*IGTA Newsletter* autumn 1993). Organizers claimed that one million lesbians and gay men marched from the United Nations and rallied in Central Park, marking a quarter of a century of gay and lesbian liberation, and demanding more human rights for the future (*Pink Paper* 334, July 1994). The march was led by a mile-long rainbow flag held by hundreds of volunteers who had 'donated £30,000 to AIDS charities in return for being able to carry the longest symbol of gay unity in history' (*Pink Paper* 334, July 1994). Sponsorship was secured from local businesses and leisure outlets (many of which are gay-owned and -run). The integration of sport into a spectacular cultural festival was a huge commercial success, netting New York City an estimated US $317 million (£230 million). The politico-economic success of Gay Games IV provided a model for future years.

Social politics have always been an important focus of the Gay Games, and they have all been held in cities with large gay communities attracted by non-discrimination policies. It has been possible, therefore, to create a high level of visibility and politicization, to raise public consciousness, and to secure sanctioning of the Gay Games by local, national and international organizations and agencies. Amsterdam is reputed to be the only major city in the world where the government actively encourages gay tourism (witness its International Gay Tourist Association), which facilitated the arrival of droves of visitors to the city for Gay Games V. The Dutch organization for the Integration of Homosexuality (COC) was open every day and organized international meetings and information services. Amnesty International, together with HIVOS, held a special human rights programme striving to support international emancipation and integration. The focus of attention was the rights of lesbians and gays in developing countries and eastern Europe. There were also 'coming out' workshops, lesbian and gay human rights workshops, Internet lesbian and gay rights training; films concerning the universality of homosexuality; and organization, communication and conflict-resolution training sessions (*Gay Games Amsterdam 1998*: 12). A conference was held to discuss aspects of contemporary homosexualities and queer sports; and another was organized around discrimination in the workplace and the Dutch government's policy to support lesbian and gay organizations in developing countries.

The endorsement of the Gay Games and gay rights by 'respectable' agents bestows on them an empowering legitimacy. Although there is still brutal oppression of homosexuality in some parts of the world and huge prejudice in most places in the world, the visibility and 'global flow' effect of the philosophy of the Gay Games has encouraged gay women and men to set up support groups and organizations even in areas where homosexuality is criminalized and punishable. The link between the local and the global has been vitally significant to lesbians who would otherwise be very isolated.

Lesbian and gay culture

The feeling of belonging to a worldwide homosexual community that rests on friendship above all else comes not only from sports participation, but also, and importantly, from the cultural activities surrounding the Gay Games. Referring to the strategy for Gay Games V in Amsterdam, Mitchell (*Observer* 2/8/98) argues that sport was used 'as a conduit to discussion and cultural assimilation, which is why there [was] as much emphasis on activities such as dance, song and art as there [was] on badminton, football, karate and the regular Olympic sports'. The Gay Games comprise one forum (amongst many) in which a positive lesbian life is applauded. At the Gay Games lesbians can immerse themselves in gay culture, celebrate their sexuality, and explore their feelings, desires and identities.

Amsterdam was the focus for eight days of sports, culture and festivities, reflecting 'the vibrant diversity of the gay and lesbian community'. The mayor of Amsterdam published a welcome to visitors:

> Besides being a great sports and cultural event, Gay Games Amsterdam 1998 is even more so an opportunity for gays and lesbians from all over the world to make new friends and to be visible, in a world that too often does

not want to acknowledge gays and lesbians in their societies. During Gay Games 1998 you can show the world that gays and lesbians are a part of our communities in all the countries of the world and that you are here to stay. … Amsterdam and her citizens are proud to have you here. Everyone can participate in Gay Games and visitors, gay and straight, are all invited to the party!

(*Gay Games Amsterdam 1998*: 4)

The sporting events were an integral part of a huge celebration of gay life and culture. Famous performers from all over the world took part in the opening and closing ceremonies in the Amsterdam Arena – the most famous stadium in the Netherlands – which for two nights became the centre of gay life, with around 50,000 participants. The highlight of the opening ceremony was the parade of over 15,000 athletes. In the Friendship Village, 'the pulsating heart of the Gay Games' (*Gay Games Amsterdam 1998*: 8) – which was specially built for the Games – people could meet, check information, buy souvenirs and gifts, eat and drink, watch performances and demonstrations, and view the Community Arts Programme. There was a Canal Parade, sponsored by Gay Business Amsterdam, with a theme of 'friendship'; there were exhibitions held in the city's museums and art galleries; a poetry high tea; a Choir Festival with approximately 50 lesbian and gay performing choirs; lesbian and gay marching bands; art exhibitions, including a lesbian and gay sport-art show; 'coming out' storytelling; theatrical performances; an open-air cinema festival; women's and men's bars; and street entertainment of all sorts. Part of the programme was a three-day women's festival of music, dance and theatre – 'all with a lesbian touch' – under the name of 'Lesbian Nations' and dedicated to the theme of androgyny. It included acrobatic acts, exotic dance performances, a bodybuilding demonstration, an exhibition of photographs taken by lesbians, entitled 'the lesbian identity', and a guided tour of 'lesbian' Amsterdam. Gay Games 1998 ended with a huge dance party based on the theme 'Dance: A Link Between Sports and Culture', emphasizing the countries and cultures of the visitors. At the closing ceremony, the specially composed Gay Games hymn was sung and the announcement that Sydney is to be the host city of Gay Games 2002 was made (*Gay Games Amsterdam 1998*: 8).

All the events surrounding the Games were important reflections and statements of identity. The position was made clear at the first Gay Games in 1986, when Rita Mae Brown gave an opening address saying, 'These games are not just a celebration of skill, they're a celebration of who we are and who we can become. It's a celebration of the best in us' (Pronger 1990: 252). The sense of 'who we are' and 'us' results from individual and group representations, from visual signifiers of difference of lesbian and gay sexualities, and in particular those which stem from the physical and sexualized body. Body significations are central in the Gay Games, in particular in its varied rituals and cultures surrounding the sports events and cultural activities.

Lesbian bodies and lifestyle

Generally speaking, in the West the sexual climate over the last hundred years has become increasingly more liberalized and lesbians have a higher (even voguish) profile than ever before – in soap operas, teenage and women's magazines, lifestyle clubs and activities, etc., and there are sometimes intrepid representations of sexuality. In a number of different ways, the Gay Games embodies these characteristics of gay culture, producing and reproducing the politics of sexuality and lesbian identity. The rituals and practices surrounding the Games spectacularize lesbian and gay activities, parody mainstream culture, sport and femininity, and provide opportunities for participants to 'dramatize their adherence to homosexual values' (Leznoff and Westley 1998: 5). For example, Nicole Eiseman, a lesbian artist, had a satirical poke at stereotypical feminine representation. She characterized *her* Gay Games hero(ine) as 'The largest girl I ever painted'. It was a caricature of a naked woman depicting huge, tanned and bulging muscles, described as follows in the *Official Souvenir Programme*: 'The vibrant form is an appreciation of the strength of women and the enjoyment of developing physical and mental capabilities' (*Official Souvenir Programme* 1998: 34). Eiseman's grotesque, spectacular female body represents an oppositional lesbian gender performance to the dominant heterosexual image of the female celebrated in mainstream sport and culture. It was one of many specifically lesbian representations symbolizing sexual identity that were incorporated into the programme.

The opening parades at Gay Games 1998 embraced flamboyant images of queerness, butchness, lesbian chic, and so on, providing an exceptional opportunity – like the Gay Pride Day and Gay Mardi Gras marches – for gay men and lesbian women to make a defiant statement about claiming a place in a dominantly heterosexual society. The 1998 Gay Games International Dyke March, in particular, encapsulated the characteristics of lesbian politics and culture. Over 14,000 lesbians took part in what was described as 'the largest dyke event in history and the second largest march up Fifth Avenue since the Vietnam War'. Although it was an unauthorized event, the police turned a 'blind eye', in order to avoid confrontation and to be seen to be non-discriminatory and sympathetic to gay rights. There were two main themes – a welfare one, highlighting 'the fight against Aids and the higher-than-average breast cancer threat to lesbians' (*Pink Paper* 334 July 1994: 1) – and a larger-than-life symbolic statement of sexual politics, described in *Diva*, the lesbian lifestyle magazine, as follows: 'The atmosphere [was] electric if sweltering, as tits, a 20 foot high vulva, dykes on stilts, and women of every shape, size, age and race [entertained] the bemused onlookers' (*Diva* August 1994: 38).

Lesbian and gay bodies, through their physical presence, physique and homoerotic appeal are at the hub of Gay Games culture. Maffesoli (1991: 19, cited in Fraser 1999: 115) points out that:

> Whether trendy exercises in sensory isolation, or various forms of body-building, or jogging, or Eastern techniques of one sort or another, the body

is being constructed as a value ... even in its most private aspects, *the body is being constructed only in order to be seen*; it is theatralized to the highest degree. Within advertising, fashion, dance, the body is adorned only to be made into a spectacle.

In all the Gay Games activities, the body is conspicuously celebrated – even in the church service at the 1998 Games, attention was paid to the body, arguably because lesbian and gay Christian men regretted that the physical aspects of friendship had been left out by the church and wanted, through worship, 'to pay attention to the body and enjoyment' (Andeweg, *Daily Friendship* 2/8/98).

Lesbians, like heterosexuals, define themselves in large part through the body rituals of sport, dress and stance, integrated with other aspects of culture, including language and music. Stylized, frequently muscularized, and erotocized lesbian bodies were the focus of advertising in the official programmes and publicity material (for example, *Friendship Gay Games 1998 Book*; *Souvenir Programme*; *Souvenir Video*). Advertisements for *Out* magazine, Durex, Randstad and *Genre* magazine – sponsors of the Games – portrayed well-muscled and sexualized images of the female body, unquestioningly aimed at the lesbian viewer. 1998 Gay Games marketing attracted masculinized, butch images and a number of women's events reinforced the butch stereotype as an erotic spectacle – for example, powerlifting and bodybuilding which consisted of '25 dykes in bikinis with seriously big muscles' (*Diva* August 1994: 38). Women were often in greater numbers than men in the training gyms, an observation also made at the 1994 Gay Games (Engels 1994). But by no means all representations were butch ones – for example, femme-style lesbians indulged in the glitz and glamour of same-sex figure skating. 'One contestant had sown 20,000 sequins onto her rainbow suit' (*Diva* August 1994: 38).[11] The variety of images of lesbian women reflected the heterogeneous character of the Gay Games lesbian community and the different sexual and stylistic orientations.

A battle over the body emerged during the skating events, when the International Skating Union (ISU) argued that the Gay Games had appropriated their rules without permission and then broken them by sanctioning same-sex couples. It refused to ratify any figure skaters that took part. To protect the futures of skaters who might want to compete in mainstream competitions, the figure skating competition was changed to a demonstration event with no medals or winners. François Marcoux, coach for figure skaters from Montreal, stated, 'The outcome is very sad, people have prepared for four years. All their dreams have gone.' Lesbian skating couples angrily described the ISU's position as a clear case of discrimination (*Gay Games Amsterdam 1998*).

Another battle over the body took place when there were criticisms of the way the Gay Games were being run. A faction within the Gay Games lesbian community argued that there was an obsession with hedonistic sex and not enough emphasis on sport; that sportsmen and women were defined by their sexuality rather than their sporting abilities; and that the extent of narcissism,

of 'kissing and fondling when successful competitors returned to their friends …
went beyond even the norms accepted in professional football and cricket!' The
critics denounced the 'meat-market' ambience of the packed gay clubs, and the
overly fetishistic and bizarre impressions portrayed of gay culture which, they
maintained, masked the serious approach to sport which most Gay Games
athletes value most highly (Engels 1994).

The consistent emphasis on the body at the Gay Games, in all its different
manifestations, is in open opposition to the heterosexual body – providing an
example of Judith Butler's (1993: 228) model of 'queer contestation'. In
common with cross-dressing, drag balls, butch-femme spectacles, gay and
lesbian marches and parades and other gay and lesbian activities that Butler
cites, in the Gay Games 'the visibility of the queer body itself assumes a political
value wherein the theatrical is not *opposed* to the political but rather draws
attention to the increasing politicization *of* theatricality' (Butler 1993: 233). At
the personal level, lesbian identities are constructed, reconstructed and
struggled over at the Gay Games which, according to Butler, is an effect of
performativity – a material process which 'not only takes place *in* time, but is
itself a temporal process' (Butler 1993: 10). Fraser (1999: 114) suggests that
'The act of agency offered by Butler's theory of performativity appears to lend
itself to an accent on the visible queer body.'

Men and women

The Gay Games has gone a long way towards breaking down conventional
gender divisions and facilitating the co-existence of lesbians and gay men.
Nevertheless, as Gloria Stein (1998: 561) points out, 'co-sexual' homosexual
culture does not compensate for

> Real, persistent structural differences in style, ideology, and access to re-
> sources among men and women. This recurring problem suggest[s] that
> while the new queer politics represent[s] the assertion of sexual difference
> which could not be assimilated into feminism, neither could gender be
> completely subsumed under sexuality. Despite their apparent commonali-
> ties, lesbians and gay men [are] often divided along the same lines as het-
> erosexual women and men.

Although at the Gay Games the narrow heterosexual distinctions between
masculinity and femininity are invalidated, there has been a history of male
domination – both in participation and in administration – similar to the male
domination of mainstream sport. Women have been increasingly asssertive over
the years and the Gay Games 1998 organizers worked for equal representation
of female and male participants and recognition of the diversity in lesbian
culture. Publicity material for Amsterdam 1998 declared that the Games were
'by, for, and about both women and men.' And to achieve this a programme
exclusively for women has been put together in addition to the sports and

cultural program that is open to everyone.' In Amsterdam, there was more equal gender representation that in previous Games. It was roughly estimated that 44 per cent of the participants were female.

The bias towards men that exists in many sports varies from country to country. In the United States, there is in general a much greater focus on equal opportunities between men and women than in other countries in the West, and in some teams – for example, Team Philadelphia – there is a very strict adherence to a philosophy of gender equality. In Australia, as well, there is close attention paid to equal representation of women and men. Outside the West there are much smaller numbers of lesbians involved in the Gay Games than gay men, and for that reason a women's outreach programme is being put in place both to examine the multiple reasons why this may be so and to provide funding to increase women's participation.

With some exceptions, men have held the key positions of authority and power – the Federation of Gay Games in particular has been very male-dominated. At the beginning of the year 2000, there were 50 directors of the Federation of Gay Games, only 12 of whom were women. Rosemary Mitchell, Tom Waddell's wife, is one of the exceptional strong female personalities who has shared decision-making power with men and has been respected by them.[12] Paula Pressley, a lesbian activist, was executive director of the 1994 New York Gay Games, and the co-president of Gay Games IV was also a woman – Jay Hill. In October 1999, Sue Emerson from England became the fourth female co-president of the Federation of Gay Games and the first non-American to hold this office. Her appointment signified a shift in the exclusively North American control of the Gay Games.

But inequalities and differences are not just at the levels of participation and administration between men and women. There are ideological and cultural distinctions as well, which separate lesbians from gay men and create divisions among Gay Games lesbians. For example, the exaggerated displays of body and sexuality, discussed above, are perceived to derive mostly from gay men, and opposition to them comes from lesbians and other gay men who want to protect the original spirit of the Gay Games. The specific incentive to address lesbian issues at the Gay Games reflects the wider discourse of sexual politics and lesbian identity. It is a struggle linked to the fashionable, rather male-oriented 'queer' movement in sport. Among some lesbians at the Gay Games there is a preference for the use of the term 'dyke' instead of 'queer', and Gay Games 'sportsdykes' want to distance themselves from narcissistic and vulgar images.[13] One of the athletes explained:

> Sex and sleaze is not how lesbians want to be perceived in the gay world. Many lesbians dissociate themselves from the idea. They are *normal* people who care about their towns, are interested in the environment, and are involved in community politics and so on. … And many lesbians who come here are passionate about sport and that's the most important reason for coming – to be able to take part in sport without the usual obstacles and

homophobic attitudes. ... This portrayal [sex and sleaze] might have been down to the fact that the symbol of Amsterdam is sex – very much aimed at the male market. Amsterdam put out the wrong message (although the organization of the Games and how it was run was fantastic). ... I found the official programme offensive with its images of naked bodies and sex. This is a total myth of what gay people are about. Hopefully Australia have heard this is not the image gay people want to project, and will take note.

This articulation reflects the tension between lesbians who prioritize sport as the reason for going to the Gay Games and lesbians who prioritize sexuality. That the Gay Games are fun, non-divisive, fundamentally non-discriminatory, and accommodating of sportsmen and women of all abilities and backgrounds – in line with Tom Waddell's original vision – is considered by some to be the most important feature of the Gay Games. There is concern that the success of the Games as an athletic festival will be masked if lesbians and gay men indulge in a sexual carnival that attracts stereotyping and places sport in the background.

Conclusion

In spite of the struggles over values and identities, the Gay Games have become a principal heroic symbol of lesbian and gay celebration, a ritual enactment of group identity, representing community, belonging and the translation of 'me' into 'us'. Whereas lesbians are almost invisible in dominant sports culture, in the Gay Games they are thrust into the limelight, and by their sheer numbers make an impact on popular consciousness. Taking part in the Gay Games is a politics of visibility which can become a source of individual and collective power (Fraser 1999: 114). Munt (1998: 23) suggests that the diversity of a lesbian community 'transposes the multiformed single subjectivity into a multicultural community, in its idealization of difference. ... The lesbian community is then presented as the embodiment of the multivalenced heroic agent.' Each lesbian, Munt argues, 'becomes an heroic fragment of the greater struggle'.

Lesbians at the Gay Games temporarily make their sexuality visible and political, in stark contrast to the often general repression and invisibility of sexuality in Western culture. Such an act of visibility is an open challenge to compulsory heterosexuality and is part of a wider movement which is challenging the sexual and cultural norms of Western societies. Altman (1998: 310) claims that 'To join a gay group is an act of affirmation that is often cathartic in its effect. Whatever the possibilities for individual liberation without full social liberation ... the act of involvement with gay liberation brings with it a new perception of the world that is remarkably radicalizing.' At the Gay Games, lesbians and gays from around the world can be open about their sexuality and need not disguise any aspect of their lifestyle – an experience which, it is claimed, 'is usually unequalled in one's lifetime' (*Unity* '94). But, for many lesbians and gay men, attendance at the Gay Games is an act of courage –

for example, for elite athletes from the West who risk being 'outed' in mainstream sport if their presence at the Gay Games is discovered. It was hoped that top international athletes would come out at the 1998 Gay Games in Amsterdam, but this did not happen. One of the organizers explained that

> Elite athletes are still nervous about negative exposure if they come out, and worried that they will lose sponsorship if they do. You can be the sleaziest top international person if you're heterosexual and still get all your endorsements. That's OK. That's allowed. But it's not allowed to be gay. ... It affects huge numbers of sportswomen who are lesbians. ... One woman on the English discus team wanted to participate in the Gay Games, then pulled out at last minute, scared to be recognised.

The fear of recognition is even greater for women from countries where homosexuality is illegal; for them, attendance at the Gay Games is associated with risk and danger. The number of women who come to the Games from such countries is minute and their identities are concealed. Those who choose to take part in the Gay Games calculate that the risks are outweighed by the sense of normality and freedom experienced in this special context, which is welcoming, 'safe' and provides collective support. The Gay Games provides for them a haven, a place for confirmation of sexuality and identity, and a setting for the renewal of personal and group politics. Plans are being made to inaugurate a Gay Winter Games – hopefully to take place in 2004, in Colorado, USA, in order to extend the opportunities to a new community of lesbian and gay sportswomen and sportsmen. At some time in the future it is hoped that the Gay Games will be held in a non-Western country in order to promote global commonality.

However, it could be argued that the campaign for sexual freedom that gay sport represents is taking place in insular, 'ghettoized' spaces and that gay sports liberation is partial and conditional – it has come only with separation and not with integration. All-gay sports teams, clubs, organizations and competitions, however popular, can create barriers between gay and straight people and provide an excuse for mainstream clubs and organizations to do nothing about their own sexual intolerance, homophobia and discrimination. So lesbian sportswomen are faced with a question about segregation or integration, about whether the increase in the numbers of clubs and outlets for gay sport is liberating or restrictive. In their own newspaper, gay people are asking the question: 'Are these clubs a symbol of our strength or will self-imposed segregation from mainstream sport inevitably hamper our progress towards greater acceptance in the heterosexual world?' (*Axiom News* 54, 29/11/99–15/12/99). At the 1998 Gay Games the EGLSF began formulating an appraisal of gay sport, and early in 1999 it produced a report entitled *Building Bridges*, which drew on a survey conducted by Rotterdam University. The report showed that the overwhelming majority of members of regular sports clubs (in Holland) that were surveyed (1600) thought that sport should not be segregated (*Axiom News* 54, 29/11/99–12/12/99) and that separation can increase disadvantages.

The gay rights group Stonewall claims that one in ten women in Western cities (fewer in the country) is a lesbian. Based on Kinsey's research on sexuality, gays are also estimated to be 10 per cent of the population, with higher percentages in some major cities and areas. The 1990 US census estimates that Washington DC's gay population is about 19 per cent of the total (*Advocate* 30 November 1993), and Judy Goldstein from the New York Gay and Lesbian Visitor's Centre estimates the city's gay population to be nearly 25 per cent. Even at 10 per cent, New York's gay and lesbian population would number roughly 80,000 people – larger than the population of many of America's largest cities, including San Francisco. But lesbians and gay men are not visible in representative numbers in mainstream sport and culture, and there is still a tendency for them to remain closeted and ghettoized, clustered in gay urban subcultures. In sport throughout the world, at all levels, there is a relatively tiny number of 'out' lesbians and gay men and, although these estimated figures of numbers of lesbians and gay men in the general population are impossible to confirm, they indicate the huge move that has to be made in order to integrate non-heterosexuals into mainstream sport and culture and to eradicate homophobia and discrimination based on sexual difference.

The organizers of gay sport for the future have a number of important questions to address, several of which were raised at the 1998 Queer Games conference, organized jointly by the Universities of Amsterdam, Nijmegen and Utrecht. Giving the keynote address, Gerd Hekma from the University of Amsterdam, asked, 'Are we "sanitizing homosexuality" by leaving sexuality out of the Gay Games in order to seek acceptance and legitimization by the larger society?' It was argued that part of this process was one of co-option into 'the dominant patriarchal mainstream society'. Further questions were raised:

- Is the cost of such a co-option the abandonment of our queerness, our challenge to conventional paradigms?

- What of challenging the class systems which exclude athletes from poor nations?

- What about adopting the strict IOC rules of 'competition' at the expense of the Gay Games' approach of playfulness?

- What can we do about the difficulties of queer participation in mainstream sports?

- What body type does the Gay Games present as ideal – as queers, we embrace both the athletically disciplined, striving for victory on the field, as well as those who just wish to 'play' in the 'games'?

- Is the tension between seeking affirmation and being queer a necessary engine for social change, reflecting our desire to be accepted as who we are?

(*Daily Friendship* 2/8/99: 15)

Many lesbian sportswomen live constantly with the tension created between their gayness and their desire for integration, which could be eased if they were courageous enough to come out in mainstream sport in greater numbers, and if more heterosexual sportswomen were prepared to stand up and speak out against heterosexism and homophobia.

6 Impaired and disabled

Building on ability

Introduction

Disability is a widespread but neglected feature of social life. It is impossible to arrive at precise global statistics for people with disabilities because of different and contested definitions, political interventions that underestimate figures for the disabled, and because many disabled people are not registered and live 'hidden' lives. Nevertheless, it is estimated that 7 to 10 per cent of the global population – in the region of 500 million people – are disabled (*WHO/68 3/12/99*; Barnes 1998: 65). Even approximate figures reveal that disabled people constitute one of the largest minority groups in the world. However, most readers of this chapter – particularly those who come from the Western world – will live the whole of their lives without having a close relationship with a young disabled friend or colleague, without ever having met a disabled sportsman or woman, and without knowing the name of a single elite disabled athlete who has won a gold medal at the Paralympic Games.

A key reason why there is a tendency for disabled and non-disabled people to live segregated lives is that disability is associated with difference and defect. Jenny Morris (1991: 170) observes that 'to non-disabled people a group of disabled people is a subject of pity, fascinated repulsion and. sometimes, fear', which, Erving Goffman (1963: 5) has argued, is because disabled people possess a stigma – 'an undesired differentness' – which pervades all social interactions and relationships. Goffman describes the visual characteristics of disability, such as blindness, amputation, cerebral palsy and paralysis, as 'physical deformities' and 'abominations of the body', marking out disabled people as abnormal, tainted and peculiar – a 'condition' which positions a person as distinct from those he calls 'normals' (1974: 80). Goffman's concept of stigma touches on the very personal and emotional feelings which, at a psychological level, separate 'the disabled community' from 'the able-bodied majority'. But, in addition, and most important, there are ideological, social and political structures of power that affect the lives of disabled people in fundamental ways and which Goffman's individualized model of stigma fails to take account of. For example, this chapter will touch on the particular relationships of disability to gender and other social divisions that affect disabled people's lived experiences, especially their involvement in sport. The following data about disability in different parts of the world sets the scene for considering different definitions and interpretations, relating them to embodiment and identity, culture and politics and, specifically, to disabled women's participation in sport.

Global data: setting the scene

The idea that disability is a medical problem affecting a small proportion of the population is no longer sustainable. According to WHO statistics for 1999, an estimated 80 per cent of the world's disabled people live in the developing world; the impairments of approximately 10 million people are caused by malnutrition; and in some countries impairments are the result of disease or war. Poverty and disability are closely intertwined, and for most disabled people the struggle for life and the lack of resources and opportunities obliterates any chance of taking part in any form of sport whatsoever, whether for rehabilitation, recreation or elite competition. The following examples point to some of the barriers facing disabled people in countries throughout the developing world:

- In the Third World, the death rate of people with a spinal injury within two years of the injury is as high today as it was in the developed world before the Second World War (Oliver 1996: 114).
- Only one in a hundred disabled people have access to any form of rehabilitation (Oliver 1996: 114).
- 80 per cent of all disabled people live in Asia and the Pacific, but they receive just 2 per cent of the total resources allocated to disabled people (24 million disabled people live in India alone)(*New Internationalist* 298, 1998: 25).
- 20 million people who need wheelchairs are without them (*New Internationalist* 298, 1998: 25).
- The wheelchairs and calipers available in developing countries are often too expensive or unsuitably designed for the people who need them (*ADD Publicity Pamphlet*).

However, Colin Barnes (1998: 65) makes the point that:

> Although there are significantly more disabled people in under-resourced, 'developing' nations of the world, the prevalence of disability is greatest in wealthier 'developed' societies. Moreover, the combination of an ageing population and new medical interventions which prolong life will ensure that the number of disabled people will increase substantially over the next few years.

Taking Europe as an example, there are around 50 million disabled people in the continent as a whole, of whom 6 million or more live in the UK and

5 million in England – in all, around one in nine of the total population (*EFDS* 2000: 7, 13; *Observer* 7/5/95; Barnes 1998: 65). However, many are not registered and the results of critical research indicate that four out of every ten adult women and men in the UK have a 'long term illness or disability' (Barnes 1998: 65). People with disabilities also comprise a significant portion of the German population – 'six million people out of 80 million, or around 7.5 per cent, had some sort of disability' (Hamilton 1997: 237–8). In North America, figures are higher – for example, Canada has a population of around 30 million, with 4.2 million people with disabilities (14 per cent) (Cassidy *et al*. 1995: 52). A survey carried out in the USA in 1986 estimated that '14 per cent (27 million) of all Americans 16 years or older were disabled' (Grimes and French 1989: 24).

In spite of the wealth of the developed world, there is a close link between disability and poverty there also. As Oliver (1996: 115) points out,

> While in the absolute sense, the material conditions of disabled people in the developed world is vastly superior to their third world counterparts, they still experience conditions of life far inferior to the rest of the population. Thus, for example, 60 per cent of disabled people in both Britain and America currently live below the poverty line.

Severe hardships are suffered by huge numbers of disabled people across the world, but it is the women and children, and those who are Black and elderly, that experience some of the worst deprivations of all. Oliver argues that, 'On any indicators, disabled women and black disabled people fare worse than their white, male counterparts' (1996: 115). In developed countries there are larger numbers of disabled women than disabled men – in part because women live longer and the likelihood of disability increases with age. Statistics from Canada indicate that girls and women have lower levels of educational achievement than both able-bodied women and disabled men, that disabled women have fewer opportunities for employment than disabled men and more of them are in low paid work, that women with disabilities face systematic discrimination in the labour market and those that do work are in the lowest paid jobs, and that women suffer from higher levels of poverty than men (Cassidy *et al*. 1995: 52–3). The position for disabled women in developing countries is far worse – they 'face exclusion and discrimination at every turn' (*ADD Publicity Pamphlet*).

Attempts to stop the causes of impairment, to improve living and working conditions, health care, social welfare and education have, understandably, had priority over the creation of a 'disability culture' and, specifically, over development programmes for disability sport. Nevertheless, the initiatives of disabled people themselves have forced a shift in thinking about definitions and discourses of disability and the engagement with, and transformation of, debates around disability politics. A radical shift in disability politics, taking place predominantly in developed countries, has been the recent attention paid to disability culture as a channel for autonomy and identity. Radical developments in disability sport are part of this shift. It is still the case, however, that relatively few disabled women from the developed world participate in sport and, for disabled women from the developing world, the chances of doing so are negligible. From whatever background, disabled sportswomen have to overcome sometimes huge ideological and practical barriers in order to participate.

Medicalizing people with impairments

Disabled activists and theorists (for example, Morris 1991, 1996; Oliver 1991, 1996) distinguish between the impairments they are born with or acquire, and the impact of the wider social context on those impairments which results in disability. In their terms, an impairment is the functional limitation within an individual caused by the lack of all or part of a limb, a defective limb, organism or mechanism of the body – including non-physical impairments which are sensory or intellectual. Disability is concerned with the social – to do with the environmental, cultural, ideological and political barriers which cause people with physical, sensory or intellectual impairments to be restricted in their opportunities and experiences. Crow (1996: 213) argues that 'misrepresentation, social exclusion and discrimination combine to disable people with impairments'. Making a similar point, Morris (1996: 10) alleges that 'Impairment does not *necessarily* create dependency and a poor quality of life; rather it is lack of control over the physical help needed which takes away people's independence.' There may be no biological reason, for example, why a paraplegic woman cannot take part in wheelchair tennis, but ideologies of the body, lack of transport, the high cost of a competition wheelchair, difficulties of gaining access to facilities, joining a club and finding people to practise with and compete against, and lack of information about disability tennis, all militate against participation. The social context, therefore, disables many paraplegic women from playing tennis, and biological impairment does not.

But, because the body is conventionally understood to be central to disability, it is difficult to recognize that disability is a social construct. There is a popular assumption that disability is an inherent, unchanging medical condition resulting in the disabled person's deviation from the 'normal' body. The emphasis on clinical diagnosis, repair of defects, the management of impairment, and rehabilitation, individualizes disability and typically reduces disabled people to a particular medical, physical or intellectual 'condition'. Disabled people's bodies and lives and experiences are thus medicalized and controlled by disability 'professionals' – doctors, physiotherapists, occupational therapists and psychologists – a process which tends to take power away from those who are disabled, to separate them from their cultural, social and economic backgrounds, and to depoliticize disability. Mitchell and Snyder (1997: 19) discuss how Michel Foucault 'turns the medicalized gaze back upon itself' and, in doing so, 'exposes a pleasure at the heart of professional activity that results in the will to produce a pathological subject of diagnosis'.

The 'medical model' of disability underpinned the emergence of sport for people with disabilities. Sir Ludwig Guttmann, one of Germany's leading brain surgeons, fled from his country to England to escape from the Nazis, and in 1944 was asked by the British government to set up the Spinal Injuries Centre at Stoke Mandeville Hospital in Aylesbury. His patients were the paralysed veterans of the Second World War who, in popular thinking, had been dramatically transformed from strong and athletic young men (mostly) and women to 'hopeless cripples'. Guttman pioneered the use of sport in their rehabilitation which, he believed, 'would encourage them to make the most of their remaining physical capabilities, provide much-needed exercise and restore mental equilibrium' (Weisman and Godfrey 1976: xii). From 1944, he introduced a range of sports to his patients, including darts, snooker, punch-ball, skittles, wheelchair polo, basketball, archery, badminton, javelin-throwing and shot putt (Guttmann 1952: 9). Several of the sports were played exclusively by men, but Guttmann valued those sports which were played by both sexes. He specifically mentions basketball because, he said, 'it was also suitable for our ladies, some of whom, like Gwen Sawkins ... became such good shots that, in our mixed teams, they even outmatched the toughest men' (Guttmann 1952: 11). But, although therapy was at the heart of the sports programme at Stoke Mandeville, it spawned a new sports movement, consolidated in 1948 when the First Stoke Mandeville Games took place, which subsequently became an annual event, increasing each time in size and variety. At the first Games there were 26 competitors from two teams competing in two sports – netball (with mixed teams) and archery (with two women out of sixteen competitors). Guttmann had a further and radical vision that 'the Stoke Mandeville Games would achieve world fame as the disabled person's equivalent of the Olympics' (Weisman and Godfrey 1976: xii). The modern global Paralympic movement has fulfilled Guttmann's dream and in recent years it has embodied a shift away from the medicalized model of disability towards a social model of disability. This is in line with a rejection by disabled people of the medicalized concept of 'normality' (able-bodiedness) and a desire to be accepted 'as they are'. Oliver (1996: 37) argues that disabled people's insistence on social change rather than individual change is part of a process of political empowerment, a position underpinned by the social model of disability.

The social model of disability

Oliver (1996: 32) explains the distinction between the medicalized and social models. In the first case, the 'problem' of disability is located 'within the individual' and stems from 'the functional limitations or psychological losses which are assumed to arise from disability'. In contrast, the social model locates the problem of disability squarely 'within society' (1996: 32) – a society that has failed to ensure that the needs of disabled people, as defined by disabled people themselves, are taken properly into account. The social model concerns itself with the social barriers that restrict the activities of people with impairments

(Thomas 1999: 14). As Morris (1996: 11) puts it, 'It means focusing, not on our impairment – what is "wrong" with our bodies and minds – but on what is wrong with the way society is organised.' It shifts the focus from impairment on to disability, using this term to refer to disabling social, environmental and attitudinal barriers rather than lack of ability.

The social model of disability was established by a group of disabled activists in Britain in the late 1960s and has gained in strength since that time (Barnes 1998: 72–6; Thomas 1999: 13). Disabled activists are involved in identity politics – they portray themselves as belonging to a community of disabled people who share a common oppression and are therefore struggling *together* in a common cause to get recognition and equality. The common oppression has been the obvious poverty, poor living standards, high levels of unemployment, and physical barriers which place limits on mobility, access and leisure activities for large numbers of disabled people. Thomas (1999: 17) claims that during the 1970s 'It became possible to see that people with impairments [were] socially excluded in every realm of social life.' The social model reflects the importance of the politicization of disability and the way in which organizations *of* disabled people (those that are run and controlled by disabled people themselves) have been threatening the hegemony of organizations *for* disabled people (those that are run and controlled by non-disabled people on their behalf). A relatively small organization of disabled people, the Union of the Physically Impaired Against Segregation (UPIAS), was formed in the early 1970s and, together with the Disabled Income Group (DIG), produced a document entitled *Fundamental Principles of Disability*, which lays out clearly the position of disabled people who reject the individualized model of disability favoured by organizations *for* the disabled:

> In our view, it is society which disables physically impaired people. Disability is something imposed on top of our impairments by the way we are unnecessarily isolated and excluded from full participation in society. Disabled people are therefore an oppressed group.
>
> (Oliver 1996: 22)

The medical and rehabilitation model of impairment and disability has subsequently been rejected by national and international organizations throughout the world that are controlled by disabled people (for example, the British Council of Organisations of Disabled People [BCODP] and the Disabled Peoples' International [DPI]).

The social model of disability has helped hugely in the struggle for equal rights for disabled people, and has facilitated the evolution of a collective identity and empowerment through activism (Crow 1996: 207). As a result, the struggle of disabled people to live independently in the community, and to be in charge of their own lives and organizations, is gaining in strength throughout the Western world. In the past, sport for disabled men and women has been provided almost exclusively by organizations set up and run by non-disabled personnel – organizations *for* disabled people. The comprehensive politicization of disability sport and the autonomy of disabled sportsmen and women may still be a long way off, but there have been recent shifts which have been influenced by these broader changes in the discourses and politics of disability and, notably, by the social model of disability – for example, initiatives to 'build on ability', to integrate disabled people into mainstream sport, and to involve disabled people in the decision-making structures of disability sport. The following brief history of sport for disabled people illustrates some of the advances that have been made over the years. Before the 1960s, female participation was minimal, and disabled women have had to struggle for equality with men within the disability sport system. For this reason, it has been argued that disabled sportswomen are doubly disadvantaged – because of their disability and because of their gender (DePauw and Gavron 1995: 209).

The early days of disability sport

The Stoke Mandeville Games are usually claimed to mark the origins of organized competitive disability sport, although there are records of events that predate those Games – notably, the World Games for the Deaf, inaugurated in 1924. Women have taken part regularly in these Games, which take place every year, but only in numbers that are approximately a quarter to a third of those of the men (DePauw and Gavron 1995: 209). Other events have been exclusively for men – for example, there was male monopoly of competitive wheelchair basketball which started in 1946 in the USA, until 1968, when it was included in the Paralympic programme. Then, in 1970, it was included for the first time in the International Stoke Mandeville Games (Weisman and Godfrey 1976: xiii–xiv; DePauw and Gavron 1995: 212).

During the Second World War and in the following few years, there was every encouragement given to women at Stoke Mandeville to take part alongside men. The very small numbers of spinally injured women in comparison to the numbers of men was in no way a threat to the overall control and dominance of men. But, once the Stoke Mandeville Games became larger, more organized, more competitive, and internationalized, women became systematically marginalized, a pattern that was reproduced throughout the Western world. The Stoke Mandeville magazine, *The Cord*, provides some evidence of the participation of women, and of attitudes to them, in the annual Games. In 1949 there were six teams in archery and three netball teams and, in all, 37 competitors. Commentaries suggest that *most* of the competitors were men. It was reported that 'Netball, in particular, was very well patronised. It seems to be as good a crowd-drawing game as soccer' (*The Cord* 1949: 23). In the action photographs, it appears that the teams were mixed with a predominance of men, although some group photographs show women all together. The games were described as fast, vigorous and even dangerous:

To a stranger, unfamiliar with the peculiar ways of paraplegics, the sight of ten wheeled chairs in hurtling pursuit of a small ball must seem odd, if not a little frightening. Even to those hardened to the hazards of netball, the sight and sound of two chairs meeting in full flight – with seemingly little catastrophe to the occupants – is always a startling experience ... But a game of netball on wheels can be enormously exciting, and the games we saw at Stoke certainly were.

(*The Cord* 1950: 19)

In 1950, javelin-throwing was introduced into the programme of events, with some female athletes (*The Cord* 1950: 23), and there was an increase in the overall numbers of competitors – 14 teams and a total of 60 competitors. One year later, in 1951, the numbers of competitors had risen to 126 and there were six sports, with demonstration events in Indian club-swinging, keep fit and table tennis.

In 1952 Guttmann organized the first international competition for wheel-chair athletes – a meeting between Britain and the Netherlands. There were 15 teams and 130 competitors in archery alone and, one year later, in 1953 there were six nations competing. By 1956 there were 21. The introduction of international competition led to a separation of the National Stoke Mandeville Games and the International Games which, once established, were held every four years and in different host countries. Although in small numbers, women were members of many of the teams that travelled to and from different countries to take part in international wheelchair events. By the mid-1950s, sport had become a common form of rehabilitation for men and women with spinal injuries, and participation in a range of different activities was considered to be medically beneficial. Women who took part in the Stoke Mandeville Games often competed in more than one sport – for example, in 1953 it was reported that 'Miss Jean Richon from France, a veteran from World War II, obviously enjoyed the fun. She took part in archery, swimming and club swinging' (Dodgson 1953: 11). The Games were considered to be an extension of treatment. Competitors were first and foremost patients for whom, it was believed, sport provided physical, psychological and social rehabilitation (*Report of the 1960 International Stoke Mandeville Games for the Paralyzed*). Their sporting performances, though praised and celebrated, were related to their identities as *disabled* people – a reminder of the essential *difference* between disabled sportsmen and women and their able-bodied counterparts. The insular context in which events took place was another symbol of difference. It is not in question that disabled sportsmen and women enjoyed taking part in the Games and were enriched by the experience – however, it was not the sporting *abilities* of the athletes that was the *raison d'être* of competition, but rather it was their *disabilities* that created a sportsworld specifically for them – separate, spatially and symbolically, from the 'real' world of sport outside. Wheelchair sport was characterized not only as different, and separate, but also as inferior. Forty years later, DePauw and Gavron (1995: 10) are still able to claim that 'Segregated events and competitions have been somewhat acceptable but are still viewed as being of less value than sport competitions for able-bodied individuals'.

The internationalization of the Stoke Mandeville Games set a pattern for the future – the Games became more and more competitive, with a greater focus on results and records, more in line with mainstream sport. All individual and team events were gender-specific with only roughly a quarter of the number of women, compared to men, taking part. There was a wide range of sports and events open to men; women had to struggle to get new events on to their programme. In 1956, for example, foil-fencing was on the women's programme for the first time, some years after it had been on the men's programme. From the 1950s, regular training sessions and increasing numbers of competitors inevitably led to an increase in skill and performance levels. The organizers of the Games reported that 'We have made progress ... with the standard of our games, and, as with the Olympic Games, we are striving to improve the skill of our sportsmen and women and break as many records as we can' (Scruton 1956: 20). 1957 marked another increase in the size of the International Stoke Mandeville Games, with 360 competitors from 24 countries (Scruton 1957: 7), and 1959 was a milestone year when track races were put on the programme for the first time. However, there were still very few women participants, and it was quite usual for individual athletes to take part in different sports and events. For example, the 'Golden Girl' of the Irish team at the 1960 International Stoke Mandeville Games was Mrs Joan Horan. Although she was the member of the national team with the most serious impairments, 'she won two gold medals – one in the St Nicolas round of the Archery, and one for the 'Crawl' in the swimming' (Close 1960: 55–6). Participation in different sports became less commonplace as the numbers of women taking part increased and standards of performance rose. Every year at the National Stoke Mandeville Games, the British team for international events was selected – competition was stiff and there were many disappointed athletes who failed to be picked. There were also consistently fewer women than men picked for the national team – for example, in 1968 there were 51 male and 22 female athletes selected to go to the International Stoke Mandeville Games in Israel the following year.

The Stoke Mandeville Games initially served athletes with spinal cord injuries, then expanded in 1976 to include other physical impairments, enabling all wheelchair-users to take part. The International Stoke Mandeville Wheelchair Sports Federation (ISMWSF) became the international governing body of wheelchair sport. It now sanctions all international competitions for those who use wheelchairs (DePauw and Gavron 1995: 29). Because the majority of people with spinal cord injuries are male – because men are the main victims of war and industrial disasters – the expansion of sporting opportunities to other wheelchair-users was a move towards equalizing opportunities for women. ISMWSF now holds annual World Wheelchair Games in 12 sports, and female participants comprise approximately one third of the total number.

Following the establishment and success of wheelchair sport competitions at national and international levels, there was growing interest in sport provision for people with different impairments. The term 'disability' has been used synonymously with impairment and a number of 'disability-specific' national and international sport organizations were set up and competition proliferated throughout the West. The International Sports Organization for the Disabled (ISOD) was established in Paris in 1964 to cater for those with disabilities other than spinal cord injuries and continues today to represent amputee, *les autres* and dwarf athletes in international competition (DePauw and Gavron 1995: 30). In 1968, the Special Olympics (an international programme of year-round sports training and competition), catering for children and adults with a learning disability, was established. The impetus for a grand multi-disability international competition, equivalent to the Olympics, came from the ISMWSF. Originally known as the Olympics for the Disabled, and renamed the Paralympic Games, the first meeting took place in Rome in 1960. Initially, the Paralympics excluded several groups of disabled athletes, but from 1972 there was gradual integration of some of the excluded groups until, in 1988, at the Seoul Paralympics, the participation of all physically disabled groups was ratified – spinal injured; amputees; blind; and athletes with cerebral palsy. In 1996, at the Atlanta Paralympics, athletes with intellectual impairments were also included (Sainsbury 1998: 1). In 1989 the International Paralympic Committee (IPC – an updated version of the previous governing body for Paralympic sport) was established with responsibility for the quadrennial Paralympics and other major competitions and for co-ordination of international sport for persons with disabilities (DePauw and Gavron 1995: 33–6). The huge growth and success of the Paralympic Games will be reflected in the Sydney 2000 Paralympics, when 125 countries will be represented by over 4000 athletes. In all, there is now a plethora of national, regional and international organizations for different sports and different disabilities across the world.

Advances and inequalities

None of these developments has been insulated from broader political discourses of disability and inequality. There have been two major equality perspectives – the first proposes that disabled people should have equal opportunities with non-disabled people; the second is concerned with equal opportunities between different groups of disabled people. Equality initiatives fit with the social model of disability, exposing first the exclusion faced by disabled people through the failure of mainstream sport to cater for them and, second, the additional discrimination faced by particular groups of disabled people. Those running the organizations (mainly White, middle-class, able-bodied men) have responded in certain respects to the changing political climate, focusing on social features of disability and to the voices of disabled sportsmen and women who want a controlling position in future developments. The hosting, since 1988, of the Paralympics in the same city as the mainstream Olympics, and the requirement that bids for the Olympic Games must include plans for the Paralympics, have raised the visibility and social significance of disability sport. Changes in the classification system used in competition, which has shifted from a disability-specific system to one based on functional ability, is also an important symbol that the bodies of disabled people are being redefined as effective rather than defective. Perhaps most significant is the integration of some disability events into popular mainstream competitions – for example, demonstration wheelchair races at the Olympic Games and full participation of disabled athletes for the first time at the Commonwealth Games to be held in Manchester, England, in 2002. The mixing of disabled sportsmen and women is a conspicuous way to displace the old medicalized images of disability, inferiority and separateness, and to replace them with demonstrations of skill, supreme athleticism and 'normality'. Recent developments in disabled sports are challenging established ideologies and redefining the terms of debates.

However, there continues at all levels to be unequal gender participation. In previous years, in certain contexts, discrimination against women was overt and harsh. In the USA, for example, women in wheelchair basketball were prohibited by the all-male and very chauvinist National Wheelchair Basketball Association (NWBA) from participating in official competitions until 1974. A year later, the first women's national tournament was held (DePauw and Gavron 1995: 212). However, during the last 20 years or so, disabled women in sport have made considerable advances. It is estimated that approximately one third of the athletes in international competitions are women but, although they are impossible to calculate accurately, the global figures for women's grassroots participation – in recreative and competitive sport – are much, much lower. Even although in some countries in the West attention has been paid to gender inequalities, there is still a marked gap between overall male and female participation. Aware of the inequalities between different groups, some organizations have created schemes to redress the imbalances. Here are two examples: one at international level, one at national level. The first example relates to Recreational Sports Development and Stimulation Disabled International (RESPO DS-DI), which has observed that those who take part in competitive sport are, in general, those who are less severely impaired and disabled. They cater, therefore, specifically for the recreational needs of individuals with severe and multiple impairments and disabilities, and particularly those in developing countries, many of whom are women (DePauw and Gavron 1995: 33). The second example is the English Federation of Disability Sport (EFDS), founded in 1998. EFDS is an umbrella body for disability sport throughout England, which has pledged to provide a new sports equity project for women and girls, Black and ethnic minorities, and those with profound and multiple disabilities – three groups that have been identified as having severe problems and low participation rates (EFDS 2000).

The reasons why fewer women than men participate in disability sport are very complex. They are linked to social divisions and to social barriers. They are also linked to ideas about difference, experience, identity and the body. The functions and malfunctions of the body influence the feelings and experiences of both disabled and non-disabled people but, as Porter (1997: xiii) argues, 'The disabled body presents a threat to the very idea of the body, the body in its pure empty form. It is this idea that informs the prevailing normativities of the body.'

Although women share with men many of the effects of impairment and disability which are circumscribed by 'the prevailing normativities of the body', they can experience them and be affected by them in very different ways.

Embodiment, sport and gender

Benson (1997: 123) points out that 'The body is ... the *medium* through which messages about identity are transmitted', and Dutton (1995: 11) explains further that:

> The body is the focal point of our individual identity, in that we not only *have* but in a sense *are* our bodies: however distinct the body may be conceptually from the 'self' which experiences it and knows it, that which experiences and knows it is by its nature an *embodied* self, a self whose social identity and whose location in time and space are contained and defined by their individual embodiment.

Embodiment has a poignancy when applied to disabled people because they are looked upon, identified, judged and represented primarily through their bodies, which are perceived in popular consciousness to be imperfect, incomplete and inadequate. Because the lack of physical impairment is treated as the norm, the impaired body immediately and conspicuously signifies difference and *ab*normality. Thus the disabled body is tied to self and identity in a most intense and evocative way. Ironically, however, theories of the body, like social theories and feminist theories, have in the main ignored the disabled body or given it inadequate treatment (Porter 1997: xiv).

Disabled people live with the tension between the imperfect body and the perfect body. The emphasis in Western societies is on mastery and perfection and the disabled body represents a trangression of this ideal. Disabled people are aware of the significance of visibility and the heightened attention placed on their bodies. There is huge pressure on them to appear as able-bodied as possible, to mask whenever possible the extent of their impairments. Seymour (1989: 14) gives a personal account:

> I develop an awareness of my body by my experience of living in my body and by means of various senses, which inform me about my own body. But the body in which I live is visible to others, it is the object of social attention. I learn about my body from the impressions I see my body make on other people. These interactions with others provide critical visual data for my self-knowledge.

But awareness of living in one's impaired body is a gendered experience. Men who have physical, sensory and intellectual impairments face a threat to their masculinity. The 'complete' and strong, aggressive, muscular body is the most tangible sign of maleness (Dutton 1995). And sight, hearing, physical and mental toughness – all associated with male bonding and forms of masculinizing culture, such as sport – also facilitate hegemonic masculinity (Connell 1995: 54; Messner 1992: 61–84). Impairment, therefore, signifies a weakening of masculine traits. Connell (1995: 54) explains that 'The constitution of masculinity through bodily performance means that gender is vulnerable when the performance cannot be sustained – for instance as a result of physical disability.' Since sport, *par excellence*, embodies hegemonic masculinity, it is popular with disabled men as a context for using their impaired bodies as a project for redefining and reclaiming their sense of maleness and of self (Sparkes and Smith 1999: 77). Writing about paraplegics, Seymour explains the different significance that sport has to men and women:

> A vital area remains by which the paraplegic man may reconstitute his masculinity. Through energetic attention to body-building, basketball, archery and many other physical activities that involve the strong muscular work of the upper trunk, shoulder and arm muscles, the paralysed man may create powerful physical definition of masculinity, which may override the other domains in which his masculinity is threatened. ... Paraplegic women, like paraplegic men, gain important functional advantages from exercise, body-building and wheelchair athletics. But such activities do not have the same powerful effect for women as they do for men since such bodily attributes are associated with masculinity and are considered to be contradictory aspects of femininity.
>
> (Seymour 1989: 114)

The sporting body represents a pivotal form of 'physical capital' for disabled men, more so than for disabled women. The concept of physical capital comes from Pierre Bourdieu's (1984) proposal that the body is a possessor of power, which exhibits value in different social fields. He recognizes that embodiment is not neutral, but is a bearer of symbolic value, integral to the maintenance of social inequalities. Highly developed muscularity has high symbolic value and is assigned a high level of physical capital. There is a clear diminution of physical capital for impaired men because they have less than perfect, strong and muscular bodies. However, disabled men train and build strength in the functioning parts of their bodies in order to create an image of the perfectible body and therefore to revitalize a feeling of masculinity. In this way, and in common with able-bodied men, disabled men are subject to the influences of representations of hegemonic masculinity. Disabled women, too, are influenced by dominant images of gender and, although in small numbers they may choose to take part in sport and become outstanding athletes who hone their bodies to perfection, many disabled women choose not to participate in sport because, in common with many able-bodied women, they are influenced more by commodified anti-athletic stereotypes of femininity.

The insistent focus on the body in commodity culture exaggerates the anxieties that disabled women feel about being 'normal' and 'feminine'. In Western societies, there is a particularly high value placed on youthfulness and the aesthetics of physical perfection and slenderness (Bordo 1990), and the disabled female body can easily become a source of embarrassment. Like able-bodied women, many disabled women have very low self-esteem and hatred of their own bodies and self-images. They experience a very personal fear of body display, which keeps them out of sport. Anna, a thalidomide victim, explains her resistance to a friend's repeated suggestion that she should join a gym:

> I really wanted to go – inside, I was dying to be physical, to have a go at 'pumping iron'. My mate kept telling me how good it was … she said she'd stick with me 'til I got used to it and she said no-one would look at me or take any notice, they were all nice and friendly people. … And I'm not badly disabled like some people, but at that time I just couldn't say yes. … I was too ashamed. It was really awful, I was so *ashamed* of my body. … It was the same thing with swimming. I just couldn't bear the thought of people looking at me. I felt *really* vulnerable.

Anna also revealed how she compared the look of her body to the idealized look of the commodified, glamorized, ultra-feminine image of flawlessness. She revealed how her body was central to her feelings of oppression. Morris (1991) makes the following observations about the beautiful/impaired body dichotomy:

> To be a disabled woman is to fail to measure up to the definition of femininity as pretty passivity. … To be considered beautiful is to give value to the absence of physical 'impairment'. … Just as beauty – and goodness – are defined by the absence of disability, so ugliness – and evil – are defined by its presence.
>
> (1991: 92, 93)

Many disabled women experience a very real sense of alienation from their bodies because of the constant reminders through popular body imagery of what they are not. Begum (1992: 77) explains that

> If a woman loses respect for her own body, and internalizes the negative messages that hang the label 'defective and undesirable' around her neck, then it is not surprising that her body becomes a source of pain, embarrassment and guilt. This can subsequently lead her to believing that her body is the enemy and she has no control over it. … Body-image has a profound impact on the way in which we perceive ourselves. A positive body-image can help to build confidence and promote self-esteem, and a negative image can affirm feelings of inferiority, worthlessness and inadequacies.

Beth, a paraplegic basketball player, rather angrily explains that incorrect assumptions are made about body imperfections and differences between disabled and non-disabled women:

> Look, able-bodied women get inhibited by all the ideas of body perfection the same as disabled women do. You know, all the beautiful. slim, 'perfect' bodies – we see them all the time – they're all around us, everywhere, you just can't escape. But then, think about it, *you're* [pointing at me] so-called 'able-bodied', but have *you* got a perfect body? Do you know *any* able-bodied women who've got perfect bodies? We've *all* got imperfect bodies – it's just more obvious for disabled women. The contrast between perfection and imperfection is more obvious.

Ironically, the focus on the perfect female body in modern society, and the increased interest in sport and fitness regimes among young non-disabled women, tends to deter many disabled women from joining in. The ideology of normality, at its most extreme characterized as 'body fascism', is a powerful form of social control – sucking able-bodied women into exercise and fitness regimes – but keeping disabled women out. But there are contradictions. Some disabled women can, and do, in common with able-bodied women, reshape and redefine their bodies through exercise regimes, cosmetic surgery, diets, drugs, adornments and prostheses. They actively construct their own bodies and the meanings attached to them through a process of discipline and self-surveillance (Foucault 1980b). Rehabilitative and corrective surgery may be performed on disabled women 'under the guise of indispensible medical treatment' but, as Meekosha (1998: 177) points out, the real purpose is 'to normalize the less than perfect body – to make it more attractive and pleasing, to fit dominant conceptions of attractiveness and desirability'.

Pride in the body

The absence of positive images of disabled women in popular magazines, such as fitness and fashion magazines, consolidates the stigma and ghettoization of disability. Radical, alternative imagery of disability was produced by the award-winning British fashion designer, Alexander McQueen. As guest editor of the September 1998 issue of the style magazine, *Dazed and Confused*, he got leading designers to dress disabled models, to show, he said, that 'beauty comes from within' and to represent disabled people as strong and proud of their disabilities. Aimee Mullins, a double amputee, was the leading model. She wore two specially designed prosthetic legs made from varnished wood. Aimee is also a disabled athlete – holding world records for the 100-metre and 200-metre sprint and the long jump. She says, 'I want to be seen as beautiful because of my disability, not in spite of it' (Quinn, *Guardian* 28/9/98).

There is, however, controversy about such initiatives. On the one hand, they are seen as part of a more general drive, led by disabled people themselves, to create positive images of disability and to stop the sidelining and marginalization of disabled people. On the other hand, there is criticism that disabled women are being commodified and sexualized in the same way as able-bodied women and that only 'better-looking' disabled women are used as models – a process which characterizes most disabled women, and expecially those with acute disabilities, as the 'real others' and divides them from those who can be represented as having characteristics closer to 'normal'. A further complexity is that some disabled women reject both the stigmatized meanings *and* the commodified meanings assigned to disability. I am referring here to those women who take pride in their impaired bodies and in their physicality and who take part in sport because they love sport. A Paralympic swimmer explained that she wants to feel physically powerful and at home with her body and in charge of her body. Her desires, she says, are the same as those of an able-bodied swimmer. In an investigation about sport and disability, Seymour (1989: 120) gives the following account of the importance of playing sport to a disabled woman:

> Pam was a highly competitive sportswoman before her accident (when she became a paraplegic). She was always very conscious of her figure, and took plenty of exercise. Being healthy for Pam was having the energy to play the sport, engage in many extra activities, as well as looking after her house and three young children. Pam conceives of herself now as very healthy. 'I lead a very stimulating life. My family have never accepted that there is anything I can't do. The only thing they will accept is that I can't go up steps.' She considered that it took at least three years before she was 'confident of myself and my ability to understand what I was – this is a matter of experience.' Pam says she is much more conscious of her body now. She watches what she eats and is constantly alert to areas of her body she can't feel.

These examples illustrate ways in which disabled people actively perform in and through the body and are active agents in the construction of body identity. The growth of disability sport reflects this trend. In recent years, both agency and identity have been mediated by radical technological innovations (Mitchell and Snyder 1997: 7), enabling women to be more active and to take part in sports and events that they could not have dreamed of participating in even some 20 years or so ago.

Agency, technology and identity

One of the first innovations to transform the lives of disabled people was the wheelchair. New wheelchair designs and technologies have conferred on disabled people an important sense of liberation and independence, an extension to the body which becomes a personal aspect of identity and self:

People like myself, who rely upon their wheelchair for mobility and independence, see it as a piece of liberating equipment. I have a certain fondness for my own little black number and feel anxious whenever it is out of my reach, panicky if it is out of my sight. I don't always like the sight of myself in it – what woman would when we live in a society whose idea of female beauty is the slim, taut, well-muscled body, dressed in skin tight skirts with stiletto heels? But I like myself well enough and enjoy wearing clothes, shoes and odd bits of adornment to suit my present shape and needs.

(Keith 1996: 76)

For wheelchair athletes, the chair signifies a body transformation, a new realm of the possible, a personal piece of technology which transfers a person into a world of speed, skill and physical perfection. Racing chairs are specially constructed so that they are aerodynamically efficient. Deborah, a Paralympian athlete, explained that 'It fits like a glove – rather like an outer layer of skin. I have to be careful what I eat, so that I can still fit into it! But it's like it's my body, "we" move together; it's like the chair and me are one.' The wheelchair, normally a symbol of weakness, of dependency, of neediness, when used for track races is transformed into a symbol of power, speed and muscularity.

The apparatuses of disability are becoming more and more sophisticated and have made it increasingly possible for disabled people to be integrated into mainstream work and social life, including sports. There are increasing numbers of performance-enhancing agents – drugs, microchip computer technologies, modern surgical techniques, state-of-the-art wheelchairs, heart pacemakers, reconstructed joints, and prostheses, etc. which are available to more and more people in the developed world and through which disabled bodies have effectively been reinvented. It is claimed that approximately 10 per cent of the US population are cyborgs in the technical sense (Mitchell and Snyder 1997: 8). The advances in technology that are applied to sport have made it possible for disabled women to perform in previously unimagined ways. Technology has provided new bodily possibilities, transforming the feel and potential of physical and psychic experiences. In elite disability sport, there are increasing numbers of athletes with mechanical, artificially designed bodies creating new sporting potential. Technology has the capacity to 'normalize' the disabled body, to produce 'supersportsmen' and 'supersportswomen'. For example, amputee athletes with carbon-fibre, spring-loaded flex-foot prostheses can already run within points of a second as fast as world-class able-bodied sprinters. Those who have the most sophisticated aids are those from the West, and they are the athletes who have the greatest chance of winning medals and breaking records. As a result, the Paralympics risk becoming a show of radical technology, rather than a show of athleticism, leaving behind those from the developing world without performance-enhancing technology at their disposal.

The different attitudes to the disabled body discussed here – attitudes about disability sport and masculinity; the alienation of disabled women from their own bodies; the commodification of the female disabled body; and the technological manipulation of the disabled body – validate the social model of disability. The disabled body is seen to be a social construct that changes according to social conditions, resources, ideas and place. The physical experience of the body is mediated by social attitudes; it is not separated from the rest of society, but is a 'lived-in' body residing in and responding to an ableist culture. But within the ableist culture, the opposition between ability and disability has become increasingly problematic since new technological developments have made possible the reshaping, remaking and empowering of actual, material bodies.

Feminism and disability

In the USA in 1989, a report resulting from extensive research, *Women and Disability Awareness Project*, was published. It concluded that

> Women with disabilities face double discrimination – discrimination based on gender and discrimination based on disability. Women who are colored face yet a third type of discrimination, as do lesbians who are disabled. The limited available statistics suggest that economically, socially, and pyschologically, women with disabilities fare worse than women who are nondisabled or men who are disabled.
>
> (Sherrill 1993: 52–3)

The *Women and Disability Awareness Project* signals the complexities of both the theory and politics of disabled women. Disabled women are not a homogeneous group – different types of disability, together with social divisions such as class, race and sexuality, create divisions and affect experience. Nevertheless, Begum (1992: 70) maintains that 'it is essential that we use our common experiences to develop a political analysis which creates bonds and forges positive strengths'. Begum's position is particularly important because mainstream feminism has not acted as an authentic representative of disabled women. Morris (1993: 58) expresses alienation and anger because of the 'failure of feminism to integrate the concerns of disabled women into its theory, methodology, research and politics'. She describes two characteristics of feminism:

> firstly, the way in which disability is generally invisible in terms of feminism's agenda; secondly, the way in which, when disability *is* a subject for research by feminists, the researchers fail to take on the subjective reality of disabled people, instead objectifying us so that the research is alienated from our experience.

Morris (1996: 2) wants to find a way of making the experiences of disabled women visible and 'sharing them with each other and with non-disabled people, in a way that – while drawing attention to the difficulties in our lives –

does not undermine our wish to assert our self-worth'. Thomas (1999: 104–20), however, is concerned about the lack of qualification of 'we' in the writing of Morris, which tends to universalize disabled women, treating them as a homogeneous group. Thomas (1999: 120) argues that disabled people are marginalized in other ways as well as because of their disabilities – 'because they are women, black, gay, older and so on'. She goes on to explain that these other social characteristics 'make up other elements of self-identities, but they do not exist in separate psychic departments and so cannot be seen as outside, or nothing to do with, disability politics. On the contrary,' she argues, 'they suffuse and enrich disability politics.' The challenge for disability feminism is to find ways to support the specific position of disabled women, as well as acknowledging and catering for differences and complexities. Many disabled women are struggling to have their needs recognized and catered for and one of their most important political demands is to live *within* the community (Morris 1991: 153), to live in a situation without prejudice and discrimination, and to have the necessary practical support which would enable them to live a full life and to join in different cultural activities, such as sport. But, as Morris (1991: 1) points out:

> Like other political movements, the disability movement, both in Britain and throughout the world, has tended to be dominated by men as both theoreticians and holders of important organisational posts. Both the movement and the development of a theory of disability have been the poorer for this as there has been an accompanying tendency to avoid confronting the personal experience of disability.

Morris (1991: 9), therefore, brings 'the perspective of feminism to an analysis of the experience of disability'. In common with other disabled feminists like Carol Thomas (1999) and Begum (1992), Morris uses the principle of making the personal political as her primary analytical tool. She places personal experiences at the centre of an understanding of women and disability, incorporating, importantly, the materiality of the human body. Her position is as follows:

> The domination by men of the disability movement has been associated with an avoidance of recognising feelings about being disabled. A feminist perspective on disability must focus, not just on the socio-economic and ideological dimensions of our oppression, but also on what it feels like to be unable to walk, to be in pain, to be incontinent, to have fits, to be unable to converse, to be blind or deaf, to have an intellectual ability which is much below average.
>
> (1991: 70)

Crow (1996: 209) also reproaches the social model of disability for denying bodily experience and focusing exclusively on the social and economic barriers.

She agrees with Morris (1991: 181) that the subjective reality of impairment is an important component of everyday life, that to experience disability is to experience the frailty of the human body, and that impairment means that bodily experiences *can* be unpleasant or difficult. Disability feminism, then, incorporates the interactions between gender and disability, combines the personal with the social, and sets the sense of the body against institutional, cultural and political structures.

But disability feminism has paid little (or no) attention to sport and sport feminists have paid little attention to disability. So, ironically, although the body is pivotal to both sport and disability, there has been no articulated feminism of disability sport. The rest of the chapter reviews examples of disabled women in sport by referring to some of the issues discussed above. In line with the perspective of disability feminism, the focus is on the relationship between personal experience and social context which signals some possibilities for a disability sport feminism.

Barriers to participation

In many respects disability sport has replicated the gender inequalities that have been inherent in modern sport since its inception in the nineteenth century (Hargreaves 1994). It is heavily male-dominated, with fewer female than male participants and fewer women than men in the 'corridors of power'. In the USA, for example, although there are more disabled women than disabled men in the population as a whole, there are significantly fewer women than men who participate in organized sports (Grimes and French 1989: 24). The 1980 US census showed that there were more men who were permanently disabled through accidents, and more women who had chronic disabling conditions, which may in part account for the discrepancy (Grimes and French 1989: 24). It is likely, however, that the more significant reasons are linked to ideologies of the body and gendered structures of power discussed earlier in this chapter.

There is very little available evidence about disabled women's childhood experiences of sport, but the following life histories suggest that negative attitudes might well be established early on. For example, Teresa, a Canadian Paralympic swimmer, experienced problems when she was a pupil at a mainstream school. She had feelings of being disabled that came – not from her impairment – but from the attitudes of able-bodied people around her. She has memories of physical education classes and horse-riding lessons, of isolation from the able-bodied majority, and of a sense of alienation from her own body:

> I was born with cerebral palsy. Physiotherapy was an important part, and was integrated into everyday life and play. Starting at about age ten, I began to have some concept of the fact that I had a disability. This started I suppose with teasing in the school yard. ... In Grade 7 (when I was about twelve) I had a new phys ed teacher who wasn't sure how to adapt activities for me, and I ... felt very uncomfortable. The result was that I ended up

isolated from the rest of the class, discouraged. By the time I learned how to serve in, say, badminton, everyone else was playing games; I didn't even know the rules. I 'dropped out' in the middle of Grade 8, with a medical exemption (PE was mandatory until Grade 9) on the advice of my English teacher. About Grade 6 I became involved with a community horseback riding program. The activity was great from a physical therapy point of view, but I became increasingly uncomfortable with some of the attitudes that I encountered, that I could never quite concretely identify. Now, with hindsight, I would characterize them as being patronizing. At this particular stable, at this particular time, there was an assumption that all people with physical disabilities were infantile/also mentally retarded; there was also a self-congratulatory air of good works done for the poor disabled kids.

The able-bodied teachers and helpers (the disability professionals), although almost certainly not intentionally patronizing, by personalizing the medicalized ideologies of defect and difference which are institutionalized in welfare organizations (schools and community programmes, for example), make people with impairments feel regulated and demeaned. The effects can be more damaging for girls and young women if gender discrimination occurs at the same time. Grimes and French (1989: 24–5) describe the joint effect of disability and gender discrimination when disabled girls are given less encouragement than boys to take part in sport at school. They argue further that 'Disabled women and girls often face enormous emotional and psychological problems. Issues of low self-esteem, inexperience with sport, fear of success and failure, which are already documented for able-bodied women, are even greater problems for disabled females' (Grimes and French 1989: 26).

In London, England, a young female volleyball player – Coral – talks about her experiences at a special school for the disabled where sport was much more a feature of boys' culture than girls' culture:

> I was born with cerebral palsy and then I fractured my back falling off a climbing frame in an adventure playground. My mum couldn't cope, so I had to go to a special school. … We had good facilities and the staff en-couraged the boys more than the girls. I think they excused themselves because most of the girls didn't want to do sport. They were more interested in 'girly' talk and all that – and, anyway, the boys were really aggressive – and football got the most attention. I didn't want to stick my neck out and be different and get stick. … Since I've left school I've found it much easier to join in – playing with adults is much more welcoming and more re-warding. It's true that the men still get more opportunities, but the atmos-phere is not so obviously anti-female.

Teresa and Coral were both deterred from participating in sport at school. Both of them later became attracted to sport through other channels and became elite sportswomen. They are exceptional. For the majority, disability and gender are structures of power that can limit the choices and outlooks of young disabled girls in relation to their participation in sport. The pattern of non-participation established in childhood is likely to be continued into adult life.

The English Federation of Disability Sport (EFDS), referred to earlier, has noted that 'inequality in other aspects of life is reflected in disability sport'. In their report, *Sport for Disabled People in England: Four Year Development Plan 2000–2004*, they point out that the experience of EFDS's member organizations is that disabled women and people from Black and ethnic minorities 'are currently almost entirely absent from their programmes and to date no real evidence is available as to the reasons why'. The report goes on to declare that 'The EFDS must research and address the reasons that lead to an absence of ethnic minorities and a gender imbalance in disability sport' (EFDS 2000: 56). EFDS has set itself a task to address equity issues for disabled people in English sport and to be able to advise and give direct support to mainstream sports providers (2000: 16). It plans, therefore, in the year 2000, to 'investigate the additional barriers for girls, women and black and ethnic minorities [by] examining demographic, geographic, social and cultural issues' (2000: 18).

The absence of research makes it difficult to give an accurate picture of the specific reasons why so few disabled women participate in sport and the specific difficulties they face if they do participate. The interviews that I have carried out confirm that some of the biggest problems relate to ignorance about resources, poverty, the high cost of equipment, lack of adequate transport, inaccessible facilities, a need for all-women sessions, and the desire for caring helpers. But many women are simply not interested in sport in the first place. Belinda, a wheelchair sportswoman, explained to me that 'Disabled girls don't have positive experiences at school and they don't see the value of leisure and sport. They see sport as an exclusive club, tightly organized, not welcoming, very male-oriented. They don't see the wider benefits.'

Belinda also introduced into the discussion a most important dimension of disability sport – the political dimension – which is normally omitted from analyses:

> Sport is separated from disability politics. Disabled sportswomen are not connected with politics and disabled organisations are not interested in sport – the primary issues are jobs, health, housing, etc. So there is no support from disability organisations – I mean those run by disabled people who are tuned in to the political debates about disability and are making demands about equality in other areas. ... We need to politicize sport – we're doing it in other areas, like the arts and theatre, but sport tends to be run by non-disabled people along the lines of non-disabled sport. And that's probably not appropriate for most disabled people – and certainly not for most disabled women.

The politicization of disability sport would address values and ethics. Disability sport would also benefit from a feminist political presence, which it lacks at present. This would bring into the open its gendered character and the fact that the majority of people in decision-making positions of power are men. Although there is a nucleus of disabled women who are keen sportswomen and have reached elite level, most disabled women prefer non-competitive recreational activities rather than competitive sport. The achievement-oriented approach, modelled on mainstream competitive sport, is favoured by many disabled men. These preferences are confirmed in a cross-cultural study carried out in the USA, Great Britain and Japan, which showed that disabled men are more likely to enter sport for reasons of achievement and status whereas women are motivated more by friendship (Fung 1992). Following interviews with 12 Australian women suffering from paralysis, Seymour (1989: 99) writes that:

> Although several of the women played sports such as tennis, netball and softball, many of them had strong commitments to less organised, more individualised activities such as cycling, sailing, dancing, walking, water-skiing, surfing and canoeing, Rosemary, who had been paralysed since birth, pushes her wheelchair around the block several times each day for exercise, and her consuming passion in life is that of football spectator. The importance of general physical *capabilities* [author's emphasis] was often expressed by even the most severely paralysed women.

Motivation and participation

In research carried out over ten years ago concerning the physical activity patterns of physically disabled women in Canada, the major reasons that disabled women gave for being physically active were to improve fitness (85 per cent), to feel better (77 per cent), to challenge abilities (68 per cent), to improve flexibility (63 per cent) and for pleasure (62 per cent). Taking up physical activity following medical advice (23 per cent) and for rehabilitation or therapeutic purposes (37 per cent) were low on the list of priorities (Watkinson and Calzonetti 1989: 24).

The eleven disabled women with whom I had interviews or email exchanges, and who came from different countries in the West (the UK, North America, Australia), were all self-motivated, and participated in sport for pleasure and fun and for a sense of physical independence – including those who were elite competitors. Those women who were involved in sport before they became disabled have found activities to take part in so that they can continue with an active lifestyle. Yvonne, who is registered blind, enjoys outdoor pursuits and rambling. She explains that, 'When you are disabled, you want things harder ... Sport gives you a zest for life, a new taste of possibilities ...'

Disabled women speak positively about the benefits they experience from taking part in sport in ways that clearly show the link between the personal and the cultural, between the physical body and the social body. Sport opens up social opportunities – the chance to meet, bond and share. It also offers, in a very intimate way, sensuous experiences of bodily physical power and freedom.

The following are extracts from the transcripts of interviews with disabled women, which illustrate the social and personal dimensions of the sport experience:

> After my accident, a lot of my so-called friends found it difficult to accept that I was permanently disabled – they couldn't handle it and gradually drifted away. I found myself in a different world – the world of the disabled – and I became separated from the non-disabled world. I'd always enjoyed sport, and playing again was like a lifeline to me. ... Although I'd lost old friends, I got lots of new ones. (Clara)

> I did play sport at school – but under duress. I always felt inferior. Now I enjoy the companionship of being with other disabled people, and I love the exercise that comes with it. (Anna)

> Sport gave me a new-found freedom. I found it such a liberating experience. For the first time I was moving my body for enjoyment – not instrumentally – to get around, to travel, to go to the toilet, to do my shopping – which was always a bit of a hassle. Now I could *enjoy* my body for the first time. (Carrie)

> I was pretty well written off. I isolated myself from the world – I was shy, introverted, absolutely hated my 'useless' body. I wanted so much to be attractive – to go out with boys. ... It was really by chance – my mother is the culprit – she brought round this girl who played table tennis in her wheelchair – it was like at a youth club – and she persuaded me to go with her one day. I used to play table tennis before my accident, so I felt a bit confident. It was great. I took all my frustrations out on the ball. I missed a lot, but I hit a lot, too, and I felt good. No one seemed to be judging me and I made friends and then went on to compete and made more friends. Now it's a way of life. I would be lost without sport. It's given me so much confidence – in my body – and with other people. (Annette)

> My identity was so tied up with my love of sport. I was a top club swimmer – went to the Nationals a couple of times and did quite well. ... When I got cancer and had my leg amputated, I was devastated. I didn't think I'd ever swim again. But I still felt the same, I imagined I *was* the same and would dream about winning a race. I knew about the Paralympics and I started to think – well, why can't I win a race again? So I found out from my physio about a club and I joined, and now – well, I didn't win – but I've got a *bronze* medal! In the water, I don't feel disabled any more – sport has the same meaning for me as it did before I lost my leg – it makes me feel powerful and good about myself – and it's put me on track for doing other things as well. I go out with able-bodied friends – if I meet new people they don't even know I'm an amputee. I do a lot of walking now – go away for

weekends with friends – I've even been to a health farm and had the whole works. It's like I've reclaimed my body – and – I know this sounds dramatic – my life. (Alice)

There are very few disabled women who take part in mainstream sport. The fear and hurt of being labelled as 'different' and inferior, or of being stigmatized or patronized, is very real. In contrast, being together with other disabled people in special groups and organizations specifically for the disabled provides a sense of inclusion rather than exclusion and a feeling of security from the fear of prejudice and discrimination. Teresa, who has described above her feelings of isolation and alienation in mainstream contexts, explains movingly how disability-specific sport transformed her life:

> One area of activity that I had never been involved in was the 'sport for disabled' community. My parents had always tried to normalize my experiences, and recruitment was mainly through rehabilitation centres, so I had never had opportunity to come across any disability sport activities. Around the time that things started to go badly in PE and riding, my mother sought out a swimming programme affiliated to the provincial wheelchair sports association (none of the other disability groups having much programming in the area at that time). I reluctantly agreed to go, one afternoon, on a trial basis. Consider that not only was I experiencing major typical teenage (girl) 'I-hate-my-body' angst, but my other current physical activities were rapidly metamorphizing into nightmares. What happened next changed my life. I had always loved swimming, and had worked as-siduously towards my Red Cross swimming badges. When I swam that Wednesday evening, the woman who was running the swimming pro-gramme was genuinely enthusiastic about my abilities. It was precisely what I needed. So I went back the next week, and the next. And I improved, and could see my improvement.

Disability-specific sport can provide a release from the taboo of disability. Disabled sportswomen are concerned with their *able*-bodiedness. Their embodied experiences are, in terms of the pleasure and pain that they feel, similar to those of able-bodied women. They want to be able to participate in sport without being viewed as objects of pity or represented as victims. Although their sporting functions may in several ways *be different from* those of non-disabled women, with learning and training, their functions can, *in common with* those of non-disabled women, be efficient and skilful. Disabled women who become elite athletes reach standards of physical excellence and supreme ability. The increasing visibility of sportswomen with disabilities helps to transcend the idea that the body is a burden and encourages other disabled women to focus on their sporting abilities. The outstanding successes of elite female disabled athletes illustrate the possibilities for a new generation of disabled sportswomen.

Disabled heroines of sport

All disabled women in sport are influenced by the particular ways in which disability and gender relations interact. But, as already discussed, disabled women are not a homogenous group, and to different degrees they are also affected by economic, practical, political and ideological barriers and by their age, class, ethnicity, nationality and sexuality, etc. To my knowledge, there has been no research into the ways in which multiple structures and forms of discrimination affect disabled women's participation in sport. This problematic is related to issues of subjectivity, difference and identity. The relatively tiny number of elite disabled sport stars, although not authentically representative of all disabled women, become heroic symbols of an imagined community and of group pride. Elite performers transform the stereotypes of disabled woman as weak, inactive victims into incredible, dynamic sports performers, blurring the able-bodied/disabled body divide. The female stars of disabled sport signal an identity which is resistant to being reduced to 'the Other'. They also symbolize a challenge to ableist ideology, a reinvention of the (dis)abled body and a redefinition of the possible. Disability sport is tied to the cultural 'politics of difference' and can be seen as a site of resistance, a freeing – specifically of disabled women – from the constraints of culture and ideology. However, it has been argued by women in the disability movement that stars and heroines can easily lead to the cult of the personality (Oliver 1996: 17). But it can also be argued that it is important to have heroic images of disabled sportswomen for popular consumption in order to change public consciousness and overturn ableism. Disabled sports heroines are active agents in the conversion from exclusion and invisibility to inclusion and visibility.

The struggle for the legitimation of disability sport for women takes place in different spaces – for example, in the community and on the international stage. Those working in community sport are, I would argue, the organic heroines, who are quietly and unassumingly challenging assumptions about disability and broadening the horizons of disability sport and disabled womanhood. But they are the unsung heroines, and it is those at the international level – the 'stars' – who have created a legitimized tradition of disabled heroines of sport. The best known are those who have achieved major sporting successes following debilitating illnesses or horrible injuries. Their often painful 'battles with their bodies' through rehabilitation, and reclaiming of their bodies through sport, transforms them automatically to heroine status. Victory through pain and/or incapacity has always been a sign of the heroic – often associated with the male body in warfare – but legitimized in relation to disabled female sporting bodies. Heroism is symbolized through bodies that suffer impairments, but then, through superhuman effort, function again, at least symbolically, as 'whole' bodies. The narrative of such disabled sporting heroines is woven around the visionary – of miracles, bravery, wonderment, fortitude, stamina, determination. The sporting context is always mainstream, the point of reference is always able-bodiedness (taken away through misfortune, but recoverable through courage). The following sportswomen are exemplars of this model of 'temporary disability'. They are all well-known in their own countries, and have been eulogized in the press; some have biographies and autobiographies to tell their stories.

In 1944, a Danish woman, Lis Hartel, was 23 years old and pregnant with her first child when she contracted polio and became 'almost entirely paralyzed' (Greenspan 1995: 26). She was at the time one of Denmark's leading dressage riders. Utterly determined to continue her riding career, she started rehabilitation when she was still pregnant and recontinued after she had delivered a healthy baby. First she had to learn to lift her arms again, to crawl, and then to walk. The process of recovery was slow and painful and reflected the extreme of personal human endeavour:

> She laid face down on the floor. A towel was put under her body, husband and mother each holding an end. They lifted her slightly from the floor and she strove to crawl forward. This was the most exhausting of all. She was almost in collapse when she was put back to bed. But she managed to crawl a few inches. As she improved, she set herself the goal of crawling a yard further each day. … Her attempts to walk were similarly painful and slow, as she advanced from crutches until after 8 months, she was able to hobble along with two crutch canes.
>
> (Mishev 1964: 117)

The transition to riding was most dramatic. She fell off her horse repeatedly, collapsed from exhaustion again and again, and was frequently close to giving up. But gradually she regained use of her thigh muscles sufficiently to keep her seat at a trot. In 1947, just three years after the polio attack, she competed in the Scandinavian Riding Championships and finished second. Then, selected to represent Denmark at the 1952 Olympic Games, amazingly, she won the silver medal (Greenspan 1995: 26). At the next Olympics, in 1956, Lis Hartel won the silver medal again.

Wilma Rudolph was especially unusual because she was a Black American from a poor family. Her particular story has been used to support the claim that the USA is a democratic society which cares and provides for people from all social groups – including those from ethnic minorities and the disabled. Rudolph was a sickly child suffering from illnesses including double pneumonia and scarlet fever, which left her unable to walk. For several years she had to endure painful treatments and massage therapy, and then 'with the help of special shoes she began walking again at the age of eight'. She tells her own story:

> Every Saturday when I was a kid my mom would take me on a bus from our home in Clarksville, Tennessee, to a Nashville hospital 60 miles away for treatment on my leg. Then during the week my brothers and sisters would take turns massaging my leg. If it wasn't for my family, I probably would never have been able to walk properly, no less run.
>
> (Greenspan 1995: 74)

At the age of 11 she shed the brace, and nine years later, at the Rome Olympics in 1960, she won three gold medals for the 100 metres, 200 metres and the 400-metre relay. She was known as 'the fastest woman in the world' and heroized in the American press as, 'The Black Gazelle' (Greenspan 1995: 74).

Two other examples of women who have overcome sickness, and returned to sport with courage and endurance, are also from the USA. Babe Didrikson was diagnosed with cancer in 1953. In 1954, just one year after an operation, she returned to competition and won the National Women's Open and the Tam O'Shanter All-American Tournament. She died two years later in 1956, at the age of 42. Ruth Heidrich underwent a double mastectomy in 1982. While she was convalescing in Hawaii in 1983, she watched the Ironman Triathlon and decided to enter it the following year – following an incredibly heavy training programme of swimming, biking and running, she did so. By 1991 she had completed six Ironman-distance triathlons and an average of 50 shorter races a year. In 1986, her heroism was recognized when she received the Strength and Courage Award from the Pacific Foundation for Cancer Research (Portz-Shovlin 1991: 110).

Three other post-trauma medal-winners come from Canada, Cuba and Sweden, respectively. Silken Laumann, who in 1991 was the women's world single sculls champion, Canadian Athlete of the Year, and favourite to win the gold medal at the Barcelona Olympics the following year, suffered horrific injuries to her leg just ten weeks before the Games. She was training in Germany when, she explains, 'I was just starting to warm up when out of nowhere was this German boat. It crashed right into my right leg, severing all the muscles, tendons and ligaments from midway up my right shin all the way down to my ankle' (Greenspan 1995: 67). The fibula was broken, five muscle groups were severed and torn from the tibia, and the initial prognosis was that she would never row again. However, Laumann went through radical, intense and painful treatment in order to keep her place in the Olympics and, against all the odds, miraculously won the bronze medal (Greenspan 1995: 67). Anna Quirot, a Black Cuban 800-metre runner, lost her daughter and was badly burned in a fire in Cuba. She came back to win a gold medal at the 1995 World Athletic Championships and a silver medal at the 1996 Olympics. Ludmila Engquist from Sweden won a medal in the 110-metre hurdles at the 1999 World Athletic Championships in Seville, Spain, a few months after she had breast cancer surgery and when she was still undergoing chemotherapy sessions.

In all these examples, the public has been supplied with graphic details of the accidents, the treatment, the struggles, and the achievements, etc., in narratives that have a framework of heroism. When sportswomen were once able-bodied there appears to be no stigma attached to the temporarily impaired (for the purposes of sport) bodily condition. The image of an able body, damaged through misfortune, becomes representative of the 'human condition'. The hidden message is that it could happen to any of us – these women are not fundamentally 'different', they are just 'damaged'. Their achievements in sport, therefore, do not represent a *crisis* of identity so much as a *strengthening* of identity. The media appropriate their bodies and their stories and re-present them as inspirational, especially, as in the case of Lis Hartel, when the women use their fame for the benefit of others. She used to make four or five appearances in different countries every year to show that recovery from polio *was* possible, and she answered hundreds of letters from polio victims with the following message: 'Never give up. However dark it may look, there is almost always a chance of making some progress which may be a milestone towards recovery. ... You can do almost anything if you only believe it hard enough' (Mishev 1964: 118).

But most disabled sportswomen are permanently impaired – either from birth or following an illness or accident – to the extent that they cannot simulate a 'whole' body. As we have seen, the ideology of ableism depicts them as distinct and different from the able-bodied population and, I would argue that for that reason, the heroic label has not been attached to them so readily. The tiny numbers of disabled sportswomen who have infiltrated the fundamentally able-bodied setting of mainstream sport are portrayed as singular and very 'special', and their position in that context is rationalized because they compete in certain sports the skills for which are not affected by their specific disability. For example, in 1984, Neroli Fairhall from New Zealand became the first wheelchair athlete to meet eligibility criteria so that she could compete in the Olympics in women's archery (DePauw and Gavron 1995: 40), and Paola Fantanal from Italy also competed in the archery competition at the 1996 Atlanta Olympics when she was in a wheelchair. Rebecca Macree, from England, who has been profoundly deaf since birth, has been a ranked player since 1995 (Finn, *The Times* 1/2/95) and was ranked 11th in the world in 1999. She continues to play as a sponsored professional on the women's squash international circuit. Marla Runyan from the USA was the first registered blind person to compete as an elite athlete in a top-class international competition. The highlights of her mainstream career were reaching the finals of the 1500 metres at the 1999 World Athletic Championships, and the 2000 Sydney Olympics when she asserted, 'I'm not a Paralympian anymore, I'm an Olympian'.

Steadward (1996: 27) argues that 'the leadership within the disability sport movement have demonstrated a deep commitment to the inclusion or integration of athletes with disabilities into able-bodied sport society, specifically into elite sport competition'. But there are still only a tiny number of disabled sportswomen who either train with or compete against their able-bodied counterparts. (The issue of integration is discussed later.) Almost all disabled sportswomen and sportsmen participate in insular, disability-specific clubs, organizations and competitions – which separates them practically and symbolically from the mainstream. The time and space separation between disability sport and mainstream events effectively ghettoizes – or at least diminishes the importance of – the achievements of those who are disabled. The consummate athleticism of elite, disabled sportswomen who win Paralympic gold medals fails to receive the same attention in the media or the same acclaim in popular consciousness as the achievements of able-bodied sportswomen. Steadward (1996: 35) argues that

Although the Paralympic Games and other world disability sport championships are premier events worthy of their own accord, there nevertheless remains a sense of segregation from the able-bodied sports community. In the past, sport opportunities for athletes with a disability have been regarded as a low-priority need, rather than a basic right, and thus the profile, visibility, and status of such sport opportunities have been perceived as second class.

The issue of representation relates to the absence, or minimal reporting, of disability sport in relation to mainstream competitions. There is also a strong bias in the media which foregrounds impairment and underrates sporting skills and achievements – elite sportswomen are constructed less frequently as *sporting* heroines and more usually as *disabled* sportswomen. In addition, there is a tendency for disabled sportsmen to get more coverage than disabled sportswomen, and for wheelchair sport to be prioritized. Elite sportswomen face discrimination based on disability and gender, compounded by discrimination against women with certain disabilities. Not surprisingly, they are constantly frustrated and annoyed by treatment which they view as demeaning. For example, when five disabled women athletes from different European and North American countries who competed at the 1994 Lillehammer Winter Paralympics were interviewed, they all agreed that 'the failure of society to recognise them as "athletes" was confirmed in their daily interactions with people. For example, they talked of being pitied; of being told they were extremely brave; and being wished a "nice vacation" when preparing to leave for the Lillehammer Paralympic Games' (Olenik *et al.* 1995: 56).

Elite disabled athletes view themselves quite differently. They have rejected the medicalized characterization of disability and are interested only in their sporting abilities and records. For them, the actual lived experience of impairment is located in a *sporting* body, one which is competent and empowering, explained here by a Paralympic wheelchair track athlete:

> I think of myself first and foremost as a *sports ... person – not* as a woman – and *not* as disabled. ... I train hard, I lift weights, I cover hundreds of miles, I go out in all weathers, I'm out on the streets when it's dark and cold when other students are dating or clubbing. ... I've got a coach, I go to physio, and I've started eating a special diet. ... I'm a *dedicated* athlete – just the same as able-bodied athletes. ... It's *very* hard work, but I like to feel strong and powerful and that's how I win gold medals – in the same way able-bodied people do. (Deborah)

The examples of elite disabled sportswomen make clear the importance of the link between culture and prejudice – a feature largely missing from the social model of disability. Thomas (1999: 40) takes the analysis further – she argues that disability is to do with the social relationships between people which she describes as a *social relational* definition. In the context of elite sport, the significance of social relations of power is very clear. Disabled sportswomen are disadvantaged because they lack power in their relations with able-bodied women, with disabled men, with the media, and with disability sport officials. What is also clear from these examples is the importance of the real experiences of disabled women (their aspirations, problems and oppressions), which point to the links between the personal and the social – a particular concern of disability feminists (Barnes 1998: 76). However, missing from these variants of the social model of disability is the failure adequately to identify disability with the body – not only to take account of the personal and sometimes painful experience of disability, but also to take account of the ways in which disabled women such as elite athletes have redefined the body's limitations, possibilities, weaknesses and strengths. Impairment can act as a restriction to social life and experience; *it can also act as a liberator*. According to Thomas (1999: 41), both impairment and impairment effects (disabilities) are 'profoundly bio-social, that is, shaped by the interaction of biological and social factors'. Looking at elite disabled sports-women, it is clear that the body is an active agent in this relationship, constantly 'in process' between the personal, experiential features of training and performance and the cultural, social and political structures which affect individual experience.

Although still in tiny numbers, only in certain contexts, and in limited ways, nevertheless, elite disabled sportswomen are becoming more visible and known to the public for their sporting achievements. For example, Tanni Grey, from the UK, who was born with spina bifida, competes in wheelchair sprint and long-distance races – i.e. 100 metres, 400 metres, 800 metres, 1500 metres, 5000 metres, the half marathon and the marathon. She has set national records, Paralympic records and world records (Hargreaves 1994: 270). The publicity surrounding her sporting triumphs has enabled her to secure sponsorship and acceptance as a sportswoman, not just as a disabled athlete. She is the best-known British female disabled athlete and has become a spokesperson for disability sport, raising its profile and pushing it towards the mainstream. She has been honoured for her contribution to disability sport with an MBE and an OBE. Diana Golden from the USA, who had her right leg amputated at the age of twelve when she was diagnosed as having bone cancer, dominated US disability skiing during the 1980s and 1990s. She won nineteen National titles and ten World Disabled Skiing Championship medals (DePauw and Gavron 1995: 49). Diana received special distinction when she became the first disabled sportswomen to receive each of the three following awards – the US Writers' Association Outstanding Com-petitor Award (1986); the US Olympic Committee Female Skier of the Year (1988); and the Flo Hyman Award from the Women's Sports Foundation (1991). Jean Driscoll (USA) became the first disabled athlete to be named the Sudafed Female Athlete of the Year and Sue Moucha (USA) became the first athlete with a disability to attend the Olympic Academy (DePauw and Gavron 1995: 41).

These disabled sportswomen are pushing at the frontiers between disability and non-disability. In sporting terms, they have achieved what – say, ten or fifteen years ago – would have been considered impossible. They have recast themselves as empowered and independent, in opposition to weak and dependent. The new narrative of ability is strengthened every time they compete and every time a record is broken. There is also an aesthetic component of self-representation – their bodies are muscular, skilful, fluid, sensuous – rendering the orthodox cultural norms and medical stereotypes of disability increasingly residual. This is the essence of body agency. Elite disabled athletes use their bodies assertively and confidently and understand the nexus between body, identity and culture. They are *active* agents in a process of change and are aware of their positions as role models for disability sport, as the following examples show.

Brenda Gilmore from the USA has a spinal cord injury and was involved in competitive wheelchair tennis from 1985 to 1989. At a personal level, she describes sport as 'crucial to my mental and physical well-being' and describes those who are active in sport as 'a group who tends to challenge life instead of waiting around for things to come to us. We are the high-profile "hot shots" that help change the image of the physically challenged by our social appeal and appearance' (DePauw and Gavron 1995: 58). Corina Robitjcho is a member of the German national wheelchair basketball team. She claims that 'Sport is my life. I can't imagine a life without sport', and to young children she says, 'If you find yourself in sport, it will be a great enrichment. Go looking for yourself and see the wonderful things that sport can give you' (DePauw and Gavron 1995: 110). Karen Farmer-Lewis, a congenital single-leg amputee (she was born without a right tibia and with a deformed right foot) has set 14 world records in track and field throwing, jumping and running events. Her message to young people is 'Don't let anyone take your dreams away. Believe in yourself. Create your own goals' (DePauw and Gavron 1995: 213). When Louise Sauvage won a gold medal in the 800-metre women's wheelchair demonstration event at the Atlanta Olympics, it was the only time the Australian flag was raised in the main stadium. Louise has five Paralympic gold medals, is a world champion, and winner of the 1997 Boston Marathon. As the most celebrated Paralympic athlete in Australia and one of the best-known sportswomen (able-bodied or disabled) in her country, she is now an official ambassador for the Sydney 2000 Paralympic Games. She is aware that wheelchair athletes, in particular, are getting more recognition: 'Sometimes it's good because at least people are noticing you and know what you're doing.' But she is also aware that the majority of disabled sportswomen remain unknown: 'Other times I think it would be nice for other athletes to get more of a profile to show the different kinds of disabilities and the range of sports we [disabled athletes] compete in' (*Women in Sport* [Australia] 1998).

Louise reflects the complex and contradictory position that disabled sportswomen find themselves in. On the one hand, 'building on ability' has become an unconscious feature of their identities and some elite athletes are benefiting from greater visibility. On the other hand, the majority of disabled women continue to face huge barriers to recognition, especially those who compete in less popular sports and those who are severely disabled. The particular problems that women face, but which are not fully understood because of lack of research, are reflected in the lower numbers of women who take part in disability sport overall and especially at the Paralympics.

Women in the Paralympic Games

In 1993, Sherrill (1993: 54) maintained that Paralympic sportswomen constituted an oppressed minority, reflected in their underrepresentation at the Paralympic Games. Four years later, Carol Mushett, IPC Executive Committee member, stated that, 'Over the last three quadrenniums, we have seen an alarming decrease in opportunity and participation by women athletes with disabilities. This trend is reflected across all sports with the exception of swimming and powerlifting' (Sherrill 1997: 33–4).

There is a recognizable pattern of unequal participation rates of women in comparison to men at the Paralympic Games. At the Barcelona Paralympics there were 3020 competitors from 82 countries taking part in 15 different sports. Of these, 2323 were male competitors and 697 were female competitors – 23 per cent of the total. Although a handful of countries had over 50 per cent of women in their teams, the majority had low percentages or none at all, and 30 countries brought no female athletes or staff. The five contingents with the highest percentages were, in descending order: Denmark (88.3 per cent); Canada (61.5 per cent); Ireland (50.6 per cent); Australia (44.8 per cent); USA (39.5 per cent) (Sherrill 1993: 33–4). In general, the teams with most women were from the developed world, and those with fewest women were from the developing world. The Paralympic Rules, set by the IPC, exacerbated the problem. They required that events could only be scheduled if a large enough number of athletes of the same gender and functional ability classification met the qualifying standards, so that three countries and two continents were represented (Sherrill 1993: 55). In some events the numbers of women were so small that this rule could not be complied with and consequently certain functional classification groups for women were cut out of the programme at the last minute, or women were entered in events they had not trained for, or put against competitors with different ability classifications (Sherrill 1993: 54–5).

At the 1996 Paralympics in Atlanta, the overall situation was similar and, in some national delegations, female percentages had dropped. There were 3195 competitors from 103 different countries, taking part in 19 different sports. The number of male competitors totalled 2415 and the number of female competitors was 780 – 24 per cent of the total. Fifty countries, mostly from the developing world, sent no female competitors – an increase of 60 per cent. The biggest Paralympic sport, track and field athletics, had 709 male and 197 female competitors (28 per cent); traditional male sports had no female teams – for example, football (87 men from 7 countries), powerlifting (142 men from 55 countries); and rugby (47 men from 6 countries); and there were no female competitors, either, in judo (67 men from 18 countries) or volleyball (225 men from 17 countries) (IPC *After Action Report*). The only sport with a higher number of female than male competitors was equestrian eventing, with 15 men and 46 women taking part (75 per cent).

In general, the countries with the largest overall number of women and the highest percentage of women in their teams were from the West, with well-established disability sport infrastructures. In many of the countries from the developing world, disabled women are treated as outcastes and are struggling for survival, and the minimal resources allocated for disability sport in those countries go primarily to men. There are also cultural and religious factors, which exacerbate gender inequalities. But, despite the existence of an international disability sport movement, very little is known about the experiences and problems of disabled sportswomen worldwide, the specific forms of patriarchy in developing countries which affect access to sport, or the influences of culture and tradition on disabled women's lives.

The focus in this chapter has been on physical disabilities, but gender inequality in sport participation is present in all disability groups. For example, since the inception of the Special Olympics in 1968 there have been far fewer male than female participants. The *Special Olympics International Report*, (n.d.: 2) states:

> Of the population with mental retardation, approximately 65% are males and 35% females. For individual sports within the Special Olympics, the percentage of males and females nearly matches the general population figures for 60% are males and 40% are females. However, there is a dramatic difference in team sports participation. 77.5% of the team sports participants are males as compared with only 22.5% females.

The low percentages of women taking part in elite disability sport reflect the general pattern of participation at lower levels. Fewer women than men take part in competitive disability sport overall – a striking example comes from Britain where, in wheelchair basketball (the largest wheelchair sport in the country), only 7 per cent of those registered in the National League are women (Grey 1997: 122). The ratio of male/female participation in wheelchair sport generally is estimated as a fairly constant four to one (Strange 1995: 1).

Gender and power

Using male domination of the IPC as the example, Sherrill (1993: 54–5) complains that 'Too few women for too long have been involved in the power structure that controls sport for athletes with disability.' In the year 2000, there is only one woman out of 22 members of the Executive Committee of the IPC. She is Carol Mushett, the technical officer. Those holding powerful positions in the other international disability sport organizations are also predominantly men. A notable exception was Liz Dendy (GB), who was the first and only female president of the CP-ISRA (Cerebral Palsy-International Sport and

Recreation Association). During her presidency she was also the only female member of the IPC (DePauw and Gavron 1995: 212). Using Britain as one example, at national level, the British Paralympic Association (BPA) has a Board of Trustees of eight people, of whom just one is female. However, seven out of the nine staff members of the BPA are female and the two highest staff positions – the general secretary and the chef de mission – are both held by women. In coaching, as well, there is gender imbalance and prejudice. There are far fewer female than male coaches at international level, and discussions with aspiring elite female athletes reveals discrimination against them by male athletes and unequal treatment from male coaches and trainers (Strange 1995: 2). The argument has been made that, in order to improve the underrepresentation of women in the Paralympics, and to prevent future discrimination against women, there should be more women representatives in the IPC and the national sports federations, there should have been more female members of the Atlanta Paralympic Committee, and there should be more women sharing in the decision-making for the Sydney 2000 Paralympic Games.

But the issue is more complex. As we have seen, those in positions of power in disability sport organizations are mostly men, but they are also mostly White and able-bodied. They are not, therefore, properly representative of disabled women in general, or of those from varied social and ethnic backgrounds. Although there are some competing disabled athletes who hold positions on governing bodies (Grey 1997: 122), in the main, disability sport organizations are organizations *for* the disabled and not *of* the disabled. The effect is that insufficient attention is paid to the *actual experience* of disability, and disabled sportswomen (and men) are unable to exercise control over decisions which affect their sporting lives in fundamental ways. Unrepresentative disability sport bodies are examples of institutionalized discrimination, which is interwoven throughout sport and throughout the fabric of society. If sport organizations were controlled and run by disabled people themselves, they could more easily challenge prejudices and promote equality and anti-discriminatory practices. The EFDS, mentioned earlier, is unusually insightful and radical about the issue of participatory democracy. Its mission plan embraces the importance of empowering disabled people so that they are involved in all aspects of the Federation and its work (EFDS 2000: 8). Even so, on the staff of the Federation there are only five people with physical or sensory impairments working in development posts, out of a total staff of 25 (EFDS 2000: 7).

Without proper representation, disabled sportswomen have had to take independent action to make demands for change. Although they have not had their own disability sport group and do not act collectively, the voices of individuals, together with the general discourse of gender equality which has gained ground throughout the sportsworld and in society, have had some influence on attitudes to gender issues in disability sports organizations. The IPC has set up a Women's Initiative to address the underrepresentation of women in Paralympic competition, and is considering a quota system, which would guarantee places for women at major games (Grey 1997: 122–3). But, although the IPC has identified the issue of representation of women in the Paralympic movement as one of the highest priority, and 'the IPC Sport Science Sub-Committee is supporting initiatives to institute a line of feminist research in this area' (Olenik *et al.* 1995: 57), it has been slow to take action. Following its failure to implement changes at the Atlanta Games to correct the problems of Barcelona, Brandoburova and Scherney (1999: 5), both disabled athletes, argue that the classification systems used for competitive disability sport continue to disadvantage women. They also claim that there are decreasing opportunities in competitive sport for severely disabled athletes – especially women – and especially in track and field athletics, the biggest of all Paralympic sports:

> We do not understand the policy of IPC that works in favour of increasingly limiting the opportunities of currently active women and severely disabled athletes, which leads to hidden discrimination of some classes and disability groups and thus reducing the sports program of the Paralympic Games. Those very Paralympic Games that represent one of the most visible examples of sport in today's society and what is more important, the deepest ambition of every athlete with a disability.

In some classes there are only two or three competitors, and severely disabled athletes are put into competitions with combined classes so that, even if they break a world record, they may do so by coming last in the race. Underrepresented classes are not considered to be challenging and getting a medal lacks value, even if the performance is outstanding. The system encourages countries only to enter women athletes and severely disabled athletes if they are in events with viable numbers, so outstanding athletes can get left out of their national team. The problem is therefore exacerbated. Although the constitution of the IPC states that there is a need to increase opportunities for the severely disabled and for female athletes and to avoid combining classes, according to Brandoburova and Scherney (1999: 5), 'they are doing nothing to make competition for these two groups fairer' and 'most female classes and those of the severely disabled are [still] underrepresented'. They explain that 'classes are officially combined almost two years before the Paralympic Games with entry standards too low for the less disabled class but unattainable for the severely disabled which are often set high above their own world record' (Brandoburova and Scherney 1999: 6). The IPC promised to redress the problem, but have failed to implement changes for the Sydney Paralympics. Brandoburova and Scherney (1999: 5) suggest that a special ruling should be made to allow participation of athletes in threatened classes to take part without a quota system, and that a decision to combine events should only be made after the last entry has been received.

Brandoburova and Scherney gained support for their proposals at the 1999 General Assembly of the European Paralympic Committee (EPC). The following recommendations were carried unanimously:

That the president and the executive committee of the EPC should approach the IPC and do everything in their power to implement the motions below.

1   To protect the most threatened classes of female athletes by adoption of a special rule applicable for the Paralympic Games that allows to have the entry standards based on the results of their respective classes which then may be combined after the final entries evaluation and in case of an insufficient number of entries in the respective class (6 participants, 4 nations). Only then such a class can be combined with another class of the least handicap.

2   To establish a working group to make possible efforts to develop a new and better system for fair competition in track and field events allowing two or more underrepresented classes compete together based on similar principles as currently used in Alpine or Cross-Country skiing (a so called KRECK-system) or functional classification as used in Swimming.

Disabled sportswomen have also been actively campaigning for several years to include more sports and events on the women's Paralympic programme. Female athletes argue that the IPC has favoured sports for men and have resisted change (Strange 1995: 3). In some ways, the struggles of disabled sportswomen replicate the past struggles of able-bodied sportswomen – a recent example is the attempt to get accepted in traditional male-dominated sports – notably wheelchair rugby and powerlifting. There has been fast-growing grassroots support for these two sports among disabled women and yet it has been a struggle for them to get Paralympic recognition. Wheelchair rugby was included as a Paralympic event for the first time in 1992, but for men only, and it remained male-specific in Atlanta and Sydney, despite the fact that women play in increasing numbers in female-only and mixed-sex teams in local contexts. But the growing popularity of women's powerlifting and the resultant lobby to make it a Paralympic sport has been more successful. The outcome of disputes and negotiations was a decision by the IPC to put women's powerlifting onto the Paralympic programme of events for the first time in Sydney 2000.

The explanation for women's low involvement in Paralympic sport is also linked to other issues. Ironically, with the move away from rehabilitation sport there is now less automatic channelling into sport for health reasons, which in turn may reduce the numbers of women available to go on to elite sport. There is also a greater range of non-Paralympic sports available to disabled women – for example, the ISMWSF is aiming to achieve 50 per cent female participation by introducing different sports for female participation (for example, hand cycling, badminton, golf and weightlifting). There are also a plethora of 'postmodern' cultural forms opening up to disabled women; for example in theatre, art and travel. So disabled women now have greater cultural choices and, when they do choose sport, in many cases they prefer non-competitive forms and friendly women-only settings. Some women, then, are making informed decisions to stay out of competitive sport. In summary, the reasons why there is a large discrepancy between male and female Paralympic participation are highly complex, linked to ableist ideologies, gendered relations of power, social and cultural barriers and personal choices.

Segregation and integration

The issue of participation is also linked to the highly topical controversy about segregation and integration.[1] This issue has institutional significance, formalized in debates in all the major disability sport organizations and, as we have already seen, it also has very personal significance. Although there is no general consensus, at an institutional level there is official commitment to the inclusion of disabled athletes (most specifically elite athletes) into mainstream sport. The segregation/integration debate in disability sport is related to, and has been influenced by, broader political considerations and disability rights discourses. It is, fundamentally, to do with the *construction of difference* between disabled and non-disabled sports groups and the associated sense of superiority and inferiority (segregation), and the *acceptance of difference* between disabled and non-disabled sports groups and the associated nurturing of 'togetherness' (integration). I am using the term 'segregation' to describe disabled people playing sport exclusively with their disabled peers, and integration when disabled people play sport alongside those who are non-disabled.

Disabled activists reject segregation. It implies being cut off from mainstream society and culture, ghettoized in insular institutions, and dissociated from able-bodied people in everyday aspects of work and living. Part of the manifesto of the Disabled People's International, which was formulated at the organization's first Congress, reads: 'We maintain that all people are of equal value. This conviction implies that disabled people have the right to participate in every sphere of society. ... We therefore reject all forms of segregation ...' (Morris 1991: 173). Segregation is fundamentally an issue of power, explained here by Morris: 'Segregation, the separation from mainstream society, is an important part of the material experience of powerlessness. Segregation takes many forms but comes about because the needs created by our disabilities are not met within society's mainstream activities' (1991: 117).

Historically, mainstream sport and disability sport have been separately resourced and separated in time and place. Mainstream sport has been, undeniably, the major beneficiary of resources and, until very recently, disabled people have been struggling as the 'Others' in separate oganizations and competitions. There has, however, been a radical change taking place over the last two decades in response to the demands of disabled athletes and disability rights campaigners. The key ideological shift has been from a disability-specific philosophy to a sport-specific philosophy. The new emphasis is on sporting ability, underpinned by a functional classification system so that sportsmen and women with different impairments but similar abilities can compete against each other. The sport and ability focus has been the initiative for integrating disabled athletes into mainstream sport – in training and in competition. This can mean, but not necessarily, that disabled and non-disabled athletes will compete against one another. The most usual model of integration is for disabled athletes to have their own events as part of a general programme so that resources are shared and disability can become incidental to sport.

To begin with, the process was experimental – for example, exhibition events for disabled athletes took place for the first time at the 1984 Winter Olympics (selected alpine and nordic events for physically impaired and blind athletes) and at the 1984 Summer Olympics (1500-metre wheelchair race for men, 800-metre wheelchair race for women), and have been included in subsequent Paralympic Games. The idea of integration was consolidated in 1990, when the IPC International Committee on Integration of Athletes with a Disability (ICI) – later renamed the Commission for Inclusion of Athletes with a Disability (CIAD) – was formed by a 'group of Canadians who envisioned the inclusion of selected full medal events for athletes with disabilities in major international competitions', in particular the Olympics and the Commonwealth Games (DePauw and Gavron 1995: 221). CIAD was effective in getting six exhibition events for disabled athletes in the 1994 Commonwealth Games in Vancouver, Canada, but unsuccessful in getting full medal events for disabled athletes at the 1998 Commonwealth Games in Malaysia, as they had hoped – a reflection of the different attitudes and controversies around the world that surround the issue of integration. As already mentioned, in 2002, at the next Commonwealth Games in Manchester, England, events for disabled athletes will be included in the programme. The IPC – who represents the 'establishment' position, has come out firmly in favour of integration. One of its objectives is 'To seek the integration of sports for athletes with disabilities into the international sports movement for able-bodied athletes, whilst safeguarding and preserving the identity of sports for disabled athletes' (IPC *publicity pack* n.d.).

Integration has been facilitated by the policies of the main sports organizations in a number of different countries, such as Australia, Canada and the USA. In Britain, disability sport is also moving closer to able-bodied sport, a process legitimized in 1989 when the report of the Minister for Sport's Review Group, *Building on Ability*, recommended that disability sport-specific organizations, working with the governing bodies of mainstream sport, should liaise to provide improved resources for elite sport for the disabled. Governing bodies were urged to 'actively encourage disabled athletes to take part in the events and competitions they organise, either in direct competition with able-bodied athletes or in parallel events' (Minister for Sport's Review Group 1989: 14, 20). But progress has been slow, comprehensive integration is still a long way off, and many governing bodies still have to be encouraged to cater equally for disabled as well as non-disabled people. In 1989, one of the missions of the

European Federation for Disability Sport was to 'mainstream' disability sport so that:

> the organisation and provision of sporting opportunity for disabled people becomes the responsibility of National Governing Bodies of sport, Local Authorities and other mainstream sport providers and disabled people will have the same individual choices afforded them as other members of society.
>
> (EFDS 2000: 8, 10)

Even incomplete integration opens up new opportunities for some elite disabled sportswomen through the sharing of resources and training with able-bodied athletes. But some athletes have had bad experiences. Rebeccah Macree, for example, 'encountered animosity from officials and other players who did not believe that she could play without hearing the ball or the score' (Finn, *The Times* 1/2/95) and, also in England, Deborah, a leading Paralympic track athlete was harassed by chauvinist able-bodied male students for using her wheelchair on the track, to the extent that she felt compelled to train on the road instead. Coral, another leading English sportswoman, explained that, 'Often in mainstream contexts, you feel like you're being patronized, they feel sorry for you. There's a sense of "do-gooding" so you feel like you're not worth much – you're different.' However, most top disabled sportswomen welcome integration – 'It's good when we're seen together, when we're all sportswomen together'; 'I think I do better training alongside able-bodied athletes'; 'It's good because we're accepted – I don't feel in any way inferior and I've made a lot of friends and we train together'; 'It's simple – we get better facilities and better coaching. Being mainstreamed is how it should be'.

'Being mainstreamed is how it should be' exemplifies the political and personal beliefs of most disabled women in sport. The hope attached to 'being mainstreamed' is that disabled sportswomen would have equal access to sport resources, equal funding and equal representation on decision-making bodies. Making it possible for disabled sportswomen to share the best resources, join mainstream clubs and train with mainstream athletes is a move in the right direction. But full inclusion, rather than accommodation, is needed so that differences between disabled and non-disabled sportswomen would be unimportant and the love of sport would take precedence. 'Being mainstreamed' should ackowledge equality as a right, not a privilege. Part of that right would be the continuance of disability sport organizations to ensure equality for those disabled sportswomen whose needs are best met through those channels. 1981 was designated the UN International Year for Disabled Persons. The motto was 'Full participation and equality' (Oliver 1996: 112). And that is what disabled sportswomen are still struggling for.

Conclusion

Disability sport is an experience that has been shaped by individuals and society. In recent years, disabled sportswomen have transformed their physical bodies, previously characterized through medical discourses as defective and pathological, into bodies that reflect ability and empowerment. Their bodies are subverted, heroic bodies, resisting inequalities and difference and undermining cultural norms. They have been shown to be plastic and changing, bodies 'in process' replacing negative images with positive ones. Disabled sportswomen are trying to produce a particular disability culture in which difference and experience are 'valid and important' (Morris 1991: 114). This represents an important form of cultural activism, which has had an emancipatory effect for individual disabled women and has helped to change public perceptions of disability. It is particularly significant because disabled people have few points of reference from mainstream culture that present them as active and powerful (Morris 1991: 85).

The story of Helen Rollason makes a fitting epilogue to this chapter. In 1990, she became the first woman to anchor the BBC's *Grandstand* sports review programme, overturning 32 years of male domination. In 1996 she was named Sports Presenter of the Year. Helen tragically died of cancer, but during her long and heroic battle against the disease she claimed that the strength and determination of disabled athletes had helped her cope with her illness. She is remembered in particular for her support of disability sports and the awards she won for her coverage of them, including the World Disabled Championships of 1990, the Blind Golfers Championship in 1991, the Paralympics of 1992 and 1996, and the Special Olympics of 1993 and 1997. Following the 1996 mainstream Olympics, when British athletes did poorly, Helen Rollason urged the media – and the nation – to support the 'real' Olympic team. Her coverage of the Paralympics was credited with transforming media and public perceptions of disability sport, focusing on positive images of sporting skill and brilliance. Jane Swan (cited in the *Guardian* 10/8/99), general secretary of the British Paralympic Association, said, 'Helen had a great rapport with the competitors because she treated them as elite athletes. Until then, the Paralympics had been treated as documentary material, focusing mainly on disability. Helen made people realize that it was sport.'

7 Struggling for a new world order

The Women's International Sport Movement[1]

Introduction

Each of the groups of women in sport represented in the preceding chapters of this book – Black women in South Africa; Muslim women in Arab countries; Aboriginal women in Australia and Canada; and lesbian women and disabled women from countries across the world – are representative of the heterogeneity of women in sport. They come from particular groups that have been historically marginalized from mainstream sport, but who, in the face of harsh forms of discrimination, have challenged one or more powerful and persistent systems of domination, including racism; religious ideologies; sexism; colonialism; and ableism. Their struggles illustrate the relations between agency and power and, as we have seen, in many cases their achievements have been remarkable and their interventions have been heroic. However, the struggles of these groups of women, and those from other marginalized groups mentioned in the first chapter, have tended to be particular struggles, not integrated fully into organized 'women in sport' developments. This chapter asks critical questions about why this is so, by looking at the recent history and development of the Women's International Sport Movement.

This is a new social movement which reputedly represents a global community of women from different countries and social and cultural groups throughout the world. It has stemmed from the establishment of international organizations and groups for women in sport and physical education – the first one founded in the late 1940s – whose leaders were almost exclusively White, Western and middle-class. Half a century later, with consolidation to 'global movement' status, most of its leaders continue to come from the developed world and have similar backgrounds to their predecessors. They have been joined by 'neo-colonial elites' from the developing world. Two key questions posed in this chapter are: whether the organizations and individuals – in their present forms and roles – which together comprise the Women's International Sport Movement, adequately represent women from marginalized groups; and whether its leaders have properly addressed the questions of marginality and representation. The questions are difficult to answer because the position of the movement is contradictory. On the one hand, it can be characterized as an exciting and radical development, but on the other hand it appears to be linked firmly to mainstream structures and values which may not be appropriate for marginalized 'outsiders'. Although members come from countries with a wide geographic spread, and member organizations claim to embody a sensitivity to difference and an understanding of the lives and problems of women in the developing world, at the same time there is a definite tendency towards neo-colonial domination. The new leadership alliance is based on Western consciousness and acculturation and has strong links to state apparatuses and the Western 'sports establishment'. The challenge that faces the leadership is to transform existing power relations in order authentically to represent women from underprivileged and marginalized backgrounds. This is a feminist issue.

Avtar Brah (1991: 168) points out that the feminist slogan 'Sisterhood is global', which was commonly used by the women's movement in the 1970s, 'failed to acknowledge the heterogeneity of the condition of being a woman'. Bearing in mind the major differences in the social circumstances of different groups of women, and their often contradictory interests, a decade ago she asked the question, 'How will feminism in the 1990s address the contradictions underlying these different womanhoods?' A similar question should be asked today in relation to the Women's International Sport Movement: 'How will sport feminism in the new millennium address the contradictions underlying the participation of women in sport from diverse backgrounds across the world?'

Brah believes that it *is* possible to develop a feminist politics that is global but, she insists:

> It demands a massive commitment together with a sustained and painstaking effort directed towards developing practices that are informed by understandings of the ways in which various structures of inequality articulate in given contexts, and shape the lives of different groups of women. We need to address how our own position – in terms of class, racism, sexuality, caste, for example – locates us within systems of power *vis-á-vis* other groups of women and men.
>
> (Brah 1991: 172)

The rest of this chapter looks at the history of the Women's International Sport Movement and examines the ways in which it is located within structures of power and in relation to difference. Its relative failure or success is related to the transformative potential of global sport feminism and will depend on whether difference is appropriated and its power dissipated or whether difference is integrated and its power intensified.

Globalization

International sport organizations have been in place since the late nineteenth century, at which time the nation state was the primary unit of understanding and analysis. Over the years, women from the First, Second and Third Worlds have been involved in the internationalization of women's sport – those from developed Western nations were exemplars of liberal democratic ideologies; women from the Eastern bloc countries were embodiments of cold war politicking between East and West; and women from poor countries in Africa and other parts of the developing world were agents for nation-building and foreign policy. But the further growth of international, supranational and transnational organizations, institutions and movements implies a shift away from 'society' and 'nation state' to 'world society'. The term 'movement' implies a global dimension that transcends nationhood, encompassing on equal terms women from the East and the West, from the developed and developing worlds, women of different races and ethnicities, and of different religions and philosophies. The focus has been on *women*, with an implied homogenization of needs and desires, and associated with a specifically global discourse of the 1990s. Robertson (1992) describes an intensification of consciousness of the world as a whole, but he argues that the economic character of international contact has been emphasized at the expense of cultural exchanges or *cultural flows* between nations, which most of all typify contemporary globalization processes. The Women's International Sport Movement is an example of a global cultural flow that links women from numerous different nation states in a common cause and that has gathered momentum over the past few years. It is one of many social movements resulting from global transformations, specifically, from an increase in the transnationalization of culture and the production of shared identities characteristic of late modernity. Women in sport from all over the world have been affected by the increased interconnectedness between countries, the encountering of other cultures, and the growth and accelerated pace and complexity of informational and cultural exchanges (Giddens 1993; Robertson 1992). In particular, ease of travel and communications by on the Internet, by email, fax and telephone have made the organization of a global women in sport movement possible. However, new technology is generally accessible only to those women from the developed world and the new elites from the developing world – a new, supposedly liberating facility which tends in practice to consolidate existing relations of power.

International Association of Physical Education and Sport for Girls and Women (IAPESGW)

The existence of the International Association of Physical Education and Sport for Girls and Women (IAPESGW) provided the spur for this new modernized movement for women in sport with its global outlook. IAPESGW was founded in 1949 by Dorothy Ainsworth, the director of Physical Education at Smith College, Massachusetts, in the USA. It became the first established international organization with an all-female membership that was concerned with the significance and values of physical education and sport to the lives of girls and women. Most of its members were physical education professionals from the West who were highly critical of the ways in which burgeoning commercialization was changing the face of sport. They were resisting 'corrupt' sport in their teaching and philosophizing and through membership of IAPESGW. In accordance with Dorothy Ainsworth's ideas, it was also claimed that IAPESGW 'embraced the globe, all of its peoples, and the diversity of their cultures' (Sloan 1994: 5).

The reality was rather different. The organization became the representative body for physical education teachers, lecturers and organizers who had been trained in colleges in the developed world – at first, they came mostly from North America and northern Europe, and then there was an increasingly strong contingent from Australia. Most members remained in the 'home' countries, some of them had migrated to developing countries and former colonies following their training, and others had come from different parts of the world to train in the West and had then returned to their countries of origin to teach. The West was at the centre of knowledge production and practices. Those who came from *outside* the West celebrated *sameness with*, rather than *difference from*, the West.

So, although the organization had an international flavour, it held a distinctly middle-class, elitist and very White Western educational and cultural hegemonic stance. In the early days, IAPESGW depended on women with professional connections and personal resources who could pay the necessary administration and travel costs needed to keep the association alive. Dorothy Ainsworth spent her own money getting women to meetings. As one past member put it, 'It brought together people of good will wanting to share what they knew and very anxious to help the countries with less well developed physical education. It really was a very "high-minded group".' But, although IAPESGW welcomed members from different parts of the world, and indeed the organization expanded to include women from a wider range of countries, and conferences were held outside North America and northern Europe, nevertheless non-White, non-Western women were viewed always as 'the Other'. (The irony was that women who themselves were in the position of the 'Other' through patriarchal domination of sport appeared to be insensitive to their own domination of less privileged women who, as a result, became *doubly* colonized.) There was no authentic representation of women from different social groups and cultural backgrounds: IAPESGW members from both the developed and the developing worlds were from elite class and educational backgrounds, the strong links with Empire remained dominant, and the association claimed proudly to be 'non-political', avoiding issues of power and difference. For example, the IAPESGW conference held in 1977 in South Africa during the time of apartheid – which included a committee of mostly White, some Coloured, but no Black African or Indian representatives – was described by one of the delegates as 'a remarkable conference in that there was no trace of political feeling in it'. Liselott Diem, IAPESGW president at the time, wanted the conference to be 'a model of co-operation among races without any discrimination or prejudice' (Hall and Pfister 1999: 20). IAPESGW accepted sponsorship from the South African Department of Sport and Recreation (Hall and Pfister 1999: 21) when apartheid was still in place and the anti-apartheid sport movement and Eastern bloc governments were maintaining the sport boycott. At no time did the conference address the politics of apartheid and human rights. Discussions about physical education remained staunchly insular. Linked to the philosophy that Western culture was advanced, 'civilizing' and superior, the aim was to transform and improve (through Western-style physical education) the lives and values of children from all ethnic and cultural backgrounds. The idea that there could be an alternative philosophy that would recognize cultures outside the West and would preserve and systematically integrate indigenous dance, play and games into school curricula and community programmes for girls and women was not on the agenda.

Belonging to IAPESGW was rather like belonging to an exclusive, subject-oriented club where physical education was given pride of place and where friendships were based on shared knowledge and a shared belief in the value of the subject to growing girls and young women. 'It was', claimed an elderly member, 'the best association I have ever belonged to.' She went on, 'It was run *by* the people who came, not *for* those who applied to come.'

In recent years, feminist writers from colonized countries have described relations such as those embodied in IAPESGW (relations of interconnectedness between 'home', be it Britain or other Western nations, and 'Empire'), as 'exploitative'. Penny Tinkler (1998: 218) argues that 'The production of Whiteness and of European ethnicities … is interwoven with the construction of the racialised "other"; "race" and ethnicity are, in many instances, implicitly if not explicitly, constructed *in relation*.' Catherine Hall (1996) calls upon us to challenge accounts of history which have contributed to narratives of Empire and notions of White ethnic superiority and stability, and other writers (Chaudhuri and Strobel 1992; hooks 1991; Ware 1992) point out that we should understand Whiteness, in common with Blackness, as a racial category, and that although the study of White Western women and imperialism may be 'unpalatable' for those of us who are White, it will help us to understand ourselves and our past as well as the history of the 'Others'.

Even into the 1980s and early 1990s, as the worlds of physical education and sport became increasingly interconnected, IAPESGW's narrow definition of culture and very strong sense of professionalism remained in place. In countries in the developing world, there was a growing interest in Western philosophies of physical education and so the association expanded. It now has over 500 members from 57 countries and all 5 continents. IAPESGW has undoubtedly sustained an important service for its members and still today 'provides opportunities for professional development and international cooperation' (IAPESGW 1998). However, it has systematically privileged Western physical education discourse and constructions as universal. In addition, until recently it has been ill at ease about locating physical education and sport in a broad social and political context, about examining developments in mainstream sport that were influencing physical education, and especially about addressing problems affecting girls and young women that were inherent to elite sport.

Women's International Sports Coalition (WISC)

It was this narrow focus, perceived to be rather conservative and inward-looking, that triggered a reaction from a few IAPESGW members who had been influenced by the women's movement. They believed that women's sport should be part of a wider feminist and political agenda. So, in 1992, at special ad hoc meetings at the annual conference of the US Women's Sports Foundation – entitled 'The Ascent of Woman' – there was an effort to set up a Women's International Sports Coalition (WISC) (Brackenridge 1992a). The vision was to '*co-ordinate globally*' the different intellectual and political approaches of the national and international organizations in existence by that time in order to create a more active, interventionist stance for women in sport. Celia Brackenridge observed that very few organizations challenged patriarchal structures and practices or linked the struggle against gender oppression in sport to wider social and political contexts. She called for a radical approach that would move beyond the liberal perspective of equal opportunities to a more critical and transformative one that would question oppressions of class, race and gender. Speaking on behalf of all the women at those meetings – who came from Australia, Belgium, Canada, Japan, the UK, and the USA – she said that its purpose was 'to recognise the value of working together across nations and to capitalise on the collective power that [women] have' (Brackenridge 1992b: 1). Another meeting was held later that year when the importance of a global perspective was reiterated.[2]

WomenSport International (WSI)

IAPESGW's continuing failure to address important issues that have a detrimental effect on females in sport was of growing concern amongst women who were working in various roles in higher education, sports medicine, government and voluntary sports agencies, and national organizations (such as the Women's Sports Foundations in the USA and England, which had been formed in 1974 and 1984 respectively). So, at the 1993 North American Society for the Sociology of Sport (NASSS) conference, where a number of these women were delegates, a decision was taken to set up a new organization, WomenSport International (WSI), which replaced the idea of the WISC coalition. The key figures in this campaign came from Australia, North America and northern Europe, and they worked rapidly to produce a constitution and an interim executive committee until such time as elections could be arranged. WomenSport International was launched officially in 1994 at the international conference in Brighton, England, which was entitled 'Women and Sport: the Challenge of Change'.

Pivotal to WSI philosophy is the notion that it should cater for a global community of women. It was formed in recognition of the 'enormous global growth in participation by women in sport and physical recreation and the shared problems facing women across many cultures' (Brackenridge 2000). In an article entitled 'Think Global, Act Global: The Future of International Women's Sport', Brackenridge (1995: 11) writes about the global aims of WSI, claiming that 'Not all women involved in sport have the opportunity to do practical work on the global level, but all can develop a global consciousness.' The organization has grown in size to 311 individual and 19 organizational memberships from 40 countries. However, over one-third of all WSI members come from the USA and, of the rest, the majority are from Canada and Mexico, Western Europe, and Australia and New Zealand. Only a smattering of members come from other countries in the world. WSI's resolve to 'go global' is reflected in lobbying and advocacy work carried out by its executive members in various international settings, notably with the International Olympic Committee (IOC) and through its representation at the 1995 Fourth United Nations World Conference on Women in Beijing (Brackenridge 1995: 7). WSI has been involved more recently in collaborative work as part of the Global Women's Sport Advocacy Community, influencing the Beijing 5 meeting – the follow-up meeting which preceded the United Nations General Session in New York in 2000 (Oglesby and Darlison 1999). The setting up of task forces to address important issues such as 'Physical Activity and Girls and Women's Health'; 'The Female Athlete Triad'; 'Masters Athletes'; 'Gender Verification'; and 'Sexual Harassment in Sport' is intended to assist and influence the position of girls and women in sport all over the world. However, there is an underlying assumption that countries outside the West are moving from a state of underdevelopment towards modernized Western models and standards of participation in sport. Although the relationship of physical activity to girls' and women's health is the focus of one of the task forces, WSI's philosophy of inclusion has been directed mostly towards competitive sport, including elite-level sport. For women in the developed world, such an approach may be greatly beneficial to those already 'in the system', but for women in the developing world it may have little significance, weakening the claim that WSI is a truly global organization. Women from the developed world are in dominant positions in the organization and, in spite of the recent incorporation of a language of exercise and health (discussed below), the privileging of models of mainstream Western sport continues.

Brighton Conference and Declaration

Self-consciousness about White, Western domination of women's international sport gained momentum during the 1990s. The attempt to reach further and further across the world to incorporate women from more and more countries was rigorously pursued in May 1994, at the time of the first international conference on women and sport, entitled 'Women, Sport and the Challenge of

Change', held in Brighton, England. The conference was the brainchild of Anita White (of the UK Sports Council). It was arranged specifically for sport policy and decision-makers at national and international levels and was funded by the (then) UK Sports Council with additional support and funding from the IOC and the British Council. Huge efforts were made, and considerable subsidies secured, in order to include delegates from the developing world, and from all continents. The success of the event was reflected in numbers: there were 280 delegates – mostly women – who came from 82 countries. The specific aim of the conference was to address and work to change the imbalances women face in sport. The outcome was *The Brighton Declaration on Women and Sport* (Sports Council 1994) – a statement of principles about equality for women in sport throughout the world. The Brighton Declaration envisions a sporting culture that will 'enable and value the full involvement of women in every aspect of sport'. It incorporates principles relating to facilities; school and junior sport; women's participation; high-performance sport; leadership in sport; education, training and development; sports information and research; resources; and domestic and international co-operation.

Anita White was a member of a European Women and Sport Group, almost exclusively from northwest Europe, who wanted to create an international initiative for women in sport. She was aware of radical work going on in Australia, Canada and New Zealand, and believed that the UK's position in the Commonwealth provided a unique opportunity to develop globally. 'What we wanted to do', she told me in an interview, 'was to get at the sport decision-makers, those men and women who were in powerful positions in sport so that we could influence *them*.' Anita believes that the Declaration was a success in so far as it got women's issues on to the international sport agenda in a creative way.

Effects of the Declaration

Between 1994 and 1998, over 200 organizations throughout the world, at international, national and local levels, adopted the Brighton Declaration (White 1998: 1). For example, it was endorsed at the first International Conference on Women and Sport held for Muslim women in Egypt in 1995, and was 'subsequently taken forward to the Supreme Council for Youth and Sport in Egypt and to the Council of Arab Ministers of Youth and Sport, who also adopted it' (White 1997: 4). It has been adopted also by the Caribbean ministers of youth and sport; the Commonwealth heads of government; the European ministers of sport; and the Supreme Council for Sport in Africa; by international physical education associations, including IAPESGW; and by the main national organizations responsible for sport in over 40 countries from the continents of Africa, North America, Asia, Oceania and Europe (White 1997: 4–5). The Brighton Declaration has provided women with a valuable 'prop' in their struggles – for example, the WSI used it effectively to lobby the IOC – the most symbolically powerful international sport organization – which had never been *pro*-active on women's issues at any time in its history.

The IOC adopted the Declaration in September 1995, responding to the unexpectedly strong and widespread international support for it. Under pressure from the WSI and other women's groups, the IOC went on: to establish, in March 1996, its own Working Group on Women; to ratify, in July 1996 in Atlanta, the Working Group's Proposals; and to set targets for female membership of National Olympic Committees and International Federations (10 per cent by 2000 and 20 per cent by 2005) (White 1997: 4–6). Also in 1996, the IOC voted for three more women members; women's weightlifting, additional hockey teams, triathlon, taekwondo, and softball were added to the Olympic programme; the Olympic Charter was amended to include the promotion of women's sport; IOC seminars on women's sport were held in Fiji and Mexico; and the IOC hosted its first World Conference on Women and Sport. And then, in 1997, there was the symbolically significant appointment of a woman – Anita Defrantz – to the position of vice president of the IOC (White 1997: 7).

Given its past history, it is difficult to believe that the IOC would have made these changes without the continued lobbying of women over the years, or unless there had been widespread public shifts in attitudes towards gender discrimination. Since the 1960s, the official rhetoric of social decision-making has wholeheartedly incorporated support for issues of equality. It is less the principle of gender equality that has to be struggled over now, but the way in which it is interpreted and whether or not, and in which ways, it is put into practice. The IOC remains a hugely privileged and self-perpetuating undemocratic body, and its members, male and female, remain part of an elite 'club' with little authentic connection to the struggles and desires of women at grassroots level. The assimilation of exceptional women, who are unrepresentative of the majority, into male discourses and structures of power, characterizes much of the change towards gender equality in the context of elite sport. Power is most certainly not located with those women that are the subjects (objects) of the discourse for change (M.A. Hall 1994: 71). It is impossible to judge how far-reaching the effects of the Brighton Conference have been, because endorsing it in order to be politically correct does not mean, necessarily, that the will is there, or the resources are available, to implement practical changes in line with philosophy.

But, most significantly, the Brighton Conference and Declaration provided a channel of empowerment for women working for female sport in countries with a wide geographic spread. White argues that many women at the conference had been working in isolation in their home countries, and that meeting other women who shared similar problems was 'energizing and very, very positive'. A general sense of empowerment was generated among women from different countries, locations and cultures. A number of delegates said they were 'inspired'. For example, during the period of the conference, a group of African women decided there should be an association for African women in sport, so they elected a working party, and mandated them to produce such an organization. There are many other examples of good practice – as defined and stimulated by the principles of the Declaration – published in a report covering the four years following the Brighton Conference. In Trinidad there was a 'Celebration of Women and Girls in Sport', which included a multimedia campaign and many and varied sporting events. Although the women who were leaders and speakers at the conference were, again, predominantly Euro-American, delegates from other parts of the world, although also elites from their countries, took the opportunity to talk together, share experiences, make plans, and take energy from a felt sense of community, which encouraged them to go home and work for improved conditions for women in sport in their own countries.

International Working Group on Women and Sport (IWG)

Another result of what was described to me as 'a massive wave of emotion and excitement and positive thinking' that came out of the Brighton Conference was the decision to hold a Second World Conference on Women and Sport in Namibia in 1998. A decision was also made to set up the International Working Group on Women and Sport (IWG). This was originally a self-elected group of women who set out to monitor the progress of the International Women and Sport Strategy and to help to plan the Namibia Conference. At the start, IWG was co-chaired by Anita White (who later became Director of Development at the UK Sports Council) and Pendukeni Iivula-Ithana (who later became Minister for Lands, Resettlement and Rehabilitation in the Namibian government). Although Africa was represented, most members of the group came from the UK, Canada, New Zealand and Australia. Because of the high costs of getting to meetings, representation from the Caribbean, Indonesia and South America, for example, was short-lived and the economic crisis in Asia militated against representation from Asian states.

From the start, the IWG has been characterized by its strong links with state apparatuses, although it has 'grafted on' some voluntary-sector representatives. Links with government gives the group the stamp of officialdom and respectability and easier access to funds and support – for example, the UK Sports Council provided the original Secretariat. The Secretariat was transferred to Canada on the basis that they would host the next conference. In order to preserve some continuity, it was agreed that leadership should reside with one of the four best-resourced Commonwealth countries, who had largely kept the movement going – that is, either Australia, Canada, New Zealand or the UK.

However, government links limit the group's autonomy and potential radicalism and, although IWG is unofficial and 'free-floating', it is comprised of women who are already active in leadership positions in other contexts, reproducing both power and privilege. (It was decided that there will be representatives in the Group from IAPESGW; WSI; the IOC Women's Working Group; and the Commonwealth Games Federation.) Outsiders have asked, 'How can I get to be on the IWG?' The present members have claimed that it is not exclusionary, that they want to make it representative of women from different parts of the world, organizations and sporting interests. It now has members from regional organizations representing Africa, Europe, Oceania and the Americas, and is trying to get one from Asia. The reality is that it is an undemocratic body, not an organization, it has no base, and no specific mission except to monitor developments. But the work of IWG is contradictory – it is precisely *because* its members are privileged that they can influence those in decision-making positions to advance the cause of women in sport. IWG thus becomes a facilitating mechanism, even although IWG members may not wield *direct* power. Anita White explains that 'My approach in trying to lead IWG has been to seize the opportunities to use such influence as we could ... mainly working through existing structures. ... I suppose it's the philosophy of using what resources you have at your disposal.' IWG members are actively promoting the principles of the Brighton Declaration through activities such as lobbying, speaking at conferences, and supporting national and regional developments. Through the involvement of politicians and government agencies, it has spearheaded an energetic and contagious growth of awareness about women's sport across the world.

Windhoek Conference

The Second World Conference on Women and Sport was held in Windhoek, Namibia, in May 1998. Its constituency was still predominantly top-level administrators and policy-makers from government agencies, sport organizations and the women's movement (WSF 1998a: 6). The Conference was entitled 'Reaching Out for Change', with the idea that women in the world of sport should 'reach out' and learn from the global women's movement and its work in other fields, such as health and education, and that far more attention should be paid to what sport can contribute to women's development as a whole and to women's empowerment (White 1997: 10). There was a speaker from the UN Commission for the Status of Women, and discussions referred to a wide range of physical activities and recreation and not just competitive sport. For example, delegates from the Nigerian Women in Sport Association have linked their work with children to education, health and social issues, including AIDS. Although there was some focus on elite, competitive sport, much more of the debate at the Windhoek Conference was concerned with women's health and well-being.

The reaching-out process also related to the location of the Conference. It enabled women from all over the African continent to come to Windhoek, most of whom are unable, for financial reasons, to attend conferences in the more usual venues in Europe and North America. There were 400 delegates from 74 countries, 200 of whom were from Africa. They came from all parts of Africa – French-speaking, English-speaking and Portuguese-speaking. Many of them had travelled in minibuses; and delegations had driven for three or four days, day and night, to get there. There was a special two-day conference before the rest of the delegates arrived, when the Africa Women in Sport Association, envisaged in Brighton, was actually launched. There was a real sense of celebration – 'great stories of exercise classes in townships, all kinds of innovations and initiatives that were really inspiring, women talking with passion about their belief in what sport could do for them'. The developing world was much better represented at Windhoek than at Brighton which, White argues, 'justified having the Conference there from the point of view of the growth of the global women and sport movement'.

Windhoek Call for Action

An outcome of the Namibia Conference was the decision to hold a Third World Conference on Women in Sport in Canada in 2002. There was also a statement entitled the 'Windhoek Call for Action', recognizing the successes of the previous four years and identifying a number of action points for the years ahead. During the four-year period following the Brighton Conference, there was a growth of awareness and acceptance of the principles of gender equity laid out in the Declaration and a remarkable start in turning the principles into practice. The four-year phase following Windhoek was especially con-cerned about connecting with the 'global women's equality movement', in particular with respect to health, education and employment. Action was called for to take account of the diversity of women's backgrounds and eliminate unequal and harmful gender relations of power at personal and institutional levels.

The Windhoek Conference and Call for Action reflect a sensitivity to difference, a growing awareness of the specific needs and desires of women from different countries and, in particular, a greater understanding of the lives and problems of women in the developing world. But we need to be cautious about labelling the Windhoek experience (which has captured the imagination and enthusiasms of women from all over the world) as a total triumph. The Call for Action is directed specifically at sports providers (at all men and women working in the plethora of public and voluntary agencies in national and international settings who have a responsibility or a direct influence on girls' and women's sport [WSF 1998a: 1]), and not at those women who are at the receiving end of policies, and who, given the chance, might have a great deal to say about them. The problem of representation is a problem for all the groups of the International Women's Sport Movement.

Problems of representation

Members of IWG continue to come predominantly from Euro-American backgrounds and are immersed in Western ideas and discourses about sport. They have tied themselves to IAPESGW and WSI, and to the Olympic and Commonwealth Movements, by co-opting women from these organizations into IWG membership. The non-democratic procedures mean that it is impossible for IWG to be authentically representative of the women it purports to represent. It is also the case that some of the key women in one organization play important roles in one or more of the other organizations or groups, so that the *same* women, with the *same* interests, the *same* ideas and the *same* connections reproduce their influence in many and different situations. They comprise a new elite – in effect, a 'women's international sport establishment'. We should not assume, either, that the conference delegates are representative of a broad constituency of women. Those who attended the Brighton and Namibia Conferences were not in general democratic representatives of groups or organizations, but were mostly paid administrators linked to local, national, government or inter-government agencies. It has been argued that 'all post-colonial societies are still subject in one way or another to overt or subtle forms of neo-colonial domination' (Ashcroft *et al.* 1995: 2) and that there has been an emergence of 'powerful local elites who manage the contradictory effects of under-development' (S. Hall 1996b: 248). Inevitably, the international move-ment embodies new elites from postcolonial countries, brought to power by independence, often educated and trained in the West, who are unrepresent-ative of woman at the grassroots in their respective countries (Ashcroft *et al.* 1998: 163).

The internal divisions which are found in all societies based, for example, on racial, linguistic and religious discrimination, affect women's opportunities in sport and separate, symbolically and in practice, women with different social and ethnic backgrounds from those who speak on their behalf. In settler/invader societies, for example, there is a real distinction of interest between the 'official' discourse of conference delegates and those of indigenous peoples. Global pressures and the influence of Eurocentric and Americanized models of sport and culture are taken for granted, and there is systematic privileging of institutionalized, highly competitive, commodified sport over the richness of pre-colonial indigenous games and cultures, which may be more authentic activities for girls and women from ethnic minority and Aboriginal groups (see Chapter 4). There is also ignorance of, or silence about, the growing movement to revive and revalue playful activities and local cultures (Laine 1993).

New elites in developing nations have mostly taken over hegemonic control from colonial elites so that, even when there is a 'filtering' or 'cascade' effect – when people in leadership positions take decisions and implement change – it is not necessarily in the way that is desired by those at the receiving end. Sharda Ugra, a sports journalist from Bombay, pointed out in 1999 that:

> In the case of India, I personally believe the real issue is the distance be-tween Indian women on the 'execs' and 'ordinary' women. The existence of this gap is a greater obstacle for women in the developing world than the culture-specific (i.e. Western, First World) nature of the global movement itself. … The elite women of the Third World – who enjoy power and access equal to their counterparts in the West – have failed the majority.

Such structures of power have contributed to the neo-colonial nature of the Women's International Sport Movement and add to the complexity of global relations within it. Additionally, those few women from the developing world who play significant roles in the International Women's Sport Movement mask the distinct racial hierarchy intrinsic to it. The leaders of the organization continue to be predominantly White, middle-class, professional Western women. This is because, in their respective Western countries, while Black (for example, Afro-Caribbean/Afro-American) women are highly visible as athletes, they become marginalized or even invisible in the executive levels of sport education and administration from which the leadership of the women's sport movement is drawn. Also marginalized or absent in powerful, decision-making positions are women from other minority groups – for example, Aboriginal women in Australia, First Nation women in North America (see Chapter 4), and British Asian women (from India, Pakistan, Sri Lanka, Bangladesh). There are two levels of neo-colonialism: the level which embodies relations of power between dominant and subordinate groups in the West; and the level which embodies relations of power between dominant Western women and those from the developing world.

Other groups of women, such as disabled women (see Chapter 6), could also claim that they are not represented because the movement maintains a very narrow view of womanhood, restricted through divisions of class, ethnicity and ability. And, although some lesbian women from countries in the West are active in leadership positions of all the component groups, homophobia continues to be a structure of exclusion for many others, and in particular for lesbian women from the developing world who suffer harsh oppression (see Chapter 5). In order to expand the social composition of the Women's International Sport Movement *globally*, it would be necessary to forge links with representative organizations of minority and oppressed groups in different countries and regions.

The issues of democracy and representation are crucial, and those groups implicated in the women's sport movement – namely IAPESGW, WSI and IWG – are struggling to become authentically global and inclusive. The new president of IAPESGW, Margaret Talbot, is clear about her task. She argues that

> I was acutely aware when I took on the Presidency of IAPESGW, that one of the most urgent tasks was to avoid the danger of 'organisational elites reproducing themselves'. We had to address the historical domination of the Association's leadership by Europeans and North Americans, and to ensure better and more effective participation and representation by women from Africa, Asia and Latin America.
>
> (personal correspondence)

She believes that IAPESGW has an important role to play in the future in forging links between so-called developed and less developed countries, and between 'Western' countries and Islamic countries, and that its most urgent focus relates to the 'World Crisis in Physical Education' (Talbot 1999: 111–13). Talbot played a leading role at the World Summit on Physical Education in 1999 in Berlin. This project was led by the International Council of Sport Science and Physical Education (ICSSPE) and was organized in response to the results of a worldwide survey showing 'the critical status of Physical Education around the world, regardless of geography or socio-economic status' (ICSSPE 1999: 4). Recommendations were sent from the conference to a meeting of ministers and senior officials responsible for physical education and sport and to the General Conference of UNESCO (ICSSPE 1999: 4) to encourage member states to ensure that sport and physical education are incorporated into school programmes. There was also IAPESGW representation, together with representatives from WSI and IWG at the Second IOC World Congress on Women and Sport in Paris in 2000. The IAPESGW executive has discussed the Beijing 5 agenda and is working collaboratively with WSI and IWG 'in the general areas of health, development, education and social justice'. At the 2001 IAPESGW Congress, further decisions will be made about working in partnership with other organizations – notably ICSSPE, which has a formal relationship with UNESCO and the IOC.

The most significant partnerships have been between the organizations of the Women's International Sport Movement itself – WSI, IAPESGW and IWG. WSI has been working during the past year on expanding what its president, Carole Oglesby, refers to as the 'global women's sport advocacy community' in the mainstream of the UN programme. By 'speaking as one' through co-operative work, there is greater potential that the international voice of women in sport will be heard and heeded. Extended co-operative links with other organizations – at national and regional levels – also strengthens the power of the lobby. The Women's Sports Foundation (WSF) in the USA and the Canadian Association for the Advancement of Women and Sport and Physical Activity (CAAWS) are examples of the numerous national bodies across the world that have effectively and collaboratively represented women in sport. ICSSPE is an example of an international body that has also played an important role in gender equity advocacy work. The role of research has become more and more significant, as well, providing substantial evidence to support arguments for equity and action. In the field of sexual harassment, in particular, evidence has been unearthed and strategies for dealing with the problem have been formulated by two leading members of WSI – Celia Brackenridge from the UK and Kari Fasting from Norway. A most significant result of their work has been the IOC resolution that, at all its regional training meetings, materials about sexual harassment will be featured. Two papers have been produced by Brackenridge and Fasting for the Council of Europe Sports Division, one of which lays out principles which should provide a basis for preventing sexual harassment, which it is hoped will be accepted by all European member states (Brackenridge and Fasting 1999: 15).

Efforts have also been made to build bridges with the mainstream women's political movement and with academic feminists who, according to Carole

Oglesby (email interview 2000), 'have always been quite separate from us and uninterested in women's sport'. Oglesby suggests that 'a transition is going on and that both movements are taking cognizance of each other'. The connection was made at Beijing 5 when there was an announcement recognizing that the passage of CEDAW (Convention to Eliminate Discrimination Against Women) – affirmed now by 170 countries – 'has had a beneficial effect on women's sport development'. IWG is now more representative of developing countries – additional members come from South America, the Caribbean and Fiji and, in common with WSI and IAPESGW, it is continuing the global expansion strategy by trying to influence decision-makers – that is, governments and non-governmental organizations (NGOs) – to keep women's and girls' exercise and sport on their respective agendas. The success of this policy was reflected at the 2000 Second IOC World Conference on Women in Sport, when there were 450 delegates from 140 countries, a growth which reflects the foundation of new organizations and new people taking the lead on women and sport in countries, when there were previously none.

There has been a change also at the level of ideas. The philosophical shift that was established in Namibia – emphasizing women's physical activity as an aspect of development and community – was confirmed as an important perspective for Beijing 5. The discourse of 'sport' was transposed to a discourse of 'healthful physical activity and active recreative lifestyle', moving the focus away from formalized, organized, competitive sport to activities which are better suited to most women and especially to those in developing countries. The 'new language' has been explained by Elizabeth Darlison (secretary general of WSI) in a written statement concerning the positive effects of physical education and active lifestyles for the health and well-being of girls, which is being sent to the commission on the status of women within the UN's Division on Advancement of Women (DAW). The topic for IAPESGW's 2001 Congress, 'Life Long Learning – Towards Active Girls and Women', reflects this shared interest in taking account of 'women's and girls' experiences from all cultures, countries and races'.

However, it is not sufficient simply to acknowledge women's different experiences. By some means, it is essential to involve women at all levels in the decision-making processes and, most importantly, those who at present lack power and freedom. I pointed out in Chapter 2 that African women from the townships have been highly critical of the South African National Sports Council's position on gender and redistribution of resources. They feel intensely that they lack power and that the establishment rhetoric about women's empowerment through sport is empty propaganda. They argue that *they understand* what is needed for physical activity and sport development in the townships far better than outsiders, that they want to *share* in decision-making procedures, but that they do not get the chance. They say that 'First World people are not aware', referring to those White (and Black elite) women who claim to be their 'representatives' in the Women's International Sport

Movement at both local and international levels. Realistically, in the present arrangements, these women have little chance of a voice in plans for the future.

Conclusion

The starting question for this chapter – whether or not a Women's International Sport Movement can ever be truly representative of the women it purports to support – should not dismiss its remarkable achievements during its brief history. Its leaders have been exceptionally energetic and determined in their efforts to change women's sport for the better, and to spread opportunities and knowledge to a wider community of women across the world. But the question does prompt us to argue for a more inclusive approach in the future. There is no doubt that the work of IWG, IAPESGW and WSI has made huge contributions to the futures of girls and women in physical education and sport, and that there is strength in their collaboration and the different emphases of their work. But if the international movement is going to grow in effectiveness, it needs to find ways of reaching those women who are marginalized in their own countries, to transform the existing sets of power relations and to 'reach out' and 'pull in' women from underprivileged backgrounds and involve them in a process of reconstruction. Leaders of the Women's International Sport Movement should pay attention to C. Wright Mills' (1959: 174) message:

> Freedom is not merely the chance to do as one pleases; neither is it merely the opportunity to choose between set alternatives. Freedom is, first of all, the chance to formulate the available choices, to argue over them – and then, the opportunity to choose.

The potentially transformative approach to women's development – the Third World Women's (TWW) empowerment perspective (see Chapter 2) – is connected to women's grassroots organizations and specifically to the experiences of women in the developing world. This perspective recognizes the interlocking of, for example, class, gender, race, ethnicity, ability and age (Chowdhry 1995: 36) and, most importantly, views women as 'participants, rather than recipients, of the development process' (Chowdhry 1995: 39). This viewpoint moves beyond the acknowledgment of diversity and listens to the voices of deprived women, values their knowledge and experiences, engages in dialogue with them, and helps them to construct their own recreation and sporting identities within the difficult lived material realities of their lives. Identity politics confronts the conflict between constructing one's own identity or having one's identity defined by others. As we have seen in the preceding chapters, the politics of recognition, of difference, of identity and of exclusion are peculiar to history and place.

More radical changes in the future would depend on whether different opinions and challenges are viewed as a threat to existing policies and plans, or whether an open forum for debate which embodies critical ideas and analysis can be established. Writing about the feminist movement and involvement with feminist politics, bell hooks issues a warning:

> Significantly, I learned that any progressive political movement grows and matures to the degree that it passionately welcomes and encourages, in theory and practice, diversity of opinion, new ideas, critical exchange, and dissent. ... Again and again, I have to insist that feminist solidarity rooted in a commitment to progressive politics must include a space for rigorous critique, for dissent, or we are doomed to reproduce in progressive communities the very forms of domination we seek to oppose.
>
> (1994: 65–7)

At present the leaders of the Women's International Sport Movement are a mixture of predominantly White, Western hegemonic elites and new developing world elites, who together are exerting specific and distinctive effects – what Stuart Hall (1996b: 254) describes as 'the contradictory effects of under-development and "emergent" new configurations of power-knowledge relations'. He goes on to argue that 'The "post-colonial" presents the coloniser equally with the colonised with "a problem of identity" ' (1996b: 337).

Different women across the world are struggling for identity, and sport has become an increasingly significant way for women to assign meaning to their lives. Female sport – and specifically the Women's International Sport Movement – is an important example of feminist cultural politics put into action through organized opposition to the domination of men in sport and through the freeing and empowering of the bodies of women from diverse backgrounds. Diversity is part of the strength and richness and political power of sportswomen, but only if communication across difference takes place. In order to deconstruct privilege and elitism, communication must happen between women from *within* nation states as well as between women from separate nation states. Women in the Women's International Sport Movement need to establish a sense of difference *and* shared experience. This will only happen if those groups of women who have been marginalized in the past – including Black women, Muslim women, Aboriginal women, lesbian women, and disabled women – are given the authority to speak for themselves and to have their personal circumstances taken notice of. The following words of Diane Coole could act as a guideline for the future development of women's sport throughout the world:

> We need to develop our understanding of difference by creating a situation in which hitherto marginalized groups can name themselves, speak for themselves, and participate in defining the terms of interaction, a situation in which we can construct an understanding of the world that is sensitive to difference.
>
> (1993: 207)

The future of a global sport feminism and the Women's International Sport Movement lies in the potential to unite women across existing divisions of culture – in relation to ability, age, class, race, religion and sexuality. Vron Ware (1992: 242) argues that 'Feminism has battled with the problem of representing the experiences of all women' and there is a 'need for a political language that will express the differences between people without losing sight of the aims and ideals that we have in common'. Global sport feminism is *defined* by difference and requires a language and a strategy that takes *account* of difference. Its future lies with coalition.

Notes

1 Introducing heroines of sport: making sense of difference and identity

1 Ann Hall is in the process of writing a history of women's sport in Canada and is painstakingly unearthing evidence of women's achievements which until now have been unknown and unpublished.

2 Race, politics and gender: women's struggles for sport in South Africa

Particular and grateful thanks for help with this chapter go to Denise Jones, who gave me much-needed information and painstakingly read and commented on earlier drafts.

1 An earlier and reduced version of this chapter, entitled 'Women's Sport, Development and Cultural Diversity: The South African Experience', was published in 1997 in *Women's Studies International Forum* 20(2): 191–220.
2 The Government of National Unity was phased out before the 1999 elections.
3 Before I went to South Africa, I had contacted a network of people actively involved in women's sport during the period of apartheid and up to the present day. Without exception, they were keen to meet me and talk to me. Venues were fixed, travel arrangements made, and meetings organized so that during a four-week period I was able to talk to around 150 people – some men, but mostly women. They were involved in different sports in varied capacities – for example, representatives from national and local organizations, including those from disabled sport organizations; sport academics, and students; those working in a range of sport codes, on sport programmes and in community schemes; girls and women who are participants, coaches, administrators and journalists. Those I talked to were from diverse backgrounds, including 'so-called' White, Indian, Coloured and African backgrounds. I conducted individual and group interviews; most interviews lasted between one and two hours. Some of the largest groups I interviewed were from Soweto and Guguletu (a township outside Cape Town); I was invited to discuss women's sport with people in their homes – in or close to Johannesburg, Soweto, Cape Town and Durban; I met mixed groups of women working in sport development, who travelled to meet me at the universities of Pretoria and the Western Cape; I talked with members of staff at the universities of Zululand and Durban-Westville; I carried out interviews with women who were active in the SACOS movement, who travelled to my hotel so that I could talk to them. I was also able to observe girls and women participating in different sports and at different venues – during training sessions, in competition and

during a public performance. Some of the women gave me their personal memorabilia – for example, photographs, newspaper cuttings, SACOS publications, competition programmes. I got other documentary evidence from the National Library of South Africa, from the Women's Bureau of South Africa, and from clubs and organizations.

4 The Population Registration Act was passed in 1950. 'Natives' were also referred to as 'Bantus' in the language of apartheid. 'Coloureds' were those considered to be of mixed racial origin – mostly of Malaysian and Indonesian descent. Those defined as 'Natives' and 'Coloureds' in the Act are subdivided further into ethnic groups.

5 The colonizers were Europeans – mostly Afrikaners, mainly of Dutch descent (although a distinctly Afrikaner identity was not consolidated until the early twentieth century), and those with British roots. The colonized refers to indigenous peoples from Africa.

6 The Human Sciences Research Council (1982) report. SANROC (n.d.: 1) has shown that the committee of the HSRC was composed 'exclusively of pro-government White sports administrators and Black government stooges'. It is likely, therefore, that the real differences are even greater.

7 The following are examples of laws which affected sports participation: Bantu Laws Amendment Act/Native Laws Amendment Act/Blacks (Urban Areas) Consolidation Act – in different ways, these Acts all restricted the movement of people into non-designated areas or to 'undesirable' gatherings; Group Areas Act – segregation of the population into different areas; Liquor Act – originally banned all mixed drinking. When revised permits were required: Pass Laws – restricted travel to away matches and for tours; Population Registration Act – all South Africans were registered as belonging to a specific racial group; Separate Amenities Act – prevented integration of ground and club facilities; Urban Areas Act – controlled Black sports facilities and restricted their use by permit. (Hain 1982: 243–4; Ramsamy 1982: 21–4).

8 'Non-racial' – a colour-blind term – demonstrated recognition of South Africa as a unified state.

9 Albert Grundlingh's (1996) article, 'Playing for Power? Rugby, Afrikaner Nationalism and Masculinity in South Africa c. 1900–c. 1970', is an exception.

10 Mixed marriages were prohibited in law.

11 Tessa Sanderson argued openly that to support Zola Budd was fundamentally racist: 'I totally believe she should never have been allowed to compete for Great Britain. The thing is I talked to the press and the press gave this big interview and said, "Tessa Blackens Zola Budd". Well, yes, I did, because at the end of the day there were a lot of Black athletes in South Africa who couldn't get a passport to get out. Now this girl walks into the British team. She ran a race which paid her £90,000. Kathy Smallwood [400 metres bronze medallist at the 1984 Olympics] and myself couldn't find sponsorship. They gave her a house – the papers gave her a house she could live in – and we were still paying our mortgage. And we held the British records and all that … And I also felt it was wrong because she lived in Bloemfontein – it was one of the most racist places in South Africa. For that alone I felt British athletics had no respect for Black athletes at that time' (personal interview 1997).

Judy Oakes is reported to have said: 'She [Budd] keeps aloof from the rest of us, she's surrounded by minders wherever she goes and she even stays in separate hotels when we are abroad. She's not a member of the British team, she's just an athlete who happens to compete in a British vest' (*Sport and Apartheid* April 1986: 1).

12 The final of the Rugby World Cup, between South Africa and New Zealand, took place in July 1995 in Johannesburg. Nelson Mandela opened the event wearing a Springbok cap and jersey – the symbols of all-White South African male sport, previously associated with Afrikaner nationalism. There was only one Black player in the South African team – Chester Williams.

13 The NSC was replaced in 2000 by the Sports Commission – a new body intended to assimilate the overlap in objectives and programmes of the NSC and the Department of Sport and Recreation.

14 Elana Meyer is a White South African woman who won a silver medal in the 10,000-metre race at the Barcelona Olympics. The race was won by Derartu Tulu from Ethiopia, who was the first Black African woman to win a gold Olympic medal on the athletics track. Hassiba Boulmerka of Algeria won a gold medal in the 1500-metre race, and Nigeria's 4 x 100-metre relay team won a gold medal. The 1992 Barcelona Olympics symbolized the breakthrough of African women into Olympic sport.

15 Three weeks before the National Netball Championships, a directive came from the NSC that there should at least 40 per cent of non-White players in all teams. The sponsors of the championships – Transnet – were up in arms and the instruction was overruled as non-constitutional. The White-dominated national federation argue that the only reason that there are fewer non-White than White members of the national squad is because of playing ability, and not racism.

16 WUS-SA is a fundraising NGO affiliated to WUS International, which consists of about 45 other national committees in other parts of the world. WUS works mainly in the field of education and training.

17 For example, in 1995 the Gender Equity Unit at the University of the Western Cape organized a Women's Studies Winter School which included seminars such as 'Moving Towards Gender Equity in Sport and Other Physical Activities'.

3 The Muslim female heroic: shorts or veils?

Special thanks to Haleh Afshar for reading and making such helpful comments on the first draft of this chapter.

1 The Qur'an is the Muslim sacred text reportedly based on Allah's (God's) revelations made to the Prophet Mohammed.

2 Ulema (mullahs, imams) – meaning 'wise men' who interpret the Qur'an and the teachings of the Prophet Mohammed.

3 The journalist was speaking at a Sports Writers' Conference in December 1991. Algerian intellectuals and reporters were extremely critical of the Imam's declaration against Hassiba Boulberka.

4 The Muslim population has risen to around 3 million in Germany (mainly Turkish), over 2 million in France (mostly North African), and around 1.5 million in the UK (mainly from Pakistan and Bangladesh).

5 In his book *The Satanic Verses*, Salman Rushdie is alleged to have blasphemed against Islam. Anyone who does so is subject to the death penalty. The Fatwa was lifted ten years later by a relatively liberal government, in September 1998, after the death of the Ayatollah, .

6 For example, in Afghanistan women are forced to wear burquas (head-to-toe black capes which cover the face with a thick 'grill' to see through) and beaten for showing their ankles (O'Kane 1998: 37); there is a wide range of 'styles of veil', from the uniform black cloaks worn by women in post-revolution Iran, to the exclusive 'designer' scarves of women of the 'new aristocracy' in Egypt' (Watson 1994: 141); in Malaysia, most Malay women have adopted some version of 'a headscarf or attractively styled veil which does not cover the face, and a long, loose two-piece dress also in an appealing co-ordination of colours and textures … to the point where it may be said to have become Malay national costume'(Nagata 1994: 78–9).

7 Tohidi (1991: 258) argues that this was the case in other countries as well – for example, Lebanon, Morocco and Pakistan.

8 Tohidi (1991: 252) writes that 'Many women, even nonreligious, nontraditional, and highly educated women, took up the veil as a symbol of solidarity and opposition to

the Shah. At rallies and demonstrations, chadors (veils) and roosaries (large scarves) were extended to the unveiled women, who felt obliged to show their solidarity with the majority.'

9 Many women were active demonstrators during the revolution of 1979, which culminated in the overthrow of the Shah and the creation of the Islamic Republic of Iran, led by the Ayatollah Khomeini.

10 The punishments for the crime of appearing without hijab are 75 lashes or imprisonment.

11 In Muslim countries, there are burgeoning women's liberation movements.

12 The Iranian Olympic Committee announced that it would not send swimmers to China in 1990 because mixed-sex events were planned (Pourhaddadi 1998: 12).

13 Especially significant because, at the Barcelona Olympics in 1992, the Iranian delegation (composed of 40 men) had refused to follow the rule set by the Organizing Committee that a young woman would hold each country's emblem at the front of each delegation. They said that they would not walk behind a woman!

14 In 1998, a group of Iranian women marked the 19th anniversary of the Iranian Revolution by climbing Mount Kilimanjaro in Tanzania.

15 At Iran's first local government elections in March 1999, moderate candidates supportive of Mohammed Khatami won sweeping victories. Khatami's aim is 'to make religious interpretation more compatible with a generation that is demanding modernisation' (Abdo *Guardian* 2/3/99). This may stop the new legislation proposed by hardliners, including the very powerful Supreme Leader Ayatollah Khomeini, to ban the voicing of any opinions that are critical of the mullahs' position about the role of women (Macleod 1998: 29).

16 This was the first time in nearly 20 years that Iranian women had been allowed to attend a men's wrestling match.

17 Public opinion was effective in preventing a ban on televised football during the World Cup – even though 'the Iranian government said it was concerned that pictures of "lewd" acts would be carried "live" into the homes of God-fearing Muslim families' (Bhatia 1998). The 1998 Football World Cup match between Iran and the USA had a 20-second delay before screening, to allow censors to edit out anything considered un-Islamic, such as images of scantily clad Western women (Hillmore 1996).

18 Although the attempt failed, as many as one-third of the National Assembly voted in favour.

19 FIS – widely known as *Intergristes* is the party representing Algeria's Muslim fundamentalist movement. In 1991, the FIS won sweeping victories in municipal elections, and in the first round of the national election (Morgan 1998: 347).

20 Boulmerka dedicated her medal to Mohamed Boudiaf, former president of Algeria, who was assassinated, allegedly by fundamentalists, in June 1992.

21 Because Boulmerka wants to be able to return to her home in Algeria, she has become cautious about talking openly about her situation as a Muslim athlete (Holder 1996).

22 The Baccalauréat is the qualifying examination for university taken by high-school students in order to continue into higher education.

23 There were 10,000 spectators at the opening ceremony and 1000 competitors from 16 Islamic nations taking part – Afghanistan, Azerbaijan, Bangladesh, Fiji, Gabon, Guinea, Indonesia, Iran, Kazakhstan, Kyrgyzstan, the Maldives, Oman, Pakistan, Syria, Turkmenistan and Yemen. Eight Muslim states failed to turn up. An official said they may have had difficulty meeting all the Islamic conditions for participation. Events took place in locations around the country in athletics, badminton, basketball, chess, equestrian events, gymnastics, handball, squash, swimming, shooting, tennis, volleyball and karate. Iran took first place, Kazakhstan was second, and Indonesia came third.

24 Professor Abdelrahman organized the conference following her attendance in 1994 at the Brighton Conference and the creation of the Brighton Declaration – see Chapter 7. The use of the term 'scientific' in the conference title denotes the analytical and theoretical framework of the conference. The conference was sponsored by the Ministry of Education, the Ministry of International Co-operation, the Supreme Council of Youth and Sport, and the Arab League. Approximately 70 per cent of the 200 delegates who attended were women, including Egyptian physical educators, the deans and faculty members from all the major Egyptian universities, and representatives from Egyptian sport organizations. From the conference came a list of 15 key recommendations, recognizing the value of sport to Muslim women in society as well as the essential contribution that sport makes to health.

25 The second conference was under the auspices of Mrs Suzan Mubarak, wife of the president of the Arab Republic of Egypt, who has pioneered work for women and children in Egypt and all over the Arab world. It was supported also by the Supreme Council of Youth and Sport. The third conference in 1999 was under the auspices of Dr Kamal El-Ganzourym, prime minister and president of the Supreme Council for Youth and Sport, and in co-operation and participation with numerous national and international sports and educational organizations.

26 'In most of the Gulf States, apart from the privileged few with their own private gyms, women do not take part in any physical education' (Holder 1996).

27 Qatar is an absolute monarchy. Sheikh Hamad rules by decree.

28 In 1999 Qatar became the first Gulf State to allow women to vote in the municipality council elections.

29 The Prophet's Hadith (the body of tradition about Mohammed that supplements the Qu'ran).

30 Details of the founders of Atlanta are as follows: Anne Marie Lizim (Belgium, ex-Secretary of State for European Affairs); Annie Sugier (a nuclear scientist and French feminist); and Linda Weil-Curiel (French human rights lawyer).

31 The following list of delegations to the 1992 Barcelona Olympics are those that were exclusively male: American Samoa (3); Bahrain (13); Botswana (6); Burkina Faso (4); Caiman Islands (10); Cook Islands (2); Djibouti (5); Eastern Samoa (5); Gambia (6); Haiti (7); Iran (40); Iraq (9); Kuwait (36); Laos (6); Lebanon (13); Libya (6); Mauritania (6); Niger (8); Oman (5); Pakistan (27); Panama (5); Qatar (31); Saudi Arabia (9); Solomon Islands (1); Sudan (6); Swaziland (5); Syria (10); Tanzania (9); Togo (6); Tonga (5); Trinidad and Tobago (7); United Arab Emirates (14); Uruguay (23); Virgin Islands (4); Yemen (13).

32 The Olympic Charter states that 'The goal of the Olympic Movement is to contribute to building a peaceful and better world by educating youth through sport practised without discrimination of any kind with regard to a country or a person on grounds of race, religion, politics, sex or otherwise.'

33 The Atlanta movement has been active since the 1992 Olympic Games, but had its official launch later, in January 1995.

34 In a brochure distributed by Iranian embassies throughout the world, the following statement is made about the Solidarity Games: 'The aim of these games is to spread the Muslim system's culture and values ... and to prevent the corruption resulting from the simultaneous presence of men and women athletes in the same place.' At the seminar on Women and Sport held at the Fourth World Conference on Women in Beijing, China, the spokesperson for the Second Muslim Women's Solidarity Games wished that they would serve as a model for the 500 million Muslim women in the world of whom, she alleged, 'Iran is morally in charge'.

35 The United Nations High Commissioner on Human Rights, Ayala Lasso, said that sex discrimination was a 'civic sin' and agreed that Atlanta was correct in asking the IOC to follow their own charter. The Council of Europe Parliamentary Assembly Resolution 1092 (1996) on discrimination against women in the field of sport – and,

more particularly, in the Olympic Games – includes statements and recomendations in general support of the philosophy and actions of Atlanta. It views the absence of women in national teams and the organization of women-only games (barring men from attending) to be infringements of fundamental human rights. The Assembly states that 'Even if there are cultural differences and traditions, this should be no argument for accepting any policy of discrimination against women in sport.' Its final recommendation is as follows:

The Assembly requests that the IOC:
i)   firmly and clearly oppose any discrimination against women in sport
ii) refuses to support any sports event based on discrimination, such as the 'Solidarity Games for Women in Islamic Countries'.

36 The Feminist Majority Foundation, which has become part of the Atlanta movement, circulated a petition to the IOC during Expo '96 for women's empowerment. Its president, Eleanor Smeal and Director of Policy and Research, Jennifer Jackman, mobilized US women to take action against the countries that block women's Olympic participation. Before the Atlanta Olympics, Dr Parvin Darabi from Iran said, 'We would like to stage a demonstration during the opening ceremonies of the Atlanta Olympics to condemn gender apartheid in Iran and other Islamic nations.' She was raising money to bring a championship woman athlete from Iran to the Atlanta Olympics to tell her story.

37 At the 1996 Olympics there were no female athletes from the following countries: Afghanistan; Brunei Darussalam; Botswana; Djibouti; Grenada; Guinea-Bissau; Haiti; Iraq; Kuwait; Libya; Mauritania; Nauru; Oman; Palestine; Papua New Guinea; Qatar; Rwanda; Senegal; Somalia; Saudi Arabia; Sudan; Togo; United Arab Emirates; Yemen.

38 The two members of the IOC Executive Commission that met the Atlanta delegation were François Carrard, Director General of the IOC, and Anita DeFrantz. The two groups agreed on certain points, but remained divided on the critical question as to whether all women should be free to compete in all Olympic disciplines, no matter the reasons given by their governments to deprive women of this universal right.

39 The following letter was presented to the IOC on 17 July 1996 in Atlanta, Georgia:

'An Open Letter to Juan Antonio Samaranch on his Birthday'

Sir,

As you are aware, we created Atlanta [Atlanta Plus] in 1992 to protest gender discrimination at the Olympic Games after the shock Opening Ceremony in Barcelona where 35 countries were composed only of men.

In January '95, the answer given to our demand was that '*the Olympic hierarchy would be reluctant to take the lead in combating sex discrimination when other international organizations such as the United Nations have not taken strong diplomatic action*' (Associated Press, 13 January 1995).

This answer was surprising since the Olympic Charter clearly states that '*all forms of discrimination with respect to a country or a person, whether for reasons of race, religion, politics, sex or any other are incompatible with the Olympic movement*'.

Nevertheless, to comply with the IOC 'hierarchy's' demand we have obtained from the United Nations Human Rights Commission, the Council of the European Parliament very clear resolutions supporting our views which you will find enclosed.

All women must be gratified that the Atlanta Games include more women than ever before. This makes it more urgent to ensure that women from all countries are allowed to compete.

This is neither a cultural/religious issue nor a woman's-only issue. To put an end to such an unacceptable situation which is in conflict with the Olympic Charter, we request the IOC:

- *to donate one cent per ticket* to a foundation which will distribute the funds to help countries that cannot afford to train women
- to exclude those countries which either practice institutionalized segregation or forbid female participation of women in the Olympics for *ideological reasons.*

Why should men of those countries be allowed to join one of the few universal gatherings of people of all nations when women of the same countries cannot share this joy and pride? Women all around the world look forward to your response.

Sincerely

Anne Marie Lizim
Annie Sugier
Linda Weil-Curiel

40 In an unpublished paper delivered at the Second Scientific Conference for Arab Women's Sport, in Alexandria, Egypt, in 1997, in a reference to the Atlanta lobby, Margaret Talbot claims that the assumption of Atlanta is that 'only Islam is the barrier' and that 'they [Atlanta] have trivialised and ridiculed women from Islamic countries'. She censured Atlanta for not consulting Muslim women from their banned countries list and concludes: 'Atlanta Plus see the situation only through their own narrow and arrogant perspectives'. Margaret Talbot is president of IAPESGW.

In response to a paper submitted by Atlanta to the International Working Group (IWG – see Chapter 7), the decision was made not to alter the Brighton Declaration to take account of gender discrimination as requested by Atlanta.

4 Aboriginal sportswomen: heroines of difference or objects of assimilation?

1 There are numerous complexities and confusions surrounding descriptions of different peoples. For example, in Canada, the term 'First Peoples' refers to all Aboriginal peoples of the country, including 'Indians', 'Inuit' and 'Metis' (mixed race). 'First Nations' is usually used to refer to Indian bands and communities, not including the Inuit and Metis (Barber 1998: 522).

Although the term 'Indian' has come to be widely accepted, particularly by the Aboriginal peoples themselves, it is also used for the people of India, who with some justification claim prior right. In Canada, 'Amerindians' (Indians specific to the Americas) is occasionally used, but 'Native' is more widely used (not accepted in the United States on the grounds that anyone born in that country is a native, regardless of racial origin). 'Aboriginal' is less commonplace, but has been accepted to some extent by Indians as well as non-Indians. Dickason prefers the term 'Amerindian', in order to avoid the ambiguities of 'Indian' and 'Native' and to be more specific than 'Aboriginal' (Dickason 1992: 15–16).

Tribal classifications can also be complex, such as 'Cree', 'Huron', 'Beaver' and 'Haida', which were imposed by Europeans and are not original Aboriginal names.

While many of the Europeanized labels have come to be accepted by the Aboriginal peoples, some have not – for instance, the tundra-dwellers of the Arctic objected to 'Eskimo' on the grounds that it was pejorative, as it had come to be popularly believed that it came from an Ojibwa term that translated as 'eaters of raw meat' despite the opinion of linguists that it derived from a Montagnais term meaning 'she nets a snowshoe'. The tundra-dwellers' term for themselves, 'Inuit' ('the people'; 'Inuk' in the singular), has been officially accepted (Dickason 1992: 15–16).

2 MacDonald (1978) distinguishes the Aborigines who resided in Canada for the last 12,000 years according to their linguistic groups (cited in Dickason 1992):

A   The Algonkian Peoples
(i   Pre-tribal Algonkians –12,000 to 4500 years ago.)
ii   Maritimes and New England – the Delaware, Malecite, Micmac and Abnaki tribes.
iii   Central Forests and Lakes Country – the Ottawa, Algonquin and Ojibway tribes.
iv   Plains – the Atsina (Gros Ventre), the Blood, Pegan and Blackfoot tribes.
v   Northwest Forests – the Naskapi, Cree, Montagnais and Beothuk (extinct) tribes.

Today, the descendants of the Algonkians live on reserves and also in cities and towns.

B   Athapascans of the North and West include the Haida, Carrier, Chilcotin, Kootenai, Interior Salish, Coast Salish, Slave, Nahani Nation, Dogrib, Hare, Yellowknife, Chipewyan, Beaver Nation, Kutchin Nation, Nicola, Tsimshaian, Gitksan, Niska, Ahten, Nabesna, Ingalik, Tananna, Koyukon, Han, Tuchone, Nahani, Goat, Kaska, Sarcee, Sekani, Beaver, Kutchin-Loucheux, Tsetsaut Tahltan, Tlingit, Tagish, and Eyak.

C   The Inuit of the Arctic Maritimes – the People of the Aleutian Islands; the Inyupik of Canada and Greenland; and the Yupik of Alaska (Arctic Mongols).

D   The Iroquoians Eastern Woodlands.

Although Native peoples comprise only 2–3 per cent of the total Canadian population, Paraschak (1997: 3) points out that 'the Inuit and Dene form the majority of the population in the Northwest Territories and live largely in isolated communities scattered across a land mass one third the size of Canada'.

3 1957 was the year when the Welfare Ordinance legislation of 1953 was implemented. It saw the repeal of (and what was interpreted as liberation from) the Aboriginals Ordinance 1918–1953, 'which had deemed all persons of Aboriginal descent to be in need of protection and control' (Tatz 1995: 273).

4 These are all-Aboriginal sports organizations and events, which will be discussed later in the chapter.

5 Charles Perkins is an Aboriginal rights campaigner and former senior government bureaucrat.

6 The 1992 Mabo decision of the high court of Australia recognized the native title of the country's indigenous Aboriginal and Torres Strait Islander peoples. It recognized that Aboriginal people had occupied the continent at the time of the first British settlement and therefore, as prior owners, had entitlement to land. Before then, 'Australia was the only British colony that had failed to recognize in law the prior land ownership of its indigenous inhabitants' (Tonkinson 1998: 289). 1993 was something of a watershed in Aboriginal politics. The Native Title Bill became law

on the last day of 1993, but for most Aborigines the content and scope of the legislation restricts the chances of granting claims, there has been opposition from several states, companies with investment and mineral exporation interests, and from individuals whose houses and farmsteads are threatened, so that the process is very slow. Those opposing the new law claim that it is divisive and racist – treating non-Aboriginals unfairly and that there should be one law applied equally to everyone ('one nation, one law'). It has been described as 'a struggle for the soul of Australia' (Reynolds 1994: 19, cited in Tonkinson 1998: 292).

7 Deadly Vibe is sponsored by the Commonwealth Department of Health and Family Services and the Commonwealth Department of Employment, Education. Training and Youth Affairs.

8 'In 1960 native people were allowed to vote in federal elections for the first time and, thus, be considered both native and Canadian' (Paraschak 1997: 4). The Canadian Constitution Act of 1982 incorporates the Charter of Rights and Freedoms, promising a 'more just, more egalitarian society, a society more respectful of individual characteristics and claims to difference' (Salee 1995: 297). The Canadian constitution gives each ethnic group the right to preserve its own particular values, identity and culture.

9 Yuendumum is a remote settlement 300 kilometres northwest of Alice Springs.

10 For example, the annual Barunga sports and cultural festival and the Pitjantjatjara Games, both founded in the 1980s.

11 The Northern Games included competing contingents from settlements in Alaska, Northwest Territories, Yukoon Territory, Arctic Quebec and Labrador (Paraschak 1991: 83).

5 Sporting lesbians: heroic symbols of sexual liberation

Particular thanks go to Sally Munt for reading the first draft of this chapter and for her enormously helpful comments.

1 For a discussion of the original example – the civil rights movement – and the struggles of indigenous peoples, see Chapter 4.

2 The gay liberation movement originated in 1969 following the Stonewall riots. Five days of rioting ensued after the police made a routine raid on the Stonewall Inn – a gay pub in Greenwich Village, New York – and the patrons refused to leave. The Stonewall rebellion describes the fight by lesbians and gay men against police harassment.

3 Terms that will be discussed later in the chapter.

4 Many significant lesbian communities preceded Stonewall, which consolidated lesbian and gay communities.

5 The myth of gender in sport is that men are *naturally* more aggressive, more competitive and more suited to sports than women.

6 The first pro golfer to come out was Muffin Spencer-Devlin, in 1996 – see the discussion on p. 148.

7 In the UK, for example, the 'state sport apparatus' refers to the Sports Council.

8 In the UK – Clause 28 refers to a section of the Local Government Act 1988, which restrains local authorities from 'promoting' homosexuality. Following this legislation, local authorities stripped lesbian and gay activities from their programmes for fear of being taken to court. It also became illegal for schools to 'promote' homosexuality, so that many teachers no longer discuss issues of sexuality with pupils for fear of reprisals and possible loss of jobs.

9 'Ur-model' can be understood as 'role model'.

10 Cultural participants are those involved in the cultural programme organized for the duration of the Games – for example, drama, music, literature, seminars, political groups, etc.

11 The rainbow motif is a symbol of freedom that has been adopted by the gay community.

12 Although Rosemary Mitchell is a lesbian and Tom Waddell was a gay man, because they both wanted a child they decided to marry and to share the parenting.

13 Sportsdykes have been influenced by the activities of DAM (Dyke Action Machine), which was set up in reaction to the failure of 'Queer Nation' (an American activist organization) to address lesbian issues adequately (Caudwell 2000: 156).

6 Impaired and disabled: building on ability

1 There has been some debate about the use of the terms 'inclusion' (to comprise or embrace as part of a whole) and 'integration' (to combine into a whole). See, for example, Steadward (1996: 28–9). Since the terms are generally used interchangeably – as they are in the above publications – I am electing to use the term 'integration' (in opposition to segregation) to cover the different examples of the 'togetherness' of disabled and able-bodied sportspeople. These terms are also used to refer to relations between different groups of disabled people – but this is not my focus here.

7 Struggling for a new world order: the Women's International Sport Movement

1 This chapter is an expanded and revised version of the following article (1999): 'The Women's International Sports Movement: Local-Global Strategies and Empowerment', in *Women's Studies International Forum* 22(5): 1–11.

2 The meeting took place at the IAPESGW Symposium of the 1992 Pre-Olympic Scientific Congress in Malaga.

Bibliography

Books

Ahmed, A. (1992) *Postmodernism and Islam*, London: Routledge.

Ahmed, A. and H. Donnan (eds) (1994a) *Islam, Globalization and Postmodernity*, London: Routledge.

—— (1994b) 'Islam in the Age of Postmodernity', in Ahmed, A. and H. Donnan (eds) *Islam, Globalization and Postmodernity*, London: Routledge, pp. 1–20.

Albrow, M. (1996) *The Global Age*, Cambridge: Polity.

Altman, D. (1998) 'The End of the Homosexual?', in Nardi, P. and B. Schneider (eds) *Social Perspectives in Lesbian and Gay Studies*, London: Routledge, pp. 306–11.

Anderson, B. (1983) *Imagined Communities*, 2nd edition, New York: Verso.

Archer, R. (1987) 'An Exceptional Case: Politics and Sport in South Africa's Townships', in Baker, W. and J. Mangan (eds) *Sport in Africa*, New York: Africaner Publishing Company, pp. 229–49.

Armstrong, J. (1996) 'Invocation: The Real Power of Aboriginal Women', in Miller, C. and P. Chuchtyk (eds) *Women of the First Nations*, Winnipeg: University of Manitoba, pp. ix–xii.

Ashcroft, B., G. Griffiths and H. Tiffin (eds) (1995) *The Post-Colonial Studies Reader*, London: Routledge.

—— (1998) 'Key Concepts', in Ashcroft, B., G. Griffiths and H. Tiffin (eds) *Key Concepts in Post-Colonial Studies*, London: Routledge.

Barber, K. (ed.) (1998) *The Canadian Oxford Dictionary*, Toronto: Oxford University Press.

Barnes, C. (1998) 'The Social Model of Disability: A Sociological Phenomenon Ignored by Sociologists', in Shakespeare, T. (ed.) *The Disability Reader*, London: Cassell, pp. 65–78.

Barret, M. and A. Phillips (eds) *Destabilizing Theory*, Oxford: Polity.

Benedict, J. (1997) *Public Heroes, Private Felons*, Boston: Northeastern University Press.

Benson, S. (1997) 'The Body, Health and Eating Disorders', in Woodward, K. (ed.) *Identity and Difference*, London: Sage, pp. 121–81.

Bertaux, D. (ed.) (1981) *Biography and Society*, Beverley Hills, CA: Sage.

Bhabha, H. (1995) 'Cultural Diversity and Cultural Differences', in Ashcroft, B., G. Griffiths and H. Tiffin (eds) *Key Concepts in Post-Colonial Studies*, London: Routledge, pp. 206–9.

Birrell, S. (1990) 'Women of Color, Critical Autobiography and Sport', in Messner, M. and D. Sabo (eds) *Sport, Men, and the Gender Order*, Champaign, IL: Human Kinetics, pp. 185–200.

Blue, A. (1994) *Martina Unauthorized*, London: Gollancz.

Booth, D. (1998) *The Race Game*, London: Frank Cass.

Bordo, Susan (1990) 'Reading the Slender Body', in Jacobus, M., E. Fox Keller and S. Shuttleworth (eds) *Body/Politics*, London: Routledge, pp. 83–112.

Bose, M. (1994) *Sporting Colours*, Bodmin, Cornwall: Hartnolls.

Bourdieu, P. (1984) *Distinction*, London: Routledge & Kegan Paul.

Brackenridge, Celia (2000) 'WomenSport International', in Christensen, K., A. Guttmann and G. Pfister (eds) *International Encyclopedia of Women and Sport*, New York: Macmillan.

Brah, A. (1991) 'Questions of Difference and International Feminism', in Aaron, J. and S. Walby (eds) *Out of the Margins*, London: Sage, pp. 168–76.

—— (1996) *Cartographies of Diaspora*, London: Routledge.

Brickhill, J. (1976) *Race Against Race*, London: International Defence and Aid Fund.

Burton Nelson, M. (1994) *The Stronger Women Get, the More Men Love Football*, New York: Harcourt Brace.

Butler, J. (1990) *Gender Trouble*, London: Routledge.

—— (1993) *Bodies That Matter*, London: Routledge.

Cahn, S. (1994) *Coming on Strong*, New York: Harcourt Brace.

Cammack, P., D. Pool and W. Tordoff (1993) *Third World Politics*, London: Macmillan.

Cassidy, B., R. Lord and N. Mandell (1995) 'Silenced and Forgotten Women: Race, Poverty, and Disability', in Mandell, N. (ed.) *Feminist Issues*, Ontario: Prentice Hall, pp. 32–66.

Caudwell, J. (2000) 'Sex and Politics: Sites of Resistance in Women's Football', in Aitchison, C. and F. Jordan (eds) *Gender, Space and Identity*, Brighton: LSA Publication 63: 151–61.

Chaudhuri, N. and M. Strobel (eds) (1992) *Western Women and Imperialism*, Bloomington and Indianapolis: Indiana University Press.

Chow, R. (1993) 'Violence in the Other Country', in Mohanty, C., A. Russo and L. Torres (eds) *Third World Women and the Politics of Feminism*, Bloomington, IN: Indiana University Press, pp. 81–100.

Chowdhry, G. (1995) 'Engendering Development?: Women in Development (WID) in International Development Regimes', in Marchand, H. and S. Parpart (eds) *Feminism/Postmodernism/Development*, London: Routledge, pp. 26–41.

Chuchryk, P. and C. Miller (1996) 'Introduction', in Miller, C. and P. Chuchryk (eds) *Women of the First Nations*, Winnipeg: University of Manitoba Press, pp. 3–10.

Churchill, W. (1999) 'The Tragedy and the Travesty: The Subversion of Indigenous Sovereignty in North America', in Johnson, T. (ed.) *Contemporary Native American Political Issues*, Walnut Creek: Alta Mira, pp. 17–71.

Clarke, G. (1995) 'Outlaws in Sport and Education? Exploring the Sporting and Education Experiences of Lesbian Physical Education Teachers', in Lawrence, L., Murdoch, E. and S. Parker (eds) in *Professional and Development Issues in Leisure, Sport and Education*, Brighton: Leisure Studies Association: 45–58.

Collins, P. (1991) *Black Feminist Thought*, London: Routledge.

Connell, R. (1987) *Gender and Power*, Cambridge: Polity.

—— (1995) *Masculinities*, Cambridge: Polity.

Coole, D. (1993) *Women in Political Theory*, 2nd edition, Hemel Hempstead: Harvester Wheatsheaf.

Cornell, S. and D. Hartmann (1998) *Ethnicity and Race*, Thousand Oaks, CA: Pine Forge.

Creedon, P. (1994) 'From Whalebone to Spandex: Women and Sports Journalism in American Magazines, Photography and Broadcasting', in Creedon, P. (ed.) *Women, Media and Sport*, London: Sage, pp. 108–58.

Crow, L. (1996) 'Including All of Our Lives: Renewing the Social Model of Disability', in Morris, J. (1991) *Pride Against Prejudice*, London: The Women's Press, pp. 206–26.

DePauw, K. and S. Gavron (1995) *Disability and Sport*, Champaign, IL: Human Kinetics.

Dickason, O. (1992) *Canada's First Nations*, Toronto, Canada: University of Oklahoma Press.

Donald, J. and A. Rattansi (1993) 'Introduction', in Donald, J. and A. Rattansi (eds) *'Race', Culture and Difference*, London: Sage, pp. 1–8.

Donnelly, P. (ed.) (1997) *Taking Sport Seriously*, Toronto, Canada: Thompson Education.

Durlik, A. (1999) 'The Past as Legacy and Project: Postcolonial Criticism in the Perspective of Indigenous Historicism', in Johnson, T. (ed.) *Contemporary Native American Political Issues*, Walnut Creek: Alta Mira, pp. 73–97.

Dutton, K. (1995) *The Perfectible Body*, London: Cassell.

Edwards, J. and J.A. Hargreaves (2000) 'Sports Feminism', in Christensen, K., A. Guttmann and G. Pfister (eds) *International Encyclopedia of Women and Sport*, New York: Macmillan Reference, pp. 395–402.

Elsdon, D. (ed.) (1995) *Male Bias in the Development Process*, 2nd edition, Manchester: Manchester University Press.

Emberley, J. (1996) 'Aboriginal Women's Writing and the Cultural Politics of Representation', in Miller, C. and P. Chuchryk (eds) (1996) *Women of the First Nations*, Winnipeg: University of Manitoba Press, pp. 97–112.

Fanon, F. (1986) *Black Skins, White Masks*, London: Pluto.

—— (1993) 'The Fact of Blackness', in Donald, J. and A. Rattansi (eds) *'Race', Culture and Difference*, London: Sage, pp. 220–42.

—— (1995) 'National Culture', in Ashcroft, B., G. Griffiths and H. Tiffin (eds) *Key Concepts in Post-Colonial Studies*, London: Routledge, pp. 153–7.

Featherstone, M., S. Lash and R. Robertson (eds) (1995) 'An Introduction', in *Global Modernities*, London: Sage, pp. 1–24.

Festle, M. (1996) *Playing Nice: Politics and Apologies*, New York: Columbia University Press.

Flax, J. (1992) 'Feminists Theorize the Political', in Butler, J. and J. Scott (eds) *Feminists Theorize the Political*, London: Routledge, pp. 450–68.

Foucault, M. (1980a) *The History of Sexuality: An Introduction*, trans R. Hurley, vol. 1, New York: Vintage.

—— (1980b) 'Body/Power', in Gordon, C. (ed.) *Michel Foucault: Power/Knowledge*, Brighton: Harvester, pp. 60–61.

Gellner, E. (1992) *Postmodernism, Reason and Religion*, London: Routledge.

—— (1994) 'Foreword', in Ahmed, A. and H. Donnan (eds) *Islam, Globalization and Postmodernity*, London: Routledge, pp. xi–xiv.

Gerholm, T. (1994) 'Two Muslim Intellectuals in the Postmodern West', in Ahmed, A. and H. Donnan (eds) *Islam, Globalization and Postmodernity*, London: Routledge, pp. 190–212.

Giddens, A. (1993) *Sociology*, Cambridge: Polity.

Glowczewski, B. (1998) '"All One but Different": Aboriginality: National Identity versus Local Diversification in Australia', in Wassmann, J. (ed.) *Pacific Answers to Western Hegemony*, Oxford/New York: Berg, pp. 335–54.

Godwell, D. (2000) 'The Olympic Branding of Aborigines: The 2000 Olympic Games and Australia's Indigenous Peoples', in Schaffer, K. (ed.) *The Olympics at the Millennium*, USA: Rutgers University Press. In press.

Goffman, E. (1963) *Stigma*, New York: Prentice Hall.

—— (1974) 'Stigma and Social Identity', in Boswell, D. and J. Wigmore (eds) *The Handicapped Person in the Community*, London: Oxford University Press, pp. 79–90.

Goolagong, E. with B. Collins, (1975) 'Prologue', in *Evonne!*, New York: Dutton.

Govender, P. (1992) 'Women and Work', in *Women and Power: Implications for development*, World University Service Women's Development programme, 13–15 August, Johannesburg, pp. 37–45.

Greenberg, J. (1997) *Getting into the Game*, Danbury, CT: Franklin Watts.

Greenspan, B. (1995) *100 Greatest Moments in Olympic History*, Los Angeles: General Publishing Group.

Grey, T. (1997) 'Elite Women Wheelchair Athletes in Australia', in Clarke, G. and B. Humberstone (eds) *Researching Women and Sport*, London: Macmillan, pp. 113–25.

Griffin, P. (1998) *Strong Women, Deep Closets*, Champaign, IL: Human Kinetics.

Griffin, P. and Genasci, J. (1990) 'Addressing Homophobia in Physical Education: Responsibilities for Teachers and Researchers', in Messner, M. and D. Sabo (eds) *Sport, Men, and the Gender Order*, Champaign, IL: Human Kinetics, 211–22.

Grundlingh, A. (1996) 'Playing for Power? Rugby, Afrikaner Nationalism and Masculinity in South Africa, c. 1900–c.1970', in Nauright, J. and T. Chandler (eds) *Making Men*, London: Frank Cass, pp. 181–204.

Guess, C. (1997) 'Deconstructing Me: On Being (Out) in the Academy', in Heywood, L. and J. Drake (eds) *Third Wave Agenda*, Minneapolis/London: University of Minnesota Press, pp. 155–67.

Guttmann, A. (1995) *Games and Empires*, New York: Columbia University Press.

Hain, P. (1971) *Don't Play with Apartheid*, London: Allen and Unwin.

—— (1982) 'The Politics of Sport Apartheid', in Hargreaves, J.A. (ed.), *Sport, Culture and Ideology*, London: Routledge & Kegan Paul, pp. 232–48.

Hall, C. (1996) 'Histories, Empires and the Post-Colonial Moment', in Chambers, I. and L. Curti (eds) *The Post-Colonial Question*, London: Routledge, pp. 65–77.

Hall, L. (1997) 'Heroes or Villains? Reconsidering British fin de siècle Sexology and its Impact', in Segal, L. (ed.) *New Sexual Agendas*, London: Macmillan, pp. 3–16.

Hall, M.A. (1994) 'Feminist Activism in Sport: A Comparative Study of Women's Sport Advocacy Organizations', in Tomlinson, A. (ed.) *Gender, Leisure and Cultural Forms*, CSRC Topic Report 4: Chelsea School Research Centre, University of Brighton.

—— (1996) *Feminism and Sporting Bodies*, Champaign, IL: Human Kinetics.

Hall, M.A. and G. Pfister (1999) *Honoring the Legacy*, Nanaimo: North Isle Printers.

Hall, S. (1996a) 'Introduction: Who Needs 'Identity'?', in Hall, S. and P. du Gay (eds) *Questions of Cultural Identity*, London: Sage Publications: 1–17.

—— (1996b) 'When was "The Post-Colonial"? Thinking at the Limit', in Chambers, I. and L. Curti (eds) *The Post-Colonial Question*, London: Routledge, pp. 242–60.

Halliday, F. (1994) 'The Politics of Islamic Fundamentalism: Iran, Tunisia and the Challenge to the Secular State', in Ahmed, A. and H. Donnan (eds) *Islam, Globalization and Postmodernity*, London: Routledge, pp. 91–113.

Hamilton, E. (1997) 'From Social Wefare to Civil Rights: The Representation of Disability in Twentieth-Century German Literature', in Mitchell, D. and S. Snyder (eds) *The Body and Physical Difference*, Michigan: University of Michigan Press, pp. 223–39.

Hargreaves, J.A. (1992) 'Sex, Gender and the Body in Sport and Leisure: Has There Been a Civilising Process?', in Dunning, E. and C. Rojek (eds) *Sport and Leisure in the Civilising Process*, London: Macmillan, pp. 161–82.

—— (1994) *Sporting Females*, London: Routledge.

Hargreaves, J.A. and D. Jones (2000) 'South Africa', in Christensen, K., A. Guttmann and G. Pfister (eds) *International Encyclopedia of Women and Sport*, New York: Macmillan, pp. 1084–8.

Herdt, G. (1998) 'Gay and Lesbian Youth, Emergent Identities, and Cultural Scenes at Home and Abroad', in Nardi, P. and B. Schneider (eds) *Social Perspectives in Lesbian and Gay Studies*, London: Routledge, pp. 279–300.

Heywood, L. and J. Drake (eds) (1997) *Third Wave Agenda*, Minneapolis: University of Minnesota Press.

hooks, b. (1982) *Ain't I A Woman*, London: Pluto.

—— (1984) *Feminist Theory*, Boston: South End.

—— (1989) *Talking Back*, Boston: South End.

—— (1991) *Yearning*, London: Tournaround.

—— (1994) *Outlaw Culture: Resisting Representations*, London: Routledge.

Jackson, S. (1999) *Heterosexuality in Question*, London: Sage.

Jones, D. (2000) 'Linking Mind and Body in a Divided Society: Sensei Nellie: Inspirational Icon in South African Karate', in Mangan, J.A. and F. Hong (eds) *Freeing the Female Body*, London: Cass.

Kandiyoti, D. (ed.) (1991) *Women, Islam and the State*, Philadelphia: Temple University Press.

Kanneh, K. (1995) 'The Difficult Politics of Wigs and Veils: Feminism and the Colonial Body', in Ashcroft, B., G. Griffiths and H. Tiffin (eds) *The Post-Colonial Studies Reader*, London: Routledge, pp. 346–48.

Karam, A. (1998) *Women, Islamisms and the State*, London: Macmillan.

Keith, L. (1996) 'Encounters with Strangers: The Public's Responses to Disabled Women and How this Affects our Sense of Self', in Morris, J. (ed.) *Encounters with Strangers*, London: The Women's Press, pp. 69–88.

Kort, M. (1994) 'Interview: Martina Navratilova', in Fox Rogers, S. (ed.) *Sportsdykes*, New York: St Martin's Press, pp. 133–42.

Laine, L. (ed.) (1993) *On the Fringes of Sport*, Sankt Augustin: Academia Verlag.

LaRocque, E. (1996) 'The Colonization of a Native Woman Scholar', in Miller, C. and P. Chuchryk (eds) *Women of the First Nations*, Winnipeg: University of Manitoba Press, pp. 11–18.

Layden, J. (1997) *Women in Sports*, Los Angeles: General Publishing.

Le Clair, J. (1992) *Winners and Losers*, Toronto: Thompson Educational.

Lenskyj, H. (1986) *Out of Bounds*, Toronto: The Women's Press.

Lessing, M. (ed.) (1994) *South African Women Today*, Cape Town: Maskew Miller Longman.

Leznoff, M. and W. Westley (1998) 'The Homosexual Community', in Nardi, P. and B. Schneider (eds) *Social Perspectives in Lesbian and Gay Studies*, London: Routledge, pp. 5–11.

Littlechild, W. (1988) 'Foreword', in Zeman, B. *To Run with Longboat*, Edmonton: GMS Ventures.

MacDonald, R. (1978) *The Uncharted Nations* , vol. 3, *The Romance of Canadian History Series*, Vancouver: Evergreen Press.

Marchand, H. and S. Parpart (eds) (1995) *Feminism/Postmodernism/Development*, London: Routledge.

Martindale, K. (1995) 'What Makes Lesbianism Unthinkable?: Theorizing Lesbianism from Adrienne Rich to Queer Theory', in Mandell, N. (ed.) *Feminist Issues*, Ontario: Prentice Hall, pp. 67–94.

Meekosha, H. (1998) 'Body Battles: Bodies, Gender and Disability', in Shakespeare, T. (ed.) *The Disability Reader*, London: Cassell, pp. 163–80.

Messner, M. (1992) *Power at Play*, Boston, MA: Beacon Press.

Miller, C. and P. Chuchryk (eds) (1996) *Women of the First Nations*, Winnipeg: University of Manitoba Press.

Mills, C. Wright (1959) *The Sociological Imagination*, Harmondsworth: Penguin.

Mishev, D. (1964) *Meet the Olympians*, Sofia, Bulgaria: Medicine and Physical Culture Publishing House.

Mitchell, D. and S. Snyder (1997) 'Introduction: Disability Studies and the Double Bind of Representation', in Mitchell, D. and S. Snyder (eds) *The Body and Physical Difference*, Michigan: University of Michigan Press, pp. 1–31.

Mitchell, J. (1971) *Women's Estate*, Harmondsworth: Penguin.

Mohanty, C. (1991) 'Cartographies of Struggle: Third World Women and the Politics of Feminism', in Mohanty, C., A. Russo and L. Torres (eds) *Third World Women and the Politics of Feminism*, Bloomington: Indiana University Press, pp. 1–47.

—— (1995) 'Under Western Eyes: Feminist Scholarship and Colonial Discourses', in Ashcroft, B., G. Griffiths and H. Tiffin (eds) *The Post-Colonial Studies Reader*, London: Routledge, pp. 259–63.

Morgan, W. (1998) 'Hassiba Boulmerka and Islamic Green: International Sports, Cultural Differences, and Their Postmodern Interpretation', in Rail, G. (ed.) *Sport and Postmodern Times*, Albany: Suny, pp. 345–65.

Morris, J. (1991) *Pride Against Prejudice*, London: The Women's Press.

—— (ed.) (1996) *Encounters with Strangers*, London: The Women's Press.

Morton, J. (1998) 'Essentially Black, Essentially Australian, Essentially Opposed: Australian Anthropology and its Uses of Aboriginal Identity', in Wassmann, J. (ed.) *Pacific Answers to Western Hegemony*, New York: Berg, pp. 355–85.

Mosely, P. (1997) 'Australian Sport and Ethnicity', in Mosely, P., R. Cashman and H. Weatherburn (eds) (1997) *Sporting Immigrants*, New South Wales: Walla Walla Press, pp. 13–42.

Moser, C. (1993) *Gender Planning and Development*, London: Routledge.

Munt, S. (1998) *Heroic Desire*, London: Cassell.

Nagata, J. (1994) 'How to Be Islamic Without Being an Islamic State: Contested Models of Development in Malaysia', in Ahmed, A. and H. Donnan (eds) *Islam, Globalization and Postmodernity*, London: Routledge, pp. 63–90.

Nardi, P and B. Schneider (eds) (1998) *Social Perspectives in Lesbian and Gay Studies*, London: Routledge.

Nzomo, M. (1995) 'Women and Democratization Struggles in Africa: What Relevance to Postmodernist Discourse?', in Marchand, H. and Parpart (eds) *Feminism/Postmodernism/ Development*, London: Routledge, pp. 131–41.

Odendaal, A. (1995) 'The Thing That is Not Round: The Untold History of Black Rugby in South Africa', in Grundlingh, A., A. Odendaal and B. Spies, *Beyond the Tryline*, South Africa: Raven, pp. 24–63.

Oliver, M. (1991) *The Politics of Disablement*, London: Macmillan.

—— (1996) *Understanding Disability*, London: Macmillan.

Oxendine, J. (1995) 'Sport for Girls and Women', in *American Indian Sports Heritage*, 2nd edition, Champaign, IL: Human Kinetics, pp. 22–6.

Pakes, F. (1990) ' "Skill to Do Comes of Doing": Purpose in Traditional Indian Winter Games', in Corbet, E. and A. Rasporich (eds) *Winter Sports in the West*, Calgary: The Historical Society of Alberta, pp. 26–37.

Paraschak, V. (1991) 'Sport Festivals and Race Relations in the Northwest Territories of Canada', in Jarvie, G. (ed.) *Sport, Racism and Ethnicity*, London: Falmer, pp. 74–93.

—— (1996a) 'An Examination of Sport for Aboriginal Females on the Six Nations Reserve, Ontario, from 1968 to 1980', in Miller, C. and P. Chuchryk (eds) *Women of the First Nations*, Winnipeg: University of Manitoba Press, pp. 83–96.

Plummer, K. (1998a) 'Afterword: The Past, Present, and Futures of the Sociology of Same-sex Relations' in Nardi, P. and B. Schneider (eds) *Social Perspectives in Lesbian and Gay Studies*, London: Routledge, pp. 605–14.

—— (1998b) 'Homosexual Categories: Some Research Problems in the Labelling Perspective of Homosexuality' in Nardi, P. and B. Schneider (eds) *Social Perspectives in Lesbian and Gay Studies*, London: Routledge, pp. 84–99.

Porter, J.(1997) 'Foreword', in Mitchell, D. and S. Snyder (eds) *The Body and Physical Difference*, Michigan: University of Michigan Press: xiii.-xiv.

Pronger, B. (1990) *The Arena of Masculinity*, London: Gay Men's Press.

Ramsamy, S. (1982) *Apartheid: The Real Hurdle*, London: International Defence and Aid Fund.

Rattansi, A. (1992) 'Changing the Subject?: Racism, Culture and Education', in Donald, J. and A. Rattansi (eds) *'Race', Culture and Difference*, London: Sage, pp. 11–48.

Roberts, C. (1993) *Against the Grain: Women in Sport in South Africa*, Cape Town: Township Publishing.

—— (ed.)(1995a) *Sportswoman*, Vlaeberg, Cape Town: Township Publishing.

—— (1995b) *Take a Chance and Play Sport*, Department of Sport and Recreation, Cape Town, South Africa: Township Publishing.

Roberts, J. (1980) *The Pelican History of the World*, Harmondsworth: Penguin.

Robertson, R. (1992) *Globalization*, London: Sage.

Runnymede Trust (1997) *Islamaphobia*, London: Runnymede Trust.

Russell, D. (1990) *Lives of Courage*, London: Virago.

Sanders, H.-R., E. Nash and M. Hoffman (1994) 'Women and Health', in Lessing, M. (ed.) *South African Women Today*, Cape Town: Maskew Miller Longman, pp. 139–63.

Segal, L. (1997) 'Sexualities', in Woodward, K. (ed.) *Identity and Difference*, London: Sage, pp. 183–238.

Seidler, V. (1994) *Recovering the Self*, London: Routledge.

Seymour, W. (1989) *Body Alterations*, London: Unwin Hyman.

Shakespeare, T. (ed.) (1998) *The Disability Reader*, London: Cassell.

Siegel, D. (1997) 'Reading Between the Waves: Feminist Historiography in a "Postfeminist" Moment', in Heywood, L. and J. Drake (eds) *Third Wave Agenda*, London: University of Minnesota Press, pp. 55–82.

Simon, W. and H. Gagnon (1998) 'Homosexuality: The Formulation of a Sociological Perspective', in Nardi, P. and B. Schneider (eds) *Social Perspectives in Lesbian and Gay Studies*, London: Routledge, pp. 59–67.

Slowikowski, S. (1993) 'On "Primitive" Physical Culture in "Civilized" Places', in Laine, L. (ed.) *On the Fringes of Sport*, Sankt Augustin: Akademia Verlag, pp. 181–7.

Sparhawk, R., M. Leslie, P. Turbow, and Z. Rose (1989) *American Women in Sport, 1887–1987*, Metuchen, NJ/London: Scarecrow.

Sparkes, A. and B. Smith (1999) 'Disrupted Selves and Narrative Reconstructions', in Sparkes, A. and M. Silvennoinen (eds) *Talking Bodies*, SoPhi: University of Jyvaskyla Press, pp. 76–92.

Stein, A. (1998) 'Sisters and Queers: The Centering of Lesbian Feminism', in Nardi, P and B. Schneider (eds) *Social Perspectives in Lesbian and Gay Studies*, London: Routledge, pp. 553–88.

Stell, M. (1991) *Half the Race*, New South Wales: Angus and Robertson.

Struna, N. (1993) 'Dominant and Subordinate Physical Cultures in Early America', in Laine, L. (ed.) *On the Fringes of Sport*, Sankt Augustin: Academia Verlag, pp. 113–32.

—— (1994) 'The Recreational Experiences of Early American Women', in Costa, D. and S. Guthrie (eds) *Women and Sport*, Champaign, IL: Human Kinetics, pp. 45–62.

Talbot, M. (1999) 'Charting the Future', in Hall, M.A. and G. Pfister (eds) *Honoring the Legacy*, Nanaimo: North Isle, pp. 108–16.

Tatz, C. (1987) *Aborigines in Sport*, S. Aus: Aus Society for Sports History.

—— (1995) *Obstacle Race*, New South Wales: University of New South Wales.

Thomas, C. (1999) *Female Forms*, Buckingham: Oxford University Press.

Thomas, G. (1990) 'Sports and Leisure in the Nineteenth Century Fur Trade', in Corbet, E. and A. Rasporich (eds) *Winter Sports in the West*, Calgary: The Historical Society of Alberta, pp. 13–25.

Tohidi, N. (1991) 'Gender and Islamic Fundamentalism: Feminist Politics in Iran', in Mohanty, C., A. Russo and L. Torres (eds) *Third World Women and the Politics of Feminism*, Bloomington: Indiana University Press, pp. 251–70.

Tonkinson, R. (1998) 'National Identity: Australia After Mabo', in Wassmann, J. (ed.) *Pacific Answers to Western Hegemony*, New York: Berg, pp. 287–310.

Tuttle, L. (1988) *Heroines*, London: Harrap.

Uwechue, R. (1978) 'Nation Building and Sport in Africa', in Lowe, B. D. Kanin and A. Strenk (eds) *Sport and International Relations*, Champaign IL: Human Kinetics, pp. 538–49.

Vamplew, W., K. Moore, J. O'Hara, R. Cashman and I. Jobling (1994) *The Oxford Companion to Australian Sport*, 2nd edition, Melbourne: Oxford University Press.

Vertinsky, P. (1990) *The Eternally Wounded Woman*, Manchester: Manchester University Press.

Walby, S. (1992) 'Post-Post-Modernism? Theorizing Social Complexity', in Barret, M. and A. Phillips (eds) *Destabilizing Theory*, Oxford: Polity, pp. 31–42.

Wallerstein, I. (1984) *The Modern World System*, New York: Academic Press.

Ware, V. (1992) *Beyond the Pale*, London: Verso.

Watson, H. (1994) 'Women and the Veil: Personal Responses to Global Processes', in Ahmed, A. and H. Donnan (eds) *Islam, Globalization and Postmodernity*, London: Routledge, pp. 141–59.

Weeks, J. (1990) *Coming Out*, London: Quartet Books.

—— (1994) *The Lesser Evil and the Greater Good: The Theory and Politics of Social Diversity*, London: Rivers Oram.

Weisman, M. and J. Godrey (1976) *So Get on with It*, Toronto: Doubleday Canada.

Weiss, A. (1994) 'Challenges for Muslim Women in a Postmodern World', in Ahmed, A. and H. Donnan (eds) *Islam, Globalization and Postmodernity*, London: Routledge, pp. 127–40.

Williams, R. (1977) *Marxism and Literature*, Oxford: Oxford University Press.

World Health Organization (1980) *International Classification of Impairments, Disabilities and Handicaps*, Geneva: World Health Organization.

Zaretsky, E. (1995) 'The Birth of Identity Politics in the 1960s: Psychoanalysis and the Public/Private Division', in Featherstone, M., S. Lash and R. Robertson (eds) *Global Modernities*, London: Sage, pp. 244–59.

Zeman, B. (1988) *To Run with Longboat*, Edmonton: GMS Ventures.

Journals, magazines, conference papers, dissertations

Because of the large volume of material referred to, it is impossible to list all newspaper and magazine articles, television programmes and Internet information that has provided a background for the research. Newspaper, magazine and television references are cited in the text only.

Abdelrahman, N. (1991) 'Women and Sport in the Islamic Society: An Analytical Study of the Viewpoints of Some Islamic Ulamas and Physical Education Specialists', unpublished paper presented at the First Islamic Countries Sports Solidarity Congress for Women, University of Alexandria, Egypt.

—— (1998) 'Egypt', *Bulletin of International Association of Physical Education and Sport for Girls and Women* 8(1): 13, 16.

Adrian, M. (1993) 'International Association of Physical Education and Sport for Girls and Women Conference Review', *Women in Sport and Physical Activity Journal* 2(1): 61–73.

Al-Hashimy, F. (1997) 'The Development of the Women's Sport Movement in Iraq', in 'Woman and Child: Future Vision from a Sport Perspective', in *Proceedings of the Second Scientific International Conference for Women and Sport*, Alexandria University, pp. 37–9.

Anderson, D. (1998) 'New Dangers Out of Africa', *Time* 24 August: 33–4.

Annecke, W. (1990) 'Women and the War in Natal', *Agenda* 7: 12–20.

Begum, N. (1992) 'Disabled Women and the Feminist Agenda', *Feminist Review* 40: 70–84.

Birrell, S. (1989) 'Racial Relations Theories and Sport: Suggestions for a More Critical Analysis', *Sociology of Sport Journal* 6: 212–27.

Brackenridge, Celia (1992a) 'Beyond "Women and Sport": A Critique of International Women's Sports Organisations', paper presented to the 1992 Olympic Scientific Congress, Malaga, Spain.

—— (1992b) 'The Future of International Women's Sports Organisations', unpublished paper presented to the Women's Sports Foundation (USA) Annual Conference, 'The Ascent of Woman', Denver, Colorado.

—— (1995) 'Think Global, Act Global: The Future of International Women's Sport', *International Council for Health, Physical Education and Recreation Journal*, 31(4): 7–11.

Brackenridge, C. and K. Fasting (1999) 'An Analysis of Codes of Practice for Preventing Sexual Harassment and Abuse to Women and Children in Sport', paper prepared for the Council of Europe Sports Division.

Brandoburova, K. and A. Scherney (1999) 'Women in Sport', *European Paralympic Committee* 6: 5–8.

Bromley, R. (1998) 'Beyond the Boundary – International Perspectives in Cultural Studies', *Ampersand* 1: 2.

Burroughs, A., L. Ashburn and L. Seebohm (1995) ' "Add Sex and Stir": Homophobic Coverage of Women's Cricket in Australia', *Journal of Sport and Social Issues* 19(3): 266–84.

Caudwell, J. (1999) 'Women's Football in the United Kingdom: Theorizing Gender and Unpacking the Butch Lesbian Image', *Journal of Sport and Social Issues*, 23(4): 390–402.

Cheska, A. Taylor (1976) 'Ball Games Played by North American Women', in Renson, R., P. De Nayer and M. Ostyn (eds) *The History, The Evolution and Diffusion of Sports and Games in Different Cultures*, Proceedings of the Fouth International HISPA Seminar, 1975, pp. 39–56.

—— (1988) 'Ethnicity, Identity, and Sport: The Persistence of Power', *International Review for the Sociology of Sport* 23(2): 85–96.

Clarke, G. (1998) 'Queering the Pitch and Coming Out to Play: Lesbians in Physical Education and Sport', *Sport, Education and Society* 3(2): 145–60.

Close, Father Leo (1960) 'Rome and the Irish', *The Cord* 3(2): 53–7.

The Cord (1949) 'Stoke Mandeville Calling' 3(1): 22–5; 'Festival of Sport, 1950: Stoke Mandeville Hospital' 3(4): 19–25.

DePauw, K. (1997) 'Sport and Physical Activity in the Life-Cycle of Girls and Women with Disabilities', *Women's Sport and Physical Activity Journal* 6(2): 225–37.

Dodgson, A. (1953) 'International Games: Stoke Mandeville, 1953', *The Cord*, 6(2): 10–17.

English Federation of Disability Sport (2000) *'Building a Fairer Sporting Society': Sport for Disabled People in England: A Four Year Development Plan 2000–2004*, London: English Federation of Disability Sport.

Fraser, M. (1999) 'Classing Queer: Politics in Competition', in Bell, V. (ed.) 'Performativity and Belonging', *Theory, Culture and Society* 16(2): 107–31.

Fung, L. (1992) 'Participation Motives in Competitive Sports: A Cross Cultural Comparison', *Adapted Physical Activity Quarterly* 9: 114–22.

Goldsmith, M. (1995) 'Sporting Boycotts as a Political Tool', in *AQ* Autumn: 11–20.

Grimes, P. and L. French (1989) 'Barriers to Disabled Women's Participation in Sports', *Journal of Physical Education, Recreation and Dance* 58(3): 24–7.

Guttmann, L. (1952) 'On the Way to an International Sports Movement for the Paralyzed', *The Cord* 5(3): 7–23.

Haffajee, F. (1995) 'The Sisterly Republic', *New Internationalist* 265: 11–13.

Hall, M.A. (1999) 'Canuck Hockey and Dykes: Why Codes of Silence Hurt Women's Sport', article prepared for *Globe and Mail* (unpublished).

Hargreaves, J.A. (1993) 'Bodies Matter! Images of Sport and Female Sexualization', in Brackenridge, C. (ed.) *Body Matters*, Leisure Studies Association: 47: 60–6.

—— (1997) 'Women's Sport, Development, and Cultural Diversity: The South African Experience', *Women's Studies International Forum* 20(2): 191–220.

Hillmore, P. (1996) 'And May the Best Devil Win …', *Observer* 21 June.

Holder, D. (1996) 'A Woman's Place is at the Games', *Independent on Sunday* 7 July.

Horn, M. (1999) Bringing Traditional Practices to Today's Reality', *Action* 22: 26.

Hornblower, M. (1992) 'Running Against the Grain', *Times International*, June: 88–91.

IAPESGW (International Association of Physical Education and Sport for Girls and Women) (1998) *Bulletin of the International Association of Physical Education and Sport for Girls and Women* 8(1).

ICSSPE (International Council of Sport Science and Physical Education) (1999) 'Results and Recommendations of the World Summit on Physical Education', Berlin, 3–5 November.

IWG (International Working Group) Women and Sport (1998) *From Brighton to Windhoek – Facing the Challenge: Summary Progress Report of the International Women and Sport Movement – 1994–1998*, United Kingdom Sports Council.

Jackson, S. (1995/6) 'Straight Talking', *Trouble and Strife* 32: 31–8.

Kadalie, R. (1995) *Women and Politics*, unpublished reader, Gender Equity Unit: University of the Western Cape, South Africa.

Lenskyj, H. (1990) 'Sexual Harassment and Sexual Abuse: An Issue for Women in Sport', *Action Magazine* 8(2): 16.

—— (1991) 'Combatting Homophobia in Sport and Physical Education', *Sociology of Sport Journal* 8(1): 61–9.

—— (1992) 'Unsafe at Home Base: Women's Experiences of Sexual Harassment in University Sport and Physical Education', *Women in Sport and Physical Activity Journal* 1(1): 19–33.

—— (1994) 'Girl-Friendly Sport and Female Values', *Women in Sport and Physical Education Journal* 3(1): 35–45.

—— (1995) 'Sport and the Threat to Gender Boundaries', *Sporting Traditions* 12()1: 47–60.

—— (1997) 'No Fear? Lesbians in Sport and Physical Education', *Women in Sport and Physical Activity Journal* 6(2): 7–22.

Littlewood, R. (1982) 'Aboriginal Associations and the Development of Ethnicity', unpublished paper, Australian National University.

Macleod, S. (1998) 'Our Veils, Ourselves', *Time* 152(4): 29.

Mahl (1995) 'Women on the Edge of Time', *New Internationalist* August: 14–16.

Manzini, M. (1992) 'Women and Power: Implications for Development', *Women and Power: Implications for Development*, World University Service Women's Development Programme, Johannesburg, 13–15 August, pp. 3–11.

Mechti, Z. and N. Sayad (1994) *Ministry For Youth Sports: Algeria: Female Sports 'Reality and Perspective'*, unpublished paper.

Meintjes, S. (1993) 'Dilemmas of Difference', *Agenda* 19: 37–42.

Merrett, C. (1986) 'Offside: Apartheid, Sports Facilities and the Boycott', *Reality: A Journal of Liberal and Radical Opinion* 18(1).

Messner, M. (1993) ' "Changing Men" and Feminist Politics in the United States', *Theory and Society* 22: 723–37.

Minister for Sport's Review Group (1989) *Building on Ability: Sport for People With Disabilities*, London: HMSO.

Morris, J. (1993) 'Feminism and Disability' *Feminist Review* 43: 57–70.

Ngcongo, N. (1993) 'Power, Culture and the African Woman', *Agenda* 19: 5–10.

Oglesby, C. and L. Darlison (1999) 'United Nations Strategic Bridges', report on behalf of WSI, IAPESGW, IWG and the Global Women's Sport Advocacy Community, unpublished.

O'Kane, M. (1998) 'Afghanistan', *New Internationalist* 298: 37.

Olenik, L., J. Matthews and R. Steadward (1995) 'Women, Disability and Sport: Unheard Voices', *Canadian Woman Studies* 15(4): 54–7.

Palmason, D. (1993) 'Women's International Sports Coalition', *Women in Sport and Physical Education Journal* 2(1): 99–101.

Palzkill, B. (1990) 'Between Gymshoes and High-Heels – The Development of a Lesbian Identity and Existence in Top Class Sport', *International Review for the Sociology of Sport* 25(3): 221–33.

Paraschak, V. (1995a) 'Aboriginal Inclusiveness in Canadian Sporting Culture: An Image Without Substance?', paper presented at the 1995 Annual International Society for the History Physical Education and Sport Conference, Cape Town, South Africa.

—— (1995b) 'Invisible But Not Absent: Aboriginal Women in Sport and Recreation', *Canadian Woman Studies* 15(4): 71–2.

—— (1996b) 'Racialized Spaces: Cultural Regulation, Aboriginal Agency and Powwows', in *Avante* 2(1): 7–18.

—— (1997) 'Variations in Race Relations: Sporting Events for Native Peoples in Canada', *Sociology of Sport Journal* 14(1): 1–21.

Portz-Shovlin, E. (1991) 'The Human Race', *Runner's World* 26(7): 110.

Pourhaddadi, F. (1998) 'A Political and Socio-Economic History of the Asian Games', unpublished B.Sc. dissertation, University of Surrey, Roehampton.

Ransom, D. (1995) 'New Dawn, Cold Light of Day', *New Internationalist*, 265: 7–10.

Reed, S. (1994a) 'Someone's on the Fairway with Dinah', *Gay Games Official IV Program*, p. 23.

—— (1994b) 'Unlevel Playing Fields', *Out*: 92–128.

Rich, A. (1980) 'Compulsory Heterosexuality and Lesbian Existence', *Signs* 5: 631–60.

SACOS (South African Congress on Sport) (1988) *SACOSSPORT Festival '88*, Cape Town: Buchu Books.

Sainsbury, A. (1998) 'The Paralympic Movement', unpublished paper presented to the British Olympic Association Annual Conference.

Saiz, I. (1998) 'The Right That Dares Not Speak Its Name', *New Internationalist* 298: 22–3.

Salee, D. (1995) 'Identities in Conflict: The Aboriginal Question and the Politics of Recognition in Quebec', *Ethnic and Racial Studies* 18(2): 277–314.

SANROC (South African Non-Racial Olympics Committee) (n.d.) *Sport in South Africa: Some Facts*, London: SANROC.

Scruton, J. (1956) 'The 1956 International Games: Stoke Mandeville', *The Cord* 8(4): 7–26;

—— (1957) 'The 1957 International Stoke Mandeville Games', *The Cord* 9(4): 7–28;

—— (1958) 'The 1958 International Stoke Mandeville Games', *The Cord* 10(4): 12–30.

Sfeir, L. (1985) 'The Status of Muslim Women in Sport: Conflict Between Cultural Tradition and Modernization', *International Review for the Sociology of Sport* 20(4): 283–305.

Sherrill, C. (1993) 'Women with Disability, Paralympics, and Reasoned Action Contact Theory', *Women in Sport and Physical Education Journal* 2(2):51–60.

—— (1997) 'Paralympic Games 1996: Feminist and Other Concerns: What's Your Excuse?', *Palaestra* 13(1): 32–8.

Sivanandan, A. (1981) 'Race, Class and Caste in South Africa: An Open Letter to No Sizwe', in *Race and Class* 22(3): 293–301.

Sloan, M. (1994) '1993 Dorothy Sears Ainsworth Award', *Bulletin of the International Association of Physical Education and Sport for Girls and Women* 4(1): 5–6.

Smith, Y. (1992) 'Women or Colour in Society and Sport' *QUEST* 44: 228–50.

Sparkes, A. (1994) 'Life Histories and the Issues of Voice: Reflections on an Emerging Relationship', *Qualitative Studies in Education* 7(2): 165–83.

Sports Council (1994) *The Brighton Declaration on Women and Sport*, Brighton: Sports Council.

Staurowsky, E. (1998a) 'An Act of Honour or Exploitation? The Cleveland Indians' Use of the Louis Francis Sockalexis Story', *Sociology of Sport Journal* 15(4): 299–316.

—— (1998b) 'Critiquing the Language of the Gender Equity debates' *Journal of Sport and Social Issues* 22 (1): 7–26.

Steadward, R. (1996) 'Integration and Sport in the Paralympic Movement', *Sport Science Review* 5(1): 26–41.

Stein, A. and K. Plummer (1994) ' "I Can't Even Think Straight": "Queer" Theory and the Missing Sexual Revolution in Sociology', *Sociological Theory* 12(1): 78–87.

Strange, M. (1995) 'The International Stoke Mandeville Wheelchair Sports Federation (ISMWSF)', International Wheelchair Games Stoke Mandeville '95, British Wheelchair Sports Federation.

Sunde, J. and V. Bozalek (1993) '(Re)searching difference', *Agenda* 19: 29–36.

Sykes, H. (1998) 'Turning the Closets Inside/Out: Towards a Queer-Feminist Theory in Women's Physical Education', *Sociology of Sport Journal* 15(2): 154–73.

Talbot, M. (1997) 'Women, Sport and Physical Education: From Policy to Practice', in 'Woman and Child: Future Vision from a Sport Perspective', in *Proceedings of the Second Scientific International Conference for Women and Sport*, Alexandria University, 21–24 October, pp. 72–84.

Thompson, J. (1993) 'The Pathetic is Political: The Educations of Heroism', *Curriculum Enquiry* 23(4): 395–407.

Tinkler, Penny (1998) 'Introduction to Special Issue: Women, Imperialism and Identity', *Women's Studies International Forum* 21(3): 217–22.

Van der Gaag (1997) *New Internationalist* 189: 31.

Villarosa, L. (1994) 'Gay Games IV', *Out*: 89–91.

Watkinson, E. and K. Calzonetti (1989) 'Physical Activity Patterns of Physically Disabled Women in Canada', *Canadian Association of Health, Physical Education and Recreation Journal* 55(6): 21–6.

White, A. (1997) 'The Growth of the International Women and Sport Movement', in 'Woman and Child: Future Vision from a Sport Perspective', in *Proceedings of the Second Scientific International Conference for Women and Sport*, Alexandria University, pp. 3–11.

—— (1998) 'Foreword', in IWG, *Women and Sport, From Brighton to Windhoek – Facing the Challenge: Summary Progress Report of the International Women and Sport Movement – 1994–1998*, United Kingdom Sports Council, p. 1.

Wiid, B. (1994) 'Action Values Towards Holistic Living: Raising the Quality of Life Within Communities', in Amusa, L. (ed.) *Health, Physical Education, Recreation, Sport and Dance in South Africa, Proceedings of the First Africa Regional Conference on Physical, Health Education, Recreation and Dance*, Botswana: African Association of Health, Physical Education and Recreation, pp. 83–9.

The Windhoek Call for Action (1998) International Working Group (IWG) on Women and Sport, 22 May.

WSF (1998a) *Women's Sports Foundation Newsletter* May.

—— (1998b) *Women's Sports Foundation Newsletter* September.

WUS-SA (World University Service South Africa) (1992) *Women and Power: Implications for Development*, World University Service Women's Development Programme, 13–15 August, Johannesburg.

Zuma, N. (1992) 'Women and Health', *Women and Power: Implications for Development*, World University Service Women's Development Programme, 13–15 August, Johannesburg, pp. 14–16.

Internet

Internet references from which quotations and data have been taken are listed below.

Oglesby, C. and E. Darlison, *WSI, IAPESGW, IWG, and the Global Women's Advocacy Community*, report written for the WomenSport International homepage: *http://www.de.psu.edu/WSI/UNITEDword.html* (8/4/99).

Excerpts from the Speech Delivered by H.E. The President of Islami Republic of Iran in the Opening Ceremony of the First Islamic Countries' Women Sports Solidarity Congress: *http:/salamiran.org/Women/Olympic/president.html* (1998).

Excerpts from the Report Delivered by Mrs Mary Benaham, FIBA Delegate, for the First Islamic Countries' Women Sports Solidarity Games:
http:/salamiran.org/Women/Olympic/fiba.html (1998).

Excerpts from the Report by Mrs Mary Alison Glen Haig, IOC President's Delegate, for the First Islamic Countries' Women Sports Solidarity Games:
http:/salamiran.org/Women/Olympic/ioc.html (1998).

The Speech Delivered by Dr Ghafouri Fard, Head of the Physical Education Organization of Islamic Republic of Iran: *http:/salamiran.org/Women/Olympic/fard.html* (1998).

http://salamiran.org/Women/General/Women And Sports.html (1998).

Name index

Abdelrahman, N. 55, 67
Abdo, G. 237
Ahmed, A. 51; and H. Donnan 48, 49, 51, 53, 70
Albrow, M. 71
Altman, D. 170
Anderson, D. 52
Annecke, W. 41
Archer, R. 19
Armstrong, J. 80
Ashcroft, B., G. Griffiths and H. Tiffin 78, 83, 85, 227

Barber, K. 240
Barnes, C. 174, 175, 179, 204
Barret, M. and A. Phillips 43
Begum, N. 187, 191, 192
Benedict, J. 3, 139
Benson, S. 185
Bertaux, D. 9
Bhatia, S. 237
Birrell, S. 8, 9, 10, 24, 132
Blue, A. 148
Booth, D. 16
Bordo, S. 187
Bose, M. 19
Bourdieu, P. 186
Brackenridge,C.220,221;andK.Fasting 229
Brah, A. 6, 78, 79, 96, 216
Brandoburova, K. and A. Scherney 209
Brickill, J. 19
Bromley, R. 48
Burroughs, A., L. Ashburn and L. Seebohm 138, 142
Burton Nelson, M. 137, 139
Butler, J. 8, 133, 136, 168

Cahn, S. 2, 134, 135, 136, 137, 152
Cammack, P., D. Pool and W. Tordoff 18
Cassidy, B., R. Lord and N. Mandell 6, 176
Caudwell, J. 151, 243
Chaudhuri, N. and M. Strobel 219
Cheska, A. Taylor 79, 81
Chow, R. 76
Chowdhry, G. 43, 231
Chuckryk, P. and C. Miller 11, 84, 85, 113, 126
Churchill, W. 80, 83, 84
Clarke, G. 137, 140, 145, 156
Collins, P. 36
Connell, R. 1, 141, 143, 186
Coole, D. 43, 232
Cornell, S. and D. Hartmann 16, 79, 83
Creedon, P. 2
Crow, L. 177, 179, 192

DePauw, K. and S. Gavron 179, 180, 181, 182, 184, 204, 205, 208, 212
Dickason, O. 80, 240,
Dodgson, A. 182
Donnelly, P. 84
Dutton, K. 2, 185

Edwards, J. and J.A. Hargreaves 133
EFDS (European Federation for Disability Sport) 213
EGLSF (European Gay and Lesbian Sports Federation)154
Elsdon, D. 43
Emberley, J. 11, 126

Fanon, F. 83, 85
Featherstone, M. 154

Subject index